COLERIDGE

Biographia Literaria

CHAPTERS I–IV, XIV–XXII

WORDSWORTH

Prefaces and Essays on Poetry

1800–1815

COLERIDGE
Biographia Literaria

CHAPTERS I–IV, XIV–XXII

WORDSWORTH
Prefaces and Essays on Poetry
1800–1815

Edited by

GEORGE SAMPSON

with an Introductory Essay by

SIR ARTHUR QUILLER-COUCH

CAMBRIDGE
AT THE UNIVERSITY PRESS
1920

CAMBRIDGE
UNIVERSITY PRESS

University Printing House, Cambridge CB2 8BS, United Kingdom

Cambridge University Press is part of the University of Cambridge.

It furthers the University's mission by disseminating knowledge in the pursuit of education, learning and research at the highest international levels of excellence.

www.cambridge.org
Information on this title: www.cambridge.org/9781107536821

First published 1920
First paperback edition 2015

A catalogue record for this publication is available from the British Library

ISBN 978-1-107-53682-1 Paperback

PREFACE

Coleridge's *Biographia Literaria* is a work of which a part is greater than the whole. It is fragmentary and discontinuous —a series of beginnings, with a conclusion that fits none of them. The separate presentation of its better portions is therefore an act of kindness to many readers, and especially to students, who (being young) dutifully endeavour to read the whole book, and find themselves dismayed, if not defeated, by the mass of imported metaphysic that Coleridge proudly dumped into the middle. This obstacle has been removed and the book is left as, indeed, it is usually read, not merely by pupils under direction, but by older persons whom habit has made wise in omission. Certainly the best of *Biographia* is to be got by a reading of its best part first. The sequence of chapters beginning abruptly at XIV and ending just as suddenly at XXII is a detachable and delightful little treatise, which, because it examines rigorously, though reverently, poems now famous and familiar, is the best introduction English readers can have to the principles of philosophical criticism—that is, to the way of intelligent enjoyment— and it is therefore offered here, with the first four chapters as preface, to all who care to enjoy a poet's interpretation of poetry unclouded by the obscurity of yesterday's philosophy. The nature of the omitted portion is indicated in the first Appendix, which contains, as well, a full quotation of the passages with any personal interest. The book thus abbreviated is meant, not as a substitute for the whole work, but as an introduction to it. It is a first reading in Coleridge's prose.

Associated with the Wordsworth chapters of *Biographia Literaria* are the Wordsworth essays on poetry out of which the book arose and without which it might never have been written.

The text is mainly that of the second edition (see p. 246); but Coleridge's characteristic italics and capitals, normalised by the editors of 1847, have been restored. Can we not hear in them the emphasis of our philosopher's declamation in those famous monologues that gave pleasure to some, pain to others, and astonishment to all?

Upon the debated subject of annotation the only remark needed is that persons who want notes may find some of these helpful and that persons who don't may treat them as not existing. Without them (and even with them) a volume that gives the best of Coleridge's imaginative criticism—the criticism that, as Pater says, is itself a kind of creation—should have its uses for many sorts of readers.

GEORGE SAMPSON.

31 *December*, 1919.

CONTENTS

Every line has been produced by me with labor pangs. I abandon poetry altogether. I leave the higher and deeper kinds to Wordsworth, the delightful, popular, and simply dignified to Southey, and reserve for myself the honourable attempt to make others feel and understand their writings, as they deserve to be felt and understood.

S. T. C. (From a Letter, *c.* 1800.)

INTRODUCTION

I

Although *Biographia Literaria* did not see the light until July 1817, for its genesis we must go back just twenty years, to July 1797, in which month Wordsworth and his sister Dorothy paid their first visit to Coleridge and were his guests for a fortnight at Nether Stowey, under the Quantock hills, in Somerset.

Since that fortnight has become for us a diuturnity, and that visit, planned by William and Dorothy for a summer jaunt, has passed into high prose and song, let us glance over the scene and the persons, beginning with the host.

Coleridge was nearing twenty-six. Some two-and-a-half years before, he had quitted Cambridge, without a degree, after an undergraduate career (in Jesus College) which comprised the Browne Gold Medal, an ungodly row in the Senate House, a bolt to London, an enlistment in the 15th Light Dragoons—which gave him, for life, "a violent antipathy to soldiers and horses"—a penitential return, an admonishment by the Master (Dr Pearce) in the presence of the Fellows, further irregularities, and this second and final bolt. I owe it to an ancient and permanently respectable Society to add that not even the present Master and Fellows of Jesus could have treated Coleridge more tenderly than did their forerunners of 1794, who, though all sign of him was lost, obtained from Christ's Hospital, and themselves granted, a reprieve of another six months. But Cambridge was no cage for this bird, and he did not return to it.

In the intervening two-years-and-a-half many things had happened to him. He had, with his Balliol friend Robert

Southey, hatched out the famous project of Pantisocracy, whereby "twelve gentlemen of good education and liberal principles" were "to embark with twelve ladies in April next," and settle in some "delightful part of the new back settlements" of America: but it never advanced nearer towards what the present-day denizens of those settlements would call a "practical proposition" than interviewing a real-estate agent who strongly represented the banks of the Susquehanna as suitable "from its excessive beauty and security from hostile Indians, bisons, and mosquitos." "Literary characters," added the agent, "make money there." Coleridge had preached a good deal, too, at set times from pulpits and continuously when any company or single soul would listen. He had written *The Fall of Robespierre* in collaboration with Southey: had published a volume of lectures, and another of poems: had edited *The Watchman*, which ran to ten numbers, and had touted the Midlands for subscribers—with serio-comic results: had been crossed in love and, on the backwash of disappointment had been carried into marriage with Miss Sara Fricker, sister of Mrs Southey. The marriage, says Mr Dykes Campbell, was not made in Heaven: and since Southey largely engineered it, we may perhaps agree.

The lady was comely, affectionate, of domestic instincts, not above roughing it. She probably deserves scarce one-tenth of the blame for what happened in the end. With the proviso that Coleridge was ever what is called "a faithful husband," we may repeat of Mrs Coleridge what we remarked just now of Cambridge, that the cage was too narrow for the bird. But, for the time, all was bliss: improvident and impecunious, yet bliss notwithstanding. In September 1796—being, rather characteristically, away on a visit at the time—Coleridge heard that he was the father of a boy (afterwards christened Hartley): hurried home; and composed three sonnets in the tumult of his feelings.

He had been disappointed in a promise of the post of assistant editor of *The Morning Chronicle*, and again of a private tutorship to the sons of a Mrs Evans, near Derby. The boys were under trusteeship, and the trustees, for some reason objected to the arrangements: but the mother, in an affectionate parting "insisted on my acceptance of £95, and she had given Mrs Coleridge all her baby-clothes, which are, I suppose very valuable."

At this crisis in his affairs Coleridge turned to a friend who truly was one of the best fellows in the world—Thomas Poole. Most of us whose fortune has drawn them into any literary or artistic set or coterie have known in it—but not remarked until afterwards as memorable—some quiet comfortable man, whose attachment had nothing to do with any talent in writing or painting or conversing. He had somehow a sense that these things, beyond him, were just splendid, and the men who did them, splendid fellows. For himself, he could ride to hounds or knock up a hundred in average cricket: but here was something his admission to which he dumbly enjoyed as a privilege. For his contribution to the improvement of mankind, he had oftener been known to lend money than to be repaid. If, by efflux of time, we come to outlive any such coterie, to look back on it, the odds are that we find a retrospective glow in the heart for old So-and-so, not only as the best of the bunch, but as the quiet man—the *punctum indifferens* to which its extravagances referred themselves for help in practical crises and for counsel, however inarticulate.

Such a man was Tom Poole, partner in his father's tannery at Nether Stowey, under the Quantocks: a young man of twenty-eight, of strong character, alert interest in public affairs, and a heart as sound as God ever put into a Briton: who deserved, in short, to be what he is—the subject of one of the best small biographies in our language[1]. Like Coleridge and Southey, in whose marvellous talk he delighted, he sympathised with the

[1] *Thomas Poole and his Friends*: by Mrs Henry Sandford, 2 vols. 1888.

French Revolution up to the days of the Terror. In private affairs they knew him as a friend, to be trusted though the heavens should fall.

To Poole, then, Coleridge made appeal to find him a house at Stowey. "My anxieties eat me up.... I want consolation—my Friend! my Brother! write and console me." Poole reported a wayside cottage to let, with a garden behind it adjoining his own: but spoke poorly of the accommodation. Coleridge would let the accommodation go hang. "I will instruct the maid in cooking," he wrote; and, next day, that he would "keep no servant"—would even be "occasional nurse." Poole still doubted. Was it wise for the poet to bury himself in so remote a spot? This caused Coleridge "unexpected and most acute pain," and he replied with a frantic letter that extends to ten pages in print. "No summary," justly observes Mr Dykes Campbell, "could do it the least justice." Poole engaged the cottage, and the Coleridges—*papa, maman et bébé*—were installed therein on the last day of 1796. The father looked around and announced to Poole, "Literature, though I shall never abandon it, will always be a secondary object with me. My poetic vanity and my political furor have been exhaled; and I would rather be an expert, self-maintaining gardener than a Milton, if I could not unite both." He seems to have repeated this in writing to Charles Lamb, eliciting the question, "And what does your worship know about farming?" Were it not better (queried Lamb) to be getting on with a projected Epic on the Origin of Evil, as something more in his friend's way?

Many word-portraits of Coleridge, as he was at this time or a little later, have come down to us: the best, of course, that incomparable one by Hazlitt in his essay *My First Acquaintance with Poets*. For this essay, it has been well said by the editor of the present volume, "the many who date an epoch in their own lives from a first reading of *Biographia* and *Lyrical Ballads* will always feel a peculiar affection.... It is Coleridge who is the hero of the story, as he always will be to ardent youth—Coleridge in the dayspring of his fancies, with hope like a fiery pillar before him[1]." But let us see him as he struck one of his guests, Dorothy Wordsworth:

"You had a great loss," she wrote to a friend, "in not seeing Coleridge. He is a wonderful man. His conversation teems with soul, mind, and spirit. Then he is so benevolent, so good tempered and cheerful and—like William—interests himself so much about every little trifle. At first I thought him very plain, that is for about three minutes. He is pale and thin, has a wide mouth, thick lips, and not very good teeth, longish loose-growing half-curling rough black hair. But if you hear him speak for five minutes you think no more of them. His eye is large and full, not dark but gray, such an eye as would receive from a heavy soul the dullest expression, but it speaks every emotion of his animated mind. It has more of the 'poet's eye in a fine frenzy rolling' than I ever witnessed. He has fine dark eyebrows, and an overhanging forehead."

"Coleridge was still Mirandola, not yet Micawber" says Mr Sampson. But I seem to find hints of Micawber in the letters about the cottage: and here is a small significant entry of the previous year. He suffered from depression, and depression brought on neuralgia, for which (he writes to Poole)

I took between 60 and 70 drops of laudanum, and sopped the Cerberus just as his mouth began to open....I have a blister under my right ear, and I take 25 drops of laudanum every five hours, the ease and spirits gained by which have enabled me to write you this flighty, but not exaggerating account.

[1] Hazlitt, *Selected Essays*, edited by George Sampson, Cambridge, 1917. Here is a part of Hazlitt's description:

His complexion was at that time clear, and even bright
As are the children of yon azure sheen.

His forehead was broad and high, light as if built of ivory, with large projecting eyebrows, and his eyes rolling beneath them like a sea with darkened lustre.

A certain tender bloom his face o'erspread,

a purple tinge as we see it in the pale thoughtful complexions of the Spanish portrait-painters, Murillo and Velasquez. His mouth was gross, voluptuous, open, eloquent; his chin good-humoured and round; but his nose, the rudder of his face, the index of the will, was small, feeble, nothing—like what he has done. It might seem that the genius of his face as from a height surveyed and projected him (with sufficient capacity and huge aspiration) into the world unknown of thought and imagination, with nothing to support or guide his veering purpose, as if Columbus had launched his adventurous course for the New World in a scallop, without oars or compass. So at least I comment on it after the event.

Now 60 to 70 drops of laudanum is no beginner's dose.

Of the two Wordsworths, William was now midway in his twenty-eighth year, but in appearance older, with a certain rusticity of movement and a cold stockish manner which helped that impression. Readers of *The Prelude* know well enough what tumultuous fires had, with the early hopes of the French Revolution, burned beneath that crust, what disappointments had congealed it and left it so hard and grey, self-opinionated and shrunken if not absolutely narrow. *The Prelude*, we must remember, was not begun until 1799, not completed until 1805: and we must remember this for two reasons: the first that the passions confessed are wonderful in the stiff man who recollected and so artlessly set them down: the second (and stranger) that, while the generous heart of his youth undoubtedly felt these poetic strivings, it was *for the time, and even at the date of which we are writing*, almost completely unable to express them. *The Borderers* was the sort of stuff Wordsworth wrote before he visited Nether Stowey. Expression came to him afterwards, as with a rush: and I am to suggest that Coleridge found the key for his genius and unlocked it.

—With Dorothy's help, no doubt. "The character of Dorothy Wordsworth," says Lord Morley, "has long taken its place in the gallery of admirable and devoted women who have inspired the work and the thoughts of great men." So let me quote of her brother's but these six well-known lines:

> The Blessing of my later years
> Was with me when a Boy:
> She gave me eyes, she gave me ears;
> And humble cares, and delicate fears;
> A heart, the fountain of sweet tears;
> And love, and thought, and joy.

with Coleridge's portrait of her on this visit, as a pendant to her's of him.

Wordsworth and his exquisite sister are with me. She is a woman indeed! in mind, I mean, and heart; for her person is such, that if you expected to see a pretty woman, you would think her rather ordinary; if you expected to see an ordinary woman, you would think her pretty! but her manners are simple, ardent, impressive. In every motion her most innocent soul outbeams so brightly, that who saw would say

> Guilt was a thing impossible in her.

Her information various. Her eye watchful in minutest observation of nature; and her taste a perfect electrometer. It binds, protrudes and draws in, at subtlest beauties and most recondite faults.

Well, there they were, with Tom Poole at the end of the garden: and to make the gaiety complete, Charles Lamb came down to spend his annual week's holiday: and to him

> to whom
> No sound is dissonant that tells of life

Coleridge, who, during their stay was confined to house and garden with a sprained ankle, addressed the beautiful verses—*This Lime-tree Bower my Prison*—

> Well, they are gone, and here must I remain,
> This lime-tree bower my prison! I have lost
> Beauties and feelings, such as would have been
> Most sweet to my remembrance even when age
> Had dimm'd mine eyes to blindness! They, meanwhile,
> Friends, whom I never more may meet again,
> On springy heath, along the hill-top edge,
> Wander in gladness....
> Yes! they wander on
> In gladness all; but thou, methinks, most glad,
> My gentle-hearted Charles! for thou hast pined
> And hunger'd after Nature, many a year,
> In the great City pent, winning thy way
> With sad yet patient soul, through evil and pain
> And strange calamity! Ah, slowly sink
> Behind the western ridge, thou glorious Sun!
> Shine in the slant beams of the sinking orb,
> Ye purple heath-flowers! richlier burn, ye clouds!
> Live in the yellow light, ye distant groves!
> And kindle, thou blue Ocean! So my friend
> Struck with deep joy may stand, as I have stood,
> Silent with swimming sense; yea, gazing round
> On the wide landscape, gaze till all doth seem
> Less gross than bodily; and of such hues
> As veil the Almighty Spirit, when yet he makes
> Spirits perceive his presence.

A delight
Comes sudden on my heart, and I am glad
As I myself were there! Nor in this bower,
This little lime-tree bower, have I not mark'd
Much that has sooth'd me. Pale beneath the blaze
Hung the transparent foliage; and I watch'd
Some broad and sunny leaf, and lov'd to see
The shadow of the leaf and stem above
Dappling its sunshine! And that walnut-tree
Was richly ting'd, and a deep radiance lay
Full on the ancient ivy, which usurps
Those fronting elms, and now, with blackest mass
Makes their dark branches gleam a lighter hue
Through the late twilight: and though now the bat
Wheels silent by, and not a swallow twitters,
Yet still the solitary humble-bee
Sings in the bean-flower! Henceforth I shall know
That Nature ne'er deserts the wise and pure;
No plot so narrow, be but Nature there,
No waste so vacant, but may well employ
Each faculty of sense, and keep the heart
Awake to Love and Beauty! and sometimes
'Tis well to be bereft of promis'd good,
That we may lift the soul, and contemplate
With lively joy the joys we cannot share.

The quotation may seem inordinately long, but it is well (I think) to dwell on it. For it pictures the small garden out of which marvels were to grow, and it reminds us, who are apt in the chaos of Coleridge's subsequent fortunes to forget it, that he was always, as Dorothy Wordsworth put it, *benevolent*, of a heart as large as it was tender; really, most naturally, loving

All things, both great and small.

Some may suggest that in all this Mrs Coleridge and the infant Hartley are conspicuously absent. I answer, "For a corrective, read the yet more exquisite *Frost at Midnight*, written some seven months later, in February, 1798."

The Wordsworths had come for a fortnight: but, charmed by Coleridge and the Quantocks, they found a dwelling at Alfoxden, some three miles away, and set up house.

Then the miracle happened. Brother, sister and friend—

these three, as Coleridge has testified—became one soul. "They saw as much of one another as if the width of a street, and not a pair of coombes, had separated their several abodes"; and in the soul of that intimacy, under the influence of Dorothy—herself the silent one, content to encourage, criticise, admire—wrapped around by the lovely solitudes of the Quantocks—Coleridge and Wordsworth found themselves poets, speaking with new voices in a new dawn. The pity and terror of the French Revolution had been, after all, a purgotion, and their eyes were clear. We may recall that this year of 1797 saw the star of Buonaparte rising over Europe from Venice to Holland and, smiling at these two young men in a corner of Somersetshire, may murmur to ourselves

Caesar dum magnus ad altum
Fulminat Euphraten bello, victorque volentes
Per populos dat jura viamque affectat Olympo.
Illo Vergilium me tempore dulcis alebat
Parthenope, studiis florentem ignobilis oti—

but Time has been on Virgil's side, and, on the whole, is already upon Coleridge's and Wordsworth's.

Or, if we will, we may, remembering that the Quantocks are but miniature hills, pretty and pastoral, westering to the high sweep of Exmoor, read a small parable into what follows. On the thirteenth of November, at half-past four in the afternoon, the three friends set off to walk to Watchet, on their way to the Exmoor country, intending to defray their expenses by the sale of a poem which the two men were to compose on the road. So they told it afterwards

And sometimes I remember days of old
When fellowship seem'd not so far to seek,
And all the world and I seem'd much less cold,
And at the rainbow's foot lay surely gold,
And hope felt strong, and life itself not weak[1].

Before the first eight miles had been covered, the plan of joint

[1] Christina Rossetti's Sonnet, *Aloof*.

authorship had broken down, and Coleridge took the poem into his sole hands. He wrought at it until the following March. On the twenty-third of that month Dorothy writes in her Journal, "Coleridge dined with us. He brought his ballad *The Ancient Mariner* finished. We walked with him to the Miner's house. A beautiful evening, very starry, the horned moon." The stars were out with excuse; to celebrate the birth of a star.

Till clomb above the Eastern bar
The horned moon......

—her heart, we perceive, echoing the poem as she had gazed, and still echoing it as she writes.

"The horned moon"—Dorothy's Journal about this time is curiously observant of the starry heavens. For an entry or two:

January 24th. The evening cold and clear. The sea of a sober grey, streaked by the deeper grey clouds. The half dead sound of the near sheep-bell, in the hollow of the sloping coombe, exquisitely soothing.

January 25th. Went to Poole's after tea. The sky spread over with one continuous cloud, whitened by the light of the moon, which, though her dim shape was seen, did not throw forth so strong a light as to chequer the earth with shadows. At once the clouds seemed to cleave asunder, and left her in the centre of a black-blue vault. She sailed along, followed by multitudes of stars, small, and bright, and sharp. Their brightness seemed concentrated.

and March 21st (the evening after that homeward walk and parting beside the Miner's house):

We drank tea at Coleridge's. A quiet shower of snow was in the air during more than half our walk. At our return the sky partially shaded with clouds. The horned moon was set. Startled two night birds from the great elm tree.

"The horned moon was set." Heaven alone knows, I say—but no one who loves Coleridge can help wistfully guessing—what Dorothy Wordsworth might have made of him, as his wife. We have, perhaps, no right to guess, but we cannot help it. He met her too late, by a little while, as it was all but too late when he met William Wordsworth. We happen upon a page of hers written four years later, at Grasmere, and before the

Journals become overfull of entries such as "sad about Coleridge," "We talked about Coleridge":

Monday, Feb. 8th, 1802. After dinner...we went towards Rydale for letters....Before we had come to the shore of the Lake we met our patient bow-bent friend (the postman)....'I have two for you in my box.' We lifted up the lid, and there they lay....We broke the seal of Coleridge's letters, and I had light enough just to see that he was not ill. I put it in my pocket. At the top of the White Moss I took it to my bosom, a safer place for it.... The moon came out suddenly when we were at John's Grove, and *a star or two besides*.

But let us not load our minds with regrets for many things that never could be. "The country becomes every day more and more lovely," wrote Wordsworth: and the splendours of that summer in the Quantocks have passed into the history of our literature. The brother and sister quitted Alfoxden in June. In September Coleridge met them in London and voyaged with them on a happy, almost rollicking, jaunt to Hamburg. The *Lyrical Ballads* had been published a few days before, Coleridge contributing *The Rime of the Ancient Mariner*, *The Nightingale*, *The Foster-Mother's Tale* and *The Dungeon*. The friends had launched their thunderbolt, and went off in high spirits. It was a real thunderbolt, too: though for the moment England took it with her habitual phlegm. Mrs Coleridge sent news that "the *Lyrical Ballads* are not liked at all, by any."

At Hamburg, after a few crowded days, the travellers separated—the Wordsworths for Goslar, Coleridge for Ratzeburg, intent on acquiring a thorough knowledge of German.

II

As everybody knows, the famous Preface to the second edition of *Lyrical Ballads*—the explicit challenge *urbi et orbi*—was written by Wordsworth; and we have to choose between the alternatives—either that he never submitted it to Coleridge before putting it into the Second Edition (which sounds incredible), or that Coleridge read it and was too indolent or too good-natured to protest. As time went on, and the public grew angry, other prefaces, notes and supplements appeared, and all these satellites were by Wordsworth. He pullulated pugnacity.

On this then we must observe:

(1) That although the two poets were at one in the main, and especially in their protest against "poetic diction" as understood by the pseudo-classical followers of Pope—the sort of people who could not write "sun" or "moon" but supposed "Dian's bright orb and Sol's imperious ray" to be no less than "the Muse" deserved—in the *Ballads* themselves the two men worked on different methods; Wordsworth endeavouring to poetise the common and familiar, Coleridge the uncommon and fantastic: and it was precisely this difference which had assigned over *The Ancient Mariner* to Coleridge's sole charge.

(2) Wordsworth, being a self-centred man, naturally in the Preface laid all the stress on his own innovation. Moreover, to quote Mr Saintsbury, "as so often happens, resentment, and a dogged determination to 'spite the fools,' made him here represent the principle as much more deliberately carried out than it actually was. And the same doggedness," Mr Saintsbury goes on, "was no doubt at the root of his repetition of this principle in all his subsequent prose observations, though, as has been clear from the first to almost all impartial observers, he never, from *Tintern Abbey* onwards, achieves his highest poetry, and very rarely achieves high poetry at all, without putting that principle in his pocket."

(3) Although the Prefaces contain much shrewd writing and some that is highly felicitous, Wordsworth had not, as Coleridge had, a trained philosophical mind. He is apt to be at sea with his vocabulary; even has small sense that terms, as they have a history, should have their bounds respected. No doubt it were asking too much of Wordsworth (as of Blake), having to say just then what he had to say, to learn that older

men had, after all, provided him with a way of saying it accurately: but it remains that, through not knowing it, Wordsworth and Blake sometimes presented old thoughts with a solemn air of discovery, and sometimes meant what they could not say, or said what they could not possibly have meant. The blame of Wordsworth's lapses into bathos may often be divided between lack of humour and lack of a sense of words—in so far as these defects can be separated: and it is noticeable that whenever Coleridge, years after, pounced on such a lapse, Wordsworth almost invariably altered the passage before his next edition. For an instance:

> His widowed Mother, for a second mate
> Espoused the teacher of the Village School;
> Who on her offspring zealously bestowed
> Needful instruction.

Even less had Wordsworth a sense of clean classification—perhaps the surest test of a trained logician. Indeed his later groupings of his work into "Poems of the Fancy," "of Sentiment," "of Reflection" and so forth make a logician's heart bleed. They are as near a *fundamentum divisionis* as the famous legend over the Oxford tradesman's shop: "*University, Pork and Family Butcher.*"

Now Coleridge *had* this skill of fence, this knowledge of dialectic, which Wordsworth lacked. And not only could he have done it better, but its having been done worse intimately concerned him. For he had been part-author of the poems, and as he quite justly said at last, in the fourth chapter of *Biographia*,

> A careful and repeated examination of these [the two volumes of the Second Edition] confirms me in the belief, that the omission of less than a hundred lines would have precluded nine-tenths of the criticism of his work.

He goes on, a page later:

> In *the critical remarks, therefore*, prefixed and annexed to the *Lyrical Ballads*, I believe, we may safely rest, as the true origin of the unexampled opposition which Mr Wordsworth's writings have been since doomed to encounter.

Yes, but not "Mr Wordsworth's writings" only. Coleridge himself had been the sufferer and had only too good occasion to protest, as he does in Chapter III, his surprise

> that, having run the critical gauntlet for a certain class of faults which I had, nothing having come before the judgment-seat in the interim, I should, year after year, quarter after quarter, month after month (not to mention sundry petty periodicals of still quicker revolution, "or weekly or diurnal") have been, for at least seventeen years consecutively, dragged forth by them into the foremost lists of the proscribed, and forced to abide the brunt of abuse for faults directly opposite, and which I had not. How shall I explain this?

He explains this quite simply, and the explanation is historically true. *Noscitur a sociis:*

> The solution appears to be this,—I was in habits of intimacy with Mr Wordsworth....

Coleridge, then, had the ability to define his poetical faith, correcting, wherever they were false, the impressions of it left implicit by Wordsworth's Prefaces. He had an absolute right to do this. One may even say he owed this to his reputation. He had further every incentive under persistent attack. Yet for seventeen years he held his tongue. Why?

"Opium," say some. "Constitutional indolence," say others. No: surely when these have been taken into full and more than full account, we must seek a third reason, and a fourth.

III

Let us go back to 1798 and to Hamburg, where on the 21st of October Coleridge said goodbye to the Wordsworths and betook him to Ratzeburg, to master the German language by assiduous study. With a sufficient stock of it, four months later, he proceeded to Göttingen, matriculated at the University, attended lectures, and, for another four months, worked like a horse—"harder than I trust in God Almighty I shall ever have occasion to work again." His chief efforts he directed "towards a grounded knowledge of the German language and literature," studying Gothic also, and making collections for a life of Lessing and for a history of the *belles lettres* in Germany before Lessing. He left Göttingen on the 24th of June and arrived home at Nether Stowey in July. In his absence his second child, an infant, had died, and the blow had almost broken Mrs Coleridge's heart.

Husband and wife spent some three months together. But in October the old magnetism draws Coleridge north, and in a few weeks he and Wordsworth are touring through the Lake Country. "Both poets were most strongly attracted by Grasmere, and with Wordsworth it became merely a question of whether he should build a house by the lake-side or, as he finally decided, to take one which was then available. Before Christmas, he and his sister had taken up their abode in Dove Cottage, which all the world now goes to see." (J. Dykes Campbell.) Coleridge did not return to Stowey as a householder. After a short interval—mostly spent in London, in writing for *The Morning Post*—he travelled with wife and family to Cumberland, for a short month enjoyed the Wordsworths' hospitality, and on July 24th moved into a house of his own—"Greta Hall," Keswick—above the shore of Derwentwater, and some twelve miles from Dove Cottage. This migration from Stowey hurt poor Tom Poole, who felt himself left in the lurch and even accused his friend of "prostration" before Wordsworth. The word, no doubt, was too vivacious, as words spoken in anger are apt to be. But probably Mrs Sandford does not overshoot the truth in guessing that "Coleridge would never have been contented to live in the West of England while Wordsworth was living in the north." The relevance of this to our enquiry will appear by and by.

IV

Coleridge, then, had spent the most of a year in Germany, separated from wife and family and friends: had come back; and within a short while was renewing his old intimacy and, to all appearance, his old relations with the Wordsworths; taking these up where he had dropped them.

But no: for the interval had worked an inward change in the man; a change deep and, as we must hold, disastrous. He had landed in Germany a poet; and a poet, so to speak, with his hand in; his mind flushed with recent poetic feats, quick with poetry to come. He embarked from Germany not yet perhaps the "archangel a little damaged" (as Charles Lamb described him some sixteen or seventeen years later) but already—and worse for us—a poet lost. Now we should not, especially in these days, employ the word "Germany" to start a prejudice: and I wish in using it to guard myself carefully from suggesting a *post hoc ergo propter hoc*: and so I shall presently discuss other explanations of the *Why*. But there is the fact, as we may handily assure ourselves by tracing the sad and significant history of *Christabel*.

Coleridge began *Christabel*, as he himself tells us, at Stowey in 1797: that is, alongside *The Ancient Mariner*. Passages in Dorothy Wordsworth's Journal between Jan. 21 and March 2, 1798, show that Coleridge's mind was working under her influence, and (says Mr Dykes Campbell) "fix unmistakably the date of composition of Part I." For proof let us first take a few scattered sentences from the Journals:

Jan. 27th. Walked from seven o'clock till half-past eight....Only once while we were in the wood the moon burst through the invisible veil which enveloped her, the shadows of the oaks blackened, and their lines became more strongly marked....The manufacturer's dog makes a large, uncouth howl, which it continues many minutes after there is no noise near it but that of the brook.

March 7th. William and I drank tea at Coleridge's. A cloudy sky. Observed nothing particularly interesting--the distant prospect obscured. One only leaf upon the top of a tree—the sole remaining leaf—danced round and round like a rag blown by the wind.

March 24th. Coleridge, the Chesters, and Ellen Cruikshank called. We walked with them through the wood....A duller night than last night: a sort of white shade over the blue sky. The stars dim. The spring continues to advance very slowly....The crooked arm of the old oak tree points upwards to the moon.

24th (*next evening*). Walked to Coleridge's after tea. Arrived at home at one o'clock. The night cloudy but not dark.

Now let us put these passages together, and behold them transmuted into poetry.

Sir Leoline, the Baron rich,
Hath a toothless mastiff bitch;
From her kennel beneath the rock
She maketh answer to the clock,
Four for the quarters, and twelve for the hour;
Ever and aye, by shine and shower,
Sixteen short howls, not over loud;
Some say, she sees my lady's shroud.

Is the night chilly and dark?
The night is chilly, but not dark.
The thin grey cloud is spread on high,
It covers but not hides the sky.
The moon is behind, and at the full;
And yet she looks both small and dull.
The night is chill, the cloud is gray:
'Tis a month before the month of May,
And the Spring comes slowly up this way....

The lady sprang up suddenly,
The lovely lady, Christabel!
It moaned as near, as near can be,
But what it is she cannot tell.—
On the other side it seems to be
Of the huge, broad-breasted, old oak tree.

The night is chill; the forest bare;
Is it the wind that moaneth bleak?
There is not wind enough in the air
To move away the ringlet curl
From the lovely lady's cheek—
There is not wind enough to twirl
The one red leaf, the last of its clan,
That dances as often as dance it can,
Hanging so light, and hanging so high,
On the topmost twig that looks up at the sky.

Coleridge, we see, goes to Germany with the poem of *Christabel* in his mind and a part of it (the best part, I would add) already written. He comes home, seeks his friends, takes up *Christabel* again, and at once Dorothy's references to it become frequent and continue until their very frequency grows pathetic:

Sunday, Aug. 31*st*, 1800. At 11 o'clock Coleridge came, when I was walking in the still clear moonshine in the garden. 4 *Oct.* We talked till twelve o'clock....Exceedingly delighted with the second part of *Christabel*.

5*th October*. Coleridge read *Christabel* a second time; we had increasing pleasure.

6*th October*. Determined not to print *Christabel* with *L*[*yrical*] *B*[*allads*].

(This would be the Second Edition of *Lyrical Ballads*, in two volumes.)

On the 22nd Coleridge is again at Dove Cottage, again reciting *Christabel*. On Nov. 1st he writes to Wedgwood that his labours on *Christabel* have been interrupted. Early next year he is busy with metaphysics, but takes a week's holiday in mid-March, "that he may make *Christabel* ready for the press." In 1803 he is reciting it to Sir Humphry Davy; "unfinished," says Davy, "as I had before heard it." Yet thirteen years pass, and at last Murray publishes it, on Byron's recommendation: but it is still a fragment. Of its treatment, before and after publication, by the critics Coleridge tells us in the last chapter of *Biographia*.

V

The story of this particular composition not only bears witness to that arrest of the poetic activity which is, for us, the real tragedy of Coleridge: it indicates pretty closely the date of that arrest, and shows it (let us admit) to have been surprisingly sharp and sudden. Now explanations based on Coleridge's opium-taking, or on his domestic unhappiness, find themselves in difficulties just here. His poetic faculty shows signs of collapse at least two years before we get evidence that his wife's fretfulness has become a felt burden to him. No doubt she had been fretting—perhaps she had been nagging—for some while: but the date at which it unhinged *his* mind, and (hypothetically) to the wreck of his poetry, is the only one pertinent to our enquiry. As for opium, we have seen that he had inured himself to a large dose as far back as November 1796; that *The Ancient Mariner* and *Christabel*, Part I, were very likely composed with help of the drug, as *Kubla Khan* admittedly was born of its immediate rapture. Let us be fair, and at this point allow it a part of the insidiousness of opium—almost a property—that it stimulates only to betray, alluring its victim with promises and leaving him *of a sudden* wrecked and stranded, helpless. But when this has been granted it remains certain that during his sojourn in Germany Coleridge worked indefatigably without (so far as we can discover) having recourse to opium; as that he returned with all his other faculties improved and at their height. Only the creative, the poetic faculty was lost—or almost lost, on the point of vanishing for ever.

I confess I find it hard to accuse opium of this singular impairment in Coleridge, of afflicting him with a paralysis which it thus localised while concurrently strengthening his industry and endurance in the severest of metaphysical studies. Between analysis and synthesis a bridge undoubtedly does lie: and a man industrious, even superhumanly industrious, in the one may find it beyond his powers to cross that bridge to the other—nay, by the build of his nature many a man does, in fact, find it impossible. I do not, for example, believe it possible that Bacon should write *Hamlet*. I am morally certain that Thomas Hobbes could not have written *Paradise Lost*, even if, in Wordsworth's phrase "he'd had the mind." ("That's just it," commented Lamb. "It only wants the mind.") But Coleridge *had*, if with an effort of will, yet securely—and, the resolution taken, easily—crossed that bridge more than once. It is a good old rule not to multiply miracles *praeter necessitatem*, and it covers choosing an everyday explanation in preference to a far-fetched one or to an incalculable one such as opium. So let us take, as at any rate handier, that vulgar experience which has translated itself into the proverb "one nail drives out another."

> One's feelings lose poetic flow
> Soon after twenty-seven or so—

writes William (Johnson) Cory, translating another common human experience, that the poet in most men dies young. The cares of this world "choke the word, and it becometh unfruitful." Or, shall we say that there was a nail, and another driven in has driven it out?

At the close of his German visit Coleridge writes to his friend Josiah Wedgwood, "I shall have bought thirty pounds worth of books, chiefly metaphysics, and with a view to the one work to which I hope to dedicate in silence (sic) the prime of my life." The books were dispatched to England. Now it is true (as Mr Shawcross points out in his excellent edition of the full *Biographia*) that Coleridge was a metaphysician long before he studied the German philosophers. In the Nether Stowey days, before ever he saw Germany, when he discussed metaphysics with Wordsworth, it was as a professional with an amateur. It appears true also that the perusal of these particular volumes was for a long time delayed, and that even with the philosophy of Kant he had yet to make acquaintance. But already at Göttingen his German friends had "lamented the too abstruse nature of his ordinary speculations." And all the letters, all the journals, all the records down to *Biographia*, bear overwhelming evidence of this—that the man came back to England intensely and furiously preoccupied with metaphysics. *This*, I suggest, and neither opium nor Mrs Coleridge's fretfulness, was the main reason why he could not recall his mind to poetry nor get *Christabel* finished in time for the second edition of *Lyrical Ballads*, though poor Dorothy would help to copy it out for him. Nay, I will go farther. *This*, I hold, too, for the real reason why, for the time, he let Wordsworth's Preface pass. He could not argue with his friend about its imperfections: could not bring himself to it. He had gone too far for that, and knew too much. He had overleapt such questions as Poetic Diction, to speculate upon the transcendentals of Poetry and through what divine operation the human mind attained to it.

VI

Here I must make an observation which, whether the reader agree with it or not, he will find not impertinent to a study of *Biographia*. The dispute between Philosophy and Poetry is at once inveterate and—if it take two to make a quarrel—no quarrel at all; since Poetry pretty steadily declines to take part in it. If it were a quarrel, it would be (I believe, perforce) internecine. As it is, the philosophers do all the talking, and cut themselves: the poets go on writing Poetry. Aristotle, though a philosopher, was wise enough to let the nature and origin of Poetry alone, or rather to dismiss them in a few words and leave his successors to fight over their meaning. Actually, for him, Poetry was the stuff which, up to his time, the poets had written. Upon this (it seems likely, early in life) he worked a number of sound inductions and left a work which, though imperfectly reported for us by a disciple, has proved durable and may even last as long as Poetry itself.

Plato, unlike Aristotle, was a poet: and just there lay his tragedy. Precisely because the poet and the philosopher were born side by side in him, and because of his superstition that philosophy, being the more rational, must therefore be the true heir of his mind, the quarrel in him became internecine; nor, though his affections tore him, could he see any end but to strangle poetry and cast the body out of his system: which he accordingly did, with the result that (if we except Tolstoi, in these later times) Signor Benedetto Croce can arraign Plato with truth and justice as "the author of the only great negation of art which appears in the history of ideas."

There is nothing tragic in the fate of most of Plato's successors in the attempt to reduce poetry to a system and explain it in terms of philosophy, for the reason that tragedy does not concern itself in the failures of men who try to jump over the moon. We derive no purgation of pity and terror from a walk through the University of Laputa.

But before speaking with necessary frankness (necessary because constrained by belief) of the great and good whose names are uttered by thousands with bated breath, let me quote what one of their most learned admirers says of them, deeming that he praises them for superior beings. I take the following from a recent book *The Philosophy of Benedetto Croce*, by Dr Wildon Carr, learned President of the Aristotelian Society. It comes from his third chapter, expounding the principles of Croce's *Estetica*; and Dr Carr is engaged to show, by the example of Ruskin, the difference that Croce detects between so "indirect an analyser" as Ruskin and the true aesthetician—a difference so afflicting that Croce "feels some embarrassment in including in the history of a science one whose whole character is the reverse of scientific."

"Ruskin," says Dr Carr, "may well stand as the type of a class of writers on aesthetic of whom many and famous examples belong to our own country and literature. They are artists who criticise art. They are deeply versed in the philosophy of art and often give us profound insight into it, but their main direction is not towards a philosophy of art indifferent to any particular production; it is towards art itself and its appreciation. We go to them, for example, to enhance our enjoyment of the work of Polycleitus or Michelangelo, of Dante or of Beethoven. We do not go to them as we go to Kant or to Schopenhauer or to Schelling or to Hegel, *whose aesthetic appreciation may be no whit above the vulgar*, for a theory of art itself."

I ask why we should *not* go to men who can teach us about Polycleitus and Michelangelo, Dante or Beethoven in preference to men who—"their aesthetic appreciation being no whit above the vulgar"—by hypothesis lack capacity to separate wrong from right, good from less good, less good from utterly bad, in the subject on which they talk? Art is art: science is science: and anything so personal as poetry, painting, sculpture must be, by its nature, an art; cannot, by refusal of its nature, be a science. It is of the essence of art to particularise. "To generalise," says Blake, roundly speaking of art, "is to be an idiot. To particularise is the great distinction of merit." If, after art has particularised *Macbeth*, *Hamlet*, *Othello* and *Lear*, a man comes along and makes an induction upon them, will he be not the likelier to make a true induction if he know good work from bad? and who so likely to know this as "the artist who criticises art"? Which is likelier to know what poetry is all about—Dante or Hegel? Hegel or Heine?

"Ah, Dante and Heine know how to do it. But Hegel can tell how it is done, or ought to be done."—Is that the answer? Indeed, Dante and Heine can do it; but even *they* cannot tell how it comes, save somehow by work and fasting. How then shall he tell who knows neither what it is nor what it is about?

May we not before assenting to any of these majestical writers who would bind the sweet influences of Pleiades, cast back on our memories and bethink that next to Spring hats and parlour games, systems of philosophy are perhaps the most fugacious of all human toys? To those who listened once and eagerly, how far and faint already sound the echoes of Mansel, and Hegel *plus* Lewes *plus* T. H. Green; counter-chiming against Bentham, John Stuart Mill, Herbert Spencer, *plus* Comte as interpreted by the Positivists! Nietzsche, Bergson, James have followed; and have passed, or are passing; even Croce they tell me is in process of being supplanted—"Where are the snows of yester-year?" "You see, my friend," writes Goldsmith's Citizen of the World, Lien Chi Altangi, "there is nothing so ridiculous that has not at some time been said by some philosopher."

Even so it has befallen that all the chapters through which, in *Biographia*, Coleridge wandered in search of the difference between Fancy and Imagination have passed into shades of a shade. They started upon the almost forgotten system of Hartley and that origin had faded for Coleridge almost before he started to trace their growth; and the editor has omitted them from this book. On the other hand Coleridge's examination of Poetic Diction, and his analysis of the beauties and defects of Wordsworth's poetry, remain as fresh as on the day they were first written, and as invaluable to anyone who would distinguish between good and bad in poetry.

And the reason, surely, lies just here. Philosophy and poetry work on different planes, and their terms belong to different categories. The one seeks to comprehend, the other to apprehend: the one, moving round, would embrace the circumference of God's purpose, the other is content to leap from a centre *within us* to a point of the circumference, and seize it by direct vision. Argument from one to the other simply declines to travel. We might as easily explain poetry through mathematics or through biology as through metaphysics. Our strongest efforts waste themselves out in logomachy: in vain grasping at the thing, by substitution of one phrase for another which, meaning the same, gets no nearer to meaning *it*.

And yet—here is no real but only a seeming paradox—hopeless as is, and probably ever will be, the attempt to make philosophy explain poetry, poetry has one right background and one only, and that background is a philosophy of life; a sense, supported by reason, of an ordered universe, of a great scheme from which the poet fetches his types or his particulars, and to which he allows us to refer them. Shakespeare had this eminently: Coleridge had it profoundly: and for this reason, when Coleridge criticises Shakespeare, we get one of the noblest enjoyments of which the human intellect is capable: deep answering height, and between them a grand orchestra set sounding. Yes, and lacking this sense of the Universal, *τὸ καθόλου*, we write in anarchy, we judge in chaos.

VII

The story of *Biographia* itself—that is, of its composition—is a story of ludicrous dilatoriness, yet may be briefly told. In March, 1815, Coleridge was collecting some "scattered and manuscript poems, sufficient to make a volume." In May he tells Wordsworth he is designing a preface for it "which I shall have done in two, or at farthest three days." Two months later he has been kept a prisoner by the necessity to amplify "a preface to an Autobiographia Literaria, sketches of my literary Life and Opinions." This next becomes "a full account (raisonné) of the controversy concerning Wordsworth's poems and theory" with (fatal accession) "a disquisition on the powers of Association...and on the generic difference between the Fancy and the Imagination." At this Coleridge writes on and on, until it becomes too long for a preface, and the whole too long for a single volume. His next proposal is to extend the work to three volumes; and his next step after that, to quarrel with his printers. Fresh publishers are found, and with them, too, differences arise: the second volume is not long enough. Fresh matter (Chapter XXII, on the Defect and Beauties of Wordsworth's Poetry) was added; and then, as the volume obstinately remained too small, he tossed in *Satyrane*, an epistolary account of his wanderings in Germany, topped up with a critique of a bad play, and gave the whole painfully to the world in July, 1817.

"The *Biographia Literaria*," says Mr Arthur Symons[1], "is the

[1] Introduction in *Everyman's Library*.

greatest book of criticism in English, and one of the most annoying books in any language." It annoys, of course, mainly by its disconnectedness, to which Coleridge himself pleaded guilty, calling it an "immethodical miscellany." It sets out with an account of the motives which led to its composition. He gets to business on lines which readers of Newman's *Apologia* will probably allow to be the most effective of lines upon which to write an inner autobiography. After some premonitory lapses, and with the confession "I have wandered far from the object in view," he arrives at Stowey and the *Lyrical Ballads*. Thence he slides off upon the "law of Association," on Hartley, on Hylozoism, on the Mystics, on Kant, Schelling and others; interjects three chapters "of digression and anecdotes, etc.," "An Affectionate Exhortation," "of requests and premonitions concerning the perusal or omission of the chapter that follows"; re-engages upon Fancy and Imagination; reaches (in Chapter XIV) his real subject; deals with it magnificently through Chapters XIV and XV: interjects a comparison between the poets of the fifteenth and sixteenth centuries and those of his own time; girds up his loins again, and through Chapters XVIII and XIX, treats us to a really superb display of archery upon the target of Poetic Diction—until we seem to hear Apollo's own bow twanging, as shot upon shot whistles into the gold; pauses, wipes his brow, lets fall some chatty well-chosen remarks, a little heated, but obviously irrelevant enough to be only his own fun, and generally suggesting the spirit of a "tea interval," upon "the Present Mode of Conducting Critical Journals"; suddenly wonders "What has become of Wordsworth?" and again "God bless my soul, it's beginning to rain and I must have left my Autobiographia in the house! Does anyone by any chance remember where he saw it last?" Nobody does, but somebody fetches out Satyrane's Letters for a substitute. That will do: "after all, you know—a mere shower!.... Well, and that old Critique on Bertram?.... Thank you—if you *insist*. Shall we go in?" We move to the house. On the threshold our august host recollects himself, turns, lifts a hand in benediction—

'ΘΕΩι ΜΟΝΩι ΔΟΞΑ'

"So sorry—must you really go?" The door is shut: and for a second time the Wedding-Guest turns away; from an entertainment superlative indeed but curiously irreconcilable with his card of invitation. Last time, he dressed for a wedding and found himself attending a confessional. This time a confessional was advertised, but its closing stages have been reminiscent rather of a Pleasant Sunday Afternoon.

VIII

As for the confession, it breaks off just at the point where it would have been most interesting: and we must turn from *Biographia* to the letters, and to the Ode *Dejection*, for the sad details of the passage through which his bright seraphic spirit plunged and reawoke an old man, eloquent but old—old!—through his loss of "the shaping spirit of imagination," through his felt insensibility (if I may use the term) to those spiritual effluences of Nature which had once set his every nerve quivering. "The Poet is dead in me," he writes to Godwin in March 1801. "My imagination... lies like a cold snuff on the circular rim of a brass candlestick," and here is a passage from the Ode, written in April 1802—a poet, for once saying a genuine, a heart-broken, farewell to Poesy. Ah, if Nature and his spirit could speak together as of yore, could thrill to each other in the old intimate way, could startle this dull pain, and provoke and make it more alive!

A grief without a pang, void, dark, and drear,
  A stifled, drowsy, unimpassioned grief,
  Which finds no natural outlet, no relief,
    In word, or sigh, or tear—

O Lady! in this wan and heartless mood,
To other thoughts by yonder throstle woo'd,
  All this long eve, so balmy and serene,
Have I been gazing on the western sky,
  And its peculiar tint of yellow green:
And still I gaze—and with how blank an eye!
And those thin clouds above, in flakes and bars,
That give away their motion to the stars;
Those stars, that glide behind them or between,
Now sparkling, now bedimmed, but always seen:
Yon crescent Moon, as fixed as if it grew
In its own cloudless, starless lake of blue;
I see them all so excellently fair,
I see, not feel, how beautiful they are!

    My genial spirits fail;
    And what can these avail
To lift the smothering weight from off my breast?
    It were a vain endeavour,
    Though I should gaze for ever
On that green light that lingers in the west:
I may not hope from outward forms to win
The passion and the life, whose fountains are within.
O Lady! we receive but what we give,
And in our life alone does Nature live:
Ours is her wedding-garment, ours her shroud!
  And would we aught behold, of higher worth,
Than that inanimate cold world allowed
To the poor loveless ever-anxious crowd,
  Ah! from the soul itself must issue forth
A light, a glory, a fair luminous cloud
    Enveloping the Earth—
And from the soul itself must there be sent
  A sweet and potent voice, of its own birth,
Of all sweet sounds the life and element!

O pure of heart! thou need'st not ask of me
What this strong music in the soul may be!
What, and wherein it doth exist,
This light, this glory, this fair luminous mist,
This beautiful and beauty-making power.
  Joy, virtuous Lady! Joy that ne'er was given,
Save to the pure, and in their purest hour,
Life, and Life's effluence, cloud at once and shower,
Joy, Lady! is the spirit and the power,
Which wedding Nature to us gives in dower
  A new Earth and new Heaven,

Undreamt of by the sensual and the proud—
Joy is the sweet voice, Joy the luminous cloud—
We in ourselves rejoice!
And thence flows all that charms or ear or sight,
All melodies the echoes of that voice,
All colours a suffusion from that light.

There was a time when, though my path was rough,
This joy within me dallied with distress,
And all misfortunes were but as the stuff
Whence Fancy made me dreams of happiness:
For hope grew round me, like the twining vine,
And fruits, and foliage, not my own, seemed mine.
But now afflictions bow me down to earth:
Nor care I that they rob me of my mirth;
But oh! each visitation
Suspends what nature gave me at my birth,
My shaping spirit of Imagination.
For not to think of what I needs must feel,
But to be still and patient, all I can;
And haply by abstruse research to steal
From my own nature all the natural man—
This was my sole resource, my only plan:
Till that which suits a part infects the whole,
And now is almost grown the habit of my soul.

In *Biographia* the narrative commits the worst fault of narrative: it breaks key. It falsettos upon irrelevant trifles; frequently at inordinate length, and not seldom with a touch of devastating facetiousness of the sort that, as practised by De Quincey, again and again stings the gentlest reader with a mad desire to arise and hurl the book across the room. (I wish indeed we could be sure De Quincey did not catch the trick from Coleridge.) Nor can I, for one, greatly prefer even to this, the "soft shower of words," as Mr Saintsbury calls it—the gradual dusky veil closing Chapter XIV. "Finally, good sense is the body of poetic genius, fancy its drapery, emotion its life, and imagination the soul"—with the rest of it. It is so pretty:

Weave a circle round him thrice,
And close your eyes with holy dread,
For he on honeydew hath fed,
And drunk the milk of Paradise.

It is *very* pretty. But who knows precisely what it means?

IX

When he turns to examine and settle the question of Poetic Diction, his sword-play becomes quite masterly. Every youth who loves letters should get this part of *Biographia* by heart, and not only for its truth but for the *way of it*. But even here I find myself in agreement with Mr Shawcross that, done otherwise, it had perhaps in the circumstances better served Coleridge's purpose. That purpose was, as we have seen, to clear himself (though late) of consent with a certain few extravagances in Wordsworth's Preface, while assenting to it generally. The circumstances were that the two men, for long dear to one another, had become estranged in 1810, owing to a rash word of Wordsworth, misreported by Basil Montagu, who was a fool to report it at all; that the breach had been healed by Crabb Robinson in 1812, was re-opened in 1813 (apparently through Wordsworth's omission to answer a tender letter of sympathy on the loss of his son) and never again thoroughly patched. Certainly few sorrows in life had caused Coleridge a worse heart-ache. I agree, then, with Mr Shawcross that if, instead of dwelling on mistakes which he allows to be few if not trivial, Coleridge had briefly cleared himself of complicity with these and gone on to elaborate—to improve—what was true and useful and (as he casually shows in the opening of Chapter XIX) of primary importance in the gospel of both, he had done a better general service to criticism, with a better personal service to Wordsworth, and at the same time avoided the suspicion that he wrote out of an embittered mind. "*Something* at least must have occurred to pervert Coleridge's vision, if he could really believe that, in his criticisms in *Biographia Literaria*, he was serving Wordsworth's cause (and this cause was his own also) to the best of his ability."

No one surely can read the book and miss to detect on page after page the wistful solicitude for Wordsworth's feelings.

Since the Nether Stowey days eighteen years had scored themselves on Coleridge, and fatally scored out promise after promise. His family life had gone to ruin. Opium had wrecked his will, and plunged in perpetual shadow the brightness of his genius which in *Kubla Khan* had shone as something ineffable. He was no longer a Michael armed and eager, but a spent old man. He was no longer a poet. In the book he never reckons himself a poet: it is always of Wordsworth he is thinking.

Yes, that is it—of Wordsworth, his friend. Broken as he is, yet he knows (he must have known) that in criticism—the matter of his discourse—he stands to Wordsworth as a giant: and the business of his self-justification *involves* the correction of Wordsworth where Wordsworth has been wrong. Yet how tenderly he handles him, how eager he is to praise, how chivalrously (as you follow the argument) he breaks ground, lowers his guard, forbears to use his own strength!

I say that, if we read *Biographia* with this in our minds, this alone will suffice to make it, for us, a beautiful book. Wordsworth read it and judged it, conscientiously, in his own way. To Crabb Robinson he confided that "the praise he considered extravagant, and the censure inconsiderate. It had given him no pleasure." It was Wordsworth who had written

> Alas! the *gratitude* of men
> Hath oftener left me mourning.

But it is not enough, in this world, to have the right within you. To be "in the right" is more satisfactory, and easier, and far safer.

ARTHUR QUILLER-COUCH

10 *December* 1919

So wenig er auch bestimmt seyn mag, andere zu belehren, so wünscht er doch sich denen mitzutheilen, die er sich gleich gesinnt weiss, (oder hofft,) deren Anzahl aber in der Breite der Welt zerstreut ist; er wünscht sein Verhältniss zu den altesten Freunden dadurch wieder anzuknüpfen, mit neuen es fortzusetzen, und in der letzten Generation sich wieder andere für seine übrige Lebenszeit zu gewinnen. Er wünscht der Jugend die Umwege zu ersparen, auf denen er sich selbst verirrte.

(GOETHE, *Einleitung in die Propyläen.*)

TRANSLATION. Little call as he may have to instruct others, he wishes nevertheless to open out his heart to such as he either knows or hopes to be of like mind with himself, but who are widely scattered in the world: he wishes to knit anew his connections with his oldest friends, to continue those recently formed, and to win other friends among the rising generation for the remaining course of his life. He wishes to spare the young those circuitous paths, on which he himself had lost his way.

BIOGRAPHIA LITERARIA

CHAPTER I.

Motives to the present work—Reception of the Author's first publication—Discipline of his taste at school—Effect of contemporary writers on youthful minds—Bowles's Sonnets—Comparison between the poets before and since Pope.

It has been my lot to have had my name introduced both in conversation, and in print, more frequently than I find it easy to explain, whether I consider the fewness, unimportance, and limited circulation of my writings, or the retirement and distance, in which I have lived, both from the literary and political world. Most often it has been connected with some charge which I could not acknowledge, or some principle which I had never entertained. Nevertheless, had I had no other motive or incitement, the reader would not have been troubled with this exculpation. What my additional purposes were, will be seen in the following pages. It will be found, that the least of what I have written concerns myself personally. I have used the narration chiefly for the purpose of giving a continuity to the work, in part for the sake of the miscellaneous reflections suggested to me by particular events, but still more as introductory to a statement of my principles in Politics, Religion, and Philosophy, and an application of the rules, deduced from philosophical principles, to poetry and criticism. But of the objects, which I proposed to myself, it was not the least important to effect, as far as possible, a settlement of the long continued controversy concerning the true nature of poetic diction; and at the same time to define with the utmost impartiality the real *poetic* character of the poet, by whose writings this controversy was first kindled, and has been since fuelled and fanned.

In the spring of 1796, when I had but little passed the verge of manhood, I published a small volume of juvenile poems.

They were received with a degree of favour, which, young as I was, I well know was bestowed on them not so much for any positive merit, as because they were considered buds of hope and promises of better works to come. The critics of that day, the most flattering, equally with the severest, concurred in objecting to them obscurity, a general turgidness of diction, and a profusion of new coined double epithets.[1] The first is the fault which a writer is the least able to detect in his own compositions: and my mind was not then sufficiently disciplined to receive the authority of others, as a substitute for my own conviction. Satisfied that the thoughts, such as they were, could not have been expressed otherwise, or at least more perspicuously, I forgot to inquire, whether the thoughts themselves did not demand a degree of attention unsuitable to the nature and objects of poetry. This remark however applies chiefly, though not exclusively, to the Religious Musings. The remainder of the charge I admitted to its full extent, and not without sincere acknowledgments both to my private and public censors for their friendly admonitions. In the after editions, I pruned the double epithets with no sparing hand, and used my best efforts to tame the swell and glitter both of thought and diction; though in truth, these parasite plants of youthful poetry had insinuated themselves into my longer poems with such intricacy of union,

[1] The authority of Milton and Shakespeare may be usefully pointed out to young authors. In the Comus and other early poems of Milton there is a superfluity of double epithets; while in the Paradise Lost we find very few, in the Paradise Regained scarce any. The same remark holds almost equally true of the Love's Labour's Lost, Romeo and Juliet, Venus and Adonis, and Lucrece, compared with the Lear, Macbeth, Othello, and Hamlet of our great Dramatist. The rule for the admission of double epithets seems to be this: either that they should be already denizens of our language, such as *blood-stained*, *terror-stricken*, *self-applauding:* or when a new epithet, or one found in books only, is hazarded, that it, at least, be one word, not two words made one by mere virtue of the printer's hyphen. A language which, like the English, is almost without cases, is indeed in its very genius unfitted for compounds. If a writer, every time a compounded word suggests itself to him, would seek for some other mode of expressing the same sense, the chances are always greatly in favour of his finding a better word. *Ut tanquam scopulum sic fugias insolens verbum*, is the wise advice of Cæsar to the Roman Orators, and the precept applies with double force to the writers in our own language. But it must not be forgotten, that the same Cæsar wrote a Treatise for the purpose of reforming the ordinary language by bringing it to a greater accordance with the principles of logic or universal grammar.

that I was often obliged to omit disentangling the weed, from the fear of snapping the flower. From that period to the date of the present work I have published nothing, with my name, which could by any possibility have come before the board of anonymous criticism. Even the three or four poems, printed with the works of a friend,[1] as far as they were censured at all, were charged with the same or similar defects, (though I am persuaded not with equal justice,)—with an EXCESS OF ORNAMENT, in addition to STRAINED AND ELABORATE DICTION. I must be permitted to add, that, even at the early period of my juvenile poems, I saw and admitted the superiority of an austerer and more natural style, with an insight not less clear, than I at present possess. My judgment was stronger than were my powers of realizing its dictates; and the faults of my language, though indeed partly owing to a wrong choice of subjects, and the desire of giving a poetic colouring to abstract and metaphysical truths, in which a new world then seemed to open upon me, did yet, in part likewise, originate in unfeigned diffidence of my own comparative talent.—During several years of my youth and early manhood, I reverenced those who had re-introduced the manly simplicity of the Greek, and of our own elder poets, with such enthusiasm as made the hope seem presumptuous of writing successfully in the same style. Perhaps a similar process has happened to others; but my earliest poems were marked by an ease and simplicity, which I have studied, perhaps with inferior success, to impress on my later compositions.

At school, (Christ's Hospital,) I enjoyed the inestimable advantage of a very sensible, though at the same time, a very severe master, the Reverend James Bowyer. He early moulded my taste to the preference of Demosthenes to Cicero, of Homer and Theocritus to Virgil, and again of Virgil to Ovid. He habituated me to compare Lucretius, (in such extracts as I then read,) Terence, and above all the chaster poems of Catullus, not only with the Roman poets of the, so called, silver and brazen ages; but with even those of the Augustan æra: and on grounds of plain sense and universal logic to see and assert the superiority of the former in the truth and nativeness both of their thoughts and diction. At the same time that we were studying the Greek

[1] See the criticisms on the Ancient Mariner, in the Monthly and Critical Reviews of the first volume of the Lyrical Ballads.

tragic poets, he made us read Shakespeare and Milton as lessons: and they were the lessons too, which required most time and trouble to *bring up*, so as to escape his censure. I learned from him, that Poetry, even that of the loftiest and, seemingly, that of the wildest odes, had a logic of its own, as severe as that of science; and more difficult, because more subtle, more complex, and dependent on more, and more fugitive causes. In the truly great poets, he would say, there is a reason assignable, not only for every word, but for the position of every word; and I well remember that, availing himself of the synonymes to the Homer of Didymus, he made us attempt to show, with regard to each, *why* it would not have answered the same purpose; and *wherein* consisted the peculiar fitness of the word in the original text.

In our own English compositions, (at least for the last three years of our school education,) he showed no mercy to phrase, metaphor, or image, unsupported by a sound sense, or where the same sense might have been conveyed with equal force and dignity in plainer words.[1] *Lute*, *harp* and *lyre*, *Muse*, *Muses*, and *inspirations*, *Pegasus*, *Parnassus*, and *Hippocrene* were all an abomination to him. In fancy I can almost hear him now, exclaiming "Harp? Harp? Lyre? Pen and ink, boy, you mean! Muse, boy, Muse? Your nurse's daughter, you mean! Pierian spring? Oh aye! the cloister-pump, I suppose!" Nay certain introductions, similes, and examples, were placed by name on a list of interdiction. Among the similes, there was, I remember, that of the manchineel fruit, as suiting equally well with too many subjects; in which however it yielded the palm at once to the example of Alexander and Clytus, which was equally good and apt, whatever might be the theme. Was it ambition? Alexander and Clytus!—Flattery? Alexander and Clytus!—Anger—drunkenness—pride—friendship—ingratitude—late repentance? Still, still Alexander and Clytus! At length, the praises of agriculture having been exemplified in the sagacious observation that, had Alexander been holding the plough, he would not have run his friend Clytus through with a spear, this tried, and serviceable old friend was banished by public edict *in sæcula sæculorum*. I have sometimes ventured

[1] This is worthy of ranking as a maxim, (*regula maxima*,) of criticism. Whatever is translatable in other and simpler words of the same language, without loss of sense or dignity, is bad. N.B. By dignity I mean the absence of ludicrous and debasing associations.

to think, that a list of this kind, or an *index expurgatorius* of certain well known and ever returning phrases, both introductory and transitional, including a large assortment of modest egoisms, and flattering illeisms, and the like, might be hung up in our Law-courts, and both Houses of Parliament, with great advantage to the public, as an important saving of national time, an incalculable relief to his Majesty's ministers, but above all, as ensuring the thanks of country attornies, and their clients, who have private bills to carry through the House.

Be this as it may, there was one custom of our master's, which I cannot pass over in silence, because I think it imitable and worthy of imitation. He would often permit our exercises, under some pretext of want of time, to accumulate, till each lad had four or five to be looked over. Then placing the whole number *abreast* on his desk, he would ask the writer, why this or that sentence might not have found as appropriate a place under this or that other thesis; and if no satisfying answer could be returned, and two faults of the same kind were found in one exercise, the irrevocable verdict followed, the exercise was torn up, and another on the same subject to be produced, in addition to the tasks of the day. The reader will, I trust, excuse this tribute of recollection to a man, whose severities, even now, not seldom furnish the dreams, by which the blind fancy would fain interpret to the mind the painful sensations of distempered sleep; but neither lessen nor dim the deep sense of my moral and intellectual obligations. He sent us to the University excellent Latin and Greek scholars, and tolerable Hebraists. Yet our classical knowledge was the least of the good gifts, which we derived from his zealous and conscientious tutorage. He is now gone to his final reward, full of years, and full of honours, even of those honours, which were dearest to his heart, as gratefully bestowed by that school, and still binding him to the interests of that school, in which he had been himself educated, and to which during his whole life he was a dedicated thing.

From causes, which this is not the place to investigate, no models of past times, however perfect, can have the same vivid effect on the youthful mind, as the productions of contemporary genius. The discipline, my mind had undergone, *Ne falleretur rotundo sono et versuum cursu, cincinnis et floribus; sed ut inspiceret quidnam subesset, quæ sedes, quod firmamentum, quis fundus verbis; an figuræ essent mera ornatura et orationis fucus; vel sanguinis e materiæ ipsius corde effluentis rubor quidam nativus et incalescentia genuina;*—removed all obstacles to the appreciation of excellence in style without diminishing my delight. That I was thus prepared for the perusal of Mr. Bowles's sonnets and earlier poems, at once increased *their* influence, and *my* enthusiasm. The great works of past ages seem to a young man things of another race, in respect of which his faculties must remain passive and submiss, even as to the stars and mountains. But the writings of a contemporary, perhaps not many years older than himself, surrounded by the same circumstances, and disciplined by the same manners, possess a *reality* for him, and inspire an actual friendship as of a man for a man. His very admiration is the wind which fans and feeds his hope. The poems themselves assume the properties of flesh and blood. To recite, to extol, to contend for them is but the payment of a debt due to one, who exists to receive it.

There are indeed modes of teaching which have produced, and are producing, youths of a very different stamp; modes of teaching, in comparison with which we have been called on to despise our great public schools, and universities,

in whose halls are hung
Armoury of the invincible knights of old—

modes, by which children are to be metamorphosed into prodigies. And prodigies with a vengeance have I known thus produced; —prodigies of self-conceit, shallowness, arrogance, and infidelity! Instead of storing the memory, during the period when the memory is the predominant faculty, with facts for the after exercise of the judgment; and instead of awakening by the noblest models the fond and unmixed LOVE and ADMIRATION, which is the natural and graceful temper of early youth; *these* nurslings of improved pedagogy are taught to dispute and decide; to suspect all but their own and their lecturer's wisdom; and to hold nothing sacred from their contempt, but their own contemptible arrogance; —boy-graduates in all the technicals, and in all the dirty passions and impudence of anonymous criticism. To such dispositions alone can the admonition of Pliny be requisite, *Neque enim debet operibus ejus obesse, quod vivit. An si inter eos, quos nunquam vidimus, floruisset, non solum libros ejus, verum etiam imagines con-*

quireremus, ejusdem nunc honor præsentis, et gratia quasi satietate languescet? At hoc pravum, malignumque est, non admirari hominem admiratione dignissimum, quia videre, complecti, nec laudare tantum, verum etiam amare contingit.

I had just entered on my seventeenth year, when the sonnets of Mr. Bowles, twenty in number, and just then published in a quarto pamphlet, were first made known and presented to me, by a schoolfellow who had quitted us for the University, and who, during the whole time that he was in our first form, (or in our school language a GRECIAN,) had been my patron and protector. I refer to Dr. Middleton, the truly learned, and every way excellent Bishop of Calcutta:

qui laudibus amplis
Ingenium celebrare meum, calamumque solebat,
Calcar agens animo validum. Non omnia terræ
Obruta; vivit amor, vivit dolor; ora negatur
Dulcia conspicere; at flere et meminisse relictum est.

It was a double pleasure to me, and still remains a tender recollection, that I should have received from a friend so revered the first knowledge of a poet, by whose works, year after year, I was so enthusiastically delighted and inspired. My earliest acquaintances will not have forgotten the undisciplined eagerness and impetuous zeal, with which I laboured to make proselytes, not only of my companions, but of all with whom I conversed, of whatever rank, and in whatever place. As my school finances did not permit me to purchase copies, I made, within less than a year and a half, more than forty transcriptions, as the best presents I could offer to those, who had in any way won my regard. And with almost equal delight did I receive the three or four following publications of the same author.

Though I have seen and known enough of mankind to be well aware, that I shall perhaps stand alone in my creed, and that it will be well, if I subject myself to no worse charge than that of singularity; I am not therefore deterred from avowing, that I regard, and ever have regarded the obligations of intellect among the most sacred of the claims of gratitude. A valuable thought, or a particular train of thoughts, gives me additional pleasure, when I can safely refer and attribute it to the conversation or correspondence of another. My obligations to Mr. Bowles were indeed important, and for radical good. At a very premature age, even before my fifteenth year, I had bewildered myself in metaphysics, and in theological controversy. Nothing else pleased me. History, and particular facts, lost all interest in my mind. Poetry —(though for a school-boy of that age, I was above par in English versification, and had already produced two or three compositions which, I may venture to say, without reference to my age, were somewhat above mediocrity, and which had gained me more credit than the sound, good sense of my old master was at all pleased with,)—poetry itself, yea, novels and romances, became insipid to me. In my friendless wanderings on our *leave-days*,[1] (for I was an orphan, and had scarcely any connections in London,) highly was I delighted, if any passenger, especially if he were dressed in black, would enter into conversation with me. For I soon found the means of directing it to my favourite subjects

> Of providence, fore-knowledge, will, and fate,
> Fix'd fate, free will, fore-knowledge absolute,
> And found no end in wandering mazes lost.

This preposterous pursuit was, beyond doubt, injurious both to my natural powers, and to the progress of my education. It would perhaps have been destructive, had it been continued; but from this I was auspiciously withdrawn, partly indeed by an accidental introduction to an amiable family, chiefly however, by the genial influence of a style of poetry, so tender and yet so manly, so natural and real, and yet so dignified and harmonious, as the sonnets and other early poems of Mr. Bowles. Well would it have been for me, perhaps, had I never relapsed into the same mental disease; if I had continued to pluck the flower and reap the harvest from the cultivated surface, instead of delving in the unwholesome quicksilver mines of metaphysic lore. And if in after time I have sought a refuge from bodily pain and mismanaged sensibility in abstruse researches, which exercised the strength and subtilty of the understanding without awakening the feelings of the heart; still there was a long and blessed interval, during which my natural faculties were allowed to expand, and my original tendencies to develope themselves;—my fancy, and the love of nature, and the sense of beauty in forms and sounds.

The second advantage, which I owe to my early perusal,

[1] The Christ's Hospital phrase, not for holidays altogether, but for those on which the boys are permitted to go beyond the precincts of the school.

and admiration of these poems, (to which let me add, though known to me at a somewhat later period, the Lewesdon Hill of Mr. Crowe) bears more immediately on my present subject. Among those with whom I conversed, there were, of course, very many who had formed their taste, and their notions of poetry, from the writings of Pope and his followers; or to speak more generally, in that school of French poetry, condensed and invigorated by English understanding, which had predominated from the last century. I was not blind to the merits cf this school, yet, as from inexperience of the world, and consequent want of sympathy with the general subjects of these poems, they gave me little pleasure, I doubtless undervalued the *kind*, and with the presumption of youth withheld from its masters the legitimate name of poets. I saw that the excellence of this kind consisted in just and acute observations on men and manners in an artificial state of society, as its matter and substance; and in the logic of wit, conveyed in smooth and strong epigrammatic couplets, as its *form*: that even when the subject was addressed to the fancy, or the intellect, as in the Rape of Lock, or the Essay on Man; nay, when it was a consecutive narration, as in that astonishing product of matchless talent and ingenuity, Pope's Translation of the Iliad; still a *point* was looked for at the end of each second line, and the whole was, as it were, a *sorites*, or, if I may exchange a logical for a grammatical metaphor, a *conjunction disjunctive*, of epigrams. Meantime the matter and diction seemed to me characterized not so much by poetic thoughts, as by thoughts *translated* into the language of poetry. On this last point, I had occasion to render my own thoughts gradually more and more plain to myself, by frequent amicable disputes concerning Darwin's Botanic Garden, which, for some years, was greatly extolled, not only by the *reading* public in general, but even by those, whose genius and natural robustness of understanding enabled them afterwards to act foremost in dissipating these "painted mists" that occasionally rise from the marshes at the foot of Parnassus. During my first Cambridge vacation, I assisted a friend in a contribution for a literary society in Devonshire: and in this I remember to have compared Darwin's work to the Russian palace of ice, glittering, cold and transitory. In the same essay too, I assigned sundry reasons, chiefly drawn from a comparison of passages in the Latin poets with the original Greek, from which they were borrowed, for the preference of Collins's odes to those of Gray; and of the simile in Shakespeare

> How like a younker or a prodigal,
> The scarfed bark puts from her native bay,
> Hugg'd and embraced by the strumpet wind!
> How like the prodigal doth she return,
> With over-weather'd ribs and ragged sails,
> Lean, rent, and beggar'd by the strumpet wind!
> (Merch. of Ven. Act II. sc. 6.)

to the imitation in the Bard;

> Fair laughs the morn, and soft the zephyr blows
> While proudly riding o'er the azure realm
> In gallant trim the gilded vessel goes,
> Youth at the prow and pleasure at the helm;
> Regardless of the sweeping whirlwind's sway,
> That hush'd in grim repose, expects its evening prey.

(in which, by the bye, the words "realm" and "sway" are rhymes dearly purchased)—I preferred the original on the ground, that in the imitation it depended wholly on the compositor's putting, or not putting, a *small capital*, both in this, and in many other passages of the same poet, whether the words should be personifications, or mere abstractions. I mention this, because, in referring various lines in Gray to their original in Shakespeare and Milton, and in the clear perception how completely all the propriety was lost in the transfer, I was, at that early period, led to a conjecture, which, many years afterwards was recalled to me from the same thought having been started in conversation, but far more ably, and developed more fully, by Mr. Wordsworth;—namely, that this style of poetry, which I have characterised above, as translations of prose thoughts into poetic language, had been kept up by, if it did not wholly arise from, the custom of writing Latin verses, and the great importance attached to these exercises, in our public schools. Whatever might have been the case in the fifteenth century, when the use of the Latin tongue was so general among learned men, that Erasmus is said to have forgotten his native language; yet in the present day it is not to be supposed, that a youth can *think* in Latin, or that he can have any other reliance on the force or fitness of his phrases, but the authority of the writer from whom he has adopted them. Consequently he must first prepare his thoughts, and then pick out, from Virgil, Horace, Ovid, or perhaps more compendiously from his Gradus, halves and quarters of lines, in which to embody them.

I never object to a certain degree of disputatiousness in a young man from the age of seventeen to that of four or five and twenty, provided I find him always arguing on one side of the question. The controversies, occasioned by my unfeigned zeal for the honour of a favourite contemporary, then known to me only by his works, were of great advantage in the formation and establishment of my taste and critical opinions. In my defence of the lines running into each other, instead of closing at each couplet; and of natural language, neither bookish, nor vulgar, neither redolent of the lamp, nor of the kennel, such as *I will remember thee*; instead of the same thought tricked up in the rag-fair finery of,

> —— thy image on her wing
> Before my FANCY's eye shall MEMORY bring,—

I had continually to adduce the metre and diction of the Greek poets from Homer to Theocritus inclusively; and still more of our elder English poets from Chaucer to Milton. Nor was this all. But as it was my constant reply to authorities brought against me from later poets of great name, that no authority could avail in opposition to TRUTH, NATURE, LOGIC, and the LAWS OF UNIVERSAL GRAMMAR; actuated too by my former passion for metaphysical investigations; I laboured at a solid foundation, on which permanently to ground my opinions, in the component faculties of the human mind itself, and their comparative dignity and importance. According to the faculty or source, from which the pleasure given by any poem or passage was derived, I estimated the merit of such poem or passage. As the result of all my reading and meditation, I abstracted two critical aphorisms, deeming them to comprise the conditions and *criteria* of poetic style;—first, that not the poem which we have *read*, but that to which we return, with the greatest pleasure, possesses the genuine power, and claims the name of *essential poetry*;—secondly, that whatever lines can be translated into other words of the same language, without diminution of their significance, either in sense or association, or in any worthy feeling, are so far vicious in their diction. Be it however observed, that I excluded from the list of worthy feelings, the pleasure derived from mere novelty in the reader, and the desire of exacting wonderment at his powers in the author.

Oftentimes since then, in perusing French tragedies, I have fancied two marks of admiration at the end of each line, as hieroglyphics of the author's own admiration at his own cleverness. Our genuine admiration of a great poet is a continuous *under-current* of feeling; it is every where present, but seldom any where as a separate excitement. I was wont boldly to affirm, that it would be scarcely more difficult to push a stone out from the Pyramids with the bare hand, than to alter a word, or the position of a word, in Milton or Shakespeare, (in their most important works at least,) without making the poet say something else, or something worse, than he does say. One great distinction, I appeared to myself to see plainly between even the characteristic faults of our elder poets, and the false beauty of the moderns. In the former, from Donne to Cowley, we find the most fantastic out-of-the-way thoughts, but in the most pure and genuine mother English; in the latter the most obvious thoughts, in language the most fantastic and arbitrary. Our faulty elder poets sacrificed the passion and passionate flow of poetry to the subtleties of intellect and to the starts of wit; the moderns to the glare and glitter of a perpetual, yet broken and heterogeneous imagery, or rather to an amphibious something, made up, half of image, and half of abstract[1] meaning. The one sacrificed the heart to the head; the other both heart and head to point and drapery.

The reader must make himself acquainted with the general style of composition that was at that time deemed poetry, in order to understand and account for the effect produced on me by the Sonnets, the Monody at Matlock, and the Hope, of Mr. Bowles; for it is peculiar to original genius to become less and less *striking*, in proportion to its success in improving the taste and judgment of its contemporaries. The poems of West, indeed, had the merit of chaste and manly diction; but they were cold, and, if I may so express it, only *dead-coloured*; while in the best of Warton's there is a stiffness, which too often gives them the appearance of imitations from the Greek. Whatever relation, therefore, of cause or impulse Percy's collection of Ballads may bear to the most *popular* poems of the present day; yet in a more sustained and elevated style, of the then living poets Cowper

[1] I remember a ludicrous instance in the poem of a young tradesman:

> No more will I endure love's pleasing pain,
> Or round my *heart's leg* tie his galling chain.

and Bowles[1] were, to the best of my knowledge, the first who combined natural thoughts with natural diction; the first who reconciled the heart with the head.

It is true, as I have before mentioned, that from diffidence in my own powers, I for a short time adopted a laborious and florid diction, which I myself deemed, if not absolutely vicious, yet of very inferior worth. Gradually, however, my practice conformed to my better judgment; and the compositions of my twenty-fourth and twenty-fifth years—(for example, the shorter blank verse poems, the lines, which now form the middle and conclusion of the poem entitled the Destiny of Nations, and the tragedy of Remorse)—are not more below my present ideal in respect of the general tissue of the style, than those of the latest date. Their faults were at least a remnant of the former leaven, and among the many who have done me the honour of putting my poems in the same class with those of my betters, the one or two, who have pretended to bring examples of affected simplicity from my volume, have been able to adduce but one instance, and that out of a copy of verses half ludicrous, half splenetic, which I intended, and had myself characterized, as *sermoni propiora*.

Every reform, however necessary, will by weak minds be carried to an excess, which will itself need reforming. The reader will excuse me for noticing, that I myself was the first to expose *risu honesto* the three sins of poetry, one or the other of which is the most likely to beset a young writer. So long ago as the publication of the second number of the Monthly Magazine, under the name of Nehemiah Higginbottom, I contributed three sonnets, the first of which had for its object to excite a good-natured laugh at the spirit of *doleful egotism*, and at the recurrence of favourite phrases, with the double defect of being at once trite and licentious;—the second was on low creeping language and

[1] Cowper's Task was published some time before the Sonnets of Mr. Bowles; but I was not familiar with it till many years afterwards. The vein of satire which runs through that excellent poem, together with the sombre hue of its religious opinions, would probably, *at that time*, have prevented its laying any strong hold on my affections. The love of nature seems to have led Thomson to a cheerful religion; and a gloomy religion to have led Cowper to a love of nature. The one would carry his fellow-men along with him into nature; the other flies to nature from his fellow-men. In chastity of diction however, and the harmony of blank verse, Cowper leaves Thomson immeasurably below him; yet still I feel the latter to have been the *born poet*.

thoughts, under the pretence of *simplicity*; the third, the phrases of which were borrowed entirely from my own poems, on the indiscriminate use of elaborate and swelling language and imagery. The reader will find them in the note below,[1] and will I trust

[1] SONNET I.

Pensive at eve, on the hard world I mused,
And my poor heart was sad; so at the Moon
I gazed, and sighed, and sighed; for ah how soon
Eve saddens into night! mine eyes perused
With tearful vacancy the dampy grass
That wept and glitter'd in the paly ray:
And I did pause me on my lonely way
And mused me on the wretched ones that pass
O'er the bleak heath of sorrow. But alas!
Most of myself I thought! when it befel,
That the soothe spirit of the breezy wood
Breath'd in mine ear: "All this is very well,
But much of one thing, is for no thing good."
Oh my poor heart's inexplicable swell!

SONNET II.

Oh I do love thee, meek Simplicity!
For of thy lays the lulling simpleness
Goes to my heart, and soothes each small distress,
Distress tho' small, yet haply great to me.
'Tis true on Lady Fortune's gentlest pad
I amble on; and yet I know not why
So sad I am! but should a friend and I
Frown, pout and part, then I am very sad.
And then with sonnets and with sympathy
My dreamy bosom's mystic woes I pall;
Now of my false friend plaining plaintively,
Now raving at mankind in general;
But whether sad or fierce, 'tis simple all,
All very simple, meek Simplicity!

SONNET III.

And this reft house is that, the which he built,
Lamented Jack! and here his malt he pil'd,
Cautious in vain! these rats, that squeak so wild,
Squeak not unconscious of their father's guilt.
Did he not see her gleaming thro' the glade!
Belike 'twas she, the maiden all forlorn.
What tho' she milk no cow with crumpled horn,
Yet, aye she haunts the dale where erst she stray'd:
And aye, beside her stalks her amorous knight!
Still on his thighs their wonted brogues are worn,

regard them as reprinted for biographical purposes alone, and not for their poetic merits. So general at that time, and so decided was the opinion concerning the characteristic vices of my style, that a celebrated physician (now, alas! no more) speaking of me in other respects with his usual kindness to a gentleman, who was about to meet me at a dinner party, could not however resist giving him a hint not to mention *The house that Jack built* in my presence, for "that I was as *sore as a boil* about that sonnet;" he not knowing that I was myself the author of it.

And thro' those brogues, still tatter'd and betorn,
His hindward charms gleam an unearthly white.
Ah! thus thro' broken clouds at night's high noon
Peeps in fair fragments forth the full-orb'd harvest-moon!

The following anecdote will not be wholly out of place here, and may perhaps amuse the reader. An amateur performer in verse expressed to a common friend a strong desire to be introduced to me, but hesitated in accepting my friend's immediate offer, on the score that "he was, he must acknowledge, the author of a confounded severe epigram on my *Ancient Mariner*, which had given me great pain." I assured my friend that, if the epigram was a good one, it would only increase my desire to become acquainted with the author, and begged to hear it recited: when, to my no less surprise than amusement, it proved to be one which I had myself some time before written and inserted in the Morning Post, to wit—

To the Author of the Ancient Mariner.

Your poem must eternal be,
Dear sir! it cannot fail,
For 'tis incomprehensible,
And without head or tail.

CHAPTER II.

Supposed irritability of men of genius brought to the test of facts—Causes and occasions of the charge—Its injustice.

I HAVE often thought, that it would be neither uninstructive nor unamusing to analyze, and bring forward into distinct consciousness, that complex feeling, with which readers in general take part against the author, in favour of the critic; and the readiness with which they apply to *all* poets the old sarcasm of Horace upon the scribblers of his time:

——*genus irritabile vatum.*

A debility and dimness of the imaginative power, and a consequent necessity of reliance on the immediate impressions of the senses, do, we know well, render the mind liable to superstition and fanaticism. Having a deficient portion of internal and proper warmth, minds of this class seek in the crowd *circum fana* for a warmth in common, which they do not possess singly. Cold and phlegmatic in their own nature, like damp hay, they heat and inflame by co-acervation; or like bees they become restless and irritable through the increased temperature of collected multitudes. Hence the German word for fanaticism, (such at least was its original import,) is derived from the swarming of bees, namely, *schwärmen, schwärmerei.* The passion being in an inverse proportion to the insight,—*that* the more vivid, as *this* the less distinct—anger is the inevitable consequence. The absence of all foundation within their own minds for that, which they yet believe both true and indispensable to their safety and happiness, cannot but produce an uneasy state of feeling, an involuntary sense of fear from which nature has no means of rescuing herself but by anger. Experience informs us that the first defence of weak minds is to recriminate.

There's no philosopher but sees,
That rage and fear are one disease;
Tho' that may burn, and this may freeze,
They're both alike the ague.

But where the ideas are vivid, and there exists an endless power of combining and modifying them, the feelings and affections blend more easily and intimately with these ideal creations than with the objects of the senses; the mind is affected by thoughts, rather than by things; and only then feels the requisite interest even for the most important events and accidents, when by means of meditation they have passed into *thoughts*. The sanity of the mind is between superstition with fanaticism on the one hand, and enthusiasm with indifference and a diseased slowness to action on the other. For the conceptions of the mind may be so vivid and adequate, as to preclude that impulse to the realizing of them, which is strongest and most restless in those, who possess more than mere *talent*, (or the faculty of appropriating and applying the knowledge of others,)—yet still want something of the creative, and self-sufficing power of absolute genius. For this reason therefore, they are men of *commanding* Genius. While the former rest content between thought and reality, as it were in an *intermundium* of which their own living spirit supplies the substance, and their imagination the ever-varying form; the latter must impress their preconceptions on the world without, in order to present them back to their own view with the satisfying degree of clearness, distinctness, and individuality. These in tranquil times are formed to exhibit a perfect poem in palace, or temple, or landscape-garden; or a tale of romance in canals that join sea with sea, or in walls of rock, which, shouldering back the billows, imitate the power, and supply the benevolence of nature to sheltered navies; or in aqueducts that, arching the wide vale from mountain to mountain, give a Palmyra to the desert. But alas! in times of tumult they are the men destined to come forth as the shaping spirit of Ruin, to destroy the wisdom of ages in order to substitute the fancies of a day, and to change kings and kingdoms, as the wind shifts and shapes the clouds.[1] The records

[1] Of old things all are over old,
Of good things none are good enough:—
We'll show that we can help to frame
A world of other stuff.

I, too, will have my Kings, that take
From me the sign of life and death:
Kingdoms shall shift about, like clouds,
Obedient to my breath.

Wordsworth's Rob Roy.

of biography seem to confirm this theory. The men of the greatest genius, as far as we can judge from their own works or from the accounts of their contemporaries, appear to have been of calm and tranquil temper in all that related to themselves. In the inward assurance of permanent fame, they seem to have been either indifferent or resigned with regard to immediate reputation. Through all the works of Chaucer there reigns a cheerfulness, a manly hilarity, which makes it almost impossible to doubt a correspondent habit of feeling in the author himself. Shakespeare's evenness and sweetness of temper were almost proverbial in his own age. That this did not arise from ignorance of his own comparative greatness, we have abundant proof in his Sonnets, which could scarcely have been known to Pope,[1] when he asserted, that our great bard—

—grew immortal in his own despite.[2]

Speaking of one whom he had celebrated, and contrasting the duration of his works with that of his personal existence, Shakespeare adds:

[1] Pope was under the common error of his age, an error far from being sufficiently exploded even at the present day. It consists (as I explained at large, and proved in detail in my public lectures,) in mistaking for the *essentials* of the Greek stage certain rules, which the wise poets imposed upon themselves, in order to render all the remaining parts of the drama consistent with those, that had been forced upon them by circumstances independent of their will; out of which circumstances the drama itself arose. The circumstances in the time of Shakespeare, which it was equally out of his power to alter, were different, and such as, in my opinion, allowed a far wider sphere, and a deeper and more human interest. Critics are too apt to forget, that *rules* are but means to an end; consequently, where the ends are different, the rules must be likewise so. We must have ascertained what the end *is*, before we can determine what the rules *ought* to be. Judging under this impression, I did not hesitate to declare my full conviction, that the consummate judgment of Shakespeare, not only in the general construction, but in all the *detail*, of his dramas, impressed me with greater wonder, than even the might of his genius, or the depth of his philosophy. The substance of these lectures I hope soon to publish; and it is but a debt of justice to myself and my friends to notice, that the first course of lectures, which differed from the following courses only, by occasionally varying the illustrations of the same thoughts, was addressed to very numerous, and I need not add, respectable audiences at the Royal Institution, before Mr. Schlegel gave his lectures on the same subjects at Vienna.

[2] Epist. to Augustus.

Your name from hence immortal life shall have,
Tho' I once gone to all the world must die;
The earth can yield me but a common grave,
When you entombed in men's eyes shall lie.
Your monument shall be my gentle verse,
Which eyes not yet created shall o'er-read;
And tongues to be your being shall rehearse,
When all the breathers of this world are dead:
You still shall live, such virtue hath my pen,
Where breath most breathes, e'en in the mouth of men.

SONNET LXXXI.

I have taken the first that occurred; but Shakespeare's readiness to praise his rivals, *ore pleno*, and the confidence of his own equality with those whom he deemed most worthy of his praise, are alike manifested in another Sonnet.

Was it the proud full sail of his great verse,
Bound for the praise of all-too-precious you,
That did my ripe thoughts in my brain inhearse,
Making their tomb, the womb wherein they grew?
Was it his spirit, by spirits taught to write
Above a mortal pitch that struck me dead?
No, neither he, nor his compeers by night
Giving him aid, my verse astonished.
He, nor that affable familiar ghost,
Which nightly gulls him with intelligence,
As victors of my silence cannot boast;
I was not sick of any fear from thence!
But when your countenance fill'd up his line,
Then lack'd I matter, that enfeebled mine. S. LXXXVI.

In Spenser, indeed, we trace a mind constitutionally tender, delicate, and, in comparison with his three great compeers, I had almost said, *effeminate*; and this additionally saddened by the unjust persecution of Burleigh, and the severe calamities, which overwhelmed his latter days. These causes have diffused over all his compositions "a melancholy grace," and have drawn forth occasional strains, the more pathetic from their gentleness. But no where do we find the least trace of irritability, and still less of quarrelsome or affected contempt of his censurers.

The same calmness, and even greater self-possession, may be affirmed of Milton, as far as his poems, and poetic character are concerned. He reserved his anger for the enemies of religion, freedom, and his country. My mind is not capable of forming a more august conception, than arises from the contemplation of this great man in his latter days;—poor, sick, old, blind, slandered, persecuted,—

Darkness before, and danger's voice behind,—

in an age in which he was as little understood by the party, *for* whom, as by that *against* whom, he had contended; and among men before whom he strode so far as to *dwarf* himself by the distance; yet still listening to the music of his own thoughts, or if additionally cheered, yet cheered only by the prophetic faith of two or three solitary individuals, he did nevertheless

——— argue not
Against Heaven's hand or will, nor bate a jot
Of heart or hope; but still bore up and steer'd
Right onward.

From others only do we derive our knowledge that Milton, in his latter day, had his scorners and detractors; and even in his day of youth and hope, that he had enemies would have been unknown to us, had they not been likewise the enemies of his country.

I am well aware, that in advanced stages of literature, when there exist many and excellent models, a high degree of talent, combined with taste and judgment, and employed in works of imagination, will acquire for a man the *name* of a great genius; though even that *analogon* of genius, which, in certain states of society, may even render his writings more popular than the absolute reality could have done, would be sought for in vain in the mind and temper of the author himself. Yet even in instances of this kind, a close examination will often detect, that the irritability, which has been attributed to the author's *genius* as its cause, did really originate in an ill conformation of body, obtuse pain, or constitutional defect of pleasurable sensation. What is charged to the *author*, belongs to the *man*, who would probably have been still more impatient, but for the humanizing influences of the very pursuit, which yet bears the blame of his irritability.

How then are we to explain the easy credence generally given to this charge, if the charge itself be not, as I have endeavoured to show, supported by experience? This seems to me of no very difficult solution. In whatever country literature is widely diffused, there will be many who mistake an intense desire to possess the reputation of poetic genius, for the actual powers, and original tendencies which constitute it. But men, whose dearest wishes are fixed on objects wholly out of their own power, become in all cases more or less impatient and prone to anger. Besides, though it may be paradoxical to assert, that a man can know one thing and believe the opposite, yet assuredly a vain person may have so habitually indulged the wish, and persevered in the attempt, to appear what he is not, as to become himself one of his own proselytes. Still, as this counterfeit and artificial persuasion must differ, even in the person's own feelings, from a real sense of inward power, what can be more natural, than that this difference should betray itself in suspicious and jealous irritability? Even as the flowery sod, which covers a hollow, may be often detected by its shaking and trembling.

But, alas! the multitude of books, and the general diffusion of literature, have produced other and more lamentable effects in the world of letters, and such as are abundant to explain, though by no means to justify, the contempt with which the best grounded complaints of injured genius are rejected as frivolous, or entertained as matter of merriment. In the days of Chaucer and Gower, our language might (with due allowance for the imperfections of a simile) be compared to a wilderness of vocal reeds, from which the favourites only of Pan or Apollo could construct even the rude *syrinx;* and from this the *constructors* alone could elicit strains of music. But now, partly by the labours of successive poets, and in part by the more artificial state of society and social intercourse, language, mechanized as it were into a barrel-organ, supplies at once both instrument and tune. Thus even the deaf may play, so as to delight the many. Sometimes (for it is with similes, as it is with jests at a wine table, one is sure to suggest another) I have attempted to illustrate the present state of our language, in its relation to literature, by a press-room of larger and smaller stereotype pieces, which, in the present Anglo-Gallican fashion of unconnected, epigrammatic periods, it requires but an ordinary portion of ingenuity to vary indefinitely, and yet still produce something, which, if not sense, will be so like it as to do as well. Perhaps better: for it spares the reader the trouble of thinking; prevents vacancy, while it indulges indolence; and secures the memory from all danger of an intellectual *plethora.* Hence of all trades, literature at present demands the least talent or information; and, of all modes of literature, the manufacturing of poems. The difference indeed between these and the works of genius is not less than between an egg and an egg-shell; yet at a distance they both look alike.

Now it is no less remarkable than true, with how little examination works of polite literature are commonly perused, not only by the mass of readers, but by men of first rate ability, till some accident or chance[1] discussion have roused their attention, and

[1] In the course of one of my Lectures, I had occasion to point out the almost faultless position and choice of words, in Pope's *original* compositions, particularly in his Satires and Moral Essays, for the purpose of comparing them with his translation of Homer, which, I do not stand alone in regarding as the main source of our *pseudo*-poetic diction. And this, by the bye, is an additional confirmation of a remark made, I believe, by Sir Joshua Reynolds, that next to the man who forms and elevates the taste of the public, he that corrupts it, is commonly the greatest genius. Among other passages, I analyzed sentence by sentence, and almost word by word, the popular lines,

As when the moon, refulgent lamp of night, &c.
(Iliad. B. viii.)

much in the same way as has been since done, in an excellent article on Chalmers's British Poets in the Quarterly Review. The impression on the audience in general was sudden and evident: and a number of enlightened and highly educated persons, who at different times afterwards addressed me on the subject, expressed their wonder, that truth so obvious should not have struck them *before*; but at the same time acknowledged—(so much had they been accustomed, in reading poetry, to receive pleasure from the separate images and phrases successively, without asking themselves whether the collective meaning was sense or nonsense)—that they might in all probability have read the same passage again twenty times with undiminished admiration, and without once reflecting, that

ἄστρα φαεινὴν ἀμφὶ σελήνην
φαίνετ' ἀριπρεπέα—

(that is, the stars around, or near the full moon, shine pre-eminently bright)—conveys a just and happy image of a moonlight sky: while it is difficult to determine whether, in the lines,

Around *her throne* the vivid planets *roll*,
And stars *unnumber'd gild* the *glowing pole*,

the sense or the diction be the more absurd. My answer was; that, though I had derived peculiar advantages from my school discipline, and though my *general* theory of poetry was the same then as now, I had yet experienced the same sensations myself, and felt almost as if I had been newly couched, when, by Mr. Wordsworth's conversation, I had been induced to re-examine with impartial strictness Gray's celebrated Elegy. I had long before detected the defects in The Bard; but the Elegy I had considered as proof against all fair attacks; and to this day I cannot read either without delight, and a portion of enthusiasm. At all events, whatever pleasure I may have lost by put them on their guard. And hence individuals below mediocrity not less in natural power than in acquired knowledge; nay, bunglers who have failed in the lowest mechanic crafts, and whose presumption is in due proportion to their want of sense and sensibility; men, who being first scribblers from idleness and ignorance, next become libellers from envy and malevolence,—have been able to drive a successful trade in the employment of the booksellers, nay, have raised themselves into temporary name and reputation with the public at large, by that most powerful of all adulation, the appeal to the bad and malignant passions of mankind.[1] But as it is the nature of scorn, envy, and

the clearer perception of the faults in certain passages, has been more than repaid to me by the additional delight with which I read the remainder.

Another instance in confirmation of these remarks occurs to me in the Faithful Shepherdess. Seward first traces Fletcher's lines;

> More foul diseases then e'er yet the hot
> Sun bred thro' his burnings, while the Dog
> Pursues the raging Lion, throwing fog
> And deadly vapour from his angry breath,
> Filling the lower world with plague and death,

to Spenser's Shepherd's Calendar,

> The rampant Lion hunts he fast
>   With dogs of noisome breath;
> Whose baleful barking brings, in haste,
>   Pine, plagues, and dreary death!

He then takes occasion to introduce Homer's simile of the appearance of Achilles' mail to Priam compared with the Dog Star; literally thus—

"For this indeed is most splendid, but it was made an evil sign, and brings many a consuming disease to wretched mortals." Nothing can be more simple as a description, or more accurate as a simile; which, (says Seward,) is thus finely translated by Mr. Pope:

> Terrific Glory! for his burning breath
> Taints the *red* air with fevers, plagues, and death!

Now here—(not to mention the tremendous bombast)—the *Dog Star*, so called, is turned into a *real* dog, a very odd dog, a fire, fever, plague, and death-breathing, *red*-air-tainting dog: and the whole *visual* likeness is lost, while the likeness in the *effects* is rendered absurd by the exaggeration. In Spenser and Fletcher the thought is justifiable; for the images are at least consistent, and it was the intention of the writers to mark the seasons by this allegory of visualized *puns*.

[1] Especially in this AGE OF PERSONALITY, this age of literary and political GOSSIPING, when the meanest insects are worshipped with a sort of Egyptian superstition, if only the brainless head be atoned for by the sting of personal malignity in the tail;—when the most vapid satires have become the objects

all malignant propensities to require a quick change of objects, such writers are sure, sooner or later, to awake from their dream of vanity to disappointment and neglect with embittered and envenomed feelings. Even during their short-lived success, sensible in spite of themselves on what a shifting foundation it rests, they resent the mere refusal of praise as a robbery, and at the justest censures kindle at once into violent and undisciplined abuse; till the acute disease changing into chronical, the more deadly as the less violent, they become the fit instruments of literary detraction and moral slander. They are then no longer to be questioned without exposing the complainant to ridicule, because, forsooth, they are *anonymous* critics, and authorized, in Andrew Marvell's phrase, as "synodical individuals" to speak of themselves *plurali majestatico*! As if literature formed a caste, like that of the Paras in Hindostan, who, however maltreated, must not dare to deem themselves wronged! As if that, which in all other cases adds a deeper dye to slander, the circumstance of its being anonymous, here acted only to make the slanderer inviolable![1] Thus, in *part*, from the accidental tempers of individuals—(men of undoubted talent, but not men of genius)—tempers rendered yet more irritable by their desire to *appear* men of genius; but still more effectively by the excesses of the mere *counterfeits* both of talent and genius; the number too being so incomparably greater of those who are *thought* to be, than of those who really *are* men of genius; and in part from the natural, but not therefore the less partial and unjust distinction, made by the

of a keen public interest, purely from the number of contemporary characters named in the patch-work notes, (which possess, however, the comparative merit of being more poetical than the text,) and because, to increase the stimulus, the author has sagaciously left his own name for whispers and conjectures. (From *The Friend*, Vol. II. Essay I. *On the Errors of Party Spirit*, pp. 9–10. 4th edit. S.C.)

[1] If it were worth while to mix together, as ingredients, half the anecdotes which I either myself know to be true, or which I have received from men incapable of intentional falsehood, concerning the characters, qualifications, and motives of our anonymous critics, whose decisions are oracles for our reading public; I might safely borrow the words of the apocryphal Daniel; "*Give me leave*, O SOVEREIGN PUBLIC, *and I shall slay this dragon without sword or staff*." For the compound would be as the "*pitch, and fat, and hair, which Daniel took, and did seethe them together, and made lumps thereof; this he put in the dragon's mouth, and so the dragon burst in sunder; and Daniel said*, LO, THESE ARE THE GODS YE WORSHIP."

public itself between *literary* and all other property;—I believe the prejudice to have arisen, which considers an unusual irascibility concerning the reception of its products as characteristic of genius.

It might correct the moral feelings of a numerous class of readers, to suppose a Review set on foot, the object of which should be to criticise all the chief works presented to the public by our ribbon-weavers, calico-printers, cabinet-makers, and china-manufacturers; which should be conducted in the same spirit, and take the same freedom with personal character, as our literary journals. They would scarcely, I think, deny their belief, not only that the *genus irritabile* would be found to include many other *species* besides that of bards; but that the irritability of *trade* would soon reduce the resentments of *poets* into mere shadow-fights in the comparison. Or is wealth the only rational object of human interest? Or even if this were admitted, has the poet no property in his works? Or is it a rare, or culpable case, that he who serves at the altar of the Muses, should be compelled to derive his maintenance from the altar, when too he has perhaps deliberately abandoned the fairest prospects of rank and opulence in order to devote himself, an entire and undistracted man, to the instruction or refinement of his fellow-citizens? Or, should we pass by all higher objects and motives, all disinterested benevolence, and even that ambition of lasting praise which is at once the crutch and ornament, which at once supports and betrays, the infirmity of human virtue,—is the character and property of the man, who labours for our intellectual pleasures, less entitled to a share of our fellow feeling, than that of the wine-merchant or milliner? Sensibility indeed, both quick and deep, is not only a characteristic feature, but may be deemed a component part, of genius. But it is not less an essential mark of true genius, that its sensibility is excited by any other cause more powerfully than by its own personal interests; for this plain reason, that the man of genius lives most in the ideal world, in which the present is still constituted by the future or the past; and because his feelings have been habitually associated with thoughts and images, to the number, clearness, and vivacity of which the sensation of *self* is always in an inverse proportion. And yet, should he perchance have occasion to repel some false charge, or to rectify some erroneous censure, nothing is more common than for the many to mistake the general liveliness of his manner and language, *whatever* is the subject, for the effects of peculiar irritation from its accidental relation to himself.[1]

For myself, if from my own feelings, or from the less suspicious test of the observations of others, I had been made aware of any literary testiness or jealousy; I trust, that I should have been, however, neither silly nor arrogant enough to have burthened the imperfection on GENIUS. But an experience—(and I should not need documents in abundance to prove my words, if I added) —a tried experience of twenty years, has taught me, that the original sin of my character consists in a careless indifference to public opinion, and to the attacks of those who influence it; that praise and admiration have become yearly less and less desirable, except as marks of sympathy; nay that it is difficult and distressing to me to think with any interest even about the sale and profit of my works, important as, in my present circumstances, such considerations must needs be. Yet it never occurred to me to believe or fancy, that the *quantum* of intellectual power bestowed on me by nature or education was in any way connected with this habit of my feelings; or that it needed any other parents or fosterers than constitutional indolence, aggravated into languor by ill-health; the accumulating embarrassments of procrastination; the mental cowardice, which is the inseparable companion of procrastination, and which makes us anxious to think and converse on any thing rather than on what concerns ourselves; in fine, all those close vexations, whether chargeable on my faults

[1] This is one instance among many of deception, by the telling of half of a fact, and omitting the other half, when it is from their mutual counteraction and neutralization, that the *whole* truth arises, as a *tertium aliquid* different from either. Thus in Dryden's famous line

Great wit (meaning genius) to madness sure is near allied.

Now if the profound sensibility, which is doubtless *one* of the components of genius, were alone considered, single and unbalanced, it might be fairly described as exposing the individual to a greater chance of mental derangement; but then a more than usual rapidity of association, a more than usual power of passing from thought to thought, and image to image, is a component equally essential; and in the due modification of each by the other the GENIUS itself consists; so that it would be just as fair to describe the earth, as in imminent danger of exorbitating, or of falling into the sun, according as the assertor of the absurdity *confined* his attention either to the projectile or to the attractive force exclusively.

or my fortunes, which leave me but little grief to spare for evils comparatively distant and alien.

Indignation at literary wrongs I leave to men born under happier stars. I cannot *afford it.* But so far from condemning those who can, I deem it a writer's duty, and think it creditable to his heart, to feel and express a resentment proportioned to the grossness of the provocation, and the importance of the object. There is no profession on earth, which requires an attention so early, so long, or so unintermitting as that of poetry; and indeed as that of literary composition in general, if it be such as at all satisfies the demands both of taste and of sound logic. How difficult and delicate a task even the mere mechanism of verse is, may be conjectured from the failure of those, who have attempted poetry late in life. Where then a man has, from his earliest youth, devoted his whole being to an object, which by the admission of all civilized nations in all ages is honourable as a pursuit, and glorious as an attainment; what of all that relates to himself and his family, if only we except his moral character, can have fairer claims to his protection, or more authorize acts of self-defence, than the elaborate products of his intellect and intellectual industry? Prudence itself would command us to show, even if defect or diversion of natural sensibility had prevented us from feeling, a due interest and qualified anxiety for the offspring and representatives of our nobler being. I know it, alas! by woful experience. I have laid too many eggs in the hot sands of this wilderness, the world, with ostrich carelessness and ostrich oblivion. The greater part indeed have been trod under foot, and are forgotten; but yet no small number have crept forth into life, some to furnish feathers for the caps of others, and still more to plume the shafts in the quivers of my enemies, of them that unprovoked have lain in wait against my soul.

Sic vos, non vobis, mellificatis, apes!

CHAPTER III.

The Author's obligations to Critics, and the probable occasion—Principles of modern Criticism—Mr. Southey's works and character.

To anonymous critics in reviews, magazines, and news-journals of various name and rank, and to satirists with or without a name, in verse or prose, or in verse-text aided by prose-comment, I do seriously believe and profess, that I owe full two-thirds of whatever reputation and publicity I happen to possess. For when the name of an individual has occurred so frequently, in so many works, for so great a length of time, the readers of these works —(which with a shelf or two of Beauties, elegant Extracts and Anas, form nine-tenths of the reading of the reading Public[1])— cannot but be familiar with the name, without distinctly remembering whether it was introduced for eulogy or for censure. And

[1] For as to the devotees of the circulating libraries, I dare not compliment their *pass-time*, or rather *kill-time*, with the name of *reading*. Call it rather a sort of beggarly day-dreaming, during which the mind of the dreamer furnishes for itself nothing but laziness, and a little mawkish sensibility; while the whole *matériel* and imagery of the doze is supplied *ab extra* by a sort of mental *camera obscura* manufactured at the printing office, which *pro tempore* fixes, reflects, and transmits the moving phantasms of one man's delirium, so as to people the barrenness of a hundred other brains afflicted with the same trance or suspension of all common sense and all definite purpose. We should therefore transfer this species of *amusement*,—(if indeed those can be said to retire *a musis*, who were never in their company, or relaxation be attributable to those, whose bows are never bent)—from the *genus*, reading, to that comprehensive class characterized by the power of reconciling the two contrary yet co-existing propensities of human nature, namely, indulgence of sloth, and hatred of vacancy. In addition to novels and tales of chivalry in prose or rhyme, (by which last I mean neither rhythm nor metre) this *genus* comprises as its *species*, gaming, swinging, or swaying on a chair or gate; spitting over a bridge; smoking; snuff-taking; *tête à tête* quarrels after dinner between husband and wife; conning word by word all the advertisements of a daily newspaper in a public house on a rainy day, &c. &c. &c.

this becomes the more likely, if (as I believe) the habit of perusing periodical works may be properly added to Averroes' catalogue of Anti-Mnemonics, or weakeners of the memory.[1] But where this has not been the case, yet the reader will be apt to suspect, that there must be something more than usually strong and extensive in a reputation, that could either require or stand so merciless and long-continued a cannonading. Without any feeling of *anger* therefore—(for which indeed, on my own account, I have no pretext)—I may yet be allowed to express some degree of *surprise*, that, after having run the critical gauntlet for a certain class of faults which I *had*, nothing having come before the judgment-seat in the interim, I should, year after year, quarter after quarter, month after month—(not to mention sundry petty periodicals of still quicker revolution, "or weekly or diurnal")— have been, for at least seventeen years consecutively, dragged forth by them into the foremost ranks of the *proscribed*, and forced to abide the brunt of abuse, for faults directly opposite, and which I certainly had not. How shall I explain this?

Whatever may have been the case with others, I certainly cannot attribute this persecution to personal dislike, or to envy, or to feelings of vindictive animosity. Not to the former, for, with the exception of a very few who are my intimate friends, and were so before they were known as authors, I have had little other acquaintance with literary characters, than what may be implied in an accidental introduction, or casual meeting in a mixed company. And as far as words and looks can be trusted, I must believe that, even in these instances, I had excited no unfriendly disposition. Neither by letter, nor in conversation, have I ever had dispute or controversy beyond the common social interchange of opinions. Nay, where I had reason to suppose my convictions fundamentally different, it has been my habit,

[1] Ex gr. *Pediculos e capillis excerptos in arenam jacere incontusos;* eating of unripe fruit; gazing on the clouds, and (*in genere*) on movable things suspended in the air; riding among a multitude of camels; frequent laughter; listening to a series of jests and humourous anecdotes,—as when (so to modernize the learned Saracen's meaning) one man's droll story of an Irishman inevitably occasions another's droll story of a Scotchman, which again, by the same sort of conjunction disjunctive, leads to some *étourderie* of a Welshman, and that again to some sly hit of a Yorkshireman;—the habit of reading tomb-stones in church-yards, &c. By the bye, this catalogue, strange as it may appear, is not insusceptible of a sound psychological commentary.

and I may add, the impulse of my nature, to assign the grounds of my belief, rather than the belief itself; and not to express dissent, till I could establish some points of complete sympathy, some grounds common to both sides, from which to commence its explanation.

Still less can I place these attacks to the charge of envy. The few pages which I have published, are of too distant a date, and the extent of their sale a proof too conclusive against their having been popular at any time, to render probable, I had almost said possible, the excitement of envy on *their* account; and the man who should envy me on any *other*,—verily he must be *envy-mad*!

Lastly, with as little semblance of reason, could I suspect any animosity towards me from vindictive feelings as the cause. I have before said, that my acquaintance with literary men has been limited and distant; and that I have had neither dispute nor controversy. From my first entrance into life, I have, with few and short intervals, lived either abroad or in retirement. My different essays on subjects of national interest, published at different times, first in the Morning Post and then in the Courier, with my courses of Lectures on the principles of criticism as applied to Shakespeare and Milton, constitute my whole publicity; the only occasions on which I *could* offend any member of the republic of letters. With one solitary exception in which my words were first misstated and then wantonly applied to an individual, I could never learn that I had excited the displeasure of any among my literary contemporaries. Having announced my intention to give a course of Lectures on the characteristic merits and defects of English poetry in its different æras; first, from Chaucer to Milton; second, from Dryden inclusively to Thomson; and third, from Cowper to the present day; I changed my plan, and confined my disquisition to the former two periods, that I might furnish no possible pretext for the unthinking to misconstrue, or the malignant to misapply my words, and having stamped their own meaning on them, to pass them as current coin in the marts of garrulity or detraction.

Praises of the unworthy are felt by ardent minds as robberies of the deserving; and it is too true, and too frequent, that Bacon, Harrington, Machiavel, and Spinoza, are *not* read, because Hume, Condillac, and Voltaire *are*. But in promiscuous company no prudent man will oppugn the merits of a contemporary in his own supposed department; contenting himself with praising in his turn those whom *he* deems excellent. If I should ever deem it my duty at all to oppose the pretensions of individuals, I would oppose them in books which could be weighed and answered, in which I could evolve the whole of my reasons and feelings, with their requisite limits and modifications; not in irrecoverable conversation, where however strong the reasons might be, the feelings that prompted them would assuredly be attributed by some one or other to envy and discontent. Besides I well know, and, I trust, have acted on that knowledge, that it must be the ignorant and injudicious who extol the unworthy; and the eulogies of critics without taste or judgment are the natural reward of authors without feeling or genius. *Sint unicuique sua præmia.*

How then, dismissing, as I do, these three causes, am I to account for attacks, the long continuance and inveteracy of which it would require all three to explain? The solution seems to be this,—*I was in habits of intimacy with Mr. Wordsworth and Mr. Southey!* This, however, transfers, rather than removes the difficulty. Be it, that, by an unconscionable extension of the old adage, *noscitur a socio*, my literary friends are never under the water-fall of criticism, but I must be wet through with the spray; yet how came the torrent to descend upon *them?*

First then, with regard to Mr. Southey. I well remember the general reception of his earlier publications; namely, the poems published with Mr. Lovell under the names of Moschus and Bion; the two volumes of poems under his own name, and the Joan of Arc. The censures of the critics by profession are extant, and may be easily referred to:—careless lines, inequality in the merit of the different poems, and (in the lighter works) a predilection for the strange and whimsical; in short, such faults as might have been anticipated in a young and rapid writer, were indeed sufficiently enforced. Nor was there at that time wanting a party spirit to aggravate the defects of a poet, who with all the courage of uncorrupted youth had avowed his zeal for a cause, which he deemed that of liberty, and his abhorrence of oppression by whatever name consecrated. But it was as little objected by others, as dreamed of by the poet himself, that he *preferred* careless and prosaic lines on rule and of forethought, or indeed that he pretended to any other art or theory of poetic diction, except that which we may all learn from Horace, Quinctilian, the admirable dialogue, *De Oratoribus*, generally attributed to Tacitus, or Strada's

Prolusions; if indeed natural good sense and the early study of the best models in his own language had not infused the same maxims more securely, and, if I may venture the expression, more vitally. All that could have been fairly deduced was, that in his taste and estimation of writers Mr. Southey agreed far more with Thomas Warton, than with Dr. Johnson. Nor do I mean to deny, that at all times Mr. Southey was of the same mind with Sir Philip Sidney in preferring an excellent ballad in the *humblest* style of poetry to twenty indifferent poems that strutted in the *highest*. And by what have his works, published since then, been characterized, each more strikingly than the preceding, but by greater splendour, a deeper pathos, profounder reflections, and a more sustained dignity of language and of metre? Distant may the period be, but whenever the time shall come, when all his works shall be collected by some editor worthy to be his biographer, I trust that an appendix of *excerpta* of all the passages, in which his writings, name, and character have been attacked, from the pamphlets and periodical works of the last twenty years, may be an accompaniment. Yet that it would prove medicinal in after times I dare not hope; for as long as there are readers to be delighted with calumny, there will be found reviewers to calumniate. And such readers will become in all probability more numerous, in proportion as a still greater diffusion of literature shall produce an increase of sciolists, and sciolism bring with it petulance and presumption. In times of old, books were as religious oracles; as literature advanced, they next became venerable preceptors; they then descended to the rank of instructive friends; and, as their numbers increased, they sank still lower to that of entertaining companions; and at present they seem degraded into culprits to hold up their hands at the bar of every self-elected, yet not the less peremptory, judge, who chooses to write from humour or interest, from enmity or arrogance, and to abide the decision "of him that reads in malice, or him that reads after dinner."

The same retrograde movement may be traced, in the relation which the authors themselves have assumed towards their readers. From the lofty address of Bacon: "these are the meditations of Francis of Verulam, which that posterity should be possessed of, he deemed *their* interest:" or from dedication to Monarch or Pontiff, in which the honour given was asserted in equipoise to the patronage acknowledged: from Pindar's

——— ἐπ' ἄλλοι-
-σι δ' ἄλλοι μεγάλοι· τὸ δ' ἔσχατον κορυ-
-φοῦται βασιλεῦσι· Μηκέτι
πάπταινε πόρσιον.
εἴη σέ τε τοῦτον
ὑψοῦ χρόνον πατεῖν, ἐμέ
τε τοσσάδε νικαφόροις
ὁμιλεῖν, πρόφαντον σοφίᾳ καθ' Ἕλ-
-λανας ἐόντα παντᾶ. OLYMP. OD. I.

there was a gradual sinking in the etiquette or allowed style of pretension.

Poets and Philosophers, rendered diffident by their very number, addressed themselves to "*learned* readers;" then aimed to conciliate the graces of "the *candid* reader;" till, the critic still rising as the author sank, the amateurs of literature collectively were erected into a municipality of judges, and addressed as THE TOWN! And now, finally, all men being supposed able to read, and all readers able to judge, the multitudinous PUBLIC, shaped into personal unity by the magic of abstraction, sits nominal despot on the throne of criticism. But, alas! as in other despotisms, it but echoes the decisions of its invisible ministers, whose intellectual claims to the guardianship of the Muses seem, for the greater part, analogous to the physical qualifications which adapt their oriental brethren for the superintendence of the Harem. Thus it is said, that St. Nepomuc was installed the guardian of bridges, because he had fallen over one, and sunk out of sight; thus too St. Cecilia is said to have been first propitiated by musicians, because, having failed in her own attempts, she had taken a dislike to the art and all its successful professors. But I shall probably have occasion hereafter to deliver my convictions more at large concerning this state of things, and its influences on taste, genius and morality.

In the Thalaba, the Madoc, and still more evidently in the unique[1] Cid, in the Kehama, and, as last, so best, the Roderick;

[1] I have ventured to call it unique; not only because I know no work of the kind in our language, (if we except a few chapters of the old translation of Froissart)—none, which uniting the charms of romance and history, keeps the imagination so constantly on the wing, and yet leaves so much for after reflection; but likewise, and chiefly, because it is a compilation, which, in the various excellencies of translation, selection, and arrangement, required and proves greater genius in the compiler, as living in the present state of society, than in the original composers.

Southey has given abundant proof, *se cogitare quam sit magnum dare aliquid in manus hominum: nec persuadere sibi posse, non sæpe tractandum quod placere et semper et omnibus cupiat.* But on the other hand, I conceive, that Mr. Southey was quite unable to comprehend, wherein could consist the crime or mischief of printing half a dozen or more playful poems; or to speak more generally, compositions which would be enjoyed or passed over according as the taste and humour of the reader might chance to be; provided they contained nothing immoral. In the present age *perituræ parcere chartæ* is emphatically an unreasonable demand. The merest trifle he ever sent abroad had tenfold better claims to its ink and paper than all the silly criticisms on it, which proved no more than that the critic was not one of those, for whom the trifle was written; and than all the grave exhortations to a greater reverence for the public—as if the passive page of a book, by having an epigram or doggrel tale impressed on it, instantly assumed at once loco-motive power and a sort of ubiquity, so as to flutter and buzz in the ear of the public to the sore annoyance of the said mysterious personage. But what gives an additional and more ludicrous absurdity to these lamentations is the curious fact, that if in a volume of poetry the critic should find poem or passage which he deems more especially worthless, he is sure to select and reprint it in the review; by which, on his own grounds, he wastes as much more paper than the author, as the copies of a fashionable review are more numerous than those of the original book; in some, and those the most prominent instances, as ten thousand to five hundred. I know nothing that surpasses the vileness of deciding on the merits of a poet or painter, —(not by characteristic defects; for where there is genius, *these* always point to his characteristic *beauties*; but)—by accidental failures or faulty passages; except the impudence of defending it, as the proper duty, and most instructive part, of criticism. Omit or pass slightly over the expression, grace, and grouping of Raffael's *figures*; but ridicule in *detail* the knitting-needles and broom-twigs, that are to represent trees in his back grounds; and never let him hear the last of his *galli-pots*! Admit, that the Allegro and Penseroso of Milton are not *without merit*; but repay yourself for this concession, by reprinting at length *the two poems on the University Carrier*! As a fair specimen of his Sonnets, quote

A Book was writ of late called Tetrachordon;

and, as characteristic of his rhythm and metre, cite his literal translation of the first and second Psalm! In order to justify yourself, you need only assert, that had you dwelt chiefly on the beauties and excellencies of the poet, the admiration of these might seduce the attention of future writers from the objects of their love and wonder, to an imitation of the few poems and passages in which the poet was most unlike himself.

But till reviews are conducted on far other principles, and with far other motives; till in the place of arbitrary dictation and petulant sneers, the reviewers support their decisions by reference to fixed canons of criticism, previously established and deduced from the nature of man; reflecting minds will pronounce it arrogance in them thus to announce themselves to men of letters, as the guides of their taste and judgment. To the purchaser and mere reader it is, at all events, an injustice. He who tells me that there are *defects* in a new work, tells me nothing which I should not have taken for granted without his information. But he, who points out and elucidates the *beauties* of an original work, does indeed give me interesting information, such as experience would not have authorized me in anticipating. And as to compositions which the authors themselves announce with

Hæc ipsi novimus esse nihil,

why should we judge by a different rule two printed works, only because the one author is alive, and the other in his grave? What literary man has not regretted the prudery of Spratt in refusing to let his friend Cowley appear in his slippers and dressing gown? I am not perhaps the only one who has derived an innocent amusement from the riddles, conundrums, tri-syllable lines, and the like, of Swift and his correspondents, in hours of languor, when to have read his more finished works would have been useless to myself, and, in some sort, an act of injustice to the author. But I am at a loss to conceive by what perversity of judgment, these relaxations of his genius could be employed to diminish his fame as the writer of Gulliver, or the Tale of a Tub. Had Mr. Southey written twice as many poems of inferior merit, or partial interest, as have enlivened the journals of the day, they would have added to his honour with good and wise men, not merely or principally as proving the versatility of his talents, but as evidences of the purity of that mind, which even in its levities never dictated a line which it need regret on any moral account.

I have in imagination transferred to the future biographer the duty of contrasting Southey's fixed and well-earned fame, with the abuse and indefatigable hostility of his anonymous critics from his early youth to his ripest manhood. But I cannot think so ill of human nature as not to believe, that these critics have already taken shame to themselves, whether they consider the object of their abuse in his moral or his literary character. For reflect but on the variety and extent of his acquirements! He stands second to no man, either as an historian or as a bibliographer; and when I regard him as a popular essayist,—(for the articles of his compositions in the reviews are, for the greater part, essays on subjects of deep or curious interest rather than criticisms on particular works)—I look in vain for any writer, who has conveyed so much information, from so many and such recondite sources, with so many just and original reflections, in a style so lively and poignant, yet so uniformly classical and perspicuous; no one, in short, who has combined so much wisdom with so much wit; so much truth and knowledge with so much life and fancy. His prose is always intelligible and always entertaining. In poetry he has attempted almost every species of composition known before, and he has added new ones; and if we except the highest lyric,—(in which how few, how very few even of the greatest minds have been fortunate)—he has attempted every species successfully;—from the political song of the day, thrown off in the playful overflow of honest joy and patriotic exultation, to the wild ballad; from epistolary ease and graceful narrative, to austere and impetuous moral declamation; from the pastoral charms and wild streaming lights of the Thalaba, in which sentiment and imagery have given permanence even to the excitement of curiosity; and from the full blaze of the Kehama, —(a gallery of finished pictures in one splendid fancy piece, in which, notwithstanding, the moral grandeur rises gradually above the brillance of the colouring and the boldness and novelty of the machinery)—to the more sober beauties of the Madoc; and lastly, from the Madoc to his Roderick, in which, retaining all his former excellencies of a poet eminently inventive and picturesque, he has surpassed himself in language and metre, in the construction of the whole, and in the splendour of particular passages.

Here then shall I conclude? No! The characters of the deceased, like the *encomia* on tombstones, as they are described with religious tenderness, so are they read, with allowing sympathy indeed, but yet with rational deduction. There are men, who deserve a higher record; men with whose characters it is the interest of their contemporaries, no less than that of posterity, to be made acquainted; while it is yet possible for impartial censure, and even for quick-sighted envy, to cross-examine the tale without offence to the courtesies of humanity; and while the eulogist, detected in exaggeration or falsehood, must pay the full penalty of his baseness in the contempt which brands the convicted flatterer. Publicly has Mr. Southey been reviled by men, who, as I would fain hope for the honour of human nature, hurled firebrands against a figure of their own imagination; publicly have his talents been depreciated, his principles denounced; as publicly do I therefore, who have known him intimately, deem it my duty to leave recorded, that it is SOUTHEY's almost unexampled felicity, to possess the best gifts of talent and genius free from all their characteristic defects. To those who remember the state of our public schools and universities some twenty years past, it will appear no ordinary praise in any man to have passed from innocence into virtue, not only free from all vicious habit, but unstained by one act of intemperance, or the degradations akin to intemperance. That scheme of head, heart, and habitual demeanour, which in his early manhood, and first controversial writings, Milton, claiming the privilege of self-defence, asserts of himself, and challenges his calumniators to disprove; this will his school-mates, his fellow-collegians, and his maturer friends, with a confidence proportioned to the intimacy of their knowledge, bear witness to, as again realized in the life of Robert Southey. But still more striking to those, who by biography or by their own experience are familiar with the general habits of genius, will appear the poet's matchless industry and perseverance in his pursuits; the worthiness and dignity of those pursuits; his generous submission to tasks of transitory interest, or such as *his* genius alone could make otherwise; and that having thus more than satisfied the claims of affection or prudence, he should yet have made for himself time and power, to achieve more, and in more various departments, than almost any other writer has done, though employed wholly on subjects of his own choice and ambition. But as Southey possesses, and is not possessed by, his genius, even so is he master even of his virtues. The regular and methodical tenor of his daily labours, which would be deemed rare in the most mechanical pursuits, and might be envied by the mere man of business, loses all semblance of formality in the dignified simplicity of his manners, in the spring and healthful cheerfulness of his spirits. Always employed, his friends find him always at leisure. No less punctual in trifles, than steadfast in the performance of highest duties, he inflicts none of those small pains and discomforts which irregular men scatter about them, and which in the aggregate so often become formidable obstacles both to happiness and utility; while on the contrary he bestows all the pleasures, and inspires all that ease of mind on those around him or connected with him, which perfect consistency, and (if such a word might be framed) absolute *reliability*, equally in small as in great concerns, cannot but inspire and bestow; when this too is softened without being weakened by kindness and gentleness. I know few men who so well deserve the character which an antient attributes to Marcus Cato, namely, that he was likest virtue, in as much as he seemed to act aright, not in obedience to any law or outward motive, but by the necessity of a happy nature, which could not act otherwise. As son, brother, husband, father, master, friend, he moves with firm yet light steps, alike unostentatious, and alike exemplary. As a writer, he has uniformly made his talents subservient to the best interests of humanity, of public virtue, and domestic piety; his cause has ever been the cause of pure religion and of liberty, of national independence and of national illumination. When future critics shall weigh out his guerdon of praise and censure, it will be Southey the poet only, that will supply them with the scanty materials for the latter. They will likewise not fail to record, that as no man was ever a more constant friend, never had poet more friends and honourers among the good of all parties; and that quacks in education, quacks in politics, and quacks in criticism were his only enemies.[1]

[1] It is not easy to estimate the effects which the example of a young man as highly distinguished for strict purity of disposition and conduct, as for intellectual power and literary acquirements, may produce on those of the same age with himself, especially on those of similar pursuits and congenial minds. For many years, my opportunities of intercourse with Mr. Southey

have been rare, and at long intervals; but I dwell with unabated pleasure on the strong and sudden, yet I trust not fleeting, influence, which my moral being underwent on my acquaintance with him at Oxford, whither I had gone at the commencement of our Cambridge vacation on a visit to an old school-fellow. Not indeed on my moral or religious principles, for *they* had never been contaminated; but in awakening the sense of the duty and dignity of making my actions accord with those principles, both in word and deed. The irregularities only not universal among the young men of my standing, which I always *knew* to be *wrong*, I then learned to feel as *degrading*; learned to know that an opposite conduct, which was at that time considered by us as the easy virtue of cold and selfish prudence, might originate in the noblest emotions, in views the most disinterested and imaginative. It is not however from grateful recollections only, that I have been impelled thus to leave these my deliberate sentiments on record; but in some sense as a debt of justice to the man, whose name has been so often connected with mine for evil to which he is a stranger. As a specimen I subjoin part of a note, from The Beauties of the Anti-jacobin, in which, having previously informed the public that I had been dishonoured at Cambridge for preaching Deism, at a time when, for my youthful ardour in defence of Christianity, I was decried as a bigot by the proselytes of French phi- (or to speak more truly, psi-) losophy, the writer concludes with these words; "since this time he has left his native country, commenced citizen of the world, *left his poor children fatherless, and his wife destitute.* Ex his disce *his friends*, LAMB and SOUTHEY." With severest truth it may be asserted, that it would not be easy to select two men more exemplary in their domestic affections than those whose names were thus printed at full length as in the same rank of morals with a denounced infidel and fugitive, who had left his children *fatherless and his wife destitute!* Is it surprising, that many good men remained longer than perhaps they otherwise would have done adverse to a party, which encouraged and openly rewarded the authors of such atrocious calumnies? *Qualis es, nescio; sed per quales agis, scio et doleo.*

CHAPTER IV.

The Lyrical Ballads with the Preface—Mr. Wordsworth's earlier poems—On Fancy and Imagination—The investigation of the distinction important to the Fine Arts.

I HAVE wandered far from the object in view, but as I fancied to myself readers who would respect the feelings that had tempted me from the main road; so I dare calculate on not a few, who will warmly sympathize with them. At present it will be sufficient for my purpose, if I have proved, that Mr. Southey's writings no more than my own furnished the original occasion to this fiction of a *new school* of poetry, and to the clamours against its supposed founders and proselytes.

As little do I believe that Mr. Wordsworth's Lyrical Ballads were in themselves the cause. I speak exclusively of the two volumes so entitled. A careful and repeated examination of these confirms me in the belief, that the omission of less than a hundred lines would have precluded nine-tenths of the criticism on this work. I hazard this declaration, however, on the supposition, that the reader has taken it up, as he would have done any other collection of poems purporting to derive their subjects or interests from the incidents of domestic or ordinary life, intermingled with higher strains of meditation which the poet utters in his own person and character; with the proviso, that these poems were perused without knowledge of, or reference to, the author's peculiar opinions, and that the reader had not had his attention previously directed to those peculiarities. In that case, as actually happened with Mr. Southey's earlier works, the lines and passages which might have offended the general taste, would have been considered as mere inequalities, and attributed to inattention, not to perversity of judgment. The men of business who had passed their lives chiefly in cities, and who might therefore be expected to derive the highest pleasure from acute notices of men and manners conveyed in easy, yet correct and pointed language; and all those who, reading but little poetry, are most stimulated with that species of it, which seems most distant from prose, would probably have passed by the volumes altogether. Others more catholic in their taste, and yet habituated to be most pleased when most excited, would have contented themselves with deciding, that the author had been successful in proportion to the elevation of his style and subject. Not a few, perhaps, might, by their admiration of the Lines written near Tintern Abbey, on revisiting the Wye, those Left upon a Yew Tree Seat, The Old Cumberland Beggar, and Ruth, have been gradually led to peruse with kindred feeling The Brothers, the Hart-leap Well, and whatever other poems in that collection may be described as holding a middle place between those written in the highest and those in the humblest style; as for instance between the Tintern Abbey, and The Thorn, or Simon Lee. Should their taste submit to no further change, and still remain unreconciled to the colloquial phrases, or the imitations of them, that are, more or less, scattered through the class last mentioned; yet even from the small number of the latter, they would have deemed them but an inconsiderable subtraction from the merit of the whole work; or, what is sometimes not unpleasing in the publication of a new writer, as serving to ascertain the natural tendency, and consequently the proper direction of the author's genius.

In the critical remarks, therefore, prefixed and annexed to the Lyrical Ballads, I believe, we may safely rest, as the true origin of the unexampled opposition which Mr. Wordsworth's writings have been since doomed to encounter. The humbler passages in the poems themselves were dwelt on and cited to justify the rejection of the theory. What in and for themselves would have been either forgotten or forgiven as imperfections, or at least comparative failures, provoked direct hostility when announced as intentional, as the result of choice after full deliberation. Thus the poems, admitted by *all* as excellent, joined with those which had pleased the far *greater* number, though they formed two-thirds of the whole work, instead of being deemed (as in all right they should have been, even if we take for granted that the reader judged aright) an atonement for the few exceptions, gave wind and fuel to the animosity against both the poems and the poet. In all perplexity there is a portion of fear, which predisposes the mind to anger. Not able to deny that the author possessed both genius and a powerful intellect, they felt *very positive*,—but yet were not *quite certain* that he might not be in the right, and they themselves in the wrong; an unquiet state of mind, which seeks alleviation by quarrelling with the occasion of it, and by wondering at the perverseness of the man, who had written a long and argumentative essay to persuade them, that

Fair is foul, and foul is fair;

in other words, that they had been all their lives admiring without judgment, and were now about to censure without reason.[1]

That this conjecture is not wide from the mark, I am induced to believe from the noticeable fact, which I can state on my own knowledge, that the same general censure has been grounded by almost every different person on some different poem. Among those, whose candour and judgment I estimate highly, I distinctly remember six who expressed their objections to the Lyrical

[1] In opinions of long continuance, and in which we have never before been molested by a single doubt, to be suddenly *convinced* of an *error*, is almost like being *convicted* of a fault. There is a state of mind, which is the direct *antithesis* of that, which takes place when we *make a bull*. The *bull* namely consists in the bringing together two incompatible thoughts, with the *sensation*, but without the *sense*, of their connection. The psychological condition, or that which constitutes the possibility, of this state, being such disproportionate vividness of two distant thoughts, as extinguishes or obscures the consciousness of the intermediate images or conceptions, or wholly abstracts the attention from them. Thus in the well known bull, "*I was a fine child, but they changed me;*" the first conception expressed in the word "*I*," is that of personal identity—*Ego contemplans:* the second expressed in the word "*me*," is the visual image or object by which the mind represents to itself its past condition, or rather, its personal identity under the form in which it imagined itself previously to have existed,—*Ego contemplatus*. Now the change of one visual image for another involves in itself no absurdity, and becomes absurd only by its immediate juxta-position with the first thought, which is rendered possible by the whole attention being successively absorbed in each singly, so as not to notice the interjacent notion, *changed*, which by its incongruity with the first thought, *I*, constitutes the bull. Add only, that this process is facilitated by the circumstance of the words *I*, and *me*, being sometimes equivalent, and sometimes having a distinct meaning; sometimes, namely, signifying the act of self-consciousness, sometimes the external image in and by which the mind represents that act to itself, the result and symbol of its individuality. Now suppose the direct contrary state, and you will have a distinct sense of the connection between two conceptions, without that *sensation* of such connection which is supplied by habit. The man *feels* as if he were standing on his head, though he cannot but *see* that he is truly standing on his feet. This, as a painful sensation, will of course have a tendency to associate itself with him who occasions it; even as persons, who have been by painful means restored from derangement, are known to feel an involuntary dislike towards their physician.

Ballads almost in the same words, and altogether to the same purport, at the same time admitting, that several of the poems had given them great pleasure; and, strange as it might seem, the composition which one cited as execrable, another quoted as his favourite. I am indeed convinced in my own mind, that could the same experiment have been tried with these volumes, as was made in the well known story of the picture, the result would have been the same; the parts which had been covered by black spots on the one day, would be found equally *albo lapide notatæ* on the succeeding.

However this may be, it was assuredly hard and unjust to fix the attention on a few separate and insulated poems with as much aversion, as if they had been so many plague-spots on the whole work, instead of passing them over in silence, as so much blank paper, or leaves of a bookseller's catalogue; especially, as no one pretended to have found in them any immorality or indelicacy; and the poems, therefore, at the worst, could only be regarded as so many light or inferior coins in a rouleau of gold, not as so much alloy in a weight of bullion. A friend whose *talents* I hold in the highest respect, but whose *judgment* and strong sound sense I have had almost continued occasion to *revere*, making the usual complaints to me concerning both the style and subjects of Mr. Wordsworth's minor poems; I admitted that there were some few of the tales and incidents, in which I could not myself find a sufficient cause for their having been recorded in metre. I mentioned Alice Fell as an instance; "Nay," replied my friend with more than usual quickness of manner, "I cannot agree with you *there*!—that, I own, *does* seem to me a remarkably pleasing poem." In the Lyrical Ballads, (for my experience does not enable me to extend the remark equally unqualified to the two subsequent volumes,) I have heard at different times, and from different individuals, every single poem *extolled* and *reprobated*, with the exception of those of loftier kind, which as was before observed, seem to have won universal praise. This fact of itself would have made me diffident in my censures, had not a still stronger ground been furnished by the strange contrast of the heat and long continuance of the opposition, with the nature of the faults stated as justifying it. The seductive faults, the *dulcia vitia* of Cowley, Marini, or Darwin might reasonably be thought capable of corrupting the public judgment for half a century, and require a twenty years war, campaign after campaign, in order to dethrone the usurper and re-establish the legitimate taste. But that a downright simpleness, under the affectation of simplicity, prosaic words in feeble metre, silly thoughts in childish phrases, and a preference of mean, degrading, or at best trivial associations and characters, should succeed in forming a school of imitators, a company of almost *religious* admirers, and this too among young men of ardent minds, liberal education, and not

—— with academic laurels unbestowed;

and that this bare and bald *counterfeit* of poetry, which is characterized as *below* criticism, should for nearly twenty years have well-nigh *engrossed* criticism, as the main, if not the only, *butt* of review, magazine, pamphlet, poem, and paragraph;—this is indeed matter of wonder. Of yet greater is it, that the contest should still continue as[1] undecided as that between Bacchus and the frogs in Aristophanes; when the former descended to the realms of the departed to bring back the spirit of old and genuine poesy;—

X. βρεκεκεκὲξ, κοὰξ, κοάξ.
Δ. ἀλλ' ἐξόλοισθ' αὐτῷ κοάξ.
οὐδὲν γάρ ἐστ' ἀλλ' ἢ κοάξ.
....
οἰμώζετ'· οὐ γάρ μοι μέλει.
X. ἀλλὰ μὴν κεκραξόμεσθά
γ' ὁπόσον ἡ φάρυγξ ἂν ἡμῶν

[2] Without however the apprehensions attributed to the *Pagan* reformer of the poetic republic. If we may judge from the preface to the recent collection of his poems, Mr. W. would have answered with Xanthias—

σὺ δ' οὐκ ἔδεισας τὸν ψόφον τῶν ῥημάτων
καὶ τὰς ἀπειλάς; ΞΑΝ. οὐ μὰ Δί', οὐδ' ἐφρόντισα.

And here let me hint to the authors of the numerous parodies, and pretended imitations of Mr. Wordsworth's style, that at once to conceal and convey wit and wisdom in the semblance of folly and dulness, as is done in the Clowns and Fools, nay even in the Dogberry of our Shakespeare, is doubtless a proof of genius, or at all events of satiric talent; but that the attempt to ridicule a silly and childish poem, by writing another still sillier and still more childish, can only prove (if it prove any thing at all) that the parodist is a still greater blockhead than the original writer, and, what is far worse, a malignant coxcomb to boot. The talent for mimicry seems strongest where the human race are most degraded. The poor, naked half human savages of New Holland were found excellent mimics: and, in civilized society, minds of the very lowest stamp alone satirize by copying. At least the difference which must blend with and balance the likeness, in order to constitute a just imitation, existing here merely in caricature, detracts from the libeller's heart, without adding an *iota* to the credit of his understanding.

χανδάνῃ δι' ἡμέρας,
βρεκεκεκὲξ, κοὰξ, κοάξ!
Δ. τούτῳ γὰρ οὐ νικήσετε.
Χ. οὐδὲ μὴν ἡμᾶς σὺ πάντως.
Δ. οὐδὲ μὴν ὑμεῖς γε δή μ'
οὐδέποτε, κεκράξομαι γὰρ,
κἂν με δέῃ, δι' ἡμέρας,
ἕως ἂν ὑμῶν ἐπικρατήσω τῷ κοάξ!
Χ. βρεκεκεκὲξ, ΚΟΑ`Ξ, ΚΟΑ´Ξ!

During the last year of my residence at Cambridge, 1794, I became acquainted with Mr. Wordsworth's first publication entitled Descriptive Sketches; and seldom, if ever, was the emergence of an original poetic genius above the literary horizon more evidently announced. In the form, style, and manner of the whole poem, and in the structure of the particular lines and periods, there is a harshness and acerbity connected and combined with words and images all a-glow, which might recall those products of the vegetable world, where gorgeous blossoms rise out of a hard and thorny rind and shell, within which the rich fruit is elaborating. The language is not only peculiar and strong, but at times knotty and contorted, as by its own impatient strength; while the novelty and struggling crowd of images, acting in conjunction with the difficulties of the style, demands always a greater closeness of attention, than poetry,—at all events, than descriptive poetry—has a right to claim. It not seldom therefore justified the complaint of obscurity. In the following extract I have sometimes fancied, that I saw an emblem of the poem itself, and of the author's genius as it was then displayed.—

'Tis storm; and, hid in mist from hour to hour,
All day the floods a deepening murmur pour;
The sky is veiled, and every cheerful sight:
Dark is the region as with coming night;
But what a sudden burst of overpowering light!
Triumphant on the bosom of the storm,
Glances the fire-clad eagle's wheeling form;
Eastward, in long perspective glittering, shine
The wood-crowned cliffs that o'er the lake recline;
Wide o'er the Alps a hundred streams unfold,
At once to pillars turned that flame with gold;
Behind his sail the peasant strives to shun
The west that burns like one dilated sun,
Where in a mighty crucible expire
The mountains, glowing hot, like coals of fire.

The poetic Psyche, in its process to full development, undergoes as many changes as its Greek namesake, the butterfly.[1] And it is remarkable how soon genius clears and purifies itself from the faults and errors of its earliest products; faults which, in its earliest compositions, are the more obtrusive and confluent, because as heterogeneous elements, which had only a temporary use, they constitute the very *ferment*, by which themselves are carried off. Or we may compare them to some diseases, which must work on the humours, and be thrown out on the surface, in order to secure the patient from their future recurrence. I was in my twenty-fourth year, when I had the happiness of knowing Mr. Wordsworth personally, and while memory lasts, I shall hardly forget the sudden effect produced on my mind, by his recitation of a manuscript poem, which still remains unpublished, but of which the stanza and tone of style were the same as those of The Female Vagrant, as originally printed in the first volume of the Lyrical Ballads. There was here no mark of strained thought, or forced diction, no crowd or turbulence of imagery; and, as the poet hath himself well described in his Lines on revisiting the Wye, manly reflection and human associations had given both variety, and an additional interest to natural objects, which, in the passion and appetite of the first love, they had seemed to him neither to need nor permit. The occasional obscurities, which had risen from an imperfect control over the resources of his native language, had almost wholly disappeared, together with that worse defect of arbitrary and illogical phrases, at once hackneyed and fantastic, which hold so distinguished a place in the *technique* of ordinary poetry, and will, more or less, alloy the earlier poems of the truest genius, unless the attention has been specifically directed to their worthlessness and incongruity.[2] I did not perceive any thing particular in the mere style

[1] The Butterfly the ancient Grecians made
The soul's fair emblem, and its only name—
But of the soul, escaped the slavish trade
Of mortal life! For in this earthly frame
Our's is the reptile's lot, much toil, much blame,
Manifold motions making little speed,
And to deform and kill the things whereon we feed.

[2] Mr. Wordsworth, even in his two earliest poems, The Evening Walk and the Descriptive Sketches, is more free from this latter defect than most of the young poets his contemporaries. It may however be exemplified, together

of the poem alluded to during its recitation, except indeed such difference as was not separable from the thought and manner; and the Spenserian stanza, which always, more or less, recalls to the reader's mind Spenser's own style, would doubtless have authorized, in my then opinion, a more frequent descent to the phrases of ordinary life, than could without an ill effect have been hazarded in the heroic couplet. It was not however the freedom from false taste, whether as to common defects, or to those more properly his own, which made so unusual an impression on my feelings immediately, and subsequently on my judgment. It was the union of deep feeling with profound thought; the fine balance of truth in observing, with the imaginative faculty in modifying, the objects observed; and above all the original gift of spreading the tone, the *atmosphere*, and with it the depth and height of the ideal world around forms, incidents, and situations, of which, for the common view, custom had bedimmed all the lustre, had dried up the sparkle and the dew drops.

This excellence, which in all Mr. Wordsworth's writings is more or less predominant, and which constitutes the character of his mind, I no sooner felt, than I sought to understand. Repeated meditations led me first to suspect,—(and a more intimate analysis of the human faculties, their appropriate marks, functions, and effects matured my conjecture into full conviction,) —that Fancy and Imagination were two distinct and widely different faculties, instead of being, according to the general belief, either two names with one meaning, or, at furthest, the lower and higher degree of one and the same power. It is not, I own, easy to conceive a more apposite translation of the Greek

with the harsh and obscure construction, in which he more often offended, in the following lines:—

'Mid stormy vapours ever driving by,
Where ospreys, cormorants, and herons cry;
Where hardly given the hopeless waste to cheer,
Denied the bread of life the foodful ear,
Dwindles the pear on autumn's latest spray,
And *apple sickens* pale in summer's ray;
Ev'n here Content has fixed her smiling reign
With Independence, child of high Disdain.

I hope, I need not say, that I have quoted these lines for no other purpose than to make my meaning fully understood. It is to be regretted that Mr. Wordsworth has not republished these two poems entire.

φαντασία than the Latin *imaginatio*; but it is equally true that in all societies there exists an instinct of growth, a certain collective, unconscious good sense working progressively to desynonymize[1] those words originally of the same meaning, which the conflux of dialects supplied to the more homogeneous languages, as the Greek and German: and which the same cause, joined with accidents of translation from original works of different countries, occasion in mixed languages like our own. The first and most important point to be proved is, that two conceptions perfectly distinct are confused under one and the same word, and—this done—to appropriate that word exclusively to the one meaning, and the synonyme, should there be one, to the other. But if,—(as will be often the case in the arts and sciences,)—no synonyme exists, we must either invent or borrow a word. In the present instance the appropriation has already begun, and been legitimated in the derivative adjective: Milton had a highly *imaginative*, Cowley a very *fanciful* mind. If therefore I should succeed in establishing the actual existence of two faculties generally different, the nomenclature would be at once determined. To the faculty by which I had characterized Milton, we should confine the term 'imagination;' while the other would be contra-distinguished as 'fancy.' Now were it once fully ascertained, that this division

[1] This is effected either by giving to the one word a general, and to the other an exclusive use; as "to put on the back" and "to indorse;" or by an actual distinction of meanings, as "naturalist," and "physician;" or by difference of relation, as "I" and "Me" (each of which the rustics of our different provinces still use in all the cases singular of the first personal pronoun). Even the mere difference, or corruption, in the *pronunciation* of the same word, if it have become general, will produce a new word with a distinct signification; thus "property" and "propriety;" the latter of which, even to the time of Charles II. was the *written* word for all the senses of both. There is a sort of *minim immortal* among the *animalcula infusoria*, which has not naturally either birth, or death, absolute beginning, or absolute end: for at a certain period a small point appears on its back, which deepens and lengthens till the creature divides into two, and the same process recommences in each of the halves now become integral. This may be a fanciful, but it is by no means a bad emblem of the formation of words, and may facilitate the conception, how immense a nomenclature may be organized from a few simple sounds by rational beings in a social state. For each new application, or excitement of the same sound, will call forth a different sensation, which cannot but affect the pronunciation. The after recollection of the sound, without the same vivid sensation, will modify it still further; till at length all trace of the original likeness is worn away.

is no less grounded in nature than that of *delirium* from *mania*, or Otway's

> Lutes, laurels, seas of milk, and ships of amber,

from Shakespeare's

> What! have his daughters brought him to this pass?

or from the preceding apostrophe to the elements; the theory of the fine arts, and of poetry in particular, could not but derive some additional and important light. It would in its immediate effects furnish a torch of guidance to the philosophical critic; and ultimately to the poet himself. In energetic minds, truth soon changes by domestication into power; and from directing in the discrimination and appraisal of the product, becomes influencive in the production. To admire on principle, is the only way to imitate without loss of originality.

It has been already hinted, that metaphysics and psychology have long been my hobby-horse. But to have a hobby-horse, and to be vain of it, are so commonly found together, that they pass almost for the same. I trust therefore, that there will be more good humour than contempt, in the smile with which the reader chastises my self-complacency, if I confess myself uncertain, whether the satisfaction from the perception of a truth new to myself may not have been rendered more poignant by the conceit, that it would be equally so to the public. There was a time, certainly, in which I took some little credit to myself, in the belief that I had been the first of my countrymen, who had pointed out the diverse meaning of which the two terms were capable, and analyzed the faculties to which they should be appropriated. Mr. W. Taylor's recent volume of synonymes I have not yet seen;[1]

[1] I ought to have added, with the exception of a single sheet which I accidentally met with at the printer's. Even from this scanty specimen, I found it impossible to doubt the talent, or not to admire the ingenuity, of the author. That his distinctions were for the greater part unsatisfactory to *my* mind, proves nothing against their accuracy; but it may possibly be serviceable to him, in case of a second edition, if I take this opportunity of suggesting the query; whether he may not have been occasionally misled, by having assumed, as to me he appears to have done, the non-existence of *any* absolute synonymes in our language? Now I cannot but think, that there are many which remain for our posterity to distinguish and appropriate, and which I regard as so much reversionary wealth in our mother tongue. When two distinct meanings are confounded under one or more words,—(and such must be the case, as sure as our knowledge is progressive and of course

but his specification of the terms in question has been clearly shown to be both insufficient and erroneous by Mr. Wordsworth in the Preface added to the late collection of his Poems. The explanation which Mr. Wordsworth has himself given, will be found to differ from mine, chiefly, perhaps as our objects are different. It could scarcely indeed happen otherwise, from the advantage I have enjoyed of frequent conversation with him on a subject to which a poem of his own first directed my attention, and my conclusions concerning which he had made more lucid to myself by many happy instances drawn from the operation of natural objects on the mind. But it was Mr. Wordsworth's purpose to consider the influences of fancy and imagination as they are manifested in poetry, and from the different effects to conclude their diversity in kind; while it is my object to investigate the seminal principle, and then from the kind to deduce the degree. My friend has drawn a masterly sketch of the branches with their *poetic* fruitage. I wish to add the trunk, and even the roots as far as they lift themselves above ground, and are visible to the naked eye of our common consciousness.

Yet even in this attempt I am aware that I shall be obliged to draw more largely on the reader's attention, than so immethodical a miscellany as this can authorize; when in such a work (the

imperfect)—erroneous consequences will be drawn, and what is true in one sense of the word will be affirmed as true *in toto*. Men of research, startled by the consequences, seek in the things themselves—(whether in or out of the mind)—for a knowledge of the fact, and having discovered the difference, remove the equivocation either by the substitution of a new word, or by the appropriation of one of the two or more words, which had before been used promiscuously. When this distinction has been so naturalized and of such general currency that the language does as it were *think* for us—(like the sliding rule which is the mechanic's safe substitute for arithmetical knowledge)—we then say, that it is evident to *common sense*. Common sense, therefore, differs in different ages. What was born and christened in the Schools passes by degrees into the world at large, and becomes the property of the market and the tea-table. At least I can discover no other meaning of the term, *common sense*, if it is to convey any specific difference from sense and judgment *in genere*, and where it is not used scholastically for the *universal reason*. Thus in the reign of Charles II. the philosophic world was called to arms by the moral sophisms of Hobbes, and the ablest writers exerted themselves in the detection of an error, which a school-boy would now be able to confute by the mere recollection, that *compulsion* and *obligation* conveyed two ideas perfectly disparate, and that what appertained to the one, had been falsely transferred to the other by a mere confusion of terms.

Ecclesiastical Polity) of such a mind as Hooker's, the judicious author, though no less admirable for the perspicuity than for the port and dignity of his language,—and though he wrote for men of learning in a learned age,—saw nevertheless occasion to anticipate and guard against "complaints of obscurity," as often as he was to trace his subject "to the highest well-spring and fountain." Which, (continues he) "because men are not accustomed to, the pains we take are more needful a great deal, than acceptable; and the matters we handle, seem by reason of newness (till the mind grow better acquainted with them) dark and intricate." I would gladly therefore spare both myself and others this labour, if I knew how without it to present an intelligible statement of my poetic creed,—not as my *opinions*, which weigh for nothing, but as deductions from established premises conveyed in such a form, as is calculated either to effect a fundamental conviction, or to receive a fundamental confutation. If I may dare once more adopt the words of Hooker, "they, unto whom we shall seem tedious, are in no wise injured by us, because it is in their own hands to spare that labour, which they are not willing to endure." Those at least, let me be permitted to add, who have taken so much pains to render me ridiculous for a perversion of taste, and have supported the charge by attributing strange notions to me on no other authority than their own conjectures, owe it to themselves as well as to me not to refuse their attention to my own statement of the theory which I do acknowledge; or shrink from the trouble of examining the grounds on which I rest it, or the arguments which I offer in its justification.

* * * * * * *

[For some account of the chapters omitted here, see Appendix I, p. 157.]

CHAPTER XIV.

Occasion of the Lyrical Ballads, and the objects originally proposed—Preface to the second edition—The ensuing controversy, its causes and acrimony—Philosophic definitions of a Poem and Poetry with scholia.

DURING the first year that Mr. Wordsworth and I were neighbours, our conversations turned frequently on the two cardinal points of poetry, the power of exciting the sympathy of the reader by a faithful adherence to the truth of nature, and the power of giving the interest of novelty by the modifying colours of imagination. The sudden charm, which accidents of light and shade, which moon-light or sun-set diffused over a known and familiar landscape, appeared to represent the practicability of combining both. These are the poetry of nature. The thought suggested itself—(to which of us I do not recollect)— that a series of poems might be composed of two sorts. In the one, the incidents and agents were to be, in part at least, supernatural; and the excellence aimed at was to consist in the interesting of the affections by the dramatic truth of such emotions, as would naturally accompany such situations, supposing them real. And real in *this* sense they have been to every human being who, from whatever source of delusion, has at any time believed himself under supernatural agency. For the second class, subjects were to be chosen from ordinary life; the characters and incidents were to be such as will be found in every village and its vicinity, where there is a meditative and feeling mind to seek after them, or to notice them, when they present themselves.

In this idea originated the plan of the LYRICAL BALLADS; in which it was agreed, that my endeavours should be directed to persons and characters supernatural, or at least romantic; yet so as to transfer from our inward nature a human interest and a semblance of truth sufficient to procure for these shadows of imagination that willing suspension of disbelief for the moment, which constitutes poetic faith. Mr. Wordsworth, on the other hand, was to propose to himself as his object, to give the charm of novelty to things of every day, and to excite a feeling analogous to the supernatural, by awakening the mind's attention from the lethargy of custom, and directing it to the loveliness and the wonders of the world before us; an inexhaustible treasure, but for which, in consequence of the film of familiarity and selfish solicitude we have eyes, yet see not, ears that hear not, and hearts that neither feel nor understand.

With this view I wrote THE ANCIENT MARINER, and was preparing among other poems, THE DARK LADIE, and the CHRISTABEL, in which I should have more nearly realized my ideal, than I had done in my first attempt. But Mr. Wordsworth's industry had proved so much more successful, and the number of his poems so much greater, that my compositions, instead of forming a balance, appeared rather an interpolation of heterogeneous matter. Mr. Wordsworth added two or three poems written in his own character, in the impassioned, lofty, and sustained diction, which is characteristic of his genius. In this form the LYRICAL BALLADS were published; and were presented by him, as an *experiment*, whether subjects, which from their nature rejected the usual ornaments and extra-colloquial style of poems in general, might not be so managed in the language of ordinary life as to produce the pleasurable interest, which it is the peculiar business of poetry to impart. To the second edition he added a preface of considerable length; in which, notwithstanding some passages of apparently a contrary import, he was understood to contend for the extension of this style to poetry of all kinds, and to reject as vicious and indefensible all phrases and forms of speech that were not included in what he (unfortunately, I think, adopting an equivocal expression) called the language of *real* life. From this preface, prefixed to poems in which it was impossible to deny the presence of original genius, however mistaken its direction might be deemed, arose the whole long-continued controversy. For from the conjunction of perceived power with supposed heresy I explain the inveteracy and in some instances, I grieve to say, the acrimonious passions, with which the controversy has been conducted by the assailants.

Had Mr. Wordsworth's poems been the silly, the childish things, which they were for a long time described as being; had they been really distinguished from the compositions of other poets merely by meanness of language and inanity of thought; had they indeed contained nothing more than what is found in the parodies and pretended imitations of them; they must have sunk at once, a dead weight, into the slough of oblivion, and have dragged the preface along with them. But year after year increased the number of Mr. Wordsworth's admirers. They were found too not in the lower classes of the reading public, but chiefly among young men of strong sensibility and meditative minds; and their admiration (inflamed perhaps in some degree by opposition) was distinguished by its intensity, I might almost say, by its *religious* fervour. These facts, and the intellectual energy of the author, which was more or less consciously felt, where it was outwardly and even boisterously denied, meeting with sentiments of aversion to his opinions, and of alarm at their consequences, produced an eddy of criticism, which would of itself have borne up the poems by the violence with which it whirled them round and round. With many parts of this preface in the sense attributed to them and which the words undoubtedly seem to authorize, I never concurred; but on the contrary objected to them as erroneous in principle, and as contradictory (in appearance at least) both to other parts of the same preface, and to the author's own practice in the greater part of the poems themselves. Mr. Wordsworth in his recent collection has, I find, degraded this prefatory disquisition to the end of his second volume, to be read or not at the reader's choice. But he has not, as far as I can discover, announced any change in his poetic creed. At all events, considering it as the source of a controversy, in which I have been honoured more than I deserve by the frequent conjunction of my name with his, I think it expedient to declare once for all, in what points I coincide with the opinions supported in that preface, and in what points I altogether differ. But in order to render myself intelligible I must previously, in as few words as possible, explain my views, first, of a Poem; and secondly, of Poetry itself, in *kind*, and in *essence*.

The office of philosophical *disquisition* consists in just *distinction*; while it is the privilege of the philosopher to preserve himself constantly aware, that distinction is not division. In order to obtain adequate notions of any truth, we must intellectually separate its distinguishable parts; and this is the technical *process* of philosophy. But having so done, we must then restore them in our conceptions to the unity, in which they actually co-exist; and this is the *result* of philosophy. A poem contains the same elements as a prose composition; the difference therefore must consist in a different combination of them, in consequence of a different object being proposed. According to the difference of the object will be the difference of the combination. It is possible, that the object may be merely to facilitate the recollection of any given facts or observations by artificial arrangement; and the composition will be a poem, merely because it is distinguished from prose by metre, or by rhyme, or by both conjointly. In this, the lowest sense, a man might attribute the name of a poem to the well known enumeration of the days in the several months;

> Thirty days hath September,
> April, June, and November, &c.

and others of the same class and purpose. And as a particular pleasure is found in anticipating the recurrence of sounds and quantities, all compositions that have this charm super-added, whatever be their contents, *may* be entitled poems.

So much for the superficial *form*. A difference of object and contents supplies an additional ground of distinction. The immediate purpose may be the communication of truths; either of truth absolute and demonstrable, as in works of science; or of facts experienced and recorded, as in history. Pleasure, and that of the highest and most permanent kind, may *result* from the *attainment* of the end; but it is not itself the immediate end. In other works the communication of pleasure may be the immediate purpose; and though truth, either moral or intellectual, ought to be the *ultimate* end, yet this will distinguish the character of the author, not the class to which the work belongs. Blest indeed is that state of society, in which the immediate purpose would be baffled by the perversion of the proper ultimate end; in which no charm of diction or imagery could exempt the BATHYLLUS even of an Anacreon, or the ALEXIS of Virgil, from disgust and aversion!

But the communication of pleasure may be the immediate object of a work not metrically composed; and that object may have been in a high degree attained, as in novels and romances. Would then the mere superaddition of metre, with or without rhyme, entitle *these* to the name of poems? The answer is, that nothing can permanently please, which does not contain in itself the reason why it is so, and not otherwise. If metre be superadded, all other parts must be made consonant with it. They must be such, as to justify the perpetual and distinct attention to each part, which an exact correspondent recurrence of accent and sound are calculated to excite. The final definition then, so deduced, may be thus worded. A poem is that species of composition, which is opposed to works of science, by proposing for its *immediate* object pleasure, not truth; and from all other species —(having *this* object in common with it)—it is discriminated by proposing to itself such delight from the *whole*, as is compatible with a distinct gratification from each component *part*.

Controversy is not seldom excited in consequence of the disputants attaching each a different meaning to the same word; and in few instances has this been more striking, than in disputes concerning the present subject. If a man chuses to call every composition a poem, which is rhyme, or measure, or both, I must leave his opinion uncontroverted. The distinction is at least competent to characterize the writer's intention. If it were subjoined, that the whole is likewise entertaining or affecting, as a tale, or as a series of interesting reflections, I of course admit this as another fit ingredient of a poem, and an additional merit. But if the definition sought for be that of a *legitimate* poem, I answer, it must be one, the parts of which mutually support and explain each other; all in their proportion harmonizing with, and supporting the purpose and known influences of metrical arrangement. The philosophic critics of all ages coincide with the ultimate judgment of all countries, in equally denying the praises of a just poem, on the one hand, to a series of striking lines or distiches, each of which, absorbing the whole attention of the reader to itself, becomes disjointed from its context, and forms a separate whole, instead of a harmonizing part; and on the other hand, to an unsustained composition, from which the reader collects rapidly the general result unattracted by the component parts. The reader should be carried forward, not merely or chiefly by the mechanical impulse of curiosity, or by a restless desire to arrive at the final solution; but by the pleasurable activity of mind excited by the attractions of the journey itself. Like the motion of a serpent, which the Egyptians made the emblem of intellectual power; or like the path of sound through the air;— at every step he pauses and half recedes, and from the retrogressive movement collects the force which again carries him onward. *Præcipitandus est* liber *spiritus*, says Petronius most happily. The epithet, *liber*, here balances the preceding verb; and it is not easy to conceive more meaning condensed in fewer words.

But if this should be admitted as a satisfactory character of a poem, we have still to seek for a definition of poetry. The writings of Plato, and Jeremy Taylor, and Burnet's Theory of the Earth, furnish undeniable proofs that poetry of the highest kind may exist without metre, and even without the contradistinguishing objects of a poem. The first chapter of Isaiah—(indeed a very large proportion of the whole book)—is poetry in the most emphatic sense; yet it would be not less irrational than strange to assert, that pleasure, and not truth was the immediate object of the prophet. In short, whatever *specific* import we attach to the word, Poetry, there will be found involved in it, as a necessary consequence, that a poem of any length neither can be, nor ought to be, all poetry. Yet if an harmonious whole is to be produced, the remaining parts must be preserved *in keeping* with the poetry; and this can be no otherwise effected than by such a studied selection and artificial arrangement, as will partake of *one*, though not a *peculiar* property of poetry. And this again can be no other than the property of exciting a more continuous and equal attention than the language of prose aims at, whether colloquial or written.

My own conclusions on the nature of poetry, in the strictest use of the word, have been in part anticipated in some of the remarks on the Fancy and Imagination in the first volume of this work. What is poetry?—is so nearly the same question with, what is a poet?—that the answer to the one is involved in the solution of the other. For it is a distinction resulting from the poetic genius itself, which sustains and modifies the images, thoughts, and emotions of the poet's own mind.

The poet, described in *ideal* perfection, brings the whole soul of man into activity, with the subordination of its faculties to each other according to their relative worth and dignity. He diffuses a tone and spirit of unity, that blends, and (as it were) *fuses*, each into each, by that synthetic and magical power, to which I would exclusively appropriate the name of Imagination. This power, first put in action by the will and understanding, and retained under their irremissive, though gentle and unnoticed, control, *laxis effertur habenis*, reveals itself in the balance or reconcilement of opposite or discordant qualities: of sameness, with difference; of the general with the concrete; the idea with the image; the individual with the representative; the sense of novelty and freshness with old and familiar objects; a more than usual state of emotion with more than usual order; judgment ever awake and steady self-possession with enthusiasm and feeling profound or vehement; and while it blends and harmonizes the natural and the artificial, still subordinates art to nature; the manner to the matter; and our admiration of the poet to our sympathy with the poetry. Doubtless, as Sir John Davies observes of the soul —(and his words may with slight alteration be applied, and even more appropriately, to the poetic Imagination)—

Doubtless this could not be, but that she turns
Bodies to *spirit* by sublimation strange,
As fire converts to fire the things it burns,
As we our food into our nature change.

From their gross matter she abstracts *their* forms,
And draws a kind of quintessence from things;
Which to her proper nature she transforms
To bear them light on her celestial wings.

Thus does she, when from *individual states*
She doth abstract the universal kinds;
Which then re-clothed in divers names and fates
Steal access through the senses to our minds.

Finally, GOOD SENSE is the BODY of poetic genius, FANCY its DRAPERY, MOTION its LIFE, and IMAGINATION the SOUL that is every where, and in each; and forms all into one graceful and intelligent whole.

CHAPTER XV.

The specific symptoms of poetic power elucidated in a critical analysis of Shakespeare's VENUS *and* ADONIS, *and* RAPE OF LUCRECE.

IN the application of these principles to purposes of practical criticism, as employed in the appraisement of works more or less imperfect, I have endeavoured to discover what the qualities in a poem are, which may be deemed promises and specific symptoms of poetic power, as distinguished from general talent determined to poetic composition by accidental motives, by an act of the will, rather than by the inspiration of a genial and productive nature. In this investigation, I could not, I thought, do better, than keep before me the earliest work of the greatest genius, that perhaps human nature has yet produced, our *myriad-minded*[1] Shakespeare. I mean the VENUS AND ADONIS, and the LUCRECE; works which give at once strong promises of the strength, and yet obvious proofs of the immaturity, of his genius. From these I abstracted the following marks, as characteristics of original poetic genius in general.

1. In the VENUS AND ADONIS, the first and most obvious excellence is the perfect sweetness of the versification; its adaptation to the subject; and the power displayed in varying the march of the words without passing into a loftier and more majestic rhythm than was demanded by the thoughts, or permitted by the propriety of preserving a sense of melody predominant. The delight in richness and sweetness of sound, even to a faulty excess, if it be evidently original, and not the result of an easily imitable mechanism, I regard as a highly favourable promise in the compositions of a young man. The man that hath not music in his soul can indeed never be a genuine poet. Imagery,—(even taken

[1] Ἀνὴρ μυριόνους, a phrase which I have borrowed from a Greek monk, who applies it to a Patriarch of Constantinople. I might have said, that I have reclaimed, rather than borrowed, it: for it seems to belong to Shakespeare, *de jure singulari, et ex privilegio naturæ.*

from nature, much more when transplanted from books, as travels, voyages, and works of natural history),—affecting incidents, just thoughts, interesting personal or domestic feelings, and with these the art of their combination or intertexture in the form of a poem,—may all by incessant effort be acquired as a trade, by a man of talent and much reading, who, as I once before observed, has mistaken an intense desire of poetic reputation for a natural poetic genius; the love of the arbitrary end for a possession of the peculiar means. But the sense of musical delight, with the power of producing it, is a gift of imagination; and this together with the power of reducing multitude into unity of effect, and modifying a series of thoughts by some one predominant thought or feeling, may be cultivated and improved, but can never be learned. It is in these that "*poeta nascitur non fit.*"

2. A second promise of genius is the choice of subjects very remote from the private interests and circumstances of the writer himself. At least I have found, that where the subject is taken immediately from the author's personal sensations and experiences, the excellence of a particular poem is but an equivocal mark, and often a fallacious pledge, of genuine poetic power. We may perhaps remember the tale of the statuary, who had acquired considerable reputation for the legs of his goddesses, though the rest of the statue accorded but indifferently with ideal beauty; till his wife, elated by her husband's praises, modestly acknowledged that she had been his constant model. In the VENUS AND ADONIS this proof of poetic power exists even to excess. It is throughout as if a superior spirit more intuitive, more intimately conscious, even than the characters themselves, not only of every outward look and act, but of the flux and reflux of the mind in all its subtlest thoughts and feelings, were placing the whole before our view; himself meanwhile unparticipating in the passions, and actuated only by that pleasurable excitement, which had resulted from the energetic fervour of his own spirit in so vividly exhibiting what it had so accurately and profoundly contemplated. I think, I should have conjectured from these poems, that even then the great instinct, which impelled the poet to the drama, was secretly working in him, prompting him—by a series and never broken chain of imagery, always vivid and, because unbroken, often minute; by the highest effort of the picturesque in words, of which words are capable, higher perhaps than was ever realized by any

other poet, even Dante not excepted;—to provide a substitute for that visual language, that constant intervention and running comment by tone, look and gesture, which in his dramatic works he was entitled to expect from the players. His Venus and Adonis seem at once the characters themselves, and the whole representation of those characters by the most consummate actors. You seem to be told nothing, but to see and hear every thing. Hence it is, from the perpetual activity of attention required on the part of the reader; from the rapid flow, the quick change, and the playful nature of the thoughts and images; and above all from the alienation, and, if I may hazard such an expression, the utter *aloofness* of the poet's own feelings, from those of which he is at once the painter and the analyst;—that though the very subject cannot but detract from the pleasure of a delicate mind, yet never was poem less dangerous on a moral account. Instead of doing as Ariosto, and as, still more offensively, Wieland has done, instead of degrading and deforming passion into appetite, the trials of love into the struggles of concupiscence;—Shakespeare has here represented the animal impulse itself, so as to preclude all sympathy with it, by dissipating the reader's notice among the thousand outward images, and now beautiful, now fanciful circumstances, which form its dresses and its scenery; or by diverting our attention from the main subject by those frequent witty or profound reflections, which the poet's ever active mind has deduced from, or connected with, the imagery and the incidents. The reader is forced into too much action to sympathize with the merely passive of our nature. As little can a mind thus roused and awakened be brooded on by mean and indistinct emotion, as the low, lazy mist can creep upon the surface of a lake, while a strong gale is driving it onward in waves and billows.

3. It has been before observed that images, however beautiful, though faithfully copied from nature, and as accurately represented in words, do not of themselves characterize the poet. They become proofs of original genius only as far as they are modified by a predominant passion; or by associated thoughts or images awakened by that passion; or when they have the effect of reducing multitude to unity, or succession to an instant; or lastly, when a human and intellectual life is transferred to them from the poet's own spirit,

Which shoots its being through earth, sea, and air.

In the two following lines for instance, there is nothing objectionable, nothing which would preclude them from forming, in their proper place, part of a descriptive poem:

> Behold yon row of pines, that shorn and bow'd
> Bend from the sea-blast, seen at twilight eve.

But with a small alteration of rhythm, the same words would be equally in their place in a book of topography, or in a descriptive tour. The same image will rise into a semblance of poetry if thus conveyed:

> Yon row of bleak and visionary pines,
> By twilight glimpse discerned, mark! how they flee
> From the fierce sea-blast, all their tresses wild
> Streaming before them.

I have given this as an illustration, by no means as an instance, of that particular excellence which I had in view, and in which Shakespeare even in his earliest, as in his latest, works surpasses all other poets. It is by this, that he still gives a dignity and a passion to the objects which he presents. Unaided by any previous excitement, they burst upon us at once in life and in power,—

> Full many a glorious morning have I seen
> *Flatter* the mountain tops with sovereign eye.

> Not mine own fears, nor the prophetic soul
> Of the wide world dreaming on things to come—

> *　*　*　*　*　*
>
> *　*　*　*　*　*

> The mortal moon hath her eclipse endured,
> And the sad augurs mock their own presage;
> Incertainties now crown themselves assur'd,
> And Peace proclaims olives of endless age.
> Now with the drops of this most balmy time
> My love looks fresh, and Death to me subscribes,
> Since spite of him, I'll live in this poor rhyme,
> While he insults o'er dull and speechless tribes.
> And thou in this shalt find thy monument,
> When tyrants' crests, and tombs of brass are spent.

As of higher worth, so doubtless still more characteristic of poetic genius does the imagery become, when it moulds and colours itself to the circumstances, passion, or character, present and foremost in the mind. For unrivalled instances of this excellence, the reader's own memory will refer him to the LEAR, OTHELLO, in short to which not of the "*great, ever living, dead man's*" dramatic works? *Inopem me copia fecit.* How true it is to nature, he has himself finely expressed in the instance of love in his 98th Sonnet.

From you have I been absent in the spring,
When proud-pied April drest in all its trim,
Hath put a spirit of youth in every thing;
That heavy Saturn laugh'd and leap'd with him.
Yet nor the lays of birds, nor the sweet smell
Of different flowers in odour and in hue,
Could make me any summer's story tell,
Or from their proud lap pluck them, where they grew:
Nor did I wonder at the lilies white,
Nor praise the deep vermilion in the rose;
They were, tho' sweet, but figures of delight,
Drawn after you, you pattern of all those.
Yet seem'd it winter still, and, you away,
As with your shadow, I with these did play!

Scarcely less sure, or if a less valuable, not less indispensable mark

Γονίμου μὲν ποιητοῦ ———
——— ὅστις ῥῆμα γενναῖον λάκοι,

will the imagery supply, when, with more than the power of the painter, the poet gives us the liveliest image of succession with the feeling of simultaneousness:—

With this, he breaketh from the sweet embrace
Of those fair arms, which bound him to her breast,
And homeward through the dark laund runs apace;—
* * * * * *
Look! how a bright star shooteth from the sky,
So glides he in the night from Venus' eye.

4. The last character I shall mention, which would prove indeed but little, except as taken conjointly with the former;—yet without which the former could scarce exist in a high degree, and (even if this were possible) would give promises only of transitory flashes and a meteoric power;—is DEPTH, and ENERGY of THOUGHT. No man was ever yet a great poet, without being at the same time a profound philosopher. For poetry is the blossom and the fragrancy of all human knowledge, human thoughts, human passions, emotions, language, In Shakespeare's *poems* the creative power and the intellectual energy wrestle as in a war embrace. Each in its excess of strength seems to threaten the extinction of the other. At length in the DRAMA they were recon-

ciled, and fought each with its shield before the breast of the other. Or like two rapid streams, that, at their first meeting within narrow and rocky banks, mutually strive to repel each other and intermix reluctantly and in tumult; but soon finding a wider channel and more yielding shores blend, and dilate, and flow on in one current and with one voice. The VENUS AND ADONIS did not perhaps allow the display of the deeper passions. But the story of Lucretia seems to favour and even demand their intensest workings. And yet we find in *Shakespeare's* management of the tale neither pathos, nor any other *dramatic* quality. There is the same minute and faithful imagery as in the former poem, in the same vivid colours, inspirited by the same impetuous vigour of thought, and diverging and contracting with the same activity of the assimilative and of the modifying faculties; and with a yet larger display, a yet wider range of knowledge and reflection; and lastly, with the same perfect dominion, often *domination*, over the whole world of language. What then shall we say? even this; that Shakespeare, no mere child of nature; no *automaton* of genius; no passive vehicle of inspiration possessed by the spirit, not possessing it; first studied patiently, meditated deeply, understood minutely, till knowledge, become habitual and intuitive, wedded itself to his habitual feelings, and at length gave birth to that stupendous power, by which he stands alone, with no equal or second in his own class; to that power, which seated him on one of the two glory-smitten summits of the poetic mountain, with Milton as his compeer not rival. While the former darts himself forth, and passes into all the forms of human character and passion, the one Proteus of the fire and the flood; the other attracts all forms and things to himself, into the unity of his own IDEAL. All things and modes of action shape themselves anew in the being of Milton: while Shakespeare becomes all things, yet for ever remaining himself. O what great men hast thou not produced, England, my country!—Truly indeed—

> *We* must be free or die, who speak the tongue,
> Which Shakespeare spake; the faith and morals hold,
> Which Milton held. In every thing we are sprung
> Of earth's first blood, have titles manifold!

CHAPTER XVI.

Striking points of difference between the Poets of the present age and those of the fifteenth and sixteenth centuries—Wish expressed for the union of the characteristic merits of both.

CHRISTENDOM, from its first settlement on feudal rights, has been so far one great body, however imperfectly organized, that a similar spirit will be found in each period to have been acting in all its members. The study of Shakespeare's *poems*—(I do not include his dramatic works, eminently as they too deserve that title)—led me to a more careful examination of the contemporary poets both in England and in other countries. But my attention was especially fixed on those of Italy, from the birth to the death of Shakespeare; that being the country in which the fine arts had been most sedulously, and hitherto most successfully cultivated. Abstracted from the degrees and peculiarities of individual genius, the properties common to the good writers of each period seem to establish one striking point of difference between the poetry of the fifteenth and sixteenth centuries, and that of the present age. The remark may perhaps be extended to the sister art of painting. At least the latter will serve to illustrate the former. In the present age the poet—(I would wish to be understood as speaking generally, and without allusion to individual names)—seems to propose to himself as his main object, and as that which is the most characteristic of his art, new and striking IMAGES; with INCIDENTS that interest the affections or excite the curiosity. Both his characters and his descriptions he renders, as much as possible, specific and individual, even to a degree of portraiture. In his diction and metre, on the other hand, he is comparatively carèless. The measure is either constructed on no previous system, and acknowledges no justifying principle but that of the writer's convenience; or else some mechanical movement is adopted, of which one couplet or stanza is so far an adequate specimen, as that the occasional differences appear evidently to arise from accident, or the qualities of the language itself, not from meditation and an intelligent purpose. And the language from Pope's translation of Homer, to Darwin's Temple of Nature,[1] may, notwithstanding some illustrious exceptions, be too faithfully characterized, as claiming to be poetical for no better reason, than that it would be intolerable in conversation or in prose. Though alas! even our prose writings, nay even the style of our more set discourses, strive to be in the fashion, and trick themselves out in the soiled and over-worn finery of the meretricious muse. It is true that of late a great improvement in this respect is observable in our most popular writers. But it is equally true, that this recurrence to plain sense and genuine mother English is far from being general; and that the composition of our novels, magazines, public harangues, and the like is commonly as trivial in thought, and yet enigmatic in expression, as if Echo and Sphinx had laid their heads together to construct it. Nay, even of those who have most rescued themselves from this contagion, I should plead inwardly guilty to the charge of duplicity or cowardice, if I withheld my conviction, that few have guarded the purity of their native tongue with that jealous care, which the sublime Dante in his tract, *De la volgare Eloquenza*, declares to be the first duty of a poet. For language is the armoury of the human mind; and at once contains the trophies of its past, and the weapons of its future conquests. *Animadverte, quam sit ab improprietate verborum pronum hominibus prolabi in errores circa ipsas res!* HOBBES: Exam. et Exmend. hod. Math. *Sat [vero], in hâc vitæ brevitate et naturæ obscuritate, rerum est, quibus cognoscendis tempus impendatur, ut [confusis et multivocis] sermonibus intelligendis illud consumere opus non sit. [Eheu! quantas strages paravere verba nubila, quæ tot dicunt ut nihil dicunt; —nubes potius, e quibus et in rebus politicis et in ecclesia turbines et tonitrua erumpunt!] Et proinde recte dictum putamus a Platone in Gorgia:* ὃς ἂν τὰ ὀνόματα εἰδεῖ, εἴσεται καὶ τὰ πράγματα*: et ab Epicteto,* ἀρχὴ παιδεύσεως ἡ τῶν ὀνομάτων ἐπίσκεψις*: et prudentissime Galenus scribit,* ἡ τῶν ὀνομάτων χρῆσις ταραχθεῖσα καὶ τὴν τῶν πραγμάτων ἐπιταράττει γνῶσιν. *Egregie vero J. C. Scaliger, in Lib. I. de Plantis:* Est primum, inquit, sapientis officium, bene sentire, ut sibi vivat: proximum, bene loqui, ut patriæ vivat. SENNERTUS *de Puls: Differentia.*

[1] First published in 1803.

Something analogous to the materials and structure of modern poetry I seem to have noticed—(but here I beg to be understood as speaking with the utmost diffidence)—in our common landscape painters. Their foregrounds and intermediate distances are comparatively unattractive: while the main interest of the landscape is thrown into the back ground, where mountains and torrents and castles forbid the eye to proceed, and nothing tempts it to trace its way back again. But in the works of the great Italian and Flemish masters, the front and middle objects of the landscape are the most obvious and determinate, the interest gradually dies away in the back ground, and the charm and peculiar worth of the picture consists, not so much in the specific objects which it conveys to the understanding in a visual language formed by the substitution of figures for words, as in the beauty and harmony of the colours, lines, and expression, with which the objects are represented. Hence novelty of subject was rather avoided than sought for. Superior excellence in the manner of treating the same subjects was the trial and test of the artist's merit.

Not otherwise is it with the more polished poets of the fifteenth and sixteenth centuries, especially those of Italy. The imagery is almost always general: sun, moon, flowers, breezes, murmuring streams, warbling songsters, delicious shades, lovely damsels cruel as fair, nymphs, naiads, and goddesses, are the materials which are common to all, and which each shaped and arranged according to his judgment or fancy, little solicitous to add or to particularize. If we make an honourable exception in favour of some English poets, the thoughts too are as little novel as the images; and the fable of their narrative poems, for the most part drawn from mythology, or sources of equal notoriety, derive their chief attractions from the manner of treating them; from impassioned flow, or picturesque arrangement. In opposition to the present age, and perhaps in as faulty an extreme, they placed the essence of poetry in the *art*. The excellence, at which they aimed, consisted in the exquisite polish of the diction, combined with perfect simplicity. This their prime object they attained by the avoidance of every word, which a *gentleman* would *not* use in dignified conversation, and of every word and phrase, which none but a *learned* man *would* use; by the studied position of words and phrases, so that not only each part should be melodious in itself, but contribute to the harmony of the whole, each note referring and conducing to the melody of all the foregoing and following words of the same period or stanza; and lastly with equal labour, the greater because unbetrayed, by the variation and various harmonies of their metrical movement. Their measures, however, were not indebted for their variety to the introduction of new metres, such as have been attempted of late in the Alonzo and Imogen, and others borrowed from the German, having in their very mechanism a specific overpowering tune, to which the generous reader humours his voice and emphasis, with more indulgence to the author than attention to the meaning or quantity of the words; but which, to an ear familiar with the *numerous* sounds of the Greek and Roman poets, has an effect not unlike that of galloping over a paved road in a German stage-waggon without springs. On the contrary, the elder bards both of Italy and England produced a far greater as well as more charming variety by countless modifications, and subtle balances of sound in the common metres of their country. A lasting and enviable reputation awaits that man of genius, who should attempt and realize a union;—who should recall the high finish, the appropriateness, the facility, the delicate proportion, and above all, the perfusive and omnipresent grace, which have preserved, as in a shrine of precious amber, the Sparrow of Catullus, the Swallow, the Grasshopper, and all the other little loves of Anacreon; and which, with bright, though diminished glories, revisited the youth and early manhood of Christian Europe, in the vales of Arno,[1] and

[1] These thoughts were suggested to me during the perusal of the Madrigals of Giovambatista Strozzi published in Florence in May 1593, by his sons Lorenzo and Filippo Strozzi, with a dedication to their paternal uncle, *Signor Leone Strozzi, Generale delle battaglie di Santa Chiesa.* As I do not remember to have seen either the poems or their author mentioned in any English work, or to have found them in any of the common collections of Italian poetry; and as the little work is of rare occurrence; I will transcribe a few specimens. I have seldom met with compositions that possessed, to my feelings, more of that satisfying *entireness*, that complete adequateness of the manner to the matter which so charms us in Anacreon, joined with the tenderness, and more than the *delicacy* of Catullus. Trifles as they are, they were probably elaborated with great care; yet in the perusal we refer them to a spontaneous energy rather than to voluntary effort. To a cultivated taste there is a delight in *perfection* for its own sake, independent of the material in which it is manifested, that none but a cultivated taste can understand or appreciate.

After what I have advanced, it would appear presumption to offer a

the groves of Isis and of Cam;—and who with these should combine the keener interest, deeper pathos, manlier reflection, and

translation; even if the attempt were not discouraged by the different genius of the English mind and language, which demands a denser body of thought as the condition of a high polish, than the Italian. I cannot but deem it likewise an advantage in the Italian tongue, in many other respects inferior to our own, that the language of poetry is more distinct from that of prose than with us. From the earlier appearance and established primacy of the Tuscan poets, concurring with the number of independent states, and the diversity of written dialects, the Italians have gained a poetic idiom, as the Greeks before them had obtained from the same causes, with greater and more various discriminations, for example, the Ionic for their heroic verses; the Attic for their iambic; and the two modes of the Doric for the lyric or sacerdotal, and the pastoral, the distinctions of which were doubtless more obvious to the Greeks themselves than they are to us.

I will venture to add one other observation before I proceed to the transcription. I am aware that the sentiments which I have avowed concerning the points of difference between the poetry of the present age, and that of the period between 1500 and 1650, are the reverse of the opinion commonly entertained. I was conversing on this subject with a friend, when the servant, a worthy and sensible woman, coming in, I placed before her two engravings, the one a pinky-coloured plate of the day, the other a masterly etching by Salvator Rosa from one of his own pictures. On pressing her to tell us, which she preferred, after a little blushing and flutter of feeling, she replied—"Why, that, Sir, to be sure! (pointing to the *ware* from the Fleet-street print shops);—it's so *neat* and elegant. T'other is such a *scratchy* slovenly thing." An artist, whose writings are scarcely less valuable than his pictures, and to whose authority more deference will be willingly paid, than I could even wish should be shown to mine, has told us, and from his own experience too, that good taste must be *acquired*, and like all other good things, is the result of thought and the submissive study of the best models. If it be asked, "But what shall I deem such?"—the answer is; *presume* those to be the best, the *reputation* of which has been matured into *fame* by the consent of ages. For wisdom always has a final majority, if not by conviction, yet by acquiescence. In addition to Sir J. Reynolds I may mention Harris of Salisbury; who in one of his philosophical disquisitions has written on the means of acquiring a just taste with the precision of Aristotle, and the elegance of Quinctilian.

MADRIGALI.

Gelido suo ruscel chiaro, e tranquillo
M'insegnò Amor di state a mezzo'l giorno;
Ardean le selve, ardean le piagge, e i colli.
Ond' io, ch' al più gran gielo ardo e sfavillo,
Subito corsi; ma si puro adorno
Girsene il vidi, che turbar no'l volli:
Sol mi specchiava, e'n dolce ombrosa sponda
Mi stava intento al mormorar dell' onda.

the fresher and more various imagery, which give a value and a

Aure dell' angoscioso viver mio
Refrigerio soave,
E dolce sì, che più non mi par grave
Ne'l arder, ne'l morir, anz' il desio;
Deh voi'l ghiaccio, e le nubi, e'l tempo rio
Discacciatene omai, che l'onda chiara,
E l'ombra non men cara
A scherzare, e cantar per suoi boschetti,
E prati festa e allegrezza alletti.

Pacifiche, ma spesso in amorosa
Guerra co' fiori, e l'erba
Alla stagione acerba
Verdi insegne del giglio e della rosa,
Movete, Aure, pian pian; che tregua ò posa,
Se non pace, io ritrove;
E so ben dove:—Oh vago, e mansueto
Sguardo, oh labbra d'ambrosia, oh rider lieto!

Hor come un scoglio stassi,
Hor come un rio se'n fugge,
Ed hor crud' orsa rugge,
Hor canta angelo pio: ma che non fassi?
E che non fammi, O sassi,
O rivi, o belue, o Dii, questa mia vaga
Non so, se ninfa, ò maga,
Non so, se donna, ò Dea,
Non so, se dolce, ò rea?

Piangendo mi baciaste,
E ridendo il negaste:
In doglia hebbivi pia,
In festa hebbivi ria:
Nacque gioia di pianti,
Dolor di riso: O amanti
Miseri, habbiate insieme
Ognor paura e speme.

Bel Fior, tu mi rimembri
La rugiadosa guancia del bel viso;
E si vera l'assembri,
Che'n te sovente, come in lei m'affiso:
E hor del vago riso,
Hor del sereno sguardo

name that will not pass away to the poets who have done honour to our own times, and to those of our immediate predecessors.

Io pur cieco riguardo. Ma qual fugge,
O Rosa, il mattin lieve?
E chi te, come neve,
E'l mio cor teco, e la mia vita strugge?

Anna mia, Anna dolce, oh sempre nuovo
E più chiaro concento,
Quanta dolcezza sento
In sol Anna dicendo? Io mi pur pruovo,
Ne quì tra noi ritruovo,
Ne trà cieli armonia,
Che del bel nome suo più dolce sia:
Altro il Cielo, altro Amore,
Altro non suona l'Ecco del mio core.

Hor che'l prato, e la selva si scolora,
Al tuo sereno ombroso
Muovine, alto Riposo,
Deh ch'io riposi una sol notte, un hora:
Han le fere, e gli augelli, ognun talora
Ha qualche pace; io quando,
Lasso! non vonne errando,
E non piango, e non grido? e qual pur forte?
Ma poichè, non sent' egli, odine, Morte.

Risi e piansi d'Amor; nè però mai
Se non in fiamma, ò 'n onda, ò 'n vento scrissi:
Spesso mercè trovai
Crudel; sempre in me morto, in altri vissi:
Hor da' più scuri Abissi al ciel m'alzai,
Hor ne pur caddi giuso;
Stanco al fin quì son chiuso.

CHAPTER XVII.

Examination of the tenets peculiar to Mr. Wordsworth—Rustic life (above all, low and rustic life) especially unfavourable to the formation of a human diction—The best parts of language the product of philosophers, not of clowns or shepherds—Poetry essentially ideal and generic—The language of Milton as much the language of real life, yea, incomparably more so than that of the cottager.

As far then as Mr. Wordsworth in his preface contended, and most ably contended, for a reformation in our poetic diction, as far as he has evinced the truth of passion, and the *dramatic* propriety of those figures and metaphors in the original poets, which, stripped of their justifying reasons, and converted into mere artifices of connection or ornament, constitute the characteristic falsity in the poetic style of the moderns; and as far as he has, with equal acuteness and clearness, pointed out the process by which this change was effected, and the resemblances between that state into which the reader's mind is thrown by the pleasurable confusion of thought from an unaccustomed train of words and images; and that state which is induced by the natural language of impassioned feeling; he undertook a useful task, and deserves all praise, both for the attempt and for the execution. The provocations to this remonstrance in behalf of truth and nature were still of perpetual recurrence before and after the publication of this preface. I cannot likewise but add, that the comparison of such poems of merit, as have been given to the public within the last ten or twelve years, with the majority of those produced previously to the appearance of that preface, leave no doubt on my mind, that Mr. Wordsworth is fully justified in believing his efforts to have been by no means ineffectual. Not only in the verses of those who have professed their admiration of his genius, but even of those who have distinguished themselves by hostility to his theory, and depreciation of his writings, are the impressions of his principles plainly visible. It is possible, that with these principles others may have been blended, which are not equally evident; and some which are unsteady and subvertible from the narrowness or imperfection of their basis. But it is more than possible, that these errors of defect or exaggeration, by kindling and feeding the controversy, may have conduced not only to the wider propagation of the accompanying truths, but that, by their frequent presentation to the mind in an excited state, they may have won for them a more permanent and practical result. A man will borrow a part from his opponent the more easily, if he feels himself justified in continuing to reject a part. While there remain important points in which he can still feel himself in the right, in which he still finds firm footing for continued resistance, he will gradually adopt those opinions, which were the least remote from his own convictions, as not less congruous with his own theory than with that which he reprobates. In like manner with a kind of instinctive prudence, he will abandon by little and little his weakest posts, till at length he seems to forget that they had ever belonged to him, or affects to consider them at most as accidental and "petty annexments," the removal of which leaves the citadel unhurt and unendangered.

My own differences from certain supposed parts of Mr. Wordsworth's theory ground themselves on the assumption, that his words had been rightly interpreted, as purporting that the proper diction for poetry in general consists altogether in a language taken, with due exceptions, from the mouths of men in real life, a language which actually constitutes the natural conversation of men under the influence of natural feelings. My objection is, first, that in *any* sense this rule is applicable only to *certain* classes of poetry; secondly, that even to these classes it is not applicable, except in such a sense, as hath never by any one (as far as I know or have read,) been denied or doubted; and lastly, that as far as, and in that degree in which it is *practicable*, it is yet as a *rule* useless, if not injurious, and therefore either need not, or ought not to be practised. The poet informs his reader, that he had generally chosen *low and rustic* life; but not *as* low and rustic, or in order to repeat that pleasure of doubtful moral effect, which persons of elevated rank and of superior refinement oftentimes derive from a happy *imitation* of the rude unpolished manners and discourse of their inferiors. For the pleasure so derived may be traced to three exciting causes. The first is the naturalness, in *fact*, of the things represented. The second is the apparent naturalness of the *representation*, as raised and qualified by an imperceptible infusion of the author's own knowledge and talent, which infusion does, indeed, constitute it an *imitation* as distinguished from a mere *copy*. The third cause may be found in the reader's conscious feeling of his superiority awakened by the contrast presented to him; even as for the same purpose the kings and great barons of yore retained, sometimes *actual* clowns and fools, but more frequently shrewd and witty fellows in that *character*. These, however, were not Mr. Wordsworth's objects. *He* chose low and rustic life, "because in that condition the essential passions of the heart find a better soil, in which they can attain their maturity, are less under restraint, and speak a plainer and more emphatic language; because in that condition of life our elementary feelings coexist in a state of greater simplicity, and consequently may be more accurately contemplated, and more forcibly communicated; because the manners of rural life germinate from those elementary feelings; and from the necessary character of rural occupations are more easily comprehended, and are more durable; and lastly, because in that condition the passions of men are incorporated with the beautiful and permanent forms of nature."

Now it is clear to me, that in the most interesting of the poems, in which the author is more or less dramatic, as THE BROTHERS, MICHAEL, RUTH, THE MAD MOTHER, and others, the persons introduced are by no means taken *from low or rustic life* in the common acceptance of those words; and it is not less clear, that the sentiments and language, as far as they can be conceived to have been really transferred from the minds and conversation of such persons, are attributable to causes and circumstances not necessarily connected with "their occupations and abode." The thoughts, feelings, language, and manners of the shepherd-farmers in the vales of Cumberland and Westmoreland, as far as they are actually adopted in those poems, may be accounted for from causes, which will and do produce the same results in *every* state of life, whether in town or country. As the two principal I rank that INDEPENDENCE, which raises a man above servitude, or daily toil for the profit of others, yet not above the necessity of industry and a frugal simplicity of domestic life; and the accompanying unambitious, but solid and religious, EDUCATION, which has rendered few books familiar, but the Bible, and the Liturgy or Hymn book. To this latter cause, indeed, which is so far *accidental*, that it is the blessing of particular countries and a particular age, not the product of particular places or employments, the poet owes the show of probability, that his personages might really feel, think, and talk with any tolerable resemblance to his representation. It is an excellent remark of Dr. Henry More's, that "a man of confined education, but of good parts, by constant reading of the Bible will naturally form a more winning and commanding rhetoric than those that are learned; the intermixture of tongues and of artificial phrases debasing *their* style." (Enthusiasmus triumphatus, Sec. xxxv.)

It is, moreover, to be considered that to the formation of healthy feelings, and a reflecting mind, *negations* involve impediments not less formidable than sophistication and vicious intermixture. I am convinced, that for the human soul to prosper in rustic life a certain vantage-ground is pre-requisite. It is not every man that is likely to be improved by a country life or by country labours. Education, or original sensibility, or both, must pre-exist, if the changes, forms, and incidents of nature are to prove a sufficient stimulant. And where these are not sufficient, the mind contracts and hardens by want of stimulants; and the man becomes selfish, sensual, gross, and hard-hearted. Let the management of the Poor Laws in Liverpool, Manchester, or Bristol be compared with the ordinary dispensation of the poor rates in agricultural villages, where the *farmers* are the overseers and guardians of the poor. If my own experience have not been particularly unfortunate, as well as that of the many respectable country clergymen with whom I have conversed on the subject, the result would engender more than scepticism concerning the desirable influences of low and rustic life in and for itself. Whatever may be concluded on the other side, from the stronger local attachments and enterprising spirit of the Swiss, and other mountaineers, applies to a particular mode of pastoral life, under forms of property that permit and beget manners truly republican, not to rustic life in general, or to the absence of artificial cultivation. On the contrary the mountaineers, whose manners have been so often eulogized, are in general better educated and greater readers than men of equal rank elsewhere. But where this is not the case, as among the peasantry of North Wales, the ancient mountains, with all their terrors and all their glories, are pictures to the blind, and music to the deaf.

I should not have entered so much into detail upon this passage, but here seems to be the point, to which all the lines of difference converge as to their source and centre;—I mean, as far as, and in whatever respect, my poetic creed *does* differ from the doctrines promulged in this preface. I adopt with full faith, the principle of Aristotle, that poetry, as poetry, is essentially *ideal*, that it avoids and excludes all *accident*; that its apparent individualities of rank, character, or occupation must be *representative* of a class; and that the *persons* of poetry must be clothed with *generic* attributes, with the *common* attributes of the class; not with such as one gifted individual might *possibly* possess, but such as from his situation it is most probable before-hand that he *would* possess. If my premises are right and my deductions legitimate, it follows that there can be no *poetic* medium between the swains of Theocritus and those of an imaginary golden age.

The characters of the vicar and the shepherd-mariner in the poem of The Brothers, and that of the shepherd of Green-head Ghyll in the Michael, have all the verisimilitude and representative quality, that the purposes of poetry can require. They are persons of a known and abiding class, and their manners and sentiments the natural product of circumstances common to the class. Take Michael for instance:

An old man, stout of heart, and strong of limb.
His bodily frame had been from youth to age
Of an unusual strength: his mind was keen,
Intense, and frugal, apt for all affairs,
And in his Shepherd's calling he was prompt
And watchful more than ordinary men.
Hence he had learned the meaning of all winds,
Of blasts of every tone; and, oftentimes,
When others heeded not, he heard the South
Make subterraneous music, like the noise
Of Bagpipers on distant Highland hills.
The Shepherd, at such warning, of his flock
Bethought him, and he to himself would say,
"The winds are now devising work for me!"
And, truly, at all times, the storm—that drives
The Traveller to a shelter—summoned him
Up to the mountains: he had been alone

Amid the heart of many thousand mists,
That came to him and left him on the heights.
So lived he till his eightieth year was past.
And grossly that man errs, who should suppose
That the green Valleys, and the Streams and Rocks,
Were things indifferent to the Shepherd's thoughts.
Fields, where with cheerful spirits he had breathed
The common air; the hills, which he so oft
Had climbed with vigorous steps; which had impressed
So many incidents upon his mind
Of hardship, skill or courage, joy or fear;
Which like a book preserved the memory
Of the dumb animals, whom he had saved,
Had fed or sheltered, linking to such acts,
So grateful in themselves, the certainty
Of honourable gain; these fields, these hills
Which were his living Being, even more
Than his own blood—what could they less? had laid
Strong hold on his affections, were to him
A pleasurable feeling of blind love,
The pleasure which there is in life itself.

On the other hand, in the poems which are pitched in a lower key, as the HARRY GILL, and THE IDIOT BOY, the *feelings* are those of human nature in general; though the poet has judiciously laid the *scene* in the country, in order to place *himself* in the vicinity of interesting images, without the necessity of ascribing a sentimental perception of their beauty to the persons of his drama. In THE IDIOT BOY, indeed, the mother's character is not so much the real and native product of a "situation where the essential passions of the heart find a better soil, in which they can attain their maturity and speak a plainer and more emphatic language," as it is an impersonation of an instinct abandoned by judgment. Hence the two following charges seem to me not wholly groundless: at least, they are the only plausible objections, which I have heard to that fine poem. The one is, that the author has not, in the poem itself, taken sufficient care to preclude from the reader's fancy the disgusting images of *ordinary morbid idiocy*, which yet it was by no means his intention to represent. He has even by the "burr, burr, burr," uncounteracted by any preceding description of the boy's beauty, assisted in recalling them. The other is, that the idiocy of the *boy* is so evenly balanced by the folly of the *mother*, as to present to the general reader rather a laughable burlesque on the blindness of anile dotage, than an analytic display of maternal affection in its ordinary workings.

In THE THORN, the poet himself acknowledges in a note the necessity of an introductory poem, in which he should have portrayed the character of the person from whom the words of the poem are supposed to proceed: a superstitious man moderately imaginative, of slow faculties and deep feelings, "a captain of a small trading vessel, for example, who, being past the middle age of life, had retired upon an annuity, or small independent income, to some village or country town of which he was not a native, or in which he had not been accustomed to live. Such men having nothing to do become credulous and talkative from indolence." But in a poem, still more in a lyric poem—and the NURSE in ROMEO AND JULIET alone prevents me from extending the remark even to dramatic *poetry*, if indeed even the Nurse can be deemed altogether a case in point—it is not possible to imitate truly a dull and garrulous discourser, without repeating the effects of dulness and garrulity. However this may be, I dare assert, that the parts —(and these form the far larger portion of the whole)—which might as well or still better have proceeded from the poet's own imagination, and have been spoken in his own character, are those which have given, and which will continue to give, universal delight; and that the passages exclusively appropriate to the supposed narrator, such as the last couplet of the third stanza;[1] the seven last lines of the tenth;[2] and the five following stanzas, with

[1] I've measured it from side to side;
'Tis three feet long, and two feet wide.

[2] Nay, rack your brain—'tis all in vain,
I'll tell you every thing I know;
But to the Thorn, and to the Pond
Which is a little step beyond,
I wish that you would go:
Perhaps, when you are at the place,
You something of her tale may trace.

I'll give you the best help I can:
Before you up the mountain go,
Up to the dreary mountain-top,
I'll tell you all I know.
'Tis now some two-and-twenty years
Since she (her name is Martha Ray)
Gave, with a maiden's true good will,
Her company to Stephen Hill;
And she was blithe and gay,
And she was happy, happy still
Whene'er she thought of Stephen Hill.

the exception of the four admirable lines at the commencement of the fourteenth, are felt by many unprejudiced and unsophisticated hearts, as sudden and unpleasant sinkings from the height

And they had fix'd the wedding-day,
The morning that must wed them both;
But Stephen to another Maid
Had sworn another oath;
And, with this other Maid, to church
Unthinking Stephen went—
Poor Martha! on that woeful day
A pang of pitiless dismay
Into her soul was sent;
A Fire was kindled in her breast,
Which might not burn itself to rest.

They say, full six months after this,
While yet the summer leaves were green,
She to the mountain-top would go,
And there was often seen.
'Tis said, a child was in her womb,
As now to any eye was plain;
She was with child, and she was mad;
Yet often she was sober sad
From her exceeding pain.
Oh me! ten thousand times I'd rather
That he had died, that cruel father!

* * * * *
* * * * *
* * * * *
* * * * *

Last Christmas when they talked of this,
Old Farmer Simpson did maintain,
That in her womb the infant wrought
About its mother's heart, and brought
Her senses back again:
And when at last her time drew near,
Her looks were calm, her senses clear.

No more I know, I wish I did,
And I would tell it all to you;
For what became of this poor child
There's none that ever knew:
And if a child was born or no,
There's no one that could ever tell;
And if 'twas born alive or dead,
There's no one knows, as I have said:
But some remember well,
That Martha Ray about this time
Would up the mountain often climb.

to which the poet had previously lifted them, and to which he again re-elevates both himself and his reader.

If then I am compelled to doubt the theory, by which the choice of *characters* was to be directed, not only *a priori*, from grounds of reason, but both from the few instances in which the poet himself *need* be supposed to have been governed by it, and from the comparative inferiority of those instances; still more must I hesitate in my assent to the sentence which immediately follows the former citation; and which I can neither admit as particular fact, nor as general rule. "The language, too, of these men has been adopted (purified indeed from what appear to be its real defects, from all lasting and rational causes of dislike or disgust) because such men hourly communicate with the best objects from which the best part of language is originally derived; and because, from their rank in society and the sameness and narrow circle of their intercourse, being less under the action of social vanity, they convey their feelings and notions in simple and unelaborated expressions." To this I reply; that a rustic's language, purified from all provincialism and grossness, and so far re-constructed as to be made consistent with the rules of grammar—(which are in essence no other than the laws of universal logic, applied to psychological materials)—will not differ from the language of any other man of common sense, however learned or refined he may be, except as far as the notions, which the rustic has to convey, are fewer and more indiscriminate. This will become still clearer, if we add the consideration—(equally important though less obvious)—that the rustic, from the more imperfect development of his faculties, and from the lower state of their cultivation, aims almost solely to convey *insulated facts*, either those of his scanty experience or his traditional belief; while the educated man chiefly seeks to discover and express those *connections* of things, or those relative *bearings* of fact to fact, from which some more or less general law is deducible. For *facts* are valuable to a wise man, chiefly as they lead to the discovery of the indwelling *law*, which is the true *being* of things, the sole solution of their modes of existence, and in the knowledge of which consists our dignity and our power.

As little can I agree with the assertion, that from the objects with which the rustic hourly communicates the best part of language is formed. For first, if to communicate with an object implies such an acquaintance with it, as renders it capable of being discriminately reflected on, the distinct knowledge of an uneducated rustic would furnish a very scanty vocabulary. The few things and modes of action requisite for his bodily conveniences would alone be individualized; while all the rest of nature would be expressed by a small number of confused general terms. Secondly, I deny that the words and combinations of words derived from the objects, with which the rustic is familiar, whether with distinct or confused knowledge, can be justly said to form the *best* part of language. It is more than probable, that many classes of the brute creation possess discriminating sounds, by which they can convey to each other notices of such objects as concern their food, shelter, or safety. Yet we hesitate to call the aggregate of such sounds a language, otherwise than metaphorically. The best part of human language, properly so called, is derived from reflection on the acts of the mind itself. It is formed by a voluntary appropriation of fixed symbols to internal acts, to processes and results of imagination, the greater part of which have no place in the consciousness of uneducated man; though in civilized society, by imitation and passive remembrance of what they hear from their religious instructors and other superiors, the most uneducated share in the harvest which they neither sowed, nor reaped. If the history of the phrases in hourly currency among our peasants were traced, a person not previously aware of the fact would be surprised at finding so large a number, which three or four centuries ago were the exclusive property of the universities and the schools; and, at the commencement of the Reformation, had been transferred from the school to the pulpit, and thus gradually passed into common life. The extreme difficulty, and often the impossibility, of finding words for the simplest moral and intellectual processes in the languages of uncivilized tribes has proved perhaps the weightiest obstacle to the progress of our most zealous and adroit missionaries. Yet these tribes are surrounded by the same nature as our peasants are; but in still more impressive forms; and they are, moreover, obliged to *particularize* many more of them. When, therefore, Mr. Wordsworth adds, "accordingly, such a language"—(meaning, as before, the language of rustic life purified from provincialism)—"arising out of repeated experience and regular feelings, is a more permanent, and a far more philosophical language, than that which is frequently substituted for it by Poets, who think that they are conferring honour upon themselves and their art in proportion as they indulge in arbitrary and capricious habits of expression;" it may be answered, that the language, which he has in view, can be attributed to rustics with no greater right, than the style of Hooker or Bacon to Tom Brown or Sir Roger L'Estrange. Doubtless, if what is peculiar to each were omitted in each, the result must needs be the same. Further, that the poet, who uses an illogical diction, or a style fitted to excite only the low and changeable pleasure of wonder by means of groundless novelty, substitutes a language of *folly* and *vanity*, not for that of the *rustic*, but for that of *good sense* and *natural feeling*.

Here let me be permitted to remind the reader, that the positions which I controvert, are contained in the sentences—"a selection of the REAL language of men;"—"the language of these men" (that is, men in low and rustic life) "has been adopted; I have proposed to myself to imitate, and, as far as is possible, to adopt the very language of men."

"Between the language of prose and that of metrical composition, there neither is, nor can be, any essential difference:" it is against these exclusively that my opposition is directed.

I object, in the very first instance, to an equivocation in the use of the word "real." Every man's language varies, according to the extent of his knowledge, the activity of his faculties, and the depth or quickness of his feelings. Every man's language has first, its *individualities*; secondly, the common properties of the *class* to which he belongs; and thirdly, words and phrases of *universal* use. The language of Hooker, Bacon, Bishop Taylor, and Burke differs from the common language of the learned class only by the superior number and novelty of the thoughts and relations which they had to convey. The language of Algernon Sidney differs not at all from that, which every well educated gentleman would wish to write, and (with due allowances for the undeliberateness, and less connected train, of thinking natural and proper to conversation) such as he would wish to talk. Neither one nor the other differ half as much from the general language of cultivated society, as the language of Mr. Wordsworth's homeliest composition differs from that of a common peasant. For "real" therefore, we must substitute *ordinary*, or *lingua communis*. And this, we have proved, is no more to be found in the phraseology of low and rustic life than in that of any other class. Omit the peculiarities of each and the result of course must be common to all. And assuredly the omissions and changes to be made in the language of rustics, before it could be transferred to any species of poem, except the drama or other professed imitation, are at least as numerous and weighty, as would be required in adapting to the same purpose the ordinary language of tradesmen and manufacturers. Not to mention, that the language so highly extolled by Mr. Wordsworth varies in every county, nay in every village, according to the accidental character of the clergyman, the existence or non-existence of schools; or even, perhaps, as the exciseman, publican, and barber happen to be, or not to be, zealous politicians, and readers of the weekly newspaper *pro bono publico*. Anterior to cultivation the *lingua communis* of every country, as Dante has well observed, exists every where in parts, and no where as a whole.

Neither is the case rendered at all more tenable by the addition of the words, "*in a state of excitement*." For the nature of a man's words, when he is strongly affected by joy, grief, or anger, must necessarily depend on the number and quality of the general truths, conceptions and images, and of the words expressing them, with which his mind had been previously stored. For the property of passion is not to *create*; but to set in increased activity. At least, whatever new connections of thoughts or images, or—(which is equally, if not more than equally, the appropriate effect of strong excitement)—whatever generalizations of truth or experience the heat of passion may produce; yet the terms of their conveyance must have pre-existed in his former conversations, and are only collected and crowded together by the unusual stimulation. It is indeed very possible to adopt in a poem the unmeaning repetitions, habitual phrases, and other blank counters, which an unfurnished or confused understanding interposes at short intervals, in order to keep hold of his subject, which is still slipping from him, and to give him time for recollection; or, in mere aid of vacancy, as in the scanty companies of a country stage the same player pops backwards and forwards, in order to prevent the appearance of empty spaces, in the procession of Macbeth, or Henry VIII. But what assistance to the poet, or ornament to the poem, these can supply, I am at a loss to conjecture. Nothing assuredly can differ either in origin or in mode more widely from the *apparent* tautologies of intense and turbulent feeling, in which the passion is greater and of longer endurance than to be exhausted or satisfied by a single representation of the image or incident exciting it. Such repetitions I admit to be a beauty of the highest kind; as illustrated by Mr. Wordsworth himself from the song of Deborah. *At her feet he bowed, he fell, he lay down: at her feet he bowed, he fell: where he bowed, there he fell down dead.* Judges v. 27.

CHAPTER XVIII.

Language of metrical composition, why and wherein essentially different from that of prose—Origin and elements of metre—Its necessary consequences, and the conditions thereby imposed on the metrical writer in the choice of his diction.

I CONCLUDE, therefore, that the attempt is impracticable; and that, were it not impracticable, it would still be useless. For the very power of making the selection implies the previous possession of the language selected. Or where can the poet have lived? And by what rules could he direct his choice, which would not have enabled him to select and arrange his words by the light of his own judgment? We do not adopt the language of a class by the mere adoption of such words exclusively, as that class would use, or at least understand; but likewise by following the *order*, in which the words of such men are wont to succeed each other. Now this order, in the intercourse of uneducated men, is distinguished from the diction of their superiors in knowledge and power, by the greater *disjunction* and *separation* in the component parts of that, whatever it be, which they wish to communicate. There is a want of that prospectiveness of mind, that *surview*, which enables a man to foresee the whole of what he is to convey, appertaining to any one point; and by this means so to subordinate and arrange the different parts according to their relative importance, as to convey it at once, and as an organized whole.

Now I will take the first stanza, on which I have chanced to open, in the Lyrical Ballads. It is one the most simple and the least peculiar in its language.

> In distant countries have I been,
> And yet I have not often seen
> A healthy Man, a Man full grown,
> Weep in the public roads alone.
> But such a one, on English ground,
> And in the broad highway, I met;

Along the broad highway he came,
His cheeks with tears were wet;
Sturdy he seemed, though he was sad;
And in his arms a Lamb he had.

The words here are doubtless such as are current in all ranks of life; and of course not less so in the hamlet and cottage than in the shop, manufactory, college, or palace. But is this the *order*, in which the rustic would have placed the words? I am grievously deceived, if the following less *compact* mode of commencing the same tale be not a far more faithful copy. "I have been in a many parts, far and near, and I don't know that I ever saw before a man crying by himself in the public road; a grown man I mean, that was neither sick nor hurt, &c. &c." But when I turn to the following stanza in The Thorn:

At all times of the day and night
This wretched Woman thither goes;
And she is known to every star,
And every wind that blows:
And there, beside the Thorn she sits,
When the blue day-light's in the skies,
And when the whirlwind's on the hill,
Or frosty air is keen and still,
And to herself she cries,
Oh misery! Oh misery!
Oh woe is me! Oh misery!

and compare this with the language of ordinary men; or with that which I can conceive at all likely to proceed, in *real* life, from *such* a narrator, as is supposed in the note to the poem; compare it either in the succession of the images or of the sentences; I am reminded of the sublime prayer and hymn of praise, which Milton, in opposition to an established liturgy, presents as a fair *specimen* of common extemporary devotion, and such as we might expect to hear from every self-inspired minister of a conventicle! And I reflect with delight, how little a mere theory, though of his own workmanship, interferes with the processes of genuine imagination in a man of true poetic genius, who possesses, as Mr. Wordsworth, if ever man did, most assuredly does possess,

The Vision and the Faculty divine.

One point then alone remains, but that the most important; its examination having been, indeed, my chief inducement for the preceding inquisition. "*There neither is nor can be any essential difference between the language of prose and metrical composition.*" Such is Mr. Wordsworth's assertion. Now prose itself, at least in all argumentative and consecutive works, differs, and ought to differ, from the language of conversation; even as[1] reading ought to differ from talking. Unless therefore the difference denied be that of the mere *words*, as materials common to all styles of writing, and not of the *style* itself in the universally admitted sense of the term, it might be naturally presumed that there must exist a still greater between the ordonnance of poetic composition and that of prose, than is expected to distinguish prose from ordinary conversation.

There are not, indeed, examples wanting in the history of literature, of apparent paradoxes that have summoned the public wonder as new and startling truths, but which, on examination, have shrunk into tame and harmless truisms; as the eyes of a cat, seen in the dark, have been mistaken for flames of fire. But Mr. Wordsworth is among the last men, to whom a delusion of this kind would be attributed by any one, who had enjoyed the slightest opportunity of understanding his mind and character.

[1] It is no less an error in teachers, than a torment to the poor children, to enforce the necessity of reading as they would talk. In order to cure them of *singing* as it is called, that is, of too great a difference, the child is made to repeat the words with his eyes from off the book; and then, indeed, his tones resemble talking, as far as his fears, tears and trembling will permit. But as soon as the eye is again directed to the printed page, the spell begins anew; for an instinctive sense tells the child's feelings, that to utter its own momentary thoughts, and to recite the written thoughts of another, as of another, and a far wiser than himself, are two widely different things; and as the two acts are accompanied with widely different feelings, so must they justify different modes of enunciation. Joseph Lancaster, among his other sophistications of the excellent Dr. Bell's invaluable system, cures this fault of *singing*, by hanging fetters and chains on the child, to the music of which, one of his school-fellows, who walks before, dolefully chants out the child's last speech and confession, birth, parentage, and education. And this soul-benumbing ignominy, this unholy and heart-hardening burlesque on the last fearful infliction of outraged law, in pronouncing the sentence to which the stern and familiarized judge not seldom bursts into tears, has been extolled as a happy and ingenious method of remedying—what? and how?—why, one extreme in order to introduce another, scarce less distant from good sense, and certainly likely to have worse moral effects, by enforcing a semblance of petulant ease and self-sufficiency, in repression, and possible after-perversion of the natural feelings. I have to beg Dr. Bell's pardon for this connection of the two names, but he knows that contrast is no less powerful a cause of association than likeness.

Where an objection has been anticipated by such an author as natural, his answer to it must needs be interpreted in some sense which either is, or has been, or is capable of being controverted. My object then must be to discover some other meaning for the term "*essential difference*" in this place, exclusive of the indistinction and community of the words themselves. For whether there ought to exist a class of words in the English, in any degree resembling the poetic dialect of the Greek and Italian, is a question of very subordinate importance. The number of such words would be small indeed, in our language; and even in the Italian and Greek, they consist not so much of different words, as of slight differences in the *forms* of declining and conjugating the same words; forms, doubtless, which having been, at some period more or less remote, the common grammatic flexions of some tribe or province, had been accidentally appropriated to poetry by the general admiration of certain master intellects, the first established lights of inspiration, to whom that dialect happened to be native.

Essence, in its primary signification, means the principle of *individuation*, the inmost principle of the *possibility* of any thing, *as* that particular thing. It is equivalent to the *idea* of a thing, whenever we use the word, idea, with philosophic precision. Existence, on the other hand, is distinguished from essence, by the superinduction of *reality*. Thus we speak of the essence, and essential properties of a circle; but we do not therefore assert, that any thing, which really *exists*, is mathematically circular. Thus too, without any tautology we contend for the *existence* of the Supreme Being; that is, for a reality correspondent to the idea. There is, next, a *secondary* use of the word essence, in which it signifies the point or ground of contra-distinction between two modifications of the same substance or subject. Thus we should be allowed to say, that the style of architecture of Westminster Abbey is *essentially* different from that of Saint Paul's, even though both had been built with blocks cut into the same form, and from the same quarry. Only in this latter sense of the term must it have been *denied* by Mr. Wordsworth (for in this sense alone is it *affirmed* by the general opinion) that the language of poetry (that is the formal construction, or architecture, of the words and phrases) is *essentially* different from that of prose. Now the burden of the proof lies with the oppugner, not with the supporters of the common belief. Mr.

Wordsworth, in consequence, assigns as the proof of his position, "that not only the language of a large portion of every good poem, even of the most elevated character, must necessarily, except with reference to the metre, in no respect differ from that of good prose, but likewise that some of the most interesting parts of the best poems will be found to be strictly the language of prose, when prose is well written. The truth of this assertion might be demonstrated by innumerable passages from almost all the poetical writings, even of Milton himself." He then quotes Gray's sonnet—

> In vain to me the smiling mornings shine,
> And reddening Phœbus lifts his golden fire;
> The birds in vain their amorous descant join,
> Or cheerful fields resume their green attire.
> These ears, alas! for other notes repine;
> *A different object do these eyes require;*
> *My lonely anguish melts no heart but mine;*
> *And in my breast the imperfect joys expire.*
> Yet morning smiles the busy race to cheer,
> And new-born pleasure brings to happier men;
> The fields to all their wonted tribute bear;
> To warm their little loves the birds complain:
> *I fruitless mourn to him that cannot hear,*
> *And weep the more, because I weep in vain.*

and adds the following remark:—"It will easily be perceived, that the only part of this Sonnet which is of any value, is the lines printed in Italics; it is equally obvious, that, except in the rhyme, and in the use of the single word "fruitless" for fruitlessly, which is so far a defect, the language of these lines does in no respect differ from that of prose."

An idealist defending his system by the fact, that when asleep we often believe ourselves awake, was well answered by his plain neighbour, "Ah, but when awake do we ever believe ourselves asleep?"—Things identical must be convertible. The preceding passage seems to rest on a similar sophism. For the question is not, whether there may not occur in prose an order of words, which would be equally proper in a poem; nor whether there are not beautiful lines and sentences of frequent occurrence in good poems, which would be equally becoming as well as beautiful in good prose; for neither the one nor the other has ever been either denied or doubted by any one. The true question must be, whether there are not modes of expression, a *construction*, and an *order* of sentences, which are in their fit and natural place in a serious prose composition, but would be disproportionate and heterogeneous in metrical poetry; and, *vice versa*, whether in the language of a serious poem there may not be an arrangement both of words and sentences, and a use and selection of (what are called) *figures of speech*, both as to their kind, their frequency, and their occasions, which on a subject of equal weight would be vicious and alien in correct and manly prose. I contend, that in both cases this unfitness of each for the place of the other frequently will and ought to exist.

And first from the *origin* of metre. This I would trace to the balance in the mind effected by that spontaneous effort which strives to hold in check the workings of passion. It might be easily explained likewise in what manner this salutary antagonism is assisted by the very state, which it counteracts; and how this balance of antagonists became organized into *metre* (in the usual acceptation of that term), by a supervening act of the will and judgment, consciously and for the foreseen purpose of pleasure. Assuming these principles, as the *data* of our argument, we deduce from them two legitimate conditions, which the critic is entitled to expect in every metrical work. First, that, as the *elements* of metre owe their existence to a state of increased excitement, so the metre itself should be accompanied by the natural language of excitement. Secondly, that as these elements are formed into metre *artificially*, by a *voluntary* act, with the design and for the purpose of blending *delight* with emotion, so the traces of present *volition* should throughout the metrical language be proportionably discernible. Now these two conditions must be reconciled and co-present. There must be not only a partnership, but a union; an interpenetration of passion and of will, of *spontaneous* impulse and of *voluntary* purpose. Again, this union can be manifested only in a frequency of forms and figures of speech, (originally the offspring of passion, but now the adopted children of power), greater than would be desired or endured, where the emotion is not voluntarily encouraged and kept up for the sake of that pleasure, which such emotion, so tempered and mastered by the will, is found capable of communicating. It not only dictates, but of itself tends to produce a more frequent employment of picturesque and vivifying language, than would be natural in any other case, in which there did not exist, as there does in the present, a previous and well understood, though tacit, *compact* between the poet and his reader, that the latter is entitled to expect, and the former bound to supply this species and degree of pleasurable excitement. We may in some measure apply to this union the answer of Polixenes, in the Winter's Tale, to Perdita's neglect of the streaked gilliflowers, because she had heard it said

> There is an art, which, in their piedness, shares
> With great creating nature.
> *Pol.* Say there be;
> Yet nature is made better by no mean,
> But nature makes that mean; so, o'er that art,
> Which, you say, adds to nature, is an art,
> That nature makes. You see, sweet maid, we marry
> *A gentler scion to the wildest stock;*
> And make conceive a bark of baser kind
> By bud of nobler race. This is an art,
> Which does mend nature,—change it rather; but
> The art itself is nature.

Secondly, I argue from the *effects* of metre. As far as metre acts in and for itself, it tends to increase the vivacity and susceptibility both of the general feelings and of the attention. This effect it produces by the continued excitement of surprise, and by the quick reciprocations of curiosity still gratified and still re-excited, which are too slight indeed to be at any one moment objects of distinct consciousness, yet become considerable in their aggregate influence. As a medicated atmosphere, or as wine during animated conversation, they act powerfully, though themselves unnoticed. Where, therefore, correspondent food and appropriate matter are not provided for the attention and feelings thus roused, there must needs be a disappointment felt; like that of leaping in the dark from the last step of a stair-case, when we had prepared our muscles for a leap of three or four.

The discussion on the powers of metre in the preface is highly ingenious and touches at all points on truth. But I cannot find any statement of its powers considered abstractly and separately. On the contrary Mr. Wordsworth seems always to estimate metre by the powers, which it exerts during, (and, as I think, in *consequence of*), its combination with other elements of poetry. Thus the previous difficulty is left unanswered, *what* the elements are, with which it must be combined, in order to produce its own effects to any pleasurable purpose. Double and tri-syllable rhymes, indeed, form a lower species of wit, and, attended to exclusively for their own sake, may became a source of momentary amusement; as in poor Smart's distich to the Welsh Squire who had promised him a hare:

> Tell me, thou son of great Cadwallader!
> Hast sent the hare? or hast thou swallow'd her?

But for any *poetic* purposes, metre resembles, (if the aptness of the simile may excuse its meanness), yeast, worthless or disagreeable by itself, but giving vivacity and spirit to the liquor with which it is proportionally combined.

The reference to THE CHILDREN IN THE WOOD by no means satisfies my judgment. We all willingly throw ourselves back for awhile into the feelings of our childhood. This ballad, therefore, we read under such recollections of our own childish feelings, as would equally endear to us poems, which Mr. Wordsworth himself would regard as faulty in the opposite extreme of gaudy and technical ornament. Before the invention of printing, and in a still greater degree, before the introduction of writing, metre, especially *alliterative* metre (whether alliterative at the beginning of the words, as in PIERCE PLOUMAN, or at the end, as in rhymes) possessed an independent value as assisting the recollection, and consequently the preservation, of any series of truths or incidents. But I am not convinced by the collation of facts, that THE CHILDREN IN THE WOOD owes either its preservation, or its popularity, to its metrical form. Mr. Marshal's repository affords a number of tales in prose inferior in pathos and general merit, some of as old a date, and many as widely popular. TOM HICKATHRIFT, JACK THE GIANT-KILLER, GOODY TWO-SHOES, and LITTLE RED RIDING-HOOD are formidable rivals. And that they have continued in prose, cannot be fairly explained by the assumption, that the comparative meanness of their thoughts and images precluded even the humblest forms of metre. The scene of GOODY TWO-SHOES in the church is perfectly susceptible of metrical narration; and, among the *Θαύματα θαυμαστότατα* even of the present age, I do not recollect a more astonishing image than that of the "whole rookery, that flew out of the giant's beard," scared by the tremendous voice, with which this monster answered the challenge of the heroic TOM HICKATHRIFT!

If from these we turn to compositions universally, and independently of all early associations, beloved and admired; would the MARIA, THE MONK, or THE POOR MAN'S Ass of Sterne, be read with more delight, or have a better chance of immortality, had they without any change in the diction been composed in rhyme, than in their present state? If I am not grossly mistaken, the general reply would be in the negative. Nay, I will confess, that, in Mr. Wordsworth's own volumes, the ANECDOTE FOR FATHERS, SIMON LEE, ALICE FELL, BEGGARS, and THE SAILOR'S MOTHER, notwithstanding the beauties which are to be found in each of them where the poet interposes the music of his own thoughts, would have been more delightful to me in prose, told and managed, as by Mr. Wordsworth they would have been, in a moral essay or pedestrian tour.

Metre in itself is simply a stimulant of the attention, and therefore excites the question: Why is the attention to be thus stimulated? Now the question cannot be answered by the pleasure of the metre itself: for this we have shown to be *conditional*, and dependent on the appropriateness of the thoughts and expressions, to which the metrical form is superadded. Neither can I conceive any other answer that can be rationally given, short of this: I write in metre, because I am about to use a language different from that of prose. Besides, where the language is not such, how interesting soever the reflections are, that are capable of being drawn by a philosophic mind from the thoughts or incidents of the poem, the metre itself must often become feeble. Take the three last stanzas of THE SAILOR'S MOTHER, for instance. If I could for a moment abstract from the effect produced on the author's feelings, as a man, by the incident at the time of its real occurrence, I would dare appeal to his own judgment, whether in the *metre* itself he found a sufficient reason for *their* being written *metrically*?

And, thus continuing, she said
"I had a Son, who many a day
Sailed on the seas; but he is dead;
In Denmark he was cast away;
And I have travelled far as Hull, to see
What clothes he might have left, or other property.

The Bird and Cage they both were his:
'Twas my Son's Bird; and neat and trim
He kept it: many voyages
This Singing-bird hath gone with him;
When last he sailed he left the Bird behind;
As it might be, perhaps, from bodings of his mind.

He to a Fellow-lodger's care
Had left it, to be watched and fed,
Till he came back again; and there
I found it when my Son was dead;
And now, God help me for my little wit!
I trail it with me, Sir! he took so much delight in it."

If disproportioning the emphasis we read these stanzas so as to make the rhymes perceptible, even *tri-syllable* rhymes could scarcely produce an equal sense of oddity and strangeness, as we feel here in finding *rhymes at all* in sentences so exclusively colloquial. I would further ask whether, but for that visionary state, into which the figure of the woman and the susceptibility of his own genius had placed the poet's imagination,—(a state, which spreads its influence and colouring over all, that co-exists with the exciting cause, and in which

The simplest, and the most familiar things
Gain a strange power of spreading awe around them,)[1]

I would ask the poet whether he would not have felt an abrupt down-fall in these verses from the preceding stanza?

The ancient Spirit is not dead;
Old times, thought I, are breathing there;
Proud was I that my country bred
Such strength, a dignity so fair:
She begged an alms, like one in poor estate;
I looked at her again, nor did my pride abate.

It must not be omitted, and is besides worthy of notice, that those stanzas furnish the only fair instance that I have been able to discover in all Mr. Wordsworth's writings, of an *actual* adoption, or true imitation, of *the real and very language of low and rustic life*, freed from provincialisms.

Thirdly, I deduce the position from all the causes elsewhere assigned, which render metre the proper form of poetry, and poetry

[1] Altered from the description of Night-Mair in the REMORSE.

Oh Heaven! 'twas frightful! Now run down and stared at
By hideous shapes that cannot be remembered;
Now seeing nothing and imagining nothing;
But only being afraid—stifled with fear!
While every goodly or familiar form
Had a strange power of spreading terror round me!

N.B. Though Shakespeare has, for his own *all-justifying* purposes, introduced the Night-*Mare* with her own foals, yet Mair means a Sister, or perhaps a Hag.

imperfect and defective without metre. Metre, therefore, having been connected with *poetry* most often and by a peculiar fitness, whatever else is combined with *metre* must, though it be not itself *essentially* poetic, have nevertheless some property in common with poetry, as an *intermedium* of affinity, a sort, (if I may dare borrow a well-known phrase from technical chemistry), of *mordaunt* between it and the super-added metre. Now poetry, Mr. Wordsworth truly affirms, does always imply PASSION; which word must be here understood in its most general sense, as an excited state of the feelings and faculties. And as every passion has its proper pulse, so will it likewise have its characteristic modes of expression. But where there exists that degree of genius and talent which entitles a writer to aim at the honours of a poet, the very *act* of poetic composition *itself* is, and is *allowed* to imply and to produce, an unusual state of excitement, which of course justifies and demands a correspondent difference of language, as truly, though not perhaps in as marked a degree, as the excitement of love, fear, rage, or jealousy. The vividness of the descriptions or declamations in Donne, or Dryden, is as much and as often derived from the force and fervour of the describer, as from the reflections, forms or incidents, which constitute their subject and materials. The wheels take fire from the mere rapidity of their motion. To what extent, and under what modifications, this may be admitted to act, I shall attempt to define in an after remark on Mr. Wordsworth's reply to this objection, or rather on his objection to this reply, as already anticipated in his preface.

Fourthly, and as intimately connected with this, if not the same argument in a more general form, I adduce the high spiritual instinct of the human being impelling us to seek unity by harmonious adjustment, and thus establishing the principle, that *all* the parts of an organized whole must be assimilated to the more *important* and *essential* parts. This and the preceding arguments may be strengthened by the reflection, that the composition of a poem is among the *imitative* arts; and that imitation, as opposed to copying, consists either in the interfusion of the SAME throughout the radically DIFFERENT, or of the different throughout a base radically the same.

Lastly, I appeal to the practice of the best poets, of all countries and in all ages, as *authorizing* the opinion, (*deduced* from all the foregoing) that in every import of the word ESSENTIAL, which would not here involve a mere truism, there may be, is, and ought to be, an *essential* difference between the language of prose and of metrical composition.

In Mr. Wordsworth's criticism of Gray's Sonnet, the reader's sympathy with his praise or blame of the different parts is taken for granted rather perhaps too easily. He has not, at least, attempted to win or compel it by argumentative analysis. In *my* conception at least, the lines rejected as of no value do, with the exception of the two first, differ as much and as little from the language of common life, as those which he has printed in italics as possessing genuine excellence. Of the five lines thus honourably distinguished, two of them differ from prose even more widely, than the lines which either precede or follow, in the position of the words.

A different object do these eyes require;
My lonely anguish melts no heart but mine;
And in my breast the imperfect joys expire.

But were it otherwise, what would this prove, but a truth, of which no man ever doubted?—*videlicet*, that there are sentences, which would be equally in their place both in verse and prose. Assuredly it does not prove the point, which alone requires proof; namely, that there are not passages, which would suit the one and not suit the other. The first line of this sonnet is distinguished from the ordinary language of men by the epithet to morning. (For we will set aside, at present, the consideration, that the particular word "smiling" is hackneyed, and, as it involves a sort of personification, not quite congruous with the common and material attribute of "*shining*.") And, doubtless, this adjunction of epithets for the purpose of additional description, where no particular attention is demanded for the quality of the thing, would be noticed as giving a poetic cast to a man's conversation. Should the sportsman exclaim, "Come boys! the rosy morning calls you up:"—he will be supposed to have some song in his head. But no one suspects this, when he says, "A wet morning shall not confine us to our beds." This then is either a defect in poetry, or it is not. Whoever should decide in the *affirmative*, I would request him to re-peruse any one poem, of any confessedly great poet from Homer to Milton, or from Æschylus to Shakespeare; and to strike out, (in thought I mean), every instance of this kind. If the number of these fancied erasures did not startle him; or if he continued to deem the work improved by their total omission; he must advance reasons of no ordinary strength and evidence, reasons grounded in the essence of human nature. Otherwise I should not hesitate to consider him as a man not so much *proof against* all authority, as *dead* to it.

The second line,

> And reddening Phœbus lifts his golden fire;—

has indeed almost as many faults as words. But then it is a bad line, not because the language is distinct from that of prose; but because it conveys incongruous images; because it confounds the cause and the effect, the real *thing* with the personified *representative* of the thing; in short, because it differs from the language of *good sense*! That the "Phœbus" is hackneyed, and a schoolboy image, is an *accidental* fault, dependent on the age in which the author wrote, and not deduced from the nature of the thing. That it is part of an exploded mythology, is an objection more deeply grounded. Yet when the torch of ancient learning was rekindled, so cheering were its beams, that our eldest poets, cut off by Christianity from all *accredited* machinery, and deprived of all *acknowledged* guardians and symbols of the great objects of nature, were naturally induced to adopt, as a *poetic* language, those fabulous personages, those forms of the supernatural[1] in nature, which had given them such dear delight in the poems of their great masters. Nay, even at this day what scholar of genial taste will not so far sympathize with them, as to read with pleasure in Petrarch, Chaucer, or Spenser, what he would perhaps condemn as puerile in a modern poet?

I remember no poet, whose writings would safelier stand the test of Mr. Wordsworth's theory, than Spenser. Yet will Mr. Wordsworth say, that the style of the following stanza is either undistinguished from prose, and the language of ordinary life? Or that it is vicious, and that the stanzas are *blots* in THE FAERY QUEEN?

> By this the Northerne wagoner had set
> His sevenfold teme behind the stedfast starre,
> That was in Ocean waves yet never wet,
> But firme is fixt and sendeth light from farre

[1] But still more by the mechanical system of philosophy which has needlessly infected our theological opinions, and teaching us to consider the world in its relation to God, as of a building to its mason, leaves the idea of omnipresence a mere abstract notion in the state-room of our reason.

To al that in the wide deepe wandring arre:
And chearfull Chaunticlere with his note shrill
Had warned once that Phœbus' fiery carre
In hast was climbing up the Easterne hill,
Full envious that night so long his roome did fill.

At last, the golden Orientall gate
Of greatest heaven gan to open fayre,
And Phœbus, fresh as brydegrome to his mate,
Came dauncing forth, shaking his deawie hayre,
And hurld his glistring beams through gloomy ayre:
Which when the wakeful Elfe perceiv'd, streightway
He started up, and did him selfe prepayre
In sun-bright armes and battailous array;
For with that Pagan proud he combat will that day.

On the contrary to how many passages, both in hymn books and in blank verse poems, could I, (were it not invidious), direct the reader's attention, the style of which is most *unpoetic*, *because*, and only because, it is the style of *prose*? He will not suppose me capable of having in my mind such verses, as

I put my hat upon my head
And walk'd into the Strand;
And there I met another man,
Whose hat was in his hand.

To such specimens it would indeed be a fair and full reply, that these lines are not bad, because they are *unpoetic*; but because they are empty of all sense and feeling; and that it were an idle attempt to prove that "an ape is not a Newton, when it is self-evident that he is not a man." But the sense shall be good and weighty, the language correct and dignified, the subject interesting and treated with feeling; and yet the style shall, notwithstanding all these merits, be justly blamable as *prosaic*, and solely because the words and the order of the words would find their appropriate place in prose, but are not suitable to *metrical* composition. The Civil Wars of Daniel is an instructive, and even interesting work; but take the following stanzas, (and from the hundred instances which abound I might probably have selected others far more striking):

And to the end we may with better ease
Discern the true discourse, vouchsafe to shew
What were the times foregoing near to these,
That these we may with better profit know.

Tell how the world fell into this disease;
And how so great distemperature did grow;
So shall we see with what degrees it came;
How things at full do soon wax out of frame.

Ten kings had from the Norman Conqu'ror reign'd
With intermix'd and variable fate,
When England to her greatest height attain'd
Of power, dominion, glory, wealth, and state;
After it had with much ado sustain'd
The violence of princes, with debate
For titles, and the often mutinies
Of nobles for their ancient liberties.

For first, the Norman, conqu'ring all by might,
By might was forc'd to keep what he had got;
Mixing our customs and the form of right
With foreign constitutions, he had brought;
Mast'ring the mighty, humbling the poorer wight,
By all severest means that could be wrought;
And, making the succession doubtful, rent
His new-got state, and left it turbulent.

Will it be contended on the one side, that these lines are mean and senseless? Or on the other, that they are not prosaic, and for *that* reason unpoetic? This poet's well-merited epithet is that of the "well-languaged Daniel;" but likewise, and by the consent of his contemporaries no less than of all succeeding critics, the "prosaic Daniel." Yet those, who thus designate this wise and amiable writer from the frequent incorrespondency of his diction to his metre in the majority of his compositions, not only deem them valuable and interesting on other accounts; but willingly admit, that there are to be found throughout his poems, and especially in his EPISTLES and in his HYMEN'S TRIUMPH, many and exquisite specimens of that style which, as the *neutral ground* of prose and verse, is common to both. A fine and almost faultless extract, eminent as for other beauties, so for its perfection in this species of diction, may be seen in Lamb's DRAMATIC SPECIMENS, a work of various interest from the nature of the selections themselves,—(all from the plays of Shakespeare's contemporaries), —and deriving a high additional value from the notes, which are full of just and original criticism, expressed with all the freshness of originality.

Among the possible effects of practical adherence to a theory, that aims to *identify* the style of prose and verse,—(if it does not indeed claim for the latter a yet nearer resemblance to the average style of men in the *vivâ voce* intercourse of real life)—we might anticipate the following as not the least likely to occur. It will happen, as I have indeed before observed, that the metre itself, the sole acknowledged difference, will occasionally become metre to the eye only. The existence of *prosaisms*, and that they detract from the merit of a poem, *must* at length be conceded, when a number of successive lines can be rendered, even to the most delicate ear, unrecognizable as verse, or as having even been intended for verse, by simply transcribing them as prose: when if the poem be in blank verse, this can be effected without any alteration, or at most by merely restoring one or two words to their proper places, from which they had been transplanted[1] for no assignable cause or reason but that of the author's convenience; but if it be in rhyme, by the mere exchange of the final word of each line for some other of the same meaning, equally appropriate, dignified and euphonic.

[1] As the ingenious gentleman under the influence of the Tragic Muse contrived to dislocate, "I wish you a good morning, Sir! Thank you, Sir, and I wish you the same," into two blank-verse heroics:—

> To you a morning good, good Sir! I wish.
> You, Sir! I thank: to you the same wish I.

In those parts of Mr. Wordsworth's works which I have thoroughly studied, I find fewer instances in which this would be practicable than I have met in many poems, where an approximation of prose has been sedulously and on system guarded against. Indeed excepting the stanzas already quoted from THE SAILOR'S MOTHER, I can recollect but one instance: that is to say, a short passage of four or five lines in THE BROTHERS, that model of English pastoral, which I never yet read with unclouded eye.—"James, pointing to its summit, over which they had all purposed to return together, informed them that he would wait for them there. They parted, and his comrades passed that way some two hours after, but they did not find him at the appointed place, *a circumstance of which they took no heed:* but one of them, going by chance into the house, which at this time was James's house, learnt *there*, that nobody had seen him all that day." The only change which has been made is in the position of the little word *there* in two instances, the position in the original being clearly such as is not adopted in ordinary conversation. The other words printed in italics were so marked because, though good and genuine English, they are not the phraseology of common conversation either in the word put in apposition, or in the connection by the genitive pronoun. Men in general would have said, "but that was a circumstance they paid no attention to, or took no notice of;" and the language is, on the theory of the preface, justified only by the narrator's being the *Vicar*. Yet if any ear *could* suspect, that these sentences were ever printed as metre, on those very words alone could the suspicion have been grounded.

The answer or objection in the preface to the anticipated remark "that metre paves the way to other distinctions," is contained in the following words. "The distinction of rhyme and metre is regular and uniform, and not, like that produced by (what is usually called) poetic diction, arbitrary, and subject to infinite caprices, upon which no calculation whatever can be made. In the one case the reader is utterly at the mercy of the poet respecting what imagery or diction he may choose to connect with the passion." But is this a *poet*, of whom a poet is speaking? No surely! rather of a fool or madman: or at best of a vain or ignorant phantast! And might not brains so wild and so deficient make just the same havock with rhymes and metres, as they are supposed to effect with modes and figures of speech? How is the reader at the *mercy* of such men? If he continue to read their nonsense, is it not his own fault? The ultimate end of criticism is much more to establish the principles of writing, than to furnish *rules* how to pass judgment on what has been written by others; if indeed it were possible that the two could be separated. But if it be asked, by what principles the poet is to regulate his own style, if he do not adhere closely to the sort and order of words which he hears in the market, wake, high-road, or plough-field? I reply; by principles, the ignorance or neglect of which would convict him of being no *poet*, but a silly or presumptuous usurper of the name! By the principles of grammar, logic, psychology! In one word by such a knowledge of the facts, material and spiritual, that most appertain to his art, as, if it have been governed and applied by *good sense*, and rendered instinctive by habit, becomes the representative and reward of our past conscious reasonings, insights, and conclusions, and acquires the name of TASTE. By what *rule* that does not leave the reader at the poet's mercy, and the poet at his own, is the latter to distinguish between the language suitable to *suppressed*, and the language, which is characteristic of *indulged*, anger? Or between that of rage and that of jealousy? Is it obtained by wandering about in search of angry or jealous people in uncultivated society, in order to copy their words? Or not far rather by the power of imagination proceeding upon the *all in each* of human nature? By *meditation*, rather than by *observation*? And by the latter in consequence only of the former? As eyes, for which the former has pre-determined their field of vision, and to which, as to *its* organ, it communicates a microscopic power? There is not, I firmly believe, a man now living, who has, from his own inward experience, a clearer intuition, than Mr. Wordsworth himself, that the last mentioned are the true sources of *genial* discrimination. Through the same process and by the same creative agency will the poet distinguish the degree and kind of the excitement produced by the very act of poetic composition. As intuitively will he know, what differences of style it at once inspires and justifies; what intermixture of conscious volition is natural to that state; and in what instances such figures and colours of speech degenerate into mere creatures of an arbitrary purpose, cold technical artifices of ornament or connection. For, even as truth is its own light and evidence, discovering at once itself and falsehood, so is it the prerogative of poetic genius to distinguish by parental instinct its proper offspring from the changelings, which the gnomes of vanity or the fairies of fashion may have laid in its cradle or called by its names. Could a rule be given from *without*, poetry would cease to be poetry, and sink into a mechanical art. It would be μόρφωσις, not ποίησις. The *rules* of the IMAGINATION are themselves the very powers of growth and production. The *words* to which they are reducible, present only the outlines and external appearance of the fruit. A deceptive counterfeit of the superficial form and colours may be elaborated; but the marble peach feels cold and heavy, and *children* only put it to their mouths. We find no difficulty in admitting as excellent, and the legitimate language of poetic fervour self-impassioned, Donne's apostrophe to the Sun in the second stanza of his PROGRESS OF THE SOUL.

> Thee, eye of heaven! this great Soul envies not;
> By thy male force is all, we have, begot.
> In the first East thou now beginn'st to shine,
> Suck'st early balm and island spices there,
> And wilt anon in thy loose-rein'd career
> At Tagus, Po, Seine, Thames, and Danow dine,
> And see at night this western world of mine:
> Yet hast thou not more nations seen than she,
> Who before thee one day began to be,
> And, thy frail light being quench'd, shall long, long outlive thee.

Or the next stanza but one:

> Great Destiny, the commissary of God,
> That hast mark'd out a path and period
> For every thing! Who, where we offspring took,
> Our ways and ends see'st at one instant: thou

Knot of all causes! Thou, whose changeless brow
Ne'er smiles nor frowns! O! vouchsafe thou to look,
And shew my story in thy eternal book, &c.

As little difficulty do we find in excluding from the honours of unaffected warmth and elevation the madness prepense of pseudo-poesy, or the startling *hysteric* of weakness over-exerting itself, which bursts on the unprepared reader in sundry odes and apostrophes to abstract terms. Such are the Odes to Jealousy, to Hope, to Oblivion, and the like, in Dodsley's collection and the magazines of that day, which seldom fail to remind me of an Oxford copy of verses on the two SUTTONS, commencing with

INOCULATION, heavenly maid! descend!

It is not to be denied that men of undoubted talents, and even poets of true, though not of first-rate genius, have from a mistaken theory deluded both themselves and others in the opposite extreme. I once read to a company of sensible and well-educated women the introductory period of Cowley's preface to his "Pindaric Odes, written in imitation of the style and manner of the odes of Pindar." "If," (says Cowley), "a man should undertake to translate Pindar, word for word, it would be thought that one madman had translated another; as may appear, when he, that understands not the original, reads the verbal traduction of him into Latin prose, than which nothing seems more raving." I then proceeded with his own free version of the second Olympic, composed for the charitable purpose of *rationalizing* the Theban Eagle.

Queen of all harmonious things,
Dancing words and speaking strings,
What God, what hero, wilt thou sing?
What happy man to equal glories bring?
Begin, begin thy noble choice,
And let the hills around reflect the image of thy voice.
Pisa does to Jove belong,
Jove and Pisa claim thy song.
The fair first-fruits of war, th' Olympic games,
Alcides offer'd up to Jove;
Alcides, too, thy strings may move,
But, oh! what man to join with these can worthy prove?
Join Theron boldly to their sacred names;
Theron the next honour claims;
Theron to no man gives place,
Is first in Pisa's and in Virtue's race;
Theron there, and he alone,
Ev'n his own swift forefathers has outgone.

One of the company exclaimed, with the full assent of the rest, that if the original were madder than this, it must be incurably mad. I then translated the ode from the Greek, and as nearly as possible, word for word; and the impression was, that in the general movement of the periods, in the form of the connections and transitions, and in the sober majesty of lofty sense, it appeared to them to approach more nearly, than any other poetry they had heard, to the style of our Bible in the prophetic books. The first strophe will suffice as a specimen:

Ye harp-controlling hymns! (or) ye hymns the sovereigns of harps!
What God? what Hero?
What Man shall we celebrate?
Truly Pisa indeed is of Jove,
But the Olympiad (or the Olympic games) did Hercules establish,
The first-fruits of the spoils of war.
But Theron for the four-horsed car,
That bore victory to him,
It behoves us now to voice aloud:
The Just, the Hospitable,
The Bulwark of Agrigentum,
Of renowned fathers
The Flower, even him
Who preserves his native city erect and safe.

But are such rhetorical caprices condemnable only for their deviation from the language of real life? and are they by no other means to be precluded, but by the rejection of all distinctions between prose and verse, save that of metre? Surely good sense, and a moderate insight into the constitution of the human mind, would be amply sufficient to prove, that such language and such combinations are the native produce neither of the fancy nor of the imagination; that their operation consists in the excitement of surprise by the juxtaposition and *apparent* reconciliation of widely different or incompatible things. As when, for instance, the hills are made to reflect the image of a *voice*. Surely, no unusual taste is requisite to see clearly, that this compulsory juxta-position is not produced by the presentation of impressive or delightful forms to the inward vision, nor by any sympathy with the modifying powers with which the genius of the poet had united and inspirited all the objects of his thought; that it is therefore a species of *wit*, a pure work of the *will*, and implies a leisure and self-possession both of thought and of feeling, incompatible with the steady fervour of a mind possessed and filled with the grandeur of its subject. To sum up the whole in one sentence. When a poem, or a part of a poem, shall be adduced, which is evidently vicious in the figures and contexture of its style, yet for the condemnation of which no reason can be assigned, except that it differs from the style in which men actually converse, then, and not till then, can I hold this theory to be either plausible, or practicable, or capable of furnishing either rule, guidance, or precaution, that might not, more easily and more safely, as well as more naturally, have been deduced in the author's own mind from considerations of grammar, logic, and the truth and nature of things, confirmed by the authority of works, whose fame is not of ONE country, nor of ONE age.

CHAPTER XIX.

Continuation—Concerning the real object which, it is probable, Mr. Wordsworth had before him in his critical preface—Elucidation and application of this.

It might appear from some passages in the former part of Mr. Wordsworth's preface, that he meant to confine his theory of style, and the necessity of a close accordance with the actual language of men, to those particular subjects from low and rustic life, which by way of experiment he had purposed to naturalize as a new species in our English poetry. But from the train of argument that follows; from the reference to Milton; and from the spirit of his critique on Gray's sonnet; those sentences appear to have been rather courtesies of modesty, than actual limitations of his system. Yet so groundless does this system appear on a close examination; and so strange and overwhelming[1] in its consequences, that I cannot, and I do not, believe that the poet did ever himself adopt it in the unqualified sense, in which his expressions have been understood by others, and which, indeed, according to all the common laws of interpretation they seem to bear. What then did he mean? I apprehend, that in the clear perception, not unaccompanied with disgust or contempt, of the gaudy affectations of a style which passed current with too many for poetic diction, (though in truth it had as little pretensions to poetry, as to logic or common sense,) he narrowed his view for the time; and feeling a justifiable preference for the language of nature and of

[1] I had in my mind the striking but untranslatable epithet, which the celebrated Mendelssohn applied to the great founder of the Critical Philosophy "*Der alleszermalmende* KANT," that is, the all-becrushing, or rather the *all-to-nothing-crushing* Kant. In the facility and force of compound epithets, the German from the number of its cases and inflections approaches to the Greek, that language so

Bless'd in the happy marriage of sweet words.

It is in the woful harshness of its sounds alone that the German need shrink from the comparison.

good sense, even in its humblest and least ornamented forms, he suffered himself to express, in terms at once too large and too exclusive, his predilection for a style the most remote possible from the false and showy splendour which he wished to explode. It is possible, that this predilection, at first merely comparative, deviated for a time into direct partiality. But the real object which he had in view, was, I doubt not, a species of excellence which had been long before most happily characterized by the judicious and amiable Garve, whose works are so justly beloved and esteemed by the Germans, in his remarks on Gellert, from which the following is literally translated. "The talent, that is required in order to make excellent verses, is perhaps greater than the philosopher is ready to admit, or would find it in his power to acquire; the talent to seek only the apt expression of the thought, and yet to find at the same time with it the rhyme and the metre. Gellert possessed this happy gift, if ever any one of our poets possessed it; and nothing perhaps contributed more to the great and universal impression which his fables made on their first publication, or conduces more to their continued popularity. It was a strange and curious phenomenon, and such as in Germany had been previously unheard of, to read verses in which every thing was expressed just as one would wish to talk, and yet all dignified, attractive, and interesting; and all at the same time perfectly correct as to the measure of the syllables and the rhyme. It is certain, that poetry when it has attained this excellence makes a far greater impression than prose. So much so indeed, that even the gratification which the very rhymes afford, becomes then no longer a contemptible or trifling gratification."[1]

However novel this phenomenon may have been in Germany at the time of Gellert, it is by no means new, nor yet of recent existence in our language. Spite of the licentiousness with which Spenser occasionally compels the orthography of his words into a subservience to his rhymes, the whole FAERY QUEEN is an almost continued instance of this beauty. Waller's song GO, LOVELY ROSE, is doubtless familiar to most of my readers; but if I had happened to have had by me the Poems of Cotton, more but far less deservedly celebrated as the author of the VIRGIL TRAVESTIED,

[1] *Sammlung einiger Abhandlungen von Christian Garve.* [Leipzig, 1779, pp. 233–4, with slight alterations. S.C.]

I should have indulged myself, and I think have gratified many, who are not acquainted with his serious works, by selecting some admirable specimens of this style. There are not a few poems in that volume, replete with every excellence of thought, image, and passion, which we expect or desire in the poetry of the milder muse; and yet so worded, that the reader sees no one reason either in the selection or the order of the words, why he might not have said the very same in an appropriate conversation, and cannot conceive how indeed he could have expressed such thoughts otherwise, without loss or injury to his meaning.

But in truth our language is, and from the first dawn of poetry ever has been, particularly rich in compositions distinguished by this excellence. The final *e*, which is now mute, in Chaucer's age was either sounded or dropt indifferently. We ourselves still use either "beloved" or "belov'd" according as the rhyme, or measure, or the purpose of more or less solemnity may require. Let the reader then only adopt the pronunciation of the poet and of the court, at which he lived, both with respect to the final *e* and to the accentuation of the last syllable: I would then venture to ask, what even in the colloquial language of elegant and unaffected women, (who are the peculiar mistresses of "pure English and undefiled,") what could we hear more natural, or seemingly more unstudied, than the following stanzas from Chaucer's Troilus and Creseide.

And after this forth to the gate he wente,
Ther as Creseide out rode a ful gode paas,
And up and doun there made he many a wente,
And to himselfe ful oft he said, Alas!
Fro hennis rode my blisse and my solas:
As wouldè blisful God now for his joie,
I might her sene agen come in to Troie!
  And to the yondir hil I gan her gide,
Alas! and there I toke of her my leve:
And yond I saw her to her fathir ride;
For sorow of whiche mine hert shall to-cleve;
And hithir home I came whan it was eve,
And here I dwel, out-cast from allè joie,
And shal, til I maie sene her efte in Troie.
  And of himselfe imaginid he ofte
To ben defaitid, pale and woxin lesse
Than he was wonte, and that men saidin softe,
What may it be? who can the sothè gesse,

Why Troilus hath al this hevinesse?
And al this n' as but his melancolie,
That he had of himselfe suche fantasie.
  Anothir time imaginin he would
That every wight, that past him by the wey,
Had of him routhe, and that thei saien should,
I am right sory, Troilus wol dey!
And thus he drove a daie yet forth or twey,
As ye have herde: suche life gan he to lede
As he that stode betwixin hope and drede:
  For which him likid in his songis shewe
Th' encheson of his wo as he best might,
And made a songe of wordis but a fewe,
Somwhat his woful herté for to light,
And whan he was from every mann'is sight
With softé voice he of his lady dere,
That absent was, gan sing as ye may here:

* * * * * *

  This song, when he thus songin had, ful sone
He fil agen into his sighis olde:
And every night, as was his wonte to done;
He stodè the bright moonè to beholde
And all his sorowe to the moone he tolde,
And said: I wis, whan thou art hornid newe,
I shall be glad, if al the world be trewe!

Another exquisite master of this species of style, where the scholar and the poet supplies the material, but the perfect well-bred gentleman the expressions and the arrangement, is George Herbert. As from the nature of the subject, and the too frequent quaintness of the thoughts, his TEMPLE; or SACRED POEMS AND PRIVATE EJACULATIONS are comparatively but little known, I shall extract two poems. The first is a sonnet, equally admirable for the weight, number, and expression of the thoughts, and for the simple dignity of the language. (Unless, indeed, a fastidious taste should object to the latter half of the sixth line.) The second is a poem of greater length, which I have chosen not only for the present purpose, but likewise as a striking example and illustration of an assertion hazarded in a former page of these sketches: namely, that the characteristic fault of our elder poets is the reverse of that, which distinguishes too many of our more recent versifiers; the one conveying the most fantastic thoughts in the most correct and natural language; the other in the most fantastic language conveying the most trivial thoughts. The latter is a riddle of words; the former an enigma of thoughts. The one reminds me of an odd passage in Drayton's IDEAS:

As other men, so I myself do muse,
Why in this sort I wrest invention so;
And why these *giddy metaphors* I use,
Leaving the path the greater part do go;
I will resolve you: *I am lunatic!*[1]

The other recalls a still odder passage in THE SYNAGOGUE: *or* THE SHADOW OF THE TEMPLE, a connected series of poems in imitation of Herbert's TEMPLE, and, in some editions, annexed to it.

O how my mind
Is gravell'd!
Not a thought,
That I can find,
But's ravell'd
All to nought!
Short ends of threds,
And narrow shreds
Of lists,
Knots, snarled ruffs,
Loose broken tufts
Of twists,
Are my torn meditations ragged clothing,
Which, wound and woven, shape a suit for nothing:
One while I think, and then I am in pain
To think how to unthink that thought again.

Immediately after these burlesque passages I cannot proceed to the extracts promised, without changing the ludicrous tone of feeling by the interposition of the three following stanzas of Herbert's.

VIRTUE.

Sweet day, so cool, so calm, so bright,
The bridal of the earth and sky,
The dew shall weep thy fall to-night;
For thou must die.

Sweet rose, whose hue angry and brave
Bids the rash gazer wipe his eye:
Thy root is ever in its grave,
And thou must die.

Sweet spring, full of sweet days and roses,
A box, where sweets compacted lie:
My music shews, ye have your closes,
And all must die.

[1] Sonnet IX.

THE BOSOM SIN:

A SONNET BY GEORGE HERBERT.

Lord, with what care hast thou begirt us round!
Parents first season us; then schoolmasters
Deliver us to laws; they send us bound
To rules of reason, holy messengers,
Pulpits and Sundays, sorrow dogging sin,
Afflictions sorted, anguish of all sizes,
Fine nets and stratagems to catch us in,
Bibles laid open, millions of surprises;
Blessings beforehand, ties of gratefulness,
The sound of Glory ringing in our ears:
Without, our shame; within, our consciences;
Angels and grace, eternal hopes and fears.
Yet all these fences and their whole array
One cunning bosom-sin blows quite away.

LOVE UNKNOWN

Dear friend, sit down, the tale is long and sad:
And in my faintings, I presume your love
Will more comply than help. A Lord I had,
And have, of whom some grounds, which may improve,
I hold for two lives, and both lives in me.
To him I brought a dish of fruit one day,
And in the middle placed my heart. But he
(I sigh to say)
Look'd on a servant, who did know his eye,
Better than you know me, or (which is one)
Than I myself. The servant instantly,
Quitting the fruit, seiz'd on my heart alone,
And threw it in a font, wherein did fall
A stream of blood, which issued from the side
Of a great rock: I well remember all,
And have good cause: there it was dipt and dyed,
And wash'd, and wrung: the very wringing yet
Enforceth tears. "Your heart was foul, I fear."
Indeed 'tis true. I did and do commit
Many a fault, more than my lease will bear;
Yet still ask'd pardon, and was not denied.
But you shall hear. After my heart was well,
And clean and fair, as I one eventide
(I sigh to tell)
Walk'd by myself abroad, I saw a large
And spacious furnace flaming, and thereon
A boiling caldron, round about whose verge
Was in great letters set AFFLICTION.
The greatness shew'd the owner. So I went
To fetch a sacrifice out of my fold,

Thinking with that, which I did thus present,
To warm his love, which I did fear grew cold.
But as my heart did tender it, the man
Who was to take it from me, slipt his hand,
And threw my heart into the scalding pan;
My heart that brought it (do you understand?)
The offerer's heart. "Your heart was hard, I fear."
Indeed 'tis true. I found a callous matter
Began to spread and to expatiate there:
But with a richer drug than scalding water
I bath'd it often, ev'n with holy blood,
Which at a board, while many drank bare wine,
A friend did steal into my cup for good,
Ev'n taken inwardly, and most divine
To supple hardnesses. But at the length
Out of the caldron getting, soon I fled
Unto my house, where to repair the strength
Which I had lost, I hasted to my bed:
But when I thought to sleep out all these faults,
(I sigh to speak)
I found that some had stuff'd the bed with thoughts,
I would say thorns. Dear, could my heart not break,
When with my pleasures ev'n my rest was gone?
Full well I understood who had been there:
For I had given the key to none but one:
It must be he. "Your heart was dull, I fear."
Indeed a slack and sleepy state of mind
Did oft possess me; so that when I pray'd,
Though my lips went, my heart did stay behind.
But all my scores were by another paid,
Who took my guilt upon him. "Truly, Friend,
For aught I hear, your Master shews to you
More favour than you wot of. Mark the end.
The font did only what was old renew:
The cauldron suppled what was grown too hard:
The thorns did quicken what was grown too dull:
All did but strive to mend what you had marr'd.
Wherefore be cheer'd, and praise him to the full
Each day, each hour, each moment of the week,
Who fain would have you be new, tender, quick."

CHAPTER XX.

The former subject continued—The neutral style, or that common to Prose and Poetry, exemplified by specimens from Chaucer, Herbert, and others.

I HAVE no fear in declaring my conviction, that the excellence defined and exemplified in the preceding chapter is not the characteristic excellence of Mr. Wordsworth's style; because I can add with equal sincerity, that it is precluded by higher powers. The praise of uniform adherence to genuine, logical English is undoubtedly his; nay, laying the main emphasis on the word *uniform*, I will dare add that, of all contemporary poets, it is *his alone*. For, in a less absolute sense of the word, I should certainly include Mr. Bowles, Lord Byron, and, as to all his later writings, Mr. Southey, the exceptions in their works being so few and unimportant. But of the specific excellence described in the quotation from Garve, I appear to find more, and more undoubted specimens in the works of others; for instance, among the minor poems of Mr. Thomas Moore, and of our illustrious Laureate. To me it will always remain a singular and noticeable fact; that a theory, which would establish this *lingua communis*, not only as the best, but as the only commendable style, should have proceeded from a poet, whose diction, next to that of Shakespeare and Milton, appears to me of all others the most *individualized* and characteristic. And let it be remembered too, that I am now interpreting, the controverted passages of Mr. Wordsworth's critical preface by the purpose and object, which he may be supposed to have intended, rather than by the sense which the words themselves must convey, if they are taken without this allowance.

A person of any taste, who had but studied three or four of Shakespeare's principal plays, would without the name affixed scarcely fail to recognise as Shakespeare's a quotation from any other play, though but of a few lines. A similar peculiarity, though in a less degree, attends Mr. Wordsworth's style, whenever he speaks in his own person; or whenever, though under a feigned name, it is clear that he himself is still speaking, as in the different *dramatis personæ* of THE RECLUSE. Even in the other poems, in which he purposes to be most dramatic, there are few in which it does not occasionally burst forth. The reader might often address the poet in his own words with reference to the persons introduced:

> It seems, as I retrace the ballad line by line
> That but half of it is theirs, and the better half is thine.

Who, having been previously acquainted with any considerable portion of Mr. Wordsworth's publications, and having studied them with a full feeling of the author's genius, would not at once claim as Wordsworthian the little poem on the rainbow?

> The Child is father of the Man, &c.

Or in the LUCY GRAY?

> No mate, no comrade Lucy knew;
> She dwelt on a wide moor;
> *The sweetest thing that ever grew*
> *Beside a human door.*

Or in the IDLE SHEPHERD-BOYS?

> Along the river's stony marge
> The Sand-lark chants a joyous song;
> The Thrush is busy in the wood,
> And carols loud and strong.
> A thousand Lambs are on the rocks,
> All newly born! both earth and sky
> Keep jubilee, and more than all,
> Those Boys with their green Coronal;
> They never hear the cry,
> That plaintive cry! which up the hill
> Comes from the depth of Dungeon-Ghyll.

Need I mention the exquisite description of the Sea-Loch in THE BLIND HIGHLAND BOY. Who but a poet tells a tale in such language to the little ones by the fire-side as—

> Yet had he many a restless dream;
> Both when he heard the Eagle scream,
> And when he heard the torrents roar,
> And heard the water beat the shore
> Near where their Cottage stood.
>
> Beside a lake their Cottage stood,
> Not small like ours, a peaceful flood;
> But one of mighty size, and strange;
> That, rough or smooth, is full of change,
> And stirring in its bed.

For to this Lake, by night and day,
The great Sea-water finds its way
Through long, long windings of the hills;
And drinks up all the pretty rills
And rivers large and strong:

Then hurries back the road it came—
Returns on errand still the same;
This did it when the earth was new;
And this for evermore will do,
As long as earth shall last.

And, with the coming of the Tide,
Come Boats and Ships that sweetly ride,
Between the woods and lofty rocks;
And to the Shepherds with their flocks
Bring tales of distant Lands.

I might quote almost the whole of his RUTH, but take the following stanzas:

But, as you have before been told,
This Stripling, sportive, gay, and bold,
And with his dancing crest
So beautiful, through savage lands
Had roamed about with vagrant bands
Of Indians in the West.

The wind, the tempest roaring high,
The tumult of a tropic sky,
Might well be dangerous food
For him, a Youth to whom was given
So much of earth—so much of Heaven,
And such impetuous blood.

Whatever in those Climes he found
Irregular in sight or sound
Did to his mind impart
A kindred impulse, seemed allied
To his own powers, and justified
The workings of his heart.

Nor less, to feed voluptuous thought,
The beauteous forms of nature wrought,
Fair trees and lovely flowers;
The breezes their own languor lent;
The stars had feelings, which they sent
Into those magic bowers.

Yet, in his worst pursuits, I ween,
That sometimes there did intervene
Pure hopes of high intent:
For passions linked to forms so fair
And stately needs must have their share
Of noble sentiment."

But from Mr. Wordsworth's more elevated compositions, which already form three-fourths of his works; and will, I trust, constitute hereafter a still larger proportion;—from these, whether in rhyme or blank verse, it would be difficult and almost superfluous to select instances of a diction peculiarly his own, of a style which cannot be imitated without its being at once recognised, as originating in Mr. Wordsworth. It would not be easy to open on any one of his loftier strains, that does not contain examples of this; and more in proportion as the lines are more excellent, and most like the author. For those, who may happen to have been less familiar with his writings, I will give three specimens taken with little choice. The first from the lines on the BOY OF WINANDER-MERE,—who

Blew mimic hootings to the silent owls,
That they might answer him.—And they would shout
Across the watery vale, and shout again,
With long halloos, and screams, and echoes loud
Redoubled and redoubled; concourse wild
Of mirth and jocund din! And, when it chanced
That pauses of deep silence mocked his skill,
Then, sometimes, in that silence, while he hung
Listening, a gentle shock of mild surprise
Has carried far into his heart the voice
Of mountain-torrents; or the visible scene[1]

[1] Mr. Wordsworth's having judiciously adopted "*concourse wild*" in this passage for "*a wild scene*" as it stood in the former edition, encourages me to hazard a remark, which I certainly should not have made in the works of a poet less austerely accurate in the use of words, than he is, to his own great honour. It respects the propriety of the word, "*scene*," even in the sentence in which it is retained. Dryden, and he only in his more careless verses, was the first, as far as my researches have discovered, who for the convenience of rhyme used this word in the vague sense, which has been since too current even in our best writers, and which (unfortunately, I think) is given as its first explanation in Dr. Johnson's Dictionary, and therefore would be taken by an incautious reader as its proper sense. In Shakespeare and Milton the word is never used without some clear reference, proper or metaphorical, to the theatre. Thus Milton;

Cedar, and pine, and fir, and branching palm
A sylvan *scene;* and, as the ranks ascend
Shade above shade, a woody *theatre*
Of stateliest view.

I object to any extension of its meaning, because the word is already more equivocal than might be wished; inasmuch as in the limited use, which I recommend, it may still signify two different things; namely, the scenery,

Would enter unawares into his mind
With all its solemn imagery, its rocks,
Its woods, and that uncertain heaven, received
Into the bosom of the steady lake.

The second shall be that noble imitation of Drayton[1] (if it was not rather a coincidence) in the lines To JOANNA.

—When I had gazed perhaps two minutes' space,
Joanna, looking in my eyes, beheld
That ravishment of mine, and laughed aloud.
The Rock, like something starting from a sleep,
Took up the Lady's voice, and laughed again!
That ancient Woman seated on *Helm-crag*
Was ready with her cavern; *Hammar-scar*,
And the tall Steep of Silver-How sent forth
A noise of laughter; southern Loughrigg heard,
And Fairfield answered with a mountain tone.
Helvellyn far into the clear blue sky
Carried the lady's voice!—old Skiddaw blew
His speaking trumpet!—back out of the clouds
From Glaramara southward came the voice:
And Kirkstone tossed it from his misty head!

The third, which is in rhyme, I take from the SONG AT THE FEAST OF BROUGHAM CASTLE, upon the restoration of Lord Clifford, the Shepherd, to the Estates and Honours of his Ancestors.

—Now another day is come,
Fitter hope, and nobler doom;
He hath thrown aside his Crook,
And hath buried deep his Book;
Armour rusting in his Halls
On the blood of Clifford calls;—

and the characters and actions presented on the stage during the presence of particular scenes. It can therefore be preserved from obscurity only by keeping the original signification full in the mind. Thus Milton again,

——Prepare thee for another scene.

[1] Which Copland scarce had spoke, but quickly every hill,
Upon her verge that stands, the neighbouring vallies fill;
Helvillon from his height, it through the mountains threw,
From whom as soon again, the sound Dunbalrase drew,
From whose stone-trophied head, it on the Wendross went,
Which, tow'rds the sea again, resounded it to Dent.
That Brodwater, therewith within her banks astound,
In sailing to the sea, told it to Egremound,
Whose buildings, walks, and streets, with echoes loud and long,
Did mightily commend old Copland for her song.
Drayton's POLYOLBION: *Song XXX.*

'Quell the Scot,' exclaims the Lance!
Bear me to the heart of France,
Is the longing of the Shield—
Tell thy name, thou trembling Field!—
Field of death, where'er thou be,
Groan thou with our victory!
Happy day, and mighty hour,
When our Shepherd, in his power,
Mailed and horsed, with lance and sword,
To his Ancestors restored,
Like a re-appearing Star,
Like a glory from afar,
First shall head the Flock of War!

Alas! the fervent Harper did not know,
That for a tranquil Soul the Lay was framed,
Who, long compelled in humble walks to go,
Was softened into feeling, soothed, and tamed.

Love had he found in huts where poor Men lie;
His daily Teachers had been Woods and Rills,
The silence that is in the starry sky,
The sleep that is among the lonely hills.

The words themselves in the foregoing extracts, are, no doubt, sufficiently common for the greater part. (But in what poem are they not so, if we except a few misadventurous attempts to translate the arts and sciences into verse?) In THE EXCURSION the number of polysyllabic (or what the common people call, *dictionary*) words is more than usually great. And so must it needs be, in proportion to the number and variety of an author's conceptions, and his solicitude to express them with precision. —But are those words *in those places* commonly employed in real life to express the same thought or outward thing? Are they the style used in the ordinary intercourse of spoken words? No! nor are the modes of connections; and still less the breaks and transitions. Would any but a poet—at least could any one without being conscious that he had expressed himself with noticeable vivacity—have described a bird singing loud by, "The thrush is *busy* in the wood?"—or have spoken of boys with a string of club-moss round their rusty·hats, as the boys "*with their green coronal?*"—or have translated a beautiful May-day into "*Both earth and sky keep jubilee?*"—or have brought all the different marks and circumstances of a sea-loch before the mind, as the actions of a living and acting power? Or have represented the reflection of the sky in the water, as "*That uncertain heaven received into the bosom of the steady lake?*" Even the grammatical construction is not unfrequently peculiar; as "The wind, the tempest roaring high, the tumult of a tropic sky, might well be *dangerous food for him*, a youth to whom was given, &c." There is a peculiarity in the frequent use of the *ἀσυνάρτητον* (that is, the omission of the connective particle before the last of several words, or several sentences used grammatically as single words, all being in the same case and governing or governed by the same verb) and not less in the construction of words by apposition ("*for him, a youth.*") In short, were there excluded from Mr. Wordsworth's poetic compositions all, that a literal adherence to the theory of his preface *would* exclude, two thirds at least of the marked beauties of his poetry must be erased. For a far greater number of lines would be sacrificed than in any other recent poet; because the pleasure received from Wordsworth's poems being less derived either from excitement of curiosity or the rapid flow of narration, the *striking* passages form a larger proportion of their value. I do not adduce it as a fair criterion of comparative excellence, nor do I even think it such; but merely as matter of fact. I affirm, that from no contemporary writer could so many lines be quoted, without reference to the poem in which they are found, for their own independent weight or beauty. From the sphere of my own experience I can bring to my recollection three persons of no every-day powers and acquirements, who had read the poems of others with more and more unalloyed pleasure, and had thought more highly of their authors, as poets; who yet have confessed to me, that from no modern work had so many passages started up anew in their minds at different times, and as different occasions had awakened a meditative mood.

CHAPTER XXI.

Remarks on the present mode of conducting critical journals.

Long have I wished to see a fair and philosophical inquisition into the character of Wordsworth, as a poet, on the evidence of his published works; and a positive, not a comparative, appreciation of their *characteristic* excellencies, deficiencies, and defects. I know no claim, that the mere *opinion* of any individual can have to weigh down the *opinion* of the author himself; against the probability of whose parental partiality we ought to set that of his having thought longer and more deeply on the subject. But I should call that investigation fair and philosophical in which the critic announces and endeavours to establish the principles, which he holds for the foundation of poetry in general, with the specification of these in their application to the different *classes* of poetry. Having thus prepared his canons of criticism for praise and condemnation, he would proceed to particularize the most striking passages to which he deems them applicable, faithfully noticing the frequent or infrequent recurrence of similar merits or defects, and *as* faithfully distinguishing what is characteristic from what is accidental, or a mere flagging of the wing. Then if his premises be rational, his deductions legitimate, and his conclusions justly applied, the reader, and possibly the poet himself, may adopt his judgment in the light of judgment and in the independence of free-agency. If he has erred, he presents his errors in a definite place and tangible form, and holds the torch and guides the way to their detection.

I most willingly admit, and estimate at a high value, the services which the Edinburgh Review, and others formed afterwards on the same plan, have rendered to society in the diffusion of knowledge. I think the commencement of the Edinburgh Review an important epoch in periodical criticism; and that it has a claim upon the gratitude of the literary republic, and indeed of the reading public at large, for having originated the scheme of reviewing those books only, which are susceptible and deserving of argumentative criticism. Not less meritorious, and far more faithfully and in general far more ably executed, is their plan of supplying the vacant place of the trash or mediocrity, wisely left to sink into oblivion by its own weight, with original essays on the most interesting subjects of the time, religious, or political; in which the titles of the books or pamphlets prefixed furnish only the name and occasion of the disquisition. I do not arraign the keenness, or asperity of its damnatory style, in and for itself, as long as the author is addressed or treated as the mere impersonation of the work then under trial. I have no quarrel with them on this account, as long as no personal allusions are admitted, and no re-commitment (for new trial) of juvenile performances, that were published, perhaps forgotten, many years before the commencement of the review: since for the forcing back of such works to public notice no motives are easily assignable, but such as are furnished to the critic by his own personal malignity; or what is still worse, by a *habit* of malignity in the form of mere wantonness.

> No private grudge they need, no personal spite:
> The *viva sectio* is its own delight!
> All enmity, all envy, they disclaim,
> Disinterested thieves of our good name:
> Cool, sober murderers of their neighbour's fame! S. T. C.

Every censure, every sarcasm respecting a publication which the critic, with the criticised work before him, can make good, is the critic's right. The writer is authorized to reply, but not to complain. Neither can any one prescribe to the critic, how soft or how hard; how friendly, or how bitter, shall be the phrases which he is to select for the expression of such reprehension or ridicule. The critic must know, what effect it is his object to produce; and with a view to this effect must he weigh his words. But as soon as the critic betrays, that he knows more of his author, than the author's publications could have told him; as soon as from this more intimate knowledge, elsewhere obtained, he avails himself of the slightest trait *against* the author; his censure instantly becomes personal injury, his sarcasms personal insults. He ceases to be a CRITIC, and takes on him the most contemptible character to which a rational creature can be degraded, that of a gossip, backbiter, and pasquillant: but with this heavy aggravation, that he steals the unquiet, the deforming passions of the world into the museum; into the very place which, next to the chapel and oratory, should be our sanctuary, and secure place of refuge; offers abominations on the altar of the Muses; and makes its sacred paling the very circle in which he conjures up the lying and profane spirit.

This determination of unlicensed personality, and of permitted and legitimate censure, (which I owe in part to the illustrious Lessing, himself a model of acute, spirited, sometimes stinging, but always argumentative and honourable, criticism) is beyond controversy the true one: and though I would not myself exercise all the rights of the latter, yet, let but the former be excluded, I submit myself to its exercise in the hands of others, without complaint and without resentment.

Let a communication be formed between any number of learned men in the various branches of science and literature; and whether the president and central committee be in London, or Edinburgh, if only they previously lay aside their individuality, and pledge themselves inwardly, as well as ostensibly, to administer judgment according to a constitution and code of laws; and if by grounding this code on the two-fold basis of universal morals and philosophic reason, independent of all foreseen application to particular works and authors, they obtain the right to speak each as the representative of their body corporate; they shall have honour and good wishes from me, and I shall accord to them their fair dignities, though self-assumed, not less cheerfully than if I could inquire concerning them in the herald's office, or turn to them in the book of peerage. However loud may be the outcries for prevented or subverted reputation, however numerous and impatient the complaints of merciless severity and insupportable despotism, I shall neither feel, nor utter aught but to the defence and justification of the critical machine. Should any literary Quixote find himself provoked by its sounds and regular movements, I should admonish him with Sancho Panza, that it is no giant but a windmill; there it stands on its own place, and its own hillock, never goes out of its way to attack any one, and to none and from none either gives or asks assistance. When the public press has poured in any part of its produce between its mill-stones, it grinds it off, one man's sack the same as another, and with whatever wind may happen to be then blowing. All the two-and-thirty winds are alike its friends. Of the whole wide atmosphere it does not desire a single finger-breadth more than what is necessary for its sails to turn round in. But this space must be left free and unimpeded. Gnats, beetles, wasps, butterflies, and the whole tribe of ephemerals and insignificants, may flit in and out and between; may hum, and buzz, and jar; may shrill their tiny pipes, and wind their puny horns, unchastised and unnoticed. But idlers and bravadoes of larger size and prouder show must beware, how they place themselves within its sweep. Much less may they presume to lay hands on the sails, the strength of which is neither greater or less than as the wind is, which drives them round. Whomsoever the remorseless arm slings aloft, or whirls along with it in the air, he has himself alone to blame; though, when the same arm throws him from it, it will more often double than break the force of his fall.

Putting aside the too manifest and too frequent interference of national party, and even PERSONAL predilection or aversion; and reserving for deeper feelings those worse and more criminal intrusions into the sacredness of private life, which not seldom merit legal rather than literary chastisement, the two principal objects and occasions which I find for blame and regret in the conduct of the review in question are: first, its unfaithfulness to its own announced and excellent plan, by subjecting to criticism works neither indecent nor immoral, yet of such trifling importance even in point of size and, according to the critic's own verdict, so devoid of all merit, as must excite in the most candid mind the suspicion, either that dislike or vindictive feelings were at work; or that there was a cold prudential pre-determination to increase the sale of the REVIEW by flattering the malignant passions of human nature. That I may not myself become subject to the charge, which I am bringing against others, by an accusation without proof, I refer to the article on Dr. Rennell's sermon in the very first number of the EDINBURGH REVIEW as an illustration of my meaning. If in looking through all the succeeding volumes the reader should find this a solitary instance, I must submit to that painful forfeiture of esteem, which awaits a groundless or exaggerated charge.

The second point of objection belongs to this review only in common with all other works of periodical criticism; at least, it applies in common to the general system of all, whatever exception there may be in favour of particular articles. Or if it attaches to The Edinburgh Review, and to its only corrival (The Quarterly), with any peculiar force, this results from the superiority of talent, acquirement, and information which both have so undeniably displayed; and which doubtless deepens the regret though not the blame. I am referring to the substitution of assertion for argument; to the frequency of arbitrary and sometimes petulant verdicts, not seldom unsupported even by a single quotation from the work condemned, which might at least have explained the critic's meaning, if it did not prove the justice of his sentence. Even where this is not the case, the extracts are too often made without reference to any general grounds or rules from which the faultiness or inadmissibility of the qualities attributed may be deduced; and without any attempt to show, that the qualities *are* attributable to the passage extracted. I have met with such extracts from Mr. Wordsworth's poems, annexed to such assertions, as led me to imagine, that the reviewer, having written his critique before he had read the work, had then *pricked with a pin* for passages, wherewith to illustrate the various branches of his preconceived opinions. By what principle of rational choice can we suppose a critic to have been directed (at least in a Christian country, and himself, we hope, a Christian) who gives the following lines, portraying the fervour of solitary devotion excited by the magnificent display of the Almighty's works, as a proof and example of an author's tendency to *downright ravings*, and absolute unintelligibility?

> O then what soul was his, when on the tops
> Of the high mountains he beheld the sun
> Rise up, and bathe the world in light! He looked—
> Ocean and earth, the solid frame of earth,
> And ocean's liquid mass, beneath him lay
> In gladness and deep joy. The clouds were touch'd,
> And in their silent faces did he read
> Unutterable love. Sound needed none,
> Nor any *voice* of joy: his spirit drank
> The spectacle! sensation, soul, and form,
> All melted into him; they swallowed up
> His animal being; in them did he live,
> And by them did he live: they were his life.

Can it be expected, that either the author or his admirers, should be induced to pay any serious attention to decisions which prove nothing but the pitiable state of the critic's own taste and sensibility? On opening the review they see a favourite passage, of the force and truth of which they had an intuitive certainty in their own inward experience confirmed, if confirmation it could receive, by the sympathy of their most enlightened friends; some of whom perhaps, even in the world's opinion, hold a higher intellectual rank than the critic himself would presume to claim. And this very passage they find selected, as the characteristic effusion of a mind *deserted by reason!*—as furnishing evidence that the writer was raving, or he could not have thus strung words together without sense or purpose! No diversity of taste seems capable of explaining such a contrast in judgment.

That I had *over-rated* the merit of a passage or poem, that I had erred concerning the *degree* of its excellence, I might be easily induced to believe or apprehend. But that lines, the sense of which I had analyzed and found consonant with all the best convictions of my understanding; and the imagery and diction of which had collected round those convictions my noblest as well as my most delightful feelings; that I should admit such lines to be mere nonsense or lunacy, is too much for the most ingenious *arguments* to effect. But that such a revolution of taste should be brought about by a few broad assertions, seems little less than impossible. On the contrary, it would require an effort of charity not to dismiss the criticism with the aphorism of the wise man, *in animam malevolam sapientia haud intrare potest.*

What then if this very critic should have cited a large number of single lines and even of long paragraphs, which he himself acknowledges to possess eminent and original beauty? What if he himself has owned, that beauties as great are scattered in abundance throughout the whole book? And yet, though under this impression, should have commenced his critique in vulgar exultation with a prophecy meant to secure its own fulfilment? With a "THIS WON'T DO!" What? if after such acknowledgments extorted from his own judgment he should proceed from charge to charge of tameness and raving; flights and flatness; and at length, consigning the author to the house of incurables, should conclude with a strain of rudest contempt evidently grounded in the distempered state of his own moral associations? Suppose too all this done without a single leading principle established or even announced, and without any one attempt at argumentative deduction, though the poet had presented a more than usual opportunity for it, by having previously made public his own principles of judgment in poetry, and supported them by a connected train of reasoning!

The office and duty of the poet is to select the most dignified as well as

The gayest, happiest attitude of things.

The reverse, for in all cases a reverse is possible, is the appropriate business of burlesque and travesty, a predominant taste for which has been always deemed a mark of a low and degraded mind. When I was at Rome, among many other visits to the tomb of Julius II., I went thither once with a Prussian artist, a man of genius and great vivacity of feeling. As we were gazing on Michael Angelo's MOSES, our conversation turned on the horns and beard of that stupendous statue; of the necessity of each to support the other; of the super-human effect of the former, and the necessity of the existence of both to give a harmony and *integrity* both to the image and the feeling excited by it. Conceive them removed, and the statue would become *un*-natural, without being *super*-natural. We called to mind the horns of the rising sun, and I repeated the noble passage from Taylor's HOLY DYING. That horns were the emblem of power and sovereignty among the Eastern nations, and are still retained as such in Abyssinia; the Achelous of the ancient Greeks; and the probable ideas and feelings, that originally suggested the mixture of the human and the brute form in the figure, by which they realized the idea of their mysterious Pan, as representing intelligence blended with a darker power, deeper, mightier, and more universal than the conscious intellect of man; than intelligence;—all these thoughts and recollections passed in procession before our minds. My companion who possessed more than his share of the hatred, which his countrymen bore to the French, had just observed to me, "A Frenchman, Sir! is the only animal in the human shape, that by no possibility can lift itself up to religion or poetry:" when, lo! two French officers of distinction and rank entered the church! "Mark you," whispered the Prussian, "the first thing, which those scoundrels will notice—(for they will begin by instantly noticing the statue in parts, without one moment's pause of admiration impressed by the whole)—will be the horns and the beard. And the associations, which they will immediately connect with them will be those of a *he-goat* and a *cuckold*." Never did man guess more luckily. Had he inherited a portion of the great legislator's prophetic powers, whose statue we had been contemplating, he could scarcely have uttered words more coincident with the result: for even as he had said, so it came to pass.

In THE EXCURSION the poet has introduced an old man, born in humble but not abject circumstances, who had enjoyed more than usual advantages of education, both from books and from the more awful discipline of nature. This person he represents, as having been driven by the restlessness of fervid feelings, and from a craving intellect to an itinerant life; and as having in consequence passed the larger portion of his time, from earliest manhood, in villages and hamlets from door to door,

> A vagrant Merchant bent beneath his load.

Now whether this be a character appropriate to a lofty didactick poem, is perhaps questionable. It presents a fair subject for controversy; and the question is to be determined by the congruity or incongruity of such a character with what shall be proved to be the essential constituents of poetry. But surely the critic who, passing by all the opportunities which such a mode of life would present to such a man; all the advantages of the liberty of nature, of solitude, and of solitary thought; all the varieties of places and seasons, through which his track had lain, with all the varying imagery they bring with them; and lastly, all the observations of men,

> Their manners, their enjoyments, and pursuits,
> Their passions and their feelings——

which the memory of these yearly journeys must have given and recalled to such a mind—the critic, I say, who from the multitude of possible associations should pass by all these in order to fix his attention exclusively on *the pin-papers*, and *stay-tapes*, which *might* have been among the wares of his pack; this critic, in my opinion, cannot be thought to possess a much higher or much healthier state of moral feeling, than the FRENCHMEN above recorded.

CHAPTER XXII.

The characteristic defects of Wordsworth's poetry, with the principles from which the judgment, that they are defects, is deduced—Their proportion to the beauties—For the greatest part characteristic of his theory only.

If Mr. Wordsworth have set forth principles of poetry which his arguments are insufficient to support, let him and those who have adopted his sentiments be set right by the confutation of those arguments, and by the substitution of more philosophical principles. And still let the due credit be given to the portion and importance of the truths, which are blended with his theory; truths, the too exclusive attention to which had occasioned its errors, by tempting him to carry those truths beyond their proper limits. If his mistaken theory have at all influenced his poetic compositions, let the effects be pointed out, and the instances given. But let it likewise be shown, how far the influence has acted; whether diffusively, or only by starts; whether the number and importance of the poems and passages thus infected be great or trifling compared with the sound portion; and lastly, whether they are inwoven into the texture of his works, or are loose and separable. The result of such a trial would evince beyond a doubt, what it is high time to announce decisively and aloud, that the *supposed* characteristics of Mr. Wordsworth's poetry, whether admired or reprobated; whether they are simplicity or simpleness; faithful adherence to essential nature, or wilful selections from human nature of its meanest forms and under the least attractive associations; are as little the *real* characteristics of his poetry at large, as of his genius and the constitution of his mind.

In a comparatively small number of poems he chose to try an experiment; and this experiment we will suppose to have failed. Yet even in these poems it is impossible not to perceive that the natural *tendency* of the poet's mind is to great objects and elevated conceptions. The poem entitled Fidelity is for the greater part written in language, as unraised and naked as any perhaps in the two volumes. Yet take the following stanza and compare it with the preceding stanzas of the same poem.

> There sometimes does a leaping Fish
> Send through the Tarn a lonely cheer;
> The Crags repeat the Raven's croak,
> In symphony austere;
> Thither the Rainbow comes—the Cloud—
> And Mists that spread the flying shroud;
> And Sun-beams; and the sounding blast,
> That, if it could, would hurry past,
> But that enormous Barrier holds it fast.

Or compare the four last lines of the concluding stanza with the former half:

> Yes, proof was plain that, since the day
> On which the Traveller thus had died,
> The Dog had watched about the spot,
> Or by his Master's side:
> *How nourish'd here through such long time*
> *He knows, who gave that love sublime,—*
> *And gave that strength of feeling, great*
> *Above all human estimate.*

Can any candid and intelligent mind hesitate in determining, which of these best represents the tendency and native character of the poet's genius? Will he not decide that the one was written because the poet *would* so write, and the other because he could not so entirely repress the force and grandeur of his mind, but that he must in some part or other of *every* composition write otherwise? In short, that his only disease is the being out of his element; like the swan, that, having amused himself, for a while, with crushing the weeds on the river's bank, soon returns to his own majestic movements on its reflecting and sustaining surface. Let it be observed that I am here supposing the imagined judge, to whom I appeal, to have already decided against the poet's theory, as far as it is different from the principles of the art, generally acknowledged.

I cannot here enter into a detailed examination of Mr. Wordsworth's works; but I will attempt to give the main results of my own judgment, after an acquaintance of many years, and repeated perusals. And though, to appreciate the defects of a great mind it is necessary to understand previously its characteristic excellences, yet I have already expressed myself with sufficient fulness, to preclude most of the ill effects that might arise from my pursuing a contrary arrangement. I will therefore commence with what I deem the prominent *defects* of his poems hitherto published.

The first *characteristic, though only occasional* defect, which I appear to myself to find in these poems is the *inconstancy* of the *style*. Under this name I refer to the sudden and unprepared transitions from lines or sentences of peculiar felicity—(at all events striking and original)—to a style, not only unimpassioned but undistinguished. He sinks too often and too abruptly to that style, which I should place in the second division of language, dividing it into the three species; *first*, that which is peculiar to poetry; *second*, that which is only proper in prose; and *third*, the neutral or common to both. There have been works, such as Cowley's Essay on Cromwell, in which prose and verse are intermixed (not as in the Consolation of Boetius, or the ARGENIS of Barclay, by the insertion of poems supposed to have been spoken or composed on occasions previously related in prose, but) the poet passing from one to the other, as the nature of the thoughts or his own feelings dictated. Yet this mode of composition does not satisfy a cultivated taste. There is something unpleasant in the being thus obliged to alternate states of feeling so dissimilar, and this too in a species of writing, the pleasure from which is in part derived from the preparation and previous expectation of the reader. A portion of that awkwardness is felt which hangs upon the introduction of songs in our modern comic operas; and to prevent which the judicious Metastasio (as to whose exquisite *taste* there can be no hesitation, whatever doubts may be entertained as to his *poetic genius*) uniformly placed the *aria* at the end of the scene, at the same time that he almost always raises and impassions the style of the recitative immediately preceding. Even in real life, the difference is great and evident between words used as the *arbitrary marks* of thought, our smooth market-coin of intercourse, with the image and superscription worn out by currency; and those which convey pictures either borrowed from *one* outward object to enliven and particularize some *other*; or used allegorically to body forth the inward state of the person speaking; or such as are at least the exponents of his peculiar turn and unusual extent of faculty. So much so indeed, that in the social circles of private life we often find a striking use of the latter put a stop to the general flow of conversation, and by the excitement arising from concentred attention produce a sort of damp and interruption for some minutes after. But in the perusal of works of literary *art*, we *prepare* ourselves for such language; and the business of the writer, like that of a painter whose subject requires unusual splendour and prominence, is so to raise the lower and neutral tints, that what in a different style would be the *commanding* colours, are here used as the means of that gentle *degradation* requisite in order to produce the effect of a *whole*. Where this is not achieved in a poem, the metre merely reminds the reader of his claims in order to disappoint them; and where this defect occurs frequently, his feelings are alternately startled by anticlimax and hyperclimax.

I refer the reader to the exquisite stanzas cited for another purpose from THE BLIND HIGHLAND BOY; and then annex, as being in my opinion instances of this *disharmony* in style, the two following:

> And one, the rarest, was a Shell,
> Which he, poor Child, had studied well:
> The Shell of a green Turtle, thin
> And hollow;—you might sit therein,
>   It was so wide, and deep.
>
> Our Highland Boy oft visited
> The house which held this prize; and, led
> By choice or chance, did thither come
> One day, when no one was at home,
>   And found the door unbarred.

Or page 172, vol. i.

> 'Tis gone—forgotten—*let me do*
> *My best*—there was a smile or two,
> I can remember them, I see
> The smiles, worth all the world to me.
> Dear Baby! I must lay thee down:
> Thou troublest me with strange alarms;
> Smiles hast Thou, sweet ones of thy own;
> I cannot keep thee in my arms;
> For they confound me: *as it is*,
> I have forgot those smiles of his!

Or page 269, vol. i.

> Thou hast a nest, for thy love and thy rest.
> And though little troubled with sloth,
> Drunken Lark! thou would'st be loth
> To be such a Traveller as I.
>   Happy, happy liver!
> *With a soul as strong as a mountain River*
> *Pouring out praise to th' Almighty Giver,*

· Joy and jollity be with us both!
Hearing thee, or else some other,
    As merry a Brother
I on the earth will go plodding on,
By myself, cheerfully, till the day is done.

The incongruity, which I appear to find in this passage, is that of the two noble lines in italics with the preceding and following. So vol. ii. page 30.

Close by a Pond, upon the further side,
He stood alone; a minute's space, I guess,
I watch'd him, he continuing motionless:
To the Pool's further margin then I drew;
He being all the while before me full in view.

Compare this with the repetition of the same image, in the next stanza but two.

And, still as I drew near with gentle pace,
Beside the little pond or moorish flood
Motionless as a Cloud the Old Man stood,
That heareth not the loud winds when they call;
And moveth altogether, if it move at all.

Or lastly, the second of the three following stanzas, compared both with the first and the third.

My former thoughts returned; the fear that kills;
And hope that is unwilling to be fed;
Cold, pain, and labour, and all fleshly ills;
And mighty Poets in their misery dead.
But now, perplex'd by what the Old Man had said,
My question eagerly did I renew,
"How is it that you live, and what is it you do?"

He with a smile did then his words repeat;
And said, that, gathering Leeches, far and wide
He travelled; stirring thus about his feet
The waters of the Ponds where they abide.
"Once I could meet with them on every side;
But they have dwindled long by slow decay;
Yet still I persevere, and find them where I may."

While he was talking thus, the lonely place,
The Old Man's shape, and speech, all troubled me:
In my mind's eye I seemed to see him pace
About the weary moors continually,
Wandering about alone and silently.

Indeed this fine poem is *especially* characteristic of the author. There is scarce a defect or excellence in his writings of which it would not present a specimen. But it would be unjust not to repeat that this defect is only occasional. From a careful reperusal of the two volumes of poems, I doubt whether the objectionable passages would amount in the whole to one hundred lines; not the eighth part of the number of pages. In THE EXCURSION the feeling of incongruity is seldom excited by the diction of any passage considered in itself, but by the sudden superiority of some other passage forming the context.

The second defect I can generalize with tolerable accuracy, if the reader will pardon an uncouth and new coined word. There is, I should say, not seldom a *matter-of-factness* in certain poems. This may be divided into, *first*, a laborious minuteness and fidelity in the representation of objects, and their positions, as they appeared to the poet himself; *secondly*, the insertion of accidental circumstances, in order to the full explanation of his living characters, their dispositions and actions; which circumstances might be necessary to establish the probability of a statement in real life, where nothing is taken for granted by the hearer; but appear superfluous in poetry, where the reader is willing to believe for his own sake. To this *accidentality* I object, as contravening the essence of poetry, which Aristotle pronounces to be σπουδαιότατον καὶ φιλοσοφώτατον γένος, the most intense, weighty and philosophical product of human art; adding, as the *reason*, that it is the most catholic and abstract. The following passage from Davenant's prefatory letter to Hobbes well expresses this truth. "When I considered the actions which I meant to describe, (those inferring the persons), I was again persuaded rather to choose those of a former age, than the present; and in a century so far removed, as might preserve me from their improper examinations, who know not the requisites of a poem, nor how much pleasure they lose, (and even the pleasures of heroic poesy are not unprofitable), who take away the liberty of a poet, and fetter his feet in the shackles of an historian. For why should a poet doubt in story to mend the intrigues of fortune by more delightful conveyances of probable fictions, because austere historians have entered into bond to truth? An obligation, which were in poets as foolish and unnecessary, as is the bondage of false martyrs, who lie in chains for a mistaken opinion. *But by this I would imply, that truth, narrative and past, is the idol of historians, (who worship a dead thing), and truth operative, and by effects continually alive, is the mistress of poets, who hath not her existence in matter, but in reason.*"

For this minute accuracy in the painting of local imagery, the lines in THE EXCURSION, pp. 96, 97, and 98, may be taken, if not as a striking instance, yet as an illustration of my meaning. It must be some strong motive—(as, for instance, that the description was necessary to the intelligibility of the tale)—which could induce me to describe in a number of verses what a draughtsman could present to the eye with incomparably greater satisfaction by half a dozen strokes of his pencil, or the painter with as many touches of his brush. Such descriptions too often occasion in the mind of a reader, who is determined to understand his author, a feeling of labour, not very dissimilar to that, with which he would construct a diagram, line by line, for a long geometrical proposition. It seems to be like taking the pieces of a dissected map out of its box. We first look at one part, and then at another, then join and dove-tail them; and when the successive acts of attention have been completed, there is a retrogressive effort of mind to behold it as a whole. The poet should paint to the imagination, not to the fancy; and I know no happier case to exemplify the distinction between these two faculties. Master-pieces of the former mode of poetic painting abound in the writings of Milton, for example:

> The fig-tree; not that kind for fruit renown'd,
> But such as at this day, to Indians known,
> In Malabar or Decan spreads her arms,
> Branching so broad and long, that in the ground
> The bended twigs take root, *and daughters grow*
> *About the mother tree, a pillar'd shade*
> *High over-arch'd, and* ECHOING WALKS BETWEEN:
> *There oft the Indian herdsman, shunning heat,*
> *Shelters in cool, and tends his pasturing herds,*
> *At loop-holes cut through thickest shade:*—

This is *creation* rather than *painting*, or if painting, yet such, and with such co-presence of the whole picture flashed at once upon the eye, as the sun paints in a camera obscura. But the poet must likewise understand and command what Bacon calls the *vestigia communia* of the senses, the latency of all in each, and more especially as by a magical *penna duplex*, the excitement of vision by sound and the exponents of sound. Thus, "The echoing walks between," may be almost said to reverse the fable in tradition of the head of Memnon, in the Egyptian statue. Such may be deservedly entitled the *creative words* in the world of imagination.

The second division respects an apparent minute adherence to *matter-of-fact* in character and incidents; *a biographical* attention to probability, and an *anxiety* of explanation and retrospect. Under this head I shall deliver, with no feigned diffidence, the results of my best reflection on the great point of controversy between Mr. Wordsworth and his objectors; namely, on *the choice of his characters*. I have already declared, and, I trust justified, my utter dissent from the mode of argument which his critics have hitherto employed. To *their* question,—"Why did you chuse such a character, or a character from such a rank of life?"—the poet might in my opinion fairly retort: why with the conception of my character did you make wilful choice of mean or ludicrous associations not furnished by me, but supplied from your own sickly and fastidious feelings? How was it, indeed, probable, that such arguments could have any weight with an author, whose plan, whose guiding principle, and main object it was to attack and subdue that state of association, which leads us to place the chief value on those things on which man DIFFERS from man, and to forget or disregard the high dignities, which belong to HUMAN NATURE, the sense and the feeling, which *may* be, and *ought* to be, found in *all* ranks? The feelings with which, as Christians, we contemplate a mixed congregation rising or kneeling before their common Maker, Mr. Wordsworth would have us entertain at *all* times, as men, and as readers; and by the excitement of this lofty, yet prideless impartiality in *poetry*, he might hope to have encouraged its continuance in *real life*. The praise of good men be his! In real life, and, I trust, even in my imagination, I honour a virtuous and wise man, without reference to the presence or absence of artificial advantages. Whether in the person of an armed baron, a laurelled bard, or of an old Pedlar, or still older Leech-gatherer, the same qualities of head and heart must claim the same reverence. And even in poetry I am not conscious, that I have ever suffered my feelings to be disturbed or offended by any thoughts or images, which the poet himself has not presented.

But yet I object, nevertheless, and for the following reasons. First, because the object in view, as an *immediate* object, belongs to the moral philosopher, and would be pursued, not only more appropriately, but in my opinion with far greater probability of success, in sermons or moral essays, than in an elevated poem. It seems, indeed, to destroy the main fundamental distinction, not only between a *poem* and *prose*, but even between philosophy and works of fiction, inasmuch as it proposes *truth* for its immediate object, instead of *pleasure*. Now till the blessed time shall come, when truth itself shall be pleasure, and both shall be so united, as to be distinguishable in words only, not in feeling, it will remain the poet's office to proceed upon that state of association, which actually exists as *general*; instead of attempting first to *make* it what it ought to be, and then to let the pleasure follow. But here is unfortunately a small *hysteron-proteron*. For the communication of pleasure is the introductory means by which alone the poet must expect to moralize his readers. Secondly: though I were to admit, for a moment, *this* argument to be groundless: yet how is the moral effect to be produced, by merely attaching the name of some low profession to powers which are *least* likely, and to qualities which are assuredly not *more* likely, to be found in it? The Poet, speaking in his own person, may at once delight and improve us by sentiments, which teach us the independence of goodness, of wisdom, and even of genius, on the favours of fortune. And having made a due reverence before the throne of Antonine, he may bow with equal awe before Epictetus among his fellow-slaves—

> ——————and rejoice
> In the plain presence of his dignity.

Who is not at once delighted and improved, when the Poet Wordsworth himself exclaims,

> Oh! many are the Poets that are sown
> By Nature; men endowed with highest gifts
> The vision and the faculty divine,
> Yet wanting the accomplishment of verse,
> Nor having e'er, as life advanced, been led
> By circumstance to take unto the height
> The measure of themselves, these favoured Beings,
> All but a scattered few, live out their time,
> Husbanding that which they possess within,
> And go to the grave, unthought of. Strongest minds
> Are often those of whom the noisy world
> Hears least.

To use a colloquial phrase, such sentiments, in such language, do one's heart good; though I for my part, have not the fullest faith in the *truth* of the observation. On the contrary I believe the instances to be exceedingly rare; and should feel almost as strong an objection to introduce such a character in a poetic fiction, as a pair of black swans on a lake, in a fancy land-scape. When I think how many, and how much better books than Homer, or even than Herodotus, Pindar or Æschylus, could have read, are in the power of almost every man, in a country where almost every man is instructed to read and write; and how restless, how difficultly hidden, the powers of genius are; and yet find even in situations the most favourable, according to Mr. Wordsworth, for the formation of a pure and poetic language; in situations which ensure familiarity with the grandest objects of the imagination; but *one* BURNS, among the shepherds of *Scotland*, and not a single poet of humble life among those of *English* lakes and mountains; I conclude, that POETIC GENIUS is not only a very delicate but a very rare plant.

But be this as it may, the feelings with which,

> I think of Chatterton, the marvellous Boy,
> The sleepless Soul, that perished in his pride;
> Of Burns, who walk'd in glory and in joy
> Behind his plough, upon the mountain-side—

are widely different from those with which I should read a *poem*, where the author, having occasion for the character of a poet and a philosopher in the fable of his narration, had chosen to make him a *chimney-sweeper*; and then, in order to remove all doubts on the subject, had *invented* an account of his birth, parentage and education, with all the strange and fortunate accidents which had concurred in making him at once poet, philosopher, and sweep! Nothing, but biography, can justify this. If it be admissible even in a *novel*, it must be one in the manner of De Foe's, that were meant to pass for histories, not in the manner of Fielding's: in THE LIFE OF MOLL FLANDERS, or COLONEL JACK, not in a TOM JONES or even a JOSEPH ANDREWS. Much less then can it be legitimately introduced in a *poem*, the characters of which, amid the strongest individualization, must still remain representative. The precepts of Horace, on this point, are grounded on the nature both of poetry and of the human mind. They are not more peremptory, than wise and prudent. For in the first place a deviation from them perplexes the reader's feelings, and all the circumstances which are feigned in order to make such accidents less improbable, divide and disquiet his faith, rather than aid and support it. Spite of all attempts, the fiction *will* appear, and unfortunately not as *fictitious* but as *false*. The reader not only *knows*, that the sentiments and language are the poet's own, and his own too in his *artificial* character, as *poet*; but by the fruitless endeavours to make him think the contrary, he is not even suffered to *forget* it. The effect is similar to that produced by an Epic Poet, when the fable and the characters are *derived* from Scripture history, as in THE MESSIAH of Klopstock, or in Cumberland's CALVARY: and not merely *suggested* by it as in the PARADISE LOST of Milton. That *illusion*, contradistinguished from *delusion*, that *negative* faith, which simply permits the images presented to work by their own force, without either denial or affirmation of their real existence by the judgment, is rendered impossible by their immediate neighbourhood to words and facts of known and absolute truth. A faith, which transcends even historic belief, must absolutely *put out* this mere poetic *analogon* of faith, as the summer sun is said to extinguish our household fires, when it shines full upon them. What would otherwise have been yielded to as pleasing fiction, is repelled as revolting falsehood. The effect produced in this latter case by the solemn belief of the reader, is in a less degree brought about in the instances, to which I have been objecting, by the baffled attempts of the author to *make* him believe.

Add to all the foregoing the seeming uselessness both of the project and of the anecdotes from which it is to derive support. Is there one word for instance, attributed to the pedlar in THE EXCURSION, characteristic of a *Pedlar?* One sentiment, that might not more plausibly, even without the aid of any previous explanation, have proceeded from any wise and beneficent old man, of a rank or profession in which the language of learning and refinement are natural and to be expected? Need the rank have been at all particularized, where nothing follows which the knowledge of that rank is to explain or illustrate? When on the contrary this information renders the man's language, feelings, sentiments, and information a riddle, which must itself be solved by episodes of anecdote? Finally when this, and this alone, could have induced a genuine *Poet* to inweave in a poem of the loftiest style, and on subjects the loftiest and of most universal interest, such minute matters of fact, (not unlike those furnished for the obituary of a magazine by the friends of some obscure "ornament of society lately deceased" in some obscure town,) as

> Among the hills of Athol he was born:
> There, on a small hereditary Farm,
> An unproductive slip of rugged ground,
> His Father dwelt; and died in poverty;
> While He, whose lowly fortune I retrace,
> The youngest of three sons, was yet a babe,
> A little One—unconscious of their loss.
> But ere he had outgrown his infant days
> His widowed Mother, for a second Mate,
> Espoused the teacher of the Village School;
> Who on her offspring zealously bestowed
> Needful instruction.
>
> From his sixth year, the Boy of whom I speak,
> In summer, tended cattle on the Hills;
> But, through the inclement and the perilous days
> Of long-continuing winter, he repaired
> To his Step-father's School,—&c.

For all the admirable passages interposed in this narration, might, with trifling alterations, have been far more appropriately, and with far greater verisimilitude, told of a poet in the character of a poet; and without incurring another defect which I shall now mention, and a sufficient illustration of which will have been here anticipated.

Third; an undue predilection for the *dramatic* form in certain poems, from which one or other of two evils result. Either the thoughts and diction are different from that of the poet, and then there arises an incongruity of style; or they are the same and indistinguishable, and then it presents a species of ventriloquism, where two are represented as talking, while in truth one man only speaks.

The fourth class of defects is closely connected with the former; but yet are such as arise likewise from an intensity of feeling disproportionate to *such* knowledge and value of the objects described, as can be fairly anticipated of men in general, even of the most cultivated classes; and with which therefore few only, and those few particularly circumstanced, can be supposed to sympathize: In this class, I comprise occasional prolixity, repetition, and an eddying, instead of progression, of thought. As instances, see pages 27, 28, and 62 of the Poems, vol. i. and the first eighty lines of the VI.th Book of THE EXCURSION.

Fifth and last; thoughts and images too great for the subject. This is an approximation to what might be called *mental* bombast, as distinguished from verbal: for, as in the latter there is a disproportion of the expressions to the thoughts so in this there is a disproportion of thought to the circumstance and occasion. This, by the bye, is a fault of which none but a man of genius is capable. It is the awkwardness and strength of Hercules with the distaff of Omphale.

It is a well known fact, that bright colours in motion both make and leave the strongest impressions on the eye. Nothing is more likely too, than that a vivid image or visual *spectrum*, thus originated, may become the link of association in recalling the feelings and images that had accompanied the original impression. But if we describe this in such lines, as

> They flash upon that inward eye,
> Which is the bliss of solitude!

in what words shall we describe the joy of retrospection, when the images and virtuous actions of a whole well-spent life, pass before that conscience which is indeed the *inward* eye: which is indeed "*the bliss of solitude?*" Assuredly we seem to sink most abruptly, not to say burlesquely, and almost as in a medley, from this couplet to—

> And then my heart with pleasure fills,
> And dances with the *daffodils*. Vol. i. p. 328.

The second instance is from vol. ii. page 12, where the poet having gone out for a day's tour of pleasure, meets early in the morning with a knot of Gipsies, who had pitched their blanket-tents and straw-beds, together with their children and asses, in some field by the road-side. At the close of the day on his return our tourist found them in the same place. "Twelve hours," says he,

> Twelve hours, twelve bounteous hours are gone, while I
> Have been a traveller under open sky,
> Much witnessing of change and cheer,
> Yet as I left I find them here!

Whereat the poet, without seeming to reflect that the poor tawny wanderers might probably have been tramping for weeks together through road and lane, over moor and mountain, and consequently must have been right glad to rest themselves, their children and cattle, for one whole day; and overlooking the obvious truth, that such repose might be quite as necessary for *them*, as a walk of the same continuance was pleasing or healthful for the more fortunate poet; expresses his indignation in a series of lines, the diction and imagery of which would have been rather above, than below the mark, had they been applied to the immense empire of China improgressive for thirty centuries:

> The weary Sun betook himself to rest:—
> —Then issued Vesper from the fulgent west,
> Cutshining, like a visible God,
> The glorious path in which he trod.
> And now, ascending, after one dark hour,
> And one night's diminution of her power,
> Behold the mighty Moon! this way
> She looks, as if at them—but they
> Regard not her:—oh, better wrong and strife,
> Better vain deeds or evil than such life!
> The silent Heavens have goings on:
> The stars have tasks—but *these* have none!

The last instance of this defect, (for I know no other than these already cited) is from the Ode, page 351, vol. ii. where, speaking of a child, "a six years' Darling of a pigmy size," he thus addresses him:

> Thou best Philosopher, who yet dost keep
> Thy heritage, thou Eye among the blind,
> That, deaf and silent, read'st the eternal deep,
> Haunted for ever by the Eternal Mind,—
> Mighty Prophet! Seer blest!
> On whom those truths do rest,
> Which we are toiling all our lives to find;
> Thou, over whom thy Immortality
> Broods like the Day, a Master o'er a Slave,
> A Presence which is not to be put by.

Now here, not to stop at the daring spirit of metaphor which connects the epithets "deaf and silent," with the apostrophized *eye:* or (if we are to refer it to the preceding word, "Philosopher"), the faulty and equivocal syntax of the passage; and without examining the propriety of making a "Master *brood* o'er a Slave," or "the *Day*" brood *at all;* we will merely ask, what does all this mean? In what sense is a child of that age a *Philosopher?* In what sense does he *read* "the eternal deep?" In what sense is he declared to be "*for ever haunted*" by the Supreme Being? or so inspired as to deserve the splendid titles of a *Mighty Prophet*, a *blessed Seer?* By reflection? by knowledge? by conscious intuition? or by *any* form or modification of consciousness? These would be tidings indeed; but such as would pre-suppose an immediate revelation to the inspired communicator, and require miracles to authenticate his inspiration. Children at this age give us no such information of themselves; and at what time were we dipped in the Lethe, which has produced such utter oblivion of a state so godlike? There are many of us that still possess some remembrances, more or less distinct, respecting themselves at six years old; pity that the worthless straws only should float, while treasures, compared with which all the mines of Golconda and Mexico were but straws, should be absorbed by some unknown gulf into some unknown abyss.

But if this be too wild and exorbitant to be suspected as having been the poet's meaning; if these mysterious gifts, faculties, and operations, are *not* accompanied with consciousness; who *else* is conscious of them? or how can it be called the child, if it be no part of the child's conscious being? For aught I know, the thinking Spirit within me may be *substantially* one with the principle of life, and of vital operation. For aught I know, it may be employed as a secondary agent in the marvellous organization and organic movements of my body. But, surely, it would be strange language to say, that *I* construct my *heart!* or that *I* propel the finer influences through my *nerves!* or that *I* compress my brain, and draw the curtains of sleep round my own eyes! Spinoza and Behmen were, on different systems, both Pantheists; and among the ancients there were philosophers, teachers of the EN KAI ΠAN, who not only taught that God was All, but that this All constituted God. Yet not even these would confound the *part*, *as* a part, with the whole, *as* the whole. Nay, in no system is the distinction between the individual and God, between the Modification, and the one only Substance, more sharply drawn, than in that of Spinoza. Jacobi indeed relates of Lessing, that, after a conversation with him at the house of the Poet, Gleim, (the Tyrtæus and Anacreon of the German Parnassus,) in which conversation Lessing had avowed privately to Jacobi his reluctance to admit any *personal* existence of the Supreme Being, or the *possibility* of personality except in a finite Intellect, and while they were sitting at table, a shower of rain came on unexpectedly.

Gleim expressed his regret at the circumstance, because they had meant to drink their wine in the garden: upon which Lessing in one of his half-earnest, half-joking moods, nodded to Jacobi, and said, "It is *I*, perhaps, that am doing *that*," i.e. *raining!*—and Jacobi answered, "or perhaps I;" Gleim contented himself with staring at them both, without asking for any explanation.

So with regard to this passage. In what sense can the magnificent attributes, above quoted, be appropriated to a *child*, which would not make them equally suitable to a *bee*, or a *dog*, or *a field of corn;* or even to a ship, or to the wind and waves that propel it? The omnipresent Spirit works equally in *them*, as in the child; and the child is equally unconscious of it as they. It cannot surely be, that the four lines, immediately following, are to contain the explanation?

> To whom the grave
> Is but a lonely bed without the sense or sight
> Of day or the warm light,
> A place of thought where we in waiting lie;—

Surely, it cannot be that this wonder-rousing apostrophe is but a comment on the little poem, "We are Seven?"—that the whole meaning of the passage is reducible to the assertion, that a *child*, who by the bye at six years old would have been better instructed in most Christian families, has no other notion of death than that of lying in a dark, cold place? And still, I hope, not as *in a place of thought!* not the frightful notion of lying *awake* in his grave! The analogy between death and sleep is too simple, too natural, to render so horrid a belief possible for children; even had they not been in the habit, as all Christian children are, of hearing the latter term used to express the former. But if the child's belief be only, that "he is not dead, but sleepeth:" wherein does it differ from that of his father and mother, or any other adult and instructed person? To form an idea of a thing's becoming nothing; or of nothing becoming a thing; is impossible to all finite beings alike, of whatever age, and however educated or uneducated. Thus it is with splendid paradoxes in general. If the words are taken in the common sense, they convey an absurdity; and if, in contempt of dictionaries and custom, they are so interpreted as to avoid the absurdity, the meaning dwindles into some bald truism. Thus you must at once understand the words *contrary* to their common import, in order to arrive at any *sense;* and *according* to their common import, if you are to receive from them any feeling of *sublimity* or *admiration*.

Though the instances of this defect in Mr. Wordsworth's poems are so few, that for themselves it would have been scarcely just to attract the reader's attention toward them; yet I have dwelt on it, and perhaps the more for this very reason. For being so very few, they cannot sensibly detract from the reputation of an author, who is even characterized by the number of profound truths in his writings, which will stand the severest analysis; and yet few as they are, they are exactly those passages which his *blind* admirers would be most likely, and best able, to imitate. But Wordsworth, where he is indeed Wordsworth, may be mimicked by copyists, he may be plundered by plagiarists; but he can not be imitated, except by those who are not born to be imitators. For without his depth of feeling and his imaginative power his *sense* would want its vital warmth and peculiarity; and without his strong sense, his *mysticism* would become *sickly*—mere fog, and dimness!

To these defects which, as appears by the extracts, are only occasional, I may oppose, with far less fear of encountering the dissent of any candid and intelligent reader, the following (for the most part correspondent) excellencies. First, an austere purity of language both grammatically and logically; in short a perfect appropriateness of the words to the meaning. Of how high value I deem this, and how particularly estimable I hold the example at the present day, has been already stated; and in part too the reasons on which I ground both the moral and intellectual importance of habituating ourselves to a strict accuracy of expression. It is noticeable, how limited an acquaintance with the master-pieces of art will suffice to form a correct and even a sensitive taste, where none but master-pieces have been seen and admired: while on the other hand, the most correct notions, and the widest acquaintance with the works of excellence of all ages and countries, will not perfectly secure us against the contagious familiarity with the far more numerous offspring of tastelessness or of a perverted taste. If this be the case, as it notoriously is, with the arts of music and painting, much more difficult will it be, to avoid the infection of multiplied and daily examples in the practice of an art, which uses words, and words only, as its instruments. In poetry, in which every line, every phrase, may pass the ordeal of deliberation and deliberate choice, it is possible, and barely possible, to attain that *ultimatum* which I have ventured to propose as the infallible test of a blameless style; namely; its *untranslatableness* in words of the same language without injury to the meaning. Be it observed, however, that I include in the *meaning* of a word not only its correspondent object, but likewise all the associations which it recalls. For language is framed to convey not the object alone, but likewise the character, mood and intentions of the person who is representing it. In poetry it *is* practicable to preserve the diction uncorrupted by the affectations and misappropriations, which promiscuous authorship, and reading not promiscuous only because it is disproportionally most conversant with the compositions of the day, have rendered general. Yet even to the poet, composing in his own province, it is an arduous work: and as the result and pledge of a watchful good sense, of fine and luminous distinction, and of complete self-possession, may justly claim all the honour which belongs to an attainment equally difficult and valuable, and the more valuable for being rare. It is at *all* times the proper food of the understanding; but in an age of corrupt eloquence it is both food and antidote.

In prose I doubt whether it be even possible to preserve our style wholly unalloyed by the vicious phraseology which meets us every where, from the sermon to the newspaper, from the harangue of the legislator to the speech from the convivial chair, announcing a *toast* or sentiment. Our chains rattle, even while we are complaining of them. The poems of Boetius rise high in our estimation when we compare them with those of his contemporaries, as Sidonius Apollinaris, and others. They might even be referred to a purer age, but that the prose, in which they are set, as jewels in a crown of lead or iron, betrays the true age of the writer. Much however may be effected by education. I believe not only from grounds of reason, but from having in great measure assured myself of the fact by actual though limited experience, that, to a youth led from his first boyhood to investigate the meaning of every word and the reason of its choice and position, Logic presents itself as an old acquaintance under new names.

On some future occasion, more especially demanding such disquisition, I shall attempt to prove the close connection between veracity and habits of mental accuracy; the beneficial after-effects of verbal precision in the preclusion of fanaticism, which masters the feelings more especially by indistinct watch-words; and to display the advantages which language alone, at least which language with incomparably greater ease and certainty than any other means, presents to the instructor of impressing modes of intellectual energy so constantly, so imperceptibly, and as it were by such elements and atoms, as to secure in due time the formation of a second nature. When we reflect, that the cultivation of the judgment is a positive command of the moral law, since the reason can give the *principle* alone, and the conscience bears witness only to the *motive*, while the application and effects must depend on the judgment: when we consider, that the greater part of our success and comfort in life depends on distinguishing the similar from the same, that which is peculiar in each thing from that which it has in common with others, so as still to select the most probable, instead of the merely possible or positively unfit, we shall learn to value earnestly and with a practical seriousness a mean, already prepared for us by nature and society, of teaching the young mind to think well and wisely by the same unremembered process and with the same never forgotten results, as those by which it is taught to speak and converse. Now how much warmer the interest is, how much more genial the feelings of reality and practicability, and thence how much stronger the impulses to imitation are, which a *contemporary* writer, and especially a contemporary *poet*, excites in youth and commencing manhood, has been treated of in the earlier pages of these sketches. I have only to add, that all the praise which is due to the exertion of such influence for a purpose so important, joined with that which must be claimed for the infrequency of the same excellence in the same perfection, belongs in full right to Mr. Wordsworth. I am far however from denying that we have poets whose *general* style possesses the same excellence, as Mr. Moore, Lord Byron, Mr. Bowles, and, in all his later and more important works, our laurel-honouring Laureate. But there are none, in whose works I do not appear to myself to find *more* exceptions, than in those of Wordsworth. Quotations or specimens would here be wholly out of place, and must be left for the critic who doubts and would invalidate the justice of this eulogy so applied.

The second characteristic excellence of Mr. Wordsworth's works is: a correspondent weight and sanity of the Thoughts and Sentiments,—won, not from books; but—from the poet's own meditative observation. They are *fresh* and have the dew upon them. His muse, at least when in her strength of wing, and when she hovers aloft in her proper element,

Makes audible a linked lay of truth,
Of truth profound a sweet continuous lay,
Not learnt, but native, her own natural notes!

Even throughout his smaller poems there is scarcely one, which is not rendered valuable by some just and original reflection.

See page 25, vol. ii.: or the two following passages in one of his humblest compositions.

O Reader! had you in your mind
Such stores as silent thought can bring,
O gentle Reader! you would find
A tale in every thing.

and

I've heard of hearts unkind, kind deeds
With coldness still returning;
Alas! the gratitude of men
Has oftener left *me* mourning.

or in a still higher strain the six beautiful quatrains, page 134.

Thus fares it still in our decay:
And yet the wiser mind
Mourns less for what age takes away
Than what it leaves behind.

The Blackbird in the summer trees,
The Lark upon the hill,
Let loose their carols when they please,
Are quiet when they will.

With Nature never do *they* wage
A foolish strife; they see
A happy youth, and their old age
Is beautiful and free:

But we are pressed by heavy laws;
And often, glad no more,
We wear a face of joy, because
We have been glad of yore.

If there is one who need bemoan
His kindred laid in earth,
The household hearts that were his own,
It is the man of mirth.

My days, my Friend, are almost gone,
My life has been approved,
And many love me; but by none
Am I enough beloved.

or the sonnet on Buonaparte, page 202, vol. ii; or finally (for a volume would scarce suffice to exhaust the instances,) the last stanza of the poem on the withered Celandine, vol. ii. p. 312.

> To be a Prodigal's Favorite—then, worse truth,
> A Miser's Pensioner—behold our lot!
> O Man! that from thy fair and shining youth
> Age might but take the things Youth needed not!

Both in respect of this and of the former excellence, Mr. Wordsworth strikingly resembles Samuel Daniel, one of the golden writers of our golden Elizabethan age, now most causelessly neglected: Samuel Daniel, whose diction bears no mark of time, no distinction of age, which has been, and as long as our language shall last, will be so far the language of the to-day and for ever, as that it is more intelligible to us, than the transitory fashions of our own particular age. A similar praise is due to his sentiments. No frequency of perusal can deprive them of their freshness. For though they are brought into the full day-light of every reader's comprehension; yet are they drawn up from depths which few in any age are privileged to visit, into which few in any age have courage or inclination to descend. If Mr. Wordsworth is not equally with Daniel alike intelligible to all readers of average understanding in all passages of his works, the comparative difficulty does not arise from the greater impurity of the ore, but from the nature and uses of the metal. A poem is not necessarily obscure, because it does not aim to be popular. It is enough, if a work be perspicuous to those for whom it is written, and

> Fit audience find, though few.

To the "Ode on the Intimations of Immortality from Recollections of early Childhood" the poet might have prefixed the lines which Dante addresses to one of his own Canzoni—

> Canzone, i' credo, che saranno radi
> Color, che tua ragione intendan bene,
> Tanto lor sei faticoso ed alto.

> O lyric song, there will be few, think I,
> Who may thy import understand aright:
> Thou art for *them* so arduous and so high!

But the ode was intended for such readers only as had been accustomed to watch the flux and reflux of their inmost nature, to venture at times into the twilight realms of consciousness, and to feel a deep interest in modes of inmost being, to which they know that the attributes of time and space are inapplicable and alien, but which yet can not be conveyed, save in symbols of time and space. For such readers the sense is sufficiently plain, and they will be as little disposed to charge Mr. Wordsworth with believing the Platonic pre-existence in the ordinary interpretation of the words, as I am to believe, that Plato himself ever meant or taught it.

Πολλά μοι ὑπ' ἀγκῶ-
νος ὠκέα βέλη
ἔνδον ἐντὶ φαρέτρας
φωνᾶντα συνετοῖσιν· ἐς
δὲ τὸ πὰν ἑρμηνέων
χατίζει. σοφὸς ὁ πολ-
λὰ εἰδὼς φυᾷ·
μαθόντες δὲ λάβροι
παγγλωσσίᾳ κόρακες ὣς
ἄκραντα γαρυέτων
Διὸς πρὸς ὄρνιχα θεῖον.

Third (and wherein he soars far above Daniel) the sinewy strength and originality of single lines and paragraphs: the frequent *curiosa felicitas* of his diction, of which I need not here give specimens, having anticipated them in a preceding page. This beauty, and as eminently characteristic of Wordsworth's poetry, his rudest assailants have felt themselves compelled to acknowledge and admire.

Fourth; the perfect truth of nature in his images and descriptions as taken immediately from nature, and proving a long and genial intimacy with the very spirit which gives the physiognomic expression to all the works of nature. Like a green field reflected in a calm and perfectly transparent lake, the image is distinguished from the reality only by its greater softness and lustre. Like the moisture or the polish on a pebble, genius neither distorts nor false-colours its objects; but on the contrary brings out many a vein and many a tint, which escape the eye of common observation, thus raising to the rank of gems what had been often kicked away by the hurrying foot of the traveller on the dusty high road of custom.

Let me refer to the whole description of skating, vol. i. page 44 to 47, especially to the lines

So through the darkness and the cold we flew,
And not a voice was idle: with the din

Meanwhile the precipices rang aloud;
The leafless trees and every icy crag
Tinkled like iron; while the distant hills
Into the tumult sent an alien sound
Of melancholy, not unnoticed, while the stars,
Eastward, were sparkling clear, and in the west
The orange sky of evening died away.

Or to the poem on THE GREEN LINNET, vol. i. p. 244. What can be more accurate yet more lovely than the two concluding stanzas?

Upon yon tuft of hazel trees,
That twinkle to the gusty breeze,
Behold him perched in ecstasies,
　　Yet seeming still to hover;
There! where the flutter of his wings
Upon his back and body flings
Shadows and sunny glimmerings,
　　That cover him all over.

While thus before my eyes he gleams,
A Brother of the Leaves he seems;
When in a moment forth he teems
　　His little song in gushes:
As if it pleased him to disdain
And mock the Form which he did feign,
While he was dancing with the train
　　Of Leaves among the bushes.

Or the description of the blue-cap, and of the noon-tide silence, p. 284; or the poem to the cuckoo, p. 299; or, lastly, though I might multiply the references to ten times the number, to the poem, so completely Wordsworth's, commencing

Three years she grew in sun and shower—

Fifth: a meditative pathos, a union of deep and subtle thought with sensibility; a sympathy with man as man; the sympathy indeed of a contemplator, rather than a fellow-sufferer or co-mate, (*spectator, haud particeps*) but of a contemplator, from whose view no difference of rank conceals the sameness of the nature; no injuries of wind or weather, of toil, or even of ignorance, wholly disguise the human face divine. The superscription and the image of the Creator still remain legible to *him* under the dark lines, with which guilt or calamity had cancelled or cross-barred it. Here the Man and the Poet lose and find themselves in each other, the one as glorified, the latter as substantiated. In this mild and philosophic pathos, Wordsworth appears to me without a compeer. Such as he *is:* so he *writes*. See vol. i. page 134 to 136, or that most affecting composition, THE AFFLICTION OF MARGARET ——— OF ———, page 165 to 168, which no mother, and, if I may judge by my own experience, no parent can read without a tear. Or turn to that genuine lyric, in the former edition, entitled, THE MAD MOTHER, page 174 to 178, of which I cannot refrain from quoting two of the stanzas, both of them for their pathos, and the former for the fine transition in the two concluding lines of the stanza, so expressive of that deranged state, in which, from the increased sensibility, the sufferer's attention is abruptly drawn off by every trifle, and in the same instant plucked back again by the one despotic thought, bringing home with it, by the blending, *fusing* power of Imagination and Passion, the alien object to which it had been so abruptly diverted, no longer an alien but an ally and an inmate.

Suck, little Babe, oh suck again!
It cools my blood; it cools my brain;
Thy lips, I feel them, Baby! they
Draw from my heart the pain away.
Oh! press me with thy little hand;
It loosens something at my chest;
About that tight and deadly band
I feel thy little fingers prest.
The breeze I see is in the tree!
It comes to cool my Babe and me.

Thy Father cares not for my breast,
'Tis thine, sweet Baby, there to rest;
'Tis all thine own!—and, if its hue
Be changed, that was so fair to view,
'Tis fair enough for thee, my dove!
My beauty, little Child, is flown,
But thou wilt live with me in love;
And what if my poor cheek be brown?
'Tis well for me, thou canst not see
How pale and wan it else would be.

Last, and pre-eminently I challenge for this poet the gift of IMAGINATION in the highest and strictest sense of the word. In the play of *Fancy*, Wordsworth, to my feelings, is not always graceful, and sometimes *recondite*. The *likeness* is occasionally too strange, or demands too peculiar a point of view, or is such as appears the creature of predetermined research, rather than spontaneous presentation. Indeed his fancy seldom displays itself, as mere and unmodified fancy. But in imaginative power, he stands nearest of all modern writers to Shakespeare and Milton; and yet in a kind perfectly unborrowed and his own. To employ his own words, which are at once an instance and an illustration, he does indeed to all thoughts and to all objects—

> ————————add the gleam,
> The light that never was, on sea or land,
> The consecration, and the Poet's dream.

I shall select a few examples as most obviously manifesting this faculty; but if I should ever be fortunate enough to render my analysis of Imagination, its origin and characters, thoroughly intelligible to the reader, he will scarcely open on a page of this poet's works without recognising, more or less, the presence and the influences of this faculty.

From the poem on the YEW TREES, vol. i. page 303, 304.

> But worthier still of note
> Are those fraternal Four of Borrowdale,
> Joined in one solemn and capacious grove;
> Huge trunks!—and each particular trunk a growth
> Of intertwisted fibres serpentine
> Up-coiling, and inveterately convolved;
> Not uninformed with Phantasy, and looks
> That threaten the profane;—a pillared shade,
> Upon whose grassless floor of red-brown hue,
> By sheddings from the pinal umbrage tinged
> Perennially—beneath whose sable roof
> Of boughs, as if for festal purpose, decked
> With unrejoicing berries, ghostly Shapes
> May meet at noontide; FEAR and trembling HOPE,
> SILENCE and FORESIGHT; DEATH, the Skeleton,
> And TIME, the Shadow; there to celebrate,
> As in a natural temple scattered o'er
> With altars undisturbed of mossy stone,
> United worship; or in mute repose
> To lie, and listen to the mountain flood
> Murmuring from Glaramara's inmost caves.

The effect of the old man's figure in the poem of RESOLUTION AND INDEPENDENCE, vol. ii. page 33.

> While he was talking thus, the lonely place,
> The Old Man's shape, and speech, all troubled me:
> In my mind's eye I seemed to see him pace
> About the weary moors continually,
> Wandering about alone and silently.

Or the 8th, 9th, 19th, 26th, 31st, and 33d, in the collection of miscellaneous sonnets—the sonnet on the subjugation of Switzerland, page 210, or the last ode, from which I especially select the two following stanzas or paragraphs, page 349 to 350.

> Our birth is but a sleep and a forgetting:
> The Soul that rises with us, our life's Star,
> Hath had elsewhere its setting,
>   And cometh from afar.
> Not in entire forgetfulness,
> And not in utter nakedness,
> But trailing clouds of glory do we come
> From God, who is our home:
> Heaven lies about us in our infancy!
> Shades of the prison-house begin to close
>   Upon the growing Boy;
> But He beholds the light, and whence it flows,
>   He sees it in his joy!
> The Youth who daily further from the East
> Must travel, still is Nature's Priest,
>   And by the vision splendid
>   Is on his way attended;
> At length the Man perceives it die away,
> And fade into the light of common day.

And page 352 to 354 of the same ode.

> O joy! that in our embers
> Is something that doth live,
> That nature yet remembers
> What was so fugitive!
> The thought of our past years in me doth breed
> Perpetual benedictions: not indeed
> For that which is most worthy to be blest;
> Delight and liberty, the simple creed
> Of Childhood, whether busy or at rest,
> With new-fledged hope still fluttering in his breast:—
> Not for these I raise
> The song of thanks and praise;
> But for those obstinate questionings
> Of sense and outward things,
> Fallings from us, vanishings;
> Blank misgivings of a Creature
> Moving about in worlds not realized,
> High instincts, before which our mortal Nature
> Did tremble like a guilty Thing surprised!
> But for those first affections,
> Those shadowy recollections,
> Which, be they what they may,
> Are yet the fountain light of all our day,
> Are yet a master light of all our seeing;

Uphold us—cherish—and have power to make
Our noisy years seem moments in the being
Of the eternal Silence; truths that wake
To perish never;
Which neither listlessness, nor mad endeavour,
Nor Man nor Boy,
Nor all that is at enmity with joy,
Can utterly abolish or destroy!
Hence, in a season of calm weather,
Though inland far we be,
Our Souls have sight of that immortal sea
Which brought us hither;
Can in a moment travel thither,—
And see the Children sport upon the shore,
And hear the mighty waters rolling evermore.

And since it would be unfair to conclude with an extract, which, though highly characteristic, must yet, from the nature of the thoughts and the subject, be interesting or perhaps intelligible, to but a limited number of readers; I will add, from the poet's last published work, a passage equally Wordsworthian; of the beauty of which, and of the imaginative power displayed therein, there can be but one opinion, and one feeling. See White Doe, page 5.

Fast the church-yard fills;—anon
Look again and they all are gone;
The cluster round the porch, and the folk
Who sate in the shade of the Prior's Oak!
And scarcely have they disappeared
Ere the prelusive hymn is heard:—
With one consent the people rejoice,
Filling the church with a lofty voice!
They sing a service which they feel:
For 'tis the sun-rise now of zeal;
And faith and hope are in their prime
In great Eliza's golden time.

A moment ends the fervent din,
And all is hushed, without and within;
For though the priest, more tranquilly,
Recites the holy liturgy,
The only voice which you can hear
Is the river murmuring near.
—When soft!—the dusky trees between,
And down the path through the open green,
Where is no living thing to be seen;
And through yon gateway, where is found,
Beneath the arch with ivy bound,
Free entrance to the church-yard ground—

And right across the verdant sod,
Towards the very house of God;
Comes gliding in with lovely gleam,
Comes gliding in serene and slow,
Soft and silent as a dream,
A solitary Doe!
White she is as lily of June,
And beauteous as the silver moon
When out of sight the clouds are driven
And she is left alone in heaven!
Or like a ship some gentle day
In sunshine sailing far away—
A glittering ship that hath the plain
Of ocean for her own domain.

* * * * *

What harmonious pensive changes
Wait upon her as she ranges
Round and through this Pile of state
Overthrown and desolate!
Now a step or two her way
Is through space of open day,
Where the enamoured sunny light
Brightens her that was so bright;
Now doth a delicate shadow fall,
Falls upon her like a breath,
From some lofty arch or wall,
As she passes underneath.

The following analogy will, I am apprehensive, appear dim and fantastic, but in reading Bartram's Travels I could not help transcribing the following lines as a sort of allegory, or connected simile and metaphor of Wordsworth's intellect and genius.—"The soil is a deep, rich, dark mould, on a deep stratum of tenacious clay; and that on a foundation of rocks, which often break through both strata, lifting their backs above the surface. The trees which chiefly grow here are the gigantic black oak; magnolia grandiflora; fraximus excelsior; platane; and a few stately tulip trees." What Mr. Wordsworth *will* produce, it is not for me to prophesy: but I could pronounce with the liveliest convictions what he is capable of producing. It is the FIRST GENUINE PHILOSOPHIC POEM.

The preceding criticism will not, I am aware, avail to overcome the prejudices of those, who have made it a business to attack and ridicule Mr. Wordsworth's compositions.

Truth and prudence might be imaged as concentric circles. The poet may perhaps have passed beyond the latter, but he has confined himself far within the bounds of the former, in designating these critics, as "too petulant to be passive to a genuine poet, and too feeble to grapple with him; *** men of palsied imaginations, in whose minds all healthy action is languid; *** who, therefore, feed as the many direct them, or with the many are greedy after vicious provocatives."

So much for the detractors from Wordsworth's merits. On the other hand, much as I might wish for their fuller sympathy, I dare not flatter myself, that the freedom with which I have declared my opinions concerning both his theory and his defects, most of which are more or less connected with his theory, either as cause or effect, will be satisfactory or pleasing to *all* the poet's admirers and advocates. More indiscriminate than mine their admiration may be: deeper and more sincere it cannot be. But I have advanced no opinion either for praise or censure, other than as texts introductory to the reasons which compel me to form it. Above all, I was fully convinced that such a criticism was not only wanted; but that, if executed with adequate ability, it must conduce, in no mean degree, to Mr. Wordsworth's *reputation*. His *fame* belongs to another age, and can neither be accelerated nor retarded....

APPENDIX I

THE OMITTED CHAPTERS

The reader may like to have the headings of the omitted chapters.

CHAP. V. *On the law of Association—Its history traced from Aristotle to Hartley.*

CHAP. VI. *That Hartley's system, as far as it differs from that of Aristotle, is neither tenable in theory, nor founded in facts.*

CHAP. VII. *Of the necessary consequence of the Hartleian Theory—Of the original mistake or equivocation which procured its admission*—Memoria technica.

CHAP. VIII. *The system of Dualism introduced by Des Cartes—Refined first by Spinoza and afterwards by Leibnitz into the doctrine of* Harmonia praestabilita—*Hylozoism—Materialism—None of these systems, or any possible theory of association, supplies or supersedes a theory of Perception, or explains the formation of the Associable.*

This chapter contains another reference to the proposed treatise: "I shall not dilate further on this subject; because it will, (if God grant health and permission), be treated of at large and systematically in a work, which I have many years been preparing, on the Productive Logos human and divine; with, and as the introduction to, a full commentary on the Gospel of St John."

CHAP. IX. *Is Philosophy possible as a science, and what are its conditions?—Giordano Bruno—Literary Aristocracy, or the existence of a tacit compact among the learned as a privileged order—The Author's obligations to the Mystics—to Immanuel Kant—The difference between the letter and the spirit of Kant's writings, and a vindication of prudence in the teaching of Philosophy—Fichte's attempt to complete the Critical system—Its partial success and ultimate failure—Obligations to Schelling; and among English writers to Saumarez.*

CHAP. X. *A chapter of digression and anecdotes, as an interlude preceding that on the nature and genesis of the Imagination or Plastic Power—On pedantry and pedantic expressions—Advice to young authors respecting publication—Various anecdotes of the Author's literary life, and the progress of his opinions in Religion and Politics.*

The following personal passages from this chapter may be quoted:

A learned and exemplary old clergyman, who many years ago went to his reward followed by the regrets and blessings of his flock, published at his own expense two volumes octavo, entitled, A NEW THEORY OF REDEMPTION. The work was most severely handled in THE MONTHLY or CRITICAL REVIEW, I forget which; and this unprovoked hostility became the good old man's favourite topic of conversation among his friends. Well! (he used to exclaim,) in the second edition, I shall have an opportunity of exposing both the ignorance and the malignity of the anonymous critic. Two or three years however passed by without any tidings from the bookseller, who had undertaken the printing and publication of the work, and who was perfectly at his ease, as the author was known to be a man of large property. At length the accounts were written for; and in the course of a few weeks they were presented by the rider for the house, in person. My old friend put on his spectacles, and holding the scroll with no very firm hand, began—"*Paper, so much:* O moderate enough—not at all beyond my expectation! *Printing, so much:* well! moderate enough! *Stitching, covers, advertisements, carriage, and so forth, so much.*"—Still nothing amiss. *Selleridge* (for orthography is no necessary part of a bookseller's literary acquirements) £3. 3*s*. "Bless me! only three guineas for the what d'ye call it—the *selleridge?*" "No more, Sir!" replied the rider. "Nay, but that is *too* moderate!" rejoined my old friend. "Only three guineas for *selling* a thousand copies of a work in two volumes?" "O Sir!" (cries the young traveller) "you have mistaken the word. There have been none of them *sold;* they have been sent back from London long ago; and this £3. 3*s*. is for the *cellaridge*, or warehouse-room in our book cellar." The work was in consequence preferred from the ominous cellar of the publisher's to the author's garret; and, on presenting a copy to an acquaintance, the old gentleman used to tell the anecdote with great humour and still greater good nature.

With equal lack of worldly knowledge, I was a far more than equal sufferer for it, at the very outset of my authorship. Toward the close of the first year from the time, that in an inauspicious hour I left the friendly cloisters, and the happy grove of quiet, ever honoured Jesus College, Cambridge, I was persuaded by sundry philanthropists and Anti-polemists to set on foot a periodical work, entitled the WATCHMAN, that, according to the general motto of the work, *all might know the truth, and that the truth might make us free!* In order to exempt it from the stamp-tax, and likewise to contribute as little as possible to the supposed guilt of a war against freedom, it was to be published on every eighth day, thirty-two pages, large octavo, closely printed, and price only four-pence. Accordingly with a flaming prospectus,—

"*Knowledge is Power*," "To cry the state of the political atmosphere," —and so forth, I set off on a tour to the North, from Bristol to Sheffield, for the purpose of procuring customers, preaching by the way in most of the great towns, as an hireless volunteer, in a blue coat and white waistcoat, that not a rag of the woman of Babylon might be seen on me. For I was at that time and long after, though a Trinitarian (that is *ad normam Platonis*) in philosophy, yet a zealous Unitarian in religion; more accurately, I was a Psilanthropist, one of those who believe our Lord to have been the real son of Joseph, and who lay the main stress on the resurrection rather than on the crucifixion. O! never can I remember those days with either shame or regret. For I was most sincere, most disinterested. My opinions were indeed in many and most important points erroneous; but my heart was single. Wealth, rank, life itself then seemed cheap to me, compared with the interests of what I believed to be the truth, and the will of my Maker. I cannot even accuse myself of having been actuated by vanity; for in the expansion of my enthusiasm I did not think of myself at all.

My campaign commenced at Birmingham; and my first attack was on a rigid Calvinist, a tallow-chandler by trade. He was a tall dingy man, in whom length was so predominant over breadth, that he might almost have been borrowed for a foundry poker. O that face! a face κατ' ἔμφασιν! I have it before me at this moment. The lank, black, twine-like hair, pingui-nitescent, cut in a straight line along the black stubble of his thin gunpowder eye-brows, that looked like a scorched after-math from a last week's shaving. His coat collar behind in perfect unison, both of colour and lustre, with the coarse yet glib cordage, which I suppose he called his hair, and which with a bend inward at the nape of the neck,—the only approach to flexure in his whole figure, —slunk in behind his waistcoat; while the countenance lank, dark, very hard, and with strong perpendicular furrows, gave me a dim notion of some one looking at me through a used gridiron, all soot, grease, and iron! But he was one of the thorough-bred, a true lover of liberty, and, as I was informed, had proved to the satisfaction of many, that Mr. Pitt was one of the horns of the second beast in THE REVELATIONS, that *spake as a dragon*. A person, to whom one of my letters of recommendation had been addressed, was my introducer. It was a new event in my life, my first stroke in the new business I had undertaken of an author, yea, and of an author trading on his own account. My companion after some imperfect sentences and a multitude of hums and haas abandoned the cause to his client; and I commenced an harangue of half an hour to Phileleutheros, the tallow-chandler, varying my notes, through the whole gamut of eloquence, from the ratiocinative to the declamatory, and in the latter from the pathetic to the indignant. I argued, I described, I promised, I prophesied; and beginning with the captivity of nations I ended with the near approach of the millennium, finishing the whole with some of my own verses describing that glorious state out of the Religious Musings:

——————— Such delights
As float to earth, permitted visitants!
When in some hour of solemn jubilee
The massive gates of Paradise are thrown
Wide open, and forth come in fragments wild
Sweet echoes of unearthly melodies,
And odours snatched from beds of amaranth,
And they, that from the crystal river of life
Spring up on freshened wing, ambrosial gales!

My taper man of lights listened with perseverant and praiseworthy patience, though, as I was afterwards told, on complaining of certain gales that were not altogether ambrosial, it was a melting day with him. "And what, Sir," he said, after a short pause, "might the cost be?" "Only four-pence,"—(O! how I felt the anti-climax, the abysmal bathos of that four-pence!)—"only four-pence, Sir, each number, to be published on every eighth day."—"That comes to a deal of money at the end of a year. And how much, did you say, there was to be for the money?"—"Thirty-two pages, Sir! large octavo, closely printed." —"Thirty and two pages? Bless me! why except what I does in a family way on the Sabbath, that's more than I ever reads, Sir! all the year round. I am as great a one, as any man in Brummagem, Sir! for liberty and truth and all them sort of things, but as to this,—no offence, I hope, Sir,—I must beg to be excused."

So ended my first canvass: from causes that I shall presently mention, I made but one other application in person. This took place at Manchester to a stately and opulent wholesale dealer in cottons. He took my letter of introduction, and, having perused it, measured me from head to foot and again from foot to head, and then asked if I had any bill or invoice of the thing. I presented my prospectus to him. He rapidly skimmed and hummed over the first side, and still more rapidly the second and concluding page; crushed it within his fingers and the palm of his hand; then most deliberately and significantly rubbed and smoothed one part against the other; and lastly putting it into his pocket turned his back on me with an "*over-run* with these articles!" and so without another syllable retired into his counting-house. And I can truly say, to my unspeakable amusement.

This, I have said, was my second and last attempt. On returning baffled from the first, in which I had vainly essayed to repeat the miracle of Orpheus with the Brummagem patriot, I dined with the tradesman who had introduced me to him. After dinner he importuned me to smoke a pipe with him, and two or three other *illuminati* of the same rank. I objected, both because I was engaged to spend the evening with a minister and his friends, and because I had never smoked except once or twice in my life-time, and then it was herb tobacco mixed with Oronooko. On the assurance, however, that the tobacco was equally mild, and seeing too that it was of a yellow colour;—not forgetting the lamentable difficulty, I have always experienced, in saying, "No," and in abstaining from what the people about me were doing,—I took half a pipe, filling the lower half of the bowl with salt. I was soon however compelled to resign it, in consequence of a giddiness and distressful feeling in my eyes, which, as I had drunk but a single glass of ale, must, I knew, have been the effect of the tobacco. Soon after, deeming myself recovered, I sallied forth to my engagement; but the walk and the fresh air brought on all the symptoms again, and, I had scarcely entered the minister's drawing-room, and opened a small pacquet of letters, which he had received from Bristol for me; ere I sank back on the sofa in a sort of swoon rather than sleep. Fortunately I had found just time enough to inform him of the confused state of my feelings, and of the occasion. For here and thus I lay, my face like a wall that is white-washing, deathy pale and with the cold drops of perspiration running down it from my forehead, while one after another there dropped in the different gentlemen, who had been invited to meet, and spend the evening with me, to the number of from fifteen to twenty. As the poison of tobacco acts but for a short time, I at length awoke from insensibility, and looked round on the party, my eyes dazzled by the candles which had been lighted in the interim. By way of relieving my embarrassment one of the gentlemen began the conversation, with "Have you seen a paper to day, Mr. Coleridge?" "Sir!" I replied, rubbing my eyes, "I am far from convinced, that a Christian is permitted to read either newspapers or any other works of merely political and temporary interest." This remark, so ludicrously inapposite to, or rather, incongruous with, the purpose, for which I was known to have visited Birmingham, and to assist me in which they were all then met, produced an involuntary and general burst of laughter; and seldom indeed have I passed so many delightful hours, as I enjoyed in that room from the moment of that laugh till an early hour the next morning. Never, perhaps, in so mixed and numerous a party have I since heard conversation sustained with such animation, enriched with such variety of information and enlivened with such a flow of anecdote. Both then and afterwards they all joined in dissuading me from proceeding with my scheme; assured me in the most friendly and yet most flattering expressions, that neither was the employment fit for me, nor

I fit for the employment. Yet, if I determined on persevering in it, they promised to exert themselves to the utmost to procure subscribers, and insisted that I should make no more applications in person, but carry on the convass by proxy. The same hospitable reception, the same dissuasion, and, that failing, the same kind exertions in my behalf, I met with at Manchester, Derby, Nottingham, Sheffield,—indeed, at every place in which I took up my sojourn. I often recall with affectionate pleasure the many respectable men who interested themselves for me, a perfect stranger to them, not a few of whom I can still name among my friends. They will bear witness for me how opposite even then my principles were to those of Jacobinism or even of democracy, and can attest the strict accuracy of the statement which I have left on record in the 10th and 11th numbers of THE FRIEND.

From this rememberable tour I returned with nearly a thousand names on the subscription list of THE WATCHMAN; yet more than half convinced, that prudence dictated the abandonment of the scheme. But for this very reason I persevered in it; for I was at that period of my life so completely hag-ridden by the fear of being influenced by selfish motives, that to know a mode of conduct to be the dictate of prudence was a sort of presumptive proof to my feelings, that the contrary was the dictate of duty. Accordingly, I commenced the work, which was announced in London by long bills in letters larger than had ever been seen before, and which, I have been informed, for I did not see them myself, eclipsed the glories even of the lottery puffs. But alas! the publication of the very first number was delayed beyond the day announced for its appearance. In the second number an essay against fast days, with a most censurable application of a text from Isaiah for its motto, lost me near five hundred of my subscribers at one blow. In the two following numbers I made enemies of all my Jacobin and democratic patrons; for, disgusted by their infidelity, and their adoption of French morals with French *psilosophy;* and perhaps thinking, that charity ought to begin nearest home; instead of abusing the government and the Aristocrats chiefly or entirely, as had been expected of me, I levelled my attacks at "modern patriotism," and even ventured to declare my belief, that whatever the motives of ministers might have been for the sedition, or as it was then the fashion to call them, the *gagging* bills, yet the bills themselves would produce an effect to be desired by all the true friends of freedom, as far as they should contribute to deter men from openly declaiming on subjects, the principles of which they had never bottomed, and from "pleading *to* the poor and ignorant, instead of pleading *for* them." At the same time I avowed my conviction, that national education and a concurring spread of the Gospel were the indispensable condition of any true political amelioration. Thus by the time the seventh number was published, I had the mortification—(but why should I say this, when in truth I cared too little for any thing that concerned my worldly interests to be at all mortified about it?)—of seeing the preceding numbers exposed in sundry old iron shops for a penny a piece. At the ninth number I dropt the work. But from the London publisher I could not obtain a shilling; he was a —— and set me at defiance. From other places I procured but little, and after such delays as rendered that little worth nothing; and I should have been inevitably thrown into jail by my Bristol printer, who refused to wait even for a month, for a sum between eighty and ninety pounds, if the money had not been paid for me by a man by no means affluent, a dear friend, who attached himself to me from my first arrival at Bristol, who has continued my friend with a fidelity unconquered by time or even by my own apparent neglect; a friend from whom I never received an advice that was not wise, nor a remonstrance that was not gentle and affectionate.

Conscientiously an opponent of the first revolutionary war, yet with my eyes thoroughly opened to the true character and impotence of the favourers of revolutionary principles in England, principles which I held in abhorrence,—(for it was part of my political creed, that whoever ceased to act as an individual by making himself a member of any society not sanctioned by his Government, forfeited the rights of a citizen)—a vehement Anti-Ministerialist, but after the invasion of Switzerland, a more vehement Anti-Gallican, and still more intensely an Anti-Jacobin, I retired to a cottage at Stowey, and provided for my scanty maintenance by writing verses for a London Morning Paper. I saw plainly, that literature was not a profession, by which I could expect to live; for I could not disguise from myself, that, whatever my talents might or might not be in other respects, yet they were not of the sort that could enable me to become a popular writer; and that whatever my opinions might be in themselves, they were almost equi-distant from all the three prominent parties, the Pittites, the Foxites, and the Democrats. Of the unsaleable nature of my writings I had an amusing memento one morning from our own servant girl. For happening to rise at an earlier hour than usual, I observed her putting an extravagant quantity of paper into the grate in order to light the fire, and mildly checked her for her wastefulness; "La, Sir!" (replied poor Nanny) "why, it is only Watchmen."

I now devoted myself to poetry and to the study of ethics and psychology; and so profound was my admiration at this time of Hartley's Essay on Man, that I gave his name to my first-born. In addition to the gentleman, my neighbour, whose garden joined on to my little orchard, and the cultivation of whose friendship had been my sole motive in choosing Stowey for my residence, I was so fortunate as to acquire, shortly after my settlement there, an invaluable blessing in the society and neighbourhood of one, to whom I could look up with equal reverence, whether I regarded him as a poet, a philosopher, or a man. His conversation extended to almost all subjects, except physics and politics; with the latter he never troubled himself. Yet neither my retirement nor my utter abstraction from all the disputes of the day could secure me in those jealous times from suspicion and obloquy, which did not stop at me, but extended to my excellent friend, whose perfect innocence was even adduced as a proof of his guilt. One of the many busy sycophants of that day,—(I here use the word sycophant in its original sense, as a wretch who *flatters* the prevailing party by *informing* against his neighbours, under pretence that they are exporters of prohibited *figs* or fancies,—for the moral application of the term it matters not which)—one of these sycophantic law-mongrels, discoursing on the politics of the neighbourhood, uttered the following deep remark: "As to Coleridge, there is not so much harm in *him*, for he is a whirl-brain that talks whatever comes uppermost; but that ——! he is the *dark* traitor. *You never hear* HIM *say a syllable on the subject*."...

Far different were the days to which these anecdotes have carried me back. The dark guesses of some zealous *Quidnunc* met with so congenial a soil in the grave alarm of a titled Dogberry of our neighbourhood, that a spy was actually sent down from the government *pour surveillance* of myself and friend. There must have been not only abundance, but variety of these " honourable men " at the disposal of Ministers: for this proved a very honest fellow. After three weeks' truly Indian perseverance in tracking us, (for we were commonly together,) during all which time seldom were we out of doors, but he contrived to be within hearing,—(and all the while utterly unsuspected; how indeed *could* such a suspicion enter our fancies?)—he not only rejected Sir Dogberry's request that he would try yet a little longer, but declared to him his belief, that both my friend and myself were as good subjects, for aught he could discover to the contrary, as any in His Majesty's dominions. He had repeatedly hid himself, he said, for hours together behind a bank at the sea-side, (our favourite seat,) and overheard our conversation. At first he fancied, that we were aware of our danger; for he often heard me talk of one *Spy Nozy*, which he was inclined to interpret of himself, and of a remarkable feature belonging to him; but he was speedily convinced that it was the name of a man who had made a book and lived long ago. Our talk ran most upon books, and we were perpetually desiring each other to look at *this*, and to listen to *that;* but he could not catch a word about politics. Once he had joined me on the road; (this occurred, as I was returning home alone from my friend's house, which was about three miles from my own cottage,) and, passing himself off as a traveller, he had entered into conversation with me, and talked of purpose in a democrat way in order to draw me out. The result, it appears, not only convinced him that I was no friend of Jacobinism; but, (he added,) I had "plainly made it out to be such a silly as well as wicked thing, that he felt ashamed though he had only *put it on.*" I distinctly remembered the occurrence, and had mentioned it immediately on my return, repeating what the traveller with his Bardolph nose had said, with my own answer; and so little did I suspect the true object of my "tempter ere accuser," that I expressed with no small pleasure my hope and belief, that the conversation had been of some service to the poor misled malcontent. This incident therefore prevented all doubt as to the truth of the report, which through a friendly medium came to me from the master of the village inn, who had been ordered to entertain the Government gentleman in his best manner, but above all to be silent concerning such a person being in his house. At length he received Sir Dogberry's commands to accompany his guest at the final interview; and, after the absolving suffrage of the *gentleman honoured with the confidence of Ministers*, answered, as follows, to the following queries? D. Well, landlord! and what do you know of the person in question? L. I see him often pass by with maister ——, my landlord, (*that is, the owner of the house,*) and sometimes with the new-comers at Holford; but I never said a word to him or he to me. D. But do you not know, that he has distributed papers and hand-bills of a seditious nature among the common people? L. No, your Honour! I never heard of such a thing. D. Have you not seen this Mr. Coleridge, or heard of, his haranguing and talking to knots and clusters of the inhabitants?—What are you grinning at, Sir? L. Beg your Honour's pardon! but I was only thinking, how they'd have stared at him. If what I have heard be true, your Honour! they would not have understood a word he said. When our Vicar was here, Dr. L. the master of the great school and Canon of Windsor, there was a great dinner party at maister ——'s; and one of the farmers, that was there, told us that he and the Doctor talked real Hebrew Greek at each other for an hour together after dinner. D. Answer the question, Sir! does he ever harangue the people? L. I hope, your Honour an't angry with me. I can say no more than I know. I never saw him talking with any one, but my landlord, and our curate, and the strange gentleman. D. Has he not been seen wandering on the hills towards the Channel, and along the shore, with books and papers in his hand, taking charts and maps of the country? L. Why, as to that, your Honour! I own, I have heard; I am sure, I would not wish to say ill of any body; but it is certain, that I have heard—D. Speak out, man! don't be afraid, you are doing your duty to your King and Government. What have you heard? L. Why, folks do say, your Honour! as how that he is a *Poet*, and that he is going to put Quantock and all about here in print; and as they be so much together, I suppose that the strange gentleman has some *consarn* in the business."—So ended this formidable inquisition, the latter part of which alone requires explanation, and at the same time entitles the anecdote to a place in my literary life. I had considered it as a defect in the admirable poem of The Task, that the subject, which gives the title to the work, was not, and indeed could not be, carried on beyond the three or four first pages, and that, throughout the poem, the connections are frequently awkward, and the transitions abrupt and arbitrary. I sought for a subject, that should give equal room and freedom for description, incident, and impassioned reflections on men, nature, and society, yet supply in itself a natural connection to the parts, and unity to the whole. Such a subject I conceived myself to have found in a stream, traced from its source in the hills among the yellow-red moss and conical glass-shaped tufts of bent, to the first break or fall, where its drops become audible, and it begins to form a channel; thence to the peat and turf barn, itself built of the same dark squares as it sheltered; to the sheepfold; to the first cultivated plot of ground; to the lonely cottage and its bleak garden won from the heath; to the hamlet, the villages, the market-town, the manufactories, and the sea-port. My walks therefore were almost daily on the top of Quantock, and among its sloping coombes. With my pencil and memorandum-book in my hand, I was *making studies*, as the artists call them, and often moulding my thoughts into verse, with the objects and imagery immediately before my senses. Many circumstances, evil and good, intervened to prevent the completion of the poem, which was to have been entitled The Brook. Had I finished the work, it was my purpose in the heat of the moment to have dedicated it to our then committee of public safety as containing the charts and maps, with which I was to have supplied the French Government in aid of their plans of invasion. And these too for a tract of coast that, from Clevedon to Minehead, scarcely permits the approach of a fishing-boat!

All my experience from my first entrance into life to the present hour is in favour of the warning maxim, that the man, who opposes *in toto* the political or religious zealots of his age, is safer from their obloquy than he who differs from them but in one or two points, or perhaps only in degree. By that transfer of the feelings of private life into the discussion of public questions, which is the queen bee in the hive of party fanaticism, the partisan has more sympathy with an intemperate opposite than with a moderate friend. We now enjoy an intermission, and long may it continue! In addition to far higher and more important merits, our present Bible societies and other numerous associations for national or charitable objects, may serve perhaps to carry off the superfluous activity and fervour of stirring minds in innocent hyperboles and the bustle of management. But the poison-tree is not dead, though the sap may for a season have subsided to its roots. At least let us not be lulled into such a notion of our entire security, as not to keep watch and ward, even on our best feelings. I have seen gross intolerance shown in support of toleration; sectarian antipathy most obtrusively displayed in the promotion of an undistinguishing comprehension of sects; and acts of cruelty, (I had almost said,) of treachery, committed in furtherance of an object vitally important to the cause of humanity; and all this by men too of naturally kind dispositions and exemplary conduct.

The magic rod of fanaticism is preserved in the very *adyta* of human nature; and needs only the re-exciting warmth of a master hand to bud forth afresh and produce the old fruits. The horror of the Peasants' war in Germany, and the direful effects of the Anabaptists' tenets, (which differed only from those of Jacobinism by the substitution of theological for philosophical jargon,) struck all Europe for a time with affright. Yet little more than a century was sufficient to obliterate all effective memory of these events. The same principles with similar though less dreadful consequences were again at work from the imprisonment of the first Charles to the restoration of his son. The fanatic maxim of extirpating fanaticism by persecution produced a civil war. The war ended in the victory of the insurgents; but the temper survived, and Milton had abundant grounds for asserting, that "Presbyter was but OLD PRIEST writ large!" One good result, thank heaven! of this zealotry was the re-establishment of the church. And now it might have been hoped, that the mischievous spirit would have been bound for a season, "and a seal set upon him, that he should deceive the *nation* no more."[1] But no! The ball of persecution was taken up with undiminished vigour by the persecuted. The same fanatic principle that, under the solemn oath and covenant, had turned cathedrals into stables, destroyed the rarest trophies of art and ancestral piety, and hunted the brightest ornaments of learning and religion into holes and corners, now marched under episcopal banners, and, having first crowded the prisons of England, emptied its whole vial of wrath on the miserable Covenanters of Scotland.[2] A merciful providence at length constrained both parties to join against a common enemy. A wise government followed; and the established church became, and now is,

[1] Revelation xx. 3.

[2] See *Laing's* History of Scotland.—*Walter Scott's* Bards, ballads, &c.

not only the brightest example, but our best and only sure bulwark, of toleration!—the true and indispensable bank against a new inundation of persecuting zeal—*Esto perpetua!*

A long interval of quiet succeeded; or rather, the exhaustion had produced a cold fit of the ague which was *symptomatized* by indifference among the many, and a tendency to infidelity or scepticism in the educated classes. At length those feelings of disgust and hatred, which for a brief while the multitude had attached to the crimes and absurdities of sectarian and democratic fanaticism, were transferred to the oppressive privileges of the *noblesse*, and the luxury, intrigues and favouritism of the continental courts. The same principles, dressed in the ostentatious garb of a fashionable philosophy, once more rose triumphant and effected the French revolution. And have we not within the last three or four years had reason to apprehend, that the detestable maxims and correspondent measures of the late French despotism had already bedimmed the public recollections of democratic phrensy; had drawn off to other objects the electric force of the feelings which had massed and upheld those recollections; and that a favourable concurrence of occasions was alone wanting to awaken the thunder and precipitate the lightning from the opposite quarter of the political heaven?

In part from constitutional indolence, which in the very hey-day of hope had kept my enthusiasm in check, but still more from the habits and influences of a classical education and academic pursuits, scarcely had a year elapsed from the commencement of my literary and political adventures before my mind sank into a state of thorough disgust and despondency, both with regard to the disputes and the parties disputant. With more than *poetic* feeling I exclaimed:

The sensual and the dark rebel in vain,
Slaves by their own compulsion! In mad game
They break their manacles, to wear the *name*
Of freedom, graven on a heavier chain.
O Liberty! with profitless endeavour
Have I pursued thee many a weary hour;
But thou nor swell'st the victor's pomp, nor ever
Didst breathe thy soul in forms of human power!
  Alike from all, howe'er they praise thee,
  (Nor prayer nor boastful name delays thee)
  From Superstition's harpy minions
  And factious Blasphemy's obscener slaves,
  Thou speedest on thy cherub pinions,
The guide of homeless winds and playmate of the waves!

I retired to a cottage in Somersetshire at the foot of Quantock, and devoted my thoughts and studies to the foundations of religion and morals....

Soon after my return from Germany I was solicited to undertake the literary and political department in the Morning Post; and I acceded to the proposal on the condition that the paper should thenceforwards be conducted on certain fixed and announced principles, and that I should neither be obliged nor requested to deviate from them in favour of any party or any event. In consequence, that Journal became and for many years continued anti-ministerial indeed, yet with a very qualified approbation of the opposition, and with far greater earnestness and zeal both anti-Jacobin and anti-Gallican. To this hour I cannot find reason to approve of the first war either in its commencement or its conduct. Nor can I understand, with what reason either Mr. Percival, (whom I am singular enough to regard as the best and wisest minister of this reign,) or the present Administration, can be said to have pursued the plans of Mr. Pitt. The love of their country, and perseverant hostility to French principles and French ambition are indeed honourable qualities common to them and to their predecessor. But it appears to me as clear as the evidence of facts can render any question of history, that the successes of the Percival and of the existing ministry have been owing to their having pursued measures the direct contrary to Mr. Pitt's. Such for instance are the concentration of the national force to one object; the abandonment of the subsidizing policy, so far at least as neither to goad nor bribe the continental courts into war, till the convictions of their subjects had rendered it a war of their own seeking; and above all, in their manly and generous reliance on the good sense of the English people, and on that loyalty which is linked to the very heart of the nation by the system of credit and the interdependence of property.

Be this as it may, I am persuaded that the Morning Post proved a far more useful ally to the Government in its most important objects, in consequence of its being generally considered as moderately anti-ministerial, than if it had been the avowed eulogist of Mr. Pitt. The few, whose curiosity or fancy should lead them to turn over the journals of that date, may find a small proof of this in the frequent charges made by the Morning Chronicle, that such and such essays or leading paragraphs had been sent from the Treasury. The rapid and unusual increase in the sale of the Morning Post is a sufficient pledge, that genuine impartiality with a respectable portion of literary talent will secure the success of a newspaper without the aid of party or ministerial patronage. But by impartiality I mean an honest and enlightened adherence to a code of intelligible principles previously announced, and faithfully referred to in support of every judgment on men and events; not indiscriminate abuse, not the indulgence of an editor's own malignant passions, and still less, if that be possible, a determination to make money by flattering the envy and cupidity, the vindictive restlessness and self-conceit of the half-witted vulgar; a determination almost fiendish, but which, I have been informed, has been boastfully avowed by one man, the most notorious of these mob-sycophants! From the commencement of the Addington administration to the present day, whatever I have written in THE MORNING POST, or (after that paper was transferred to other proprietors) in THE COURIER, has been in defence or furtherance of the measures of Government.

> Things of this nature scarce survive that night
> That gives them birth; they perish in the sight;
> Cast by so far from *after-life*, that there
> Can scarcely aught be said, but that *they were!*

Yet in these labours I employed, and, in the belief of partial friends wasted, the prime and manhood of my intellect. Most assuredly, they added nothing to my fortune or my reputation. The industry of the week supplied the necessities of the week. From government or the friends of government I not only never received remuneration, nor ever expected it; but I was never honoured with a single acknowledgment, or expression of satisfaction. Yet the retrospect is far from painful or matter of regret. I am not indeed silly enough to take as any thing more than a violent hyperbole of party debate, Mr. Fox's assertion that the *late* war (I trust that the epithet is not prematurely applied) was a war produced by the Morning Post; or I should be proud to have the words inscribed on my tomb. As little do I regard the circumstance, that I was a specified object of Buonaparte's resentment during my residence in Italy in consequence of those essays in the Morning Post during the peace of Amiens. Of this I was warned, directly, by Baron Von Humboldt, the Prussian Plenipotentiary, who at that time was the minister of the Prussian court at Rome; and indirectly, through his secretary, by Cardinal Fesch himself. Nor do I lay any greater weight on the confirming fact, that an order for my arrest was sent from Paris, from which danger I was rescued by the kindness of a noble Benedictine, and the gracious connivance of that good old man, the present Pope. For the late tyrant's vindictive appetite was omnivorous, and preyed equally on a Duc d'Enghien,[1] and the writer of a newspaper paragraph.

[1] I seldom think of the murder of this illustrious Prince without recollecting the lines of Valerius Flaccus:

> ——————— super ipsius ingens
> Instat fama viri, virtusque haud læta tyranno;
> Ergo anteire metus, juvenemque exstinguere pergit.
>
> Argonaut. I. 29.

Like a true vulture,[1] Napoleon with an eye not less telescopic, and with a taste equally coarse in his ravin, could descend from the most dazzling heights to pounce on the leveret in the brake, or even on the field mouse amid the grass. But I do derive a gratification from the knowledge, that my essays contributed to introduce the practice of placing the questions and events of the day in a moral point of view; in giving a dignity to particular measures by tracing their policy or impolicy to permanent principles, and an interest to principles by the application of them to individual measures. In Mr. Burke's writings indeed the germs of almost all political truths may be found. But I dare assume to myself the merit of having first explicitly defined and analyzed the nature of Jacobinism; and that in distinguishing the Jacobin from the republican, the democrat, and the mere demagogue, I both rescued the word from remaining a mere term of abuse, and put on their guard many honest minds, who even in their heat of zeal against Jacobinism, admitted or supported principles from which the worst parts of that system may be legitimately deduced. That these are not necessary practical results of such principles, we owe to that fortunate inconsequence of our nature, which permits the heart to rectify the errors of the understanding. The detailed examination of the consular Government and its pretended constitution, and the proof given by me, that it was a consummate despotism in masquerade, extorted a recantation even from the Morning Chronicle, which had previously extolled this constitution as the perfection of a wise and regulated liberty. On every great occurrence I endeavoured to discover in past history the event, that most nearly resembled it. I procured, wherever it was possible, the contemporary historians, memorialists, and pamphleteers. Then fairly subtracting the points of difference from those of likeness, as the balance favoured the former or the latter, I conjectured that the result would be the same or different. In the series of essays entitled "A comparison of France under Napoleon with Rome under the first Cæsars," and in those which followed " On the probable final restoration of the Bourbons," I feel myself authorized to affirm, by the effect produced on many intelligent men, that, were the dates wanting, it might have been suspected that the essays had been written within the last twelve months. The same plan I pursued at the commencement of the Spanish revolution, and with the same success, taking the war of the United Provinces with Philip II. as the ground work of the comparison. I have mentioned this from no motives of vanity, nor even from motives of self defence, which would justify a certain degree of egotism, especially

1 *Θηρᾷ δὲ καὶ τὸν χῆνα καὶ τὴν δορκάδα,*
Καὶ τὸν λαγωὸν, καὶ τὸ τῶν ταύρων γένος.
Manuel Phile, *De Animal. Proprietat.* sect. i. l. 12.

if it be considered, how often and grossly I have been attacked for sentiments, which I had exerted my best powers to confute and expose, and how grievously these charges acted to my disadvantage while I was in Malta. Or rather they would have done so, if my own feelings had not precluded the wish of a settled establishment in that island. But I have mentioned it from the full persuasion that, armed with the two-fold knowledge of history and the human mind, a man will scarcely err in his judgment concerning the sum total of any future national event, if he have been able to procure the original documents of the past, together with the authentic accounts of the present, and if he have a philosophic tact for what is truly important in facts, and in most instances therefore for such facts as the dignity of history has excluded from the volumes of our modern compilers, by the courtesy of the age entitled historians.

To have lived in vain must be a painful thought to any man, and especially so to him who has made literature his profession. I should therefore rather condole than be angry with the mind, which could attribute to no worthier feelings than those of vanity or self love, the satisfaction which I acknowledge myself to have enjoyed from the republication of my political essays (either whole or as extracts) not only in many of our own provincial papers, but in the federal journals throughout America. I regarded it as some proof of my not having laboured altogether in vain, that from the articles written by me shortly before and at the commencement of the late unhappy war with America, not only the sentiments were adopted, but in some instances the very language, in several of the Massachusetts state papers.

But no one of these motives nor all conjointly would have impelled me to a statement so uncomfortable to my own feelings, had not my character been repeatedly attacked, by an unjustifiable intrusion on private life, as of a man incorrigibly idle, and who intrusted not only with ample talents, but favoured with unusual opportunities of improving them, had nevertheless suffered them to rust away without any efficient exertion, either for his own good or that of his fellow creatures. Even if the compositions, which I have made public, and that too in a form the most certain of an extensive circulation, though the least flattering to an author's self-love, had been published in books, they would have filled a respectable number of volumes, though every passage of merely temporary interest were omitted. My prose writings have been charged with a disproportionate demand on the attention; with an excess of refinement in the mode of arriving at truths; with beating the ground for that which might have been run down by the eye; with the length and laborious construction of my periods; in short with obscurity and the love of paradox. But my severest critics have not pretended to have found in my compositions triviality, or traces of a mind that shrunk from the toil of thinking. No one has charged me with tricking out in other words the thoughts of others, or with hashing up anew the *cramben jam decies coctam* of English literature or philosophy. Seldom have I written that in a day, the acquisition or investigation of which had not cost me the previous labour of a month.

But are books the only channel through which the stream of intellectual usefulness can flow? Is the diffusion of truth to be estimated by publications; or publications by the truth, which they diffuse or at least contain? I speak it in the excusable warmth of a mind stung by an accusation, which has not only been advanced in reviews of the widest circulation, not only registered in the bulkiest works of periodical literature, but by frequency of repetition has become an admitted fact in private literary circles, and thoughtlessly repeated by too many who call themselves my friends, and whose own recollections ought to have suggested a contrary testimony. Would that the criterion of a scholar's utility were the number and moral value of the truths, which he has been the means of throwing into the general circulation; or the number and value of the minds, whom by his conversation or letters, he has excited into activity, and supplied with the germs of their after-growth! A distinguished rank might not indeed, even then, be awarded to my exertions; but I should dare look forward with confidence to an honourable acquittal. I should dare appeal to the numerous and respectable audiences, which at different times and in different places honoured my lecture rooms with their attendance, whether the points of view from which the subjects treated of were surveyed, whether the grounds of my reasoning were such, as they had heard or read elsewhere, or have since found in previous publications. I can conscientiously declare, that the complete success of the REMORSE on the first night of its representation did not give me as great or as heart-felt a pleasure, as the observation that the pit and boxes were crowded with faces familiar to me, though of individuals whose names I did not know, and of whom I knew nothing, but that they had attended one or other of my courses of lectures. It is an excellent though perhaps somewhat vulgar proverb, that there are cases where a man may be as well "*in for a pound as for a penny.*" To those, who from ignorance of the serious injury I have received from this rumour of having dreamed away my life to no purpose, injuries which I unwillingly remember at all, much less am disposed to record in a sketch of my literary life; or to those, who from their own feelings, or the gratification they derive from thinking contemptuously of others, would like Job's comforters attribute these complaints, extorted from me by the sense of wrong, to self conceit or presumptuous vanity, I have already furnished such ample materials, that I shall gain nothing by withholding the remainder. I will not therefore hesitate to ask the consciences of those, who from their long acquaintance with me and with the circumstances are best qualified to decide or be my judges, whether the restitution of the *suum cuique* would increase or detract from my literary reputation. In this exculpation I hope to be understood as speaking of myself comparatively, and in proportion to the claims, which others are entitled to make on my time or my talents. By what I *have* effected, am I to be judged by my fellow men; what I *could* have done, is a question for my own conscience. On my own account I may perhaps have had sufficient reason to lament my deficiency in self-control, and the neglect of concentering my powers to the realization of some permanent work. But to verse rather than to prose, if to either, belongs the voice of mourning for

> Keen pangs of Love, awakening as a babe
> Turbulent, with an outcry in the heart;
> And fears self-willed that shunned the eye of hope;
> And hope that scarce would know itself from fear;
> Sense of past youth, and manhood come in vain,
> And genius given and knowledge won in vain;
> And all which I had culled in wood-walks wild,
> And all which patient toil had reared, and all,
> Commune with thee had opened out—but flowers
> Strewed on my corpse, and borne upon my bier,
> In the same coffin, for the self-same grave!

These will exist, for the future, I trust, only in the poetic strains, which the feelings at the time called forth. In those only, gentle reader,

> Affectus animi varios, bellumque sequacis
> Perlegis invidiæ, curasque revolvis inanes,
> Quas humilis tenero stylus olim effudit in ævo.
> Perlegis et lacrymas, et quod pharetratus acuta
> Ille puer puero fecit mihi cuspide vulnus.
> Omnia paulatim consumit longior ætas,
> Vivendoque simul morimur, rapimurque manendo.
> Ipse mihi collatus enim non ille videbor;
> Frons alia est, moresque alii, nova mentis imago,
> Vox aliudque sonat—Jamque observatio vitæ
> Multa dedit—lugere nihil, ferre omnia; jamque
> Paulatim lacrymas rerum experientia tersit.

CHAP. XI. *An affectionate exhortation to those who in early life feel themselves disposed to become authors.*

The beginning of this chapter may be quoted:

It was a favourite remark of the late Mr. Whitbread's, that no man does any thing from a single motive. The separate motives, or rather moods of mind, which produced the preceding reflections and anecdotes have been laid open to the reader in each separate instance. But an interest in the welfare of those, who at the present time may be in circumstances not dissimilar to my own at my first entrance into life, has been the constant accompaniment, and (as it were) the under-song of all my feelings. Whitehead exerting the prerogative of his laureatship addressed to youthful poets a poetic Charge, which is perhaps the best, and certainly the most interesting, of his works. With no other privilege than that of sympathy and sincere good wishes, I would address an affectionate exhortation to the youthful *literati*, grounded on my own experience. It will be but short; for the beginning, middle, and end converge to one charge: *never pursue literature as a trade.* With the exception of one extraordinary man, I have never known an individual, least of all an individual of genius, healthy or happy without a *profession*, that is, some *regular* employment, which does not depend on the will of the moment, and which can be carried on so far *mechanically* that an average *quantum* only of health, spirits, and intellectual exertion are requisite to its faithful discharge. Three hours of leisure, unannoyed by any alien anxiety, and looked forward to with delight as a change and recreation, will suffice to realize in literature a larger product of what is truly genial, than weeks of compulsion. Money, and immediate reputation form only an arbitrary and accidental end of literary labour. The hope of increasing them by any given exertion will often prove a stimulant to industry; but the necessity of acquiring them will in all works of genius convert the stimulant into a narcotic. Motives by excess reverse their very nature, and instead of exciting, stun and stupify the mind. For it is one contradistinction of genius from talent, that its predominant end is always comprised in the means; and this is one of the many points, which establish an analogy between genius and virtue. Now though talents may exist without genius, yet as genius cannot exist, certainly not manifest itself, without talents, I would advise every scholar, who feels the genial power working within him, so far to make a division between the two, as that he should devote his talents to the acquirement of competence in some known trade or profession, and his genius to objects of his tranquil and unbiassed choice; while the consciousness of being actuated in both alike by the sincere desire to perform his duty, will alike ennoble both. "My dear young friend," (I would say) "suppose yourself established in any honourable occupation. From the manufactory or counting house, from the law-court, or from having visited your last patient, you return at evening,

> Dear tranquil time, when the sweet sense of Home
> Is sweetest————

to your family, prepared for its social enjoyments, with the very countenances of your wife and children brightened, and their voice of welcome made doubly welcome, by the knowledge that, as far as *they* are concerned, you have satisfied the demands of the day by the labour of the day. Then, when you retire into your study, in the books on your shelves you revisit so many venerable friends with whom you can converse. Your own spirit scarcely less free from personal anxieties than the great minds, that in those books are still living for you! Even your writing desk with its blank paper and all its other implements will appear as a chain of flowers, capable of linking your feelings as well as thoughts to events and characters past or to come; not a chain of iron, which binds you down to think of the future and the remote by recalling the claims and feelings of the peremptory present. But why should I say *retire?* The habits of active life and daily intercourse with the stir of the world will tend to give you such self-command, that the presence of your family will be no interruption. Nay, the social silence, or undisturbing voices of a wife or sister will be like a restorative atmosphere, or soft music which moulds a dream without becoming its object. If facts are required to prove the possibility of combining weighty performances in literature with full and independent employment, the works of Cicero and Xenophon among the ancients; of Sir Thomas More, Bacon, Baxter, or to refer at once to later and contemporary instances, Darwin and Roscoe, are at once decisive of the question.

CHAP. XII. *A Chapter of requests and premonitions concerning the perusal or omission of the chapter that follows.*

The concluding paragraph of this chapter should be noticed:

I shall now proceed to the nature and *genesis* of the Imagination; but I must first take leave to notice, that after a more accurate perusal of Mr. Wordsworth's remarks on the Imagination, in his preface to the new edition of his poems, I find that my conclusions are not so consentient with his as, I confess, I had taken for granted. In an article contributed by me to Mr. Southey's Omniana, *On the soul and its organs of sense*, are the following sentences. "These (the human faculties) I would arrange under the different senses and powers: as the eye, the ear, the touch, &c.; the imitative power, voluntary and automatic; the imagination, or shaping and modifying power; the fancy, or the aggregative and associative power; the understanding, or the regulative, substantiating and realizing power; the speculative reason, *vis theoretica et scientifica*, or the power by which we produce, or aim to produce unity, necessity, and universality in all our knowledge by means of principles *a priori*[1]; the will, or practical reason; the faculty of choice (*Germanice*, Willkühr) and (distinct both from the moral will and the choice,) the *sensation* of volition, which I have found reason to include under the head of single and double touch." To this, as far as it relates to the subject in question, namely the words (*the aggregative and associative power*) Mr. Wordsworth's "objection is only that the definition is too general. To aggregate and to associate, to evoke and to combine, belong as well to the Imagination as to the Fancy." I reply, that if, by the power of evoking and combining, Mr. Wordsworth means the same as, and no more than, I meant by the aggregative and associative, I continue to deny, that it belongs at all to the Imagination; and I am disposed to conjecture, that he has mistaken the co-presence of Fancy with Imagination for the operation of the latter singly. A man may work with two very different tools at the same moment; each has its share in the work, but the work effected by each is distinct and different. But it will probably appear in the next chapter, that deeming it necessary to go back much further than Mr. Wordsworth's subject required or permitted, I have attached a meaning to both Fancy and Imagination, which he had not in view, at least while he was writing that preface. He will judge. Would to Heaven, I might meet with many such readers! I will conclude with the words of Bishop Jeremy Taylor: "He to whom all things are one, who draweth all things to one, and seeth all things in one, may enjoy true peace and rest of spirit."[2]

CHAP. XIII. *On the imagination, or esemplastic power.*

After beginning this chapter Coleridge breaks off and gives an elaborate excuse for not pursuing either it or the whole subject. The last paragraph may be quoted.

The IMAGINATION then I consider either as primary, or secondary. The primary IMAGINATION I hold to be the living power and prime agent of all human perception, and as a repetition in the finite mind of the eternal act of creation in the infinite I AM. The secondary I consider as an echo of the former, co-existing with the conscious will,

[1] This phrase, *a priori*, is in common most grossly misunderstood, and an absurdity burdened on it, which it does not deserve! By knowledge *a priori*, we do not mean, that we can know any thing previously to experience, which would be a contradiction in terms; but that having once known it by occasion of experience (that is, something acting upon us from without) we then know that it must have pre-existed, or the experience itself would have been impossible. By experience only I know, that I have eyes; but then my reason convinces me, that I must have had eyes in order to the experience.

[2] Jer. Taylor's *Via pacis*.

yet still as identical with the primary in the *kind* of its agency, and differing only in *degree*, and in the *mode* of its operation. It dissolves, diffuses, dissipates, in order to re-create: or where this process is rendered impossible, yet still at all events it struggles to idealize and to unify. It is essentially *vital*, even as all objects (*as* objects) are essentially fixed and dead.

FANCY, on the contrary, has no other counters to play with, but fixities and definities. The Fancy is indeed no other than a mode of Memory emancipated from the order of time and space; while it is blended with, and modified by that empirical phenomenon of the will, which we express by the word Choice. But equally with the ordinary memory the Fancy must receive all its materials ready made from the law of association.

For Chapters XIV to XXII see text. The conclusion of Chapter XXII, omitted from the text, reads thus:

How small the proportion of the defects are to the beauties, I have repeatedly declared; and that no one of them originates in deficiency of poetic genius. Had they been more and greater, I should still, as a friend to his literary character in the present age, consider an analytic display of them as *pure gain*; if only it removed, as surely to all reflecting minds even the foregoing analysis must have removed, the strange mistake, so slightly grounded yet so widely and industriously propagated, of Mr. Wordsworth's turn for *simplicity!* I am not half as much irritated by hearing his enemies abuse him for vulgarity of style, subject, and conception; as I am disgusted with the gilded side of the same meaning, as displayed by some affected admirers, with whom he is, forsooth, a " sweet, simple poet! " and *so* natural, that little master Charles and his younger sister are *so* charmed with them, that they play at "Goody Blake," or at "Johnny and Betty Foy!"

Were the collection of poems, published with these biographical sketches, important enough, (which I am not vain enough to believe,) to deserve such a distinction; *even as I have done, so would I be done unto.*

For more than eighteen months have the volume of Poems, entitled SIBYLLINE LEAVES, and the present volumes, up to this page, been printed, and ready for publication. But, ere I speak of myself in the tones, which are alone natural to me under the circumstances of late years, I would fain present myself to the Reader as I was in the first dawn of my literary life:

> When Hope grew round me, like the climbing vine,
> And fruits, and foliage, not my own, seem'd mine!

For this purpose I have selected from the letters, which I wrote home from Germany, those which appeared likely to be most interesting, and at the same time most pertinent to the title of this work.

After Chapter XXII come *Satyrane's Letters, I, II and III*, reprinted from *The Friend*. These embody recollections of Coleridge's visit to Germany in 1798, and, to use the distinction always associated with him, they are " objective " rather than " subjective."

Chap. XXIII has no title. It contains a lengthy criticism of Maturin's play called *Bertram* reprinted from *The Courier* Aug. 29, Sept. 7, 9, 10 and 11, 1816.

CHAP. XXIV. *Conclusion.*

A personal passage from this chapter may be quoted:

I shall not make this an excuse, however, for troubling my readers with any complaints or explanations, with which, as readers, they have little or no concern. It may suffice, (for the present at least,) to declare, that the causes that have delayed the publication of these volumes for so long a period after they had been printed off, were not connected with any neglect of my own; and that they would form an instructive comment on the chapter concerning *authorship as a trade*, addressed to young men of genius in the first volume of this work. I remember the ludicrous effect produced on my mind by the first sentence of an auto-biography, which, happily for the writer, was as meagre in incidents as it is well possible for the life of an individual to be—" The *eventful* life which I am about to record, from the hour in which I rose into existence on this planet, &c." Yet when, notwithstanding this warning example of self-importance before me, I review my own life, I cannot refrain from applying the same epithet to it, and with more than ordinary emphasis—and no private feeling, that affected myself only, should prevent me from *publishing* the same, (for *write* it I assuredly shall, should life and leisure be granted me,) if continued reflection should strengthen my present belief, that my history would add its contingent to the enforcement of one important truth, to wit, that we must not only love our neighbours as ourselves, but ourselves likewise as our neighbours; and that we can do neither unless we love God above both.

Who lives, that's not
Depraved or depraves? Who dies, *that bears*
Not one spurn to the grave—of their friends' gift?

Strange as the delusion may appear, yet it is most true, that three years ago I did not know or believe that I had an enemy in the world: and now even my strongest sensations of gratitude are mingled with fear, and I reproach myself for being too often disposed to ask,—Have I one friend?—During the many years which intervened between the composition and the publication of the CHRISTABEL, it became almost as well known among literary men as if it had been on common sale; the same references were made to it, and the same liberties taken with it, even to the very names of the imaginary persons in the poem. From almost all of our most celebrated poets, and from some with whom I had no personal acquaintance, I either received or heard of expressions of admiration that, (I can truly say,) appeared to myself utterly disproportionate to a work, that pretended to be nothing more than a common Faery Tale. Many, who had allowed no merit to my other poems, whether printed or manuscript, and who have frankly told me as much, uniformly made an exception in favour of the CHRISTABEL and the poem entitled LOVE. Year after year, and in societies of the most different kinds, I had been entreated to recite it: and the result was still the same in all, and altogether different in this respect from the effect produced by the occasional recitation of any other poems I had composed.—This before the publication. And since then, with very few exceptions, I have heard nothing but abuse, and this too in a spirit of bitterness at least as disproportionate to the pretensions of the poem, had it been the most pitiably below mediocrity, as the previous eulogies, and far more inexplicable....This may serve as a warning to authors, that in their calculations on the probable reception of a poem, they must subtract to a large amount from the panegyric, which may have encouraged them to publish it, however unsuspicious and however various the sources of this panegyric may have been. And, first, allowances must be made for private enmity, of the very existence of which they had perhaps entertained no suspicion—for personal enmity behind the mask of anonymous criticism: secondly for the necessity of a certain proportion of abuse and ridicule in a Review, in order to make it saleable, in consequence of which, if they have no friends behind the scenes, the chance must needs be against them; but lastly and chiefly, for the excitement and temporary sympathy of feeling, which the recitation of the poem by an admirer, especially if he be at once a warm admirer and a man of acknowledged celebrity, calls forth in the audience. For this is really a species of animal magnetism, in which the enkindling reciter, by perpetual comment of looks and tones, lends his own will and apprehensive faculty to his auditors. They *live* for the time within the dilated sphere of his intellectual being. It is equally possible, though not equally common, that a reader left to himself should sink below the poem, as that the poem left to itself should flag beneath the feelings of the reader.—But, in my own instance, I had the additional misfortune of having been gossiped about, as devoted to metaphysics, and worse than all, to a system incomparably nearer to the visionary flights of Plato, and even to the jargon of the Mystics, than to the established tenets of Locke. Whatever therefore appeared with my name was condemned beforehand, as predestined metaphysics. In a dramatic poem, which had been submitted by me to a gentleman of great influence in the theatrical world, occurred the following passage:—

> O we are querulous creatures! Little less
> Than all things can suffice to make us happy:
> And little more than nothing is enough
> To make us wretched.

Aye, here now! (exclaimed the critic) here come Coleridge's *Metaphysics!* And the very same motive (that is, not that the lines were unfit for the present state of our immense theatres; but that they were *metaphysics*[1]) was assigned elsewhere for the rejection of the two following passages. The first is spoken in answer to a usurper, who had rested his plea on the circumstance, that he had been chosen by the acclamations of the people.—

> What people? How convened? or, if convened,
> Must not the magic power that charms together
> Millions of men in council, needs have power
> To win or wield them? Rather, O far rather
> Shout forth thy titles to yon circling mountains,
> And with a thousand-fold reverberation
> Make the rocks flatter thee, and the volleying air,
> Unbribed, shout back to thee, King Emerick!
> By wholesome laws to embank the sovereign power,
> To deepen by restraint, and by prevention
> Of lawless will to amass and guide the flood
> In its majestic channel, is man's task
> And the true patriot's glory! In all else
> Men safelier trust to Heaven, than to themselves
> When least themselves: even in those whirling crowds
> Where folly is contagious, and too oft
> Even wise men leave their better sense at home,
> To chide and wonder at them, when returned.

The second passage is in the mouth of an old and experienced courtier, betrayed by the man in whom he had most trusted.

[1] Poor unlucky Metaphysics! and what are they? A single sentence expresses the object and thereby the contents of this science. Γνῶθι σεαυτόν:

> *Nosce te ipsum,*
> *Tuque Deum, quantum licet, inque Deo omnia noscas.*

Know thyself: and so shalt thou know God, as far as is permitted to a creature, and in God all things.—Surely, there is a strange—nay, rather a too natural—aversion in many to know themselves.

And yet Sarolta, simple, inexperienced,
Could see him as he was, and often warned me.
Whence learned she this?—O she was innocent!
And to be innocent is Nature's wisdom!
The fledge-dove knows the prowlers of the air,
Feared soon as seen, and flutters back to shelter.
And the young steed recoils upon his haunches,
The never-yet-seen adder's hiss first heard.
O surer than suspicion's hundred eyes
Is that fine sense, which to the pure in heart,
By mere oppugnancy of their own goodness,
Reveals the approach of evil.

As therefore my character as a writer could not easily be more injured by an overt act than it was already in consequence of the report, I published a work, a large portion of which was professedly metaphysical. A long delay occurred between its first annunciation and its appearance; it was reviewed therefore by anticipation with a malignity, so avowedly and exclusively personal, as is, I believe, unprecedented even in the present contempt of all common humanity that disgraces and endangers the liberty of the press. After its appearance, the author of this lampoon undertook to review it in the Edinburgh Review; and under the single condition, that he should have written what he himself really thought, and have criticised the work as he would have done had its author been indifferent to him, I should have chosen that man myself, both from the vigour and the originality of his mind, and from his particular acuteness in speculative reasoning, before all others.—I remembered Catullus's lines,

Desine de quoquam quicquam bene velle mereri,
  Aut aliquem fieri posse putare pium.
Omnia sunt ingrata: nihil fecisse benigne est:
  Immo, etiam tædet, tædet obestque magis;
Ut mihi, quem nemo gravius nec acerbius urget,
  Quam modo qui me unum atque unicum amicum habuit.

But I can truly say, that the grief with which I read this rhapsody of predetermined insult, had the rhapsodist himself for its whole and sole object.

[The reviewer referred to is Hazlitt. The "autobiography" promised in this paragraph was never written.]

APPENDIX II

WORDSWORTH'S PREFACE TO *LYRICAL BALLADS*

[This is the final form of the Preface. The earlier versions will be found in *Lyrical Ballads* edited by George Sampson (Methuen). See also the notes to this Appendix.]

The first Volume of these Poems has already been submitted to general perusal. It was published, as an experiment, which, I hoped, might be of some use to ascertain, how far, by fitting to metrical arrangement a selection of the real language of men in a state of vivid sensation, that sort of pleasure and that quantity of pleasure may be imparted, which a Poet may rationally endeavour to impart.

I had formed no very inaccurate estimate of the probable effect of those Poems: I flattered myself that they who should be pleased with them would read them with more than common pleasure: and, on the other hand, I was well aware, that by those who should dislike them, they would be read with more than common dislike. The result has differed from my expectation in this only, that a greater number have been pleased than I ventured to hope I should please.

. . . .

Several of my Friends are anxious for the success of these Poems, from a belief, that, if the views with which they were composed were indeed realised, a class of Poetry would be produced, well adapted to interest mankind permanently, and not unimportant in the quality, and in the multiplicity of its moral relations: and on this account they have advised me to prefix a systematic defence of the theory upon which the Poems were written. But I was unwilling to undertake the task, knowing that on this occasion the Reader would look coldly upon my arguments, since I might be suspected of having been principally influenced by the selfish and foolish hope of *reasoning* him into an approbation of these particular Poems: and I was still more unwilling to undertake the task, because, adequately to display the opinions, and fully to enforce the arguments, would require a space wholly disproportionate to a preface. For, to treat the subject with the clearness and coherence of which it is susceptible, it would be necessary to give a full account of the present state of the public taste in this country, and to determine how far this taste is healthy or depraved; which, again, could not be determined, without pointing out in what manner language and the human mind act and re-act on each other, and without retracing the revolutions, not of literature alone, but likewise of society itself. I have therefore altogether declined to enter regularly upon this defence; yet I am sensible, that there would be something like impropriety in abruptly obtruding upon the Public, without a few words of introduction, Poems so materially different from those upon which general approbation is at present bestowed.

It is supposed, that by the act of writing in verse an Author makes a formal engagement that he will gratify certain known habits of association; that he not only thus apprises the Reader that certain classes of ideas and expressions will be found in his book, but that others will be carefully excluded. This exponent or symbol held forth by metrical language must in different eras of literature have excited very different expectations: for example, in the age of Catullus, Terence, and Lucretius, and that of Statius or Claudian; and in our own country, in the age of Shakspeare and Beaumont and Fletcher, and that of Donne and Cowley, or Dryden, or Pope. I will not take upon me to determine the exact import of the promise which, by the act of writing in verse, an Author in the present day makes to his reader: but it will undoubtedly appear to many persons that I have not fulfilled the terms of an engagement thus voluntarily contracted. They who have been accustomed to the gaudiness and inane phraseology of many modern writers, if they persist in reading this book to its conclusion, will, no doubt, frequently have to struggle with feelings of strangeness and awkwardness: they will look round for poetry, and will be induced to inquire by what species of courtesy these attempts can be permitted to assume that title. I hope therefore the reader will not censure me for attempting to state what I have proposed to myself to perform; and also (as far as the limits of a preface will permit) to explain some of the chief reasons which have determined me in the choice of my purpose: that at least he may be spared any unpleasant feeling of disappointment, and that I myself may be protected from one of the most dishonourable accusations which can be brought against an Author; namely, that of an indolence which prevents him from endeavouring to ascertain what is his duty, or, when his duty is ascertained, prevents him from performing it.

The principal object, then, proposed in these Poems was to choose incidents and situations from common life, and to relate or describe them, throughout, as far as was possible in a selection of language really used by men, and, at the same time, to throw over them a certain colouring of imagination, whereby ordinary things should be presented to the mind in an unusual aspect; and, further, and above all, to make these incidents and situations interesting by tracing in them, truly though not ostentatiously, the primary laws of our nature: chiefly, as far as regards the manner in which we associate ideas in a state of excitement. Humble and rustic life was generally chosen, because, in that condition, the essential passions of the heart find a better soil in which they can attain their maturity, are less under restraint, and speak a plainer and more emphatic language; because in that condition of life our elementary feelings coexist in a state of greater simplicity, and, consequently, may be more accurately contemplated, and more forcibly communicated; because the manners of rural life germinate from those elementary feelings, and, from the necessary character of rural occupations, are more easily comprehended, and are more durable; and, lastly, because in that condition the passions of men are incorporated with the beautiful and permanent forms of nature. The language, too, of these men has been adopted (purified indeed from what appear to be its real defects, from all lasting and rational causes of dislike or disgust) because such men hourly communicate with the best objects from which the best part of language is originally derived; and because, from their rank in society and the sameness and narrow circle of their intercourse, being less under the influence of social vanity, they convey their feelings and notions in simple and unelaborated expressions. Accordingly, such a language, arising out of repeated experience and regular feelings, is a more permanent, and a far more philosophical language, than that which is frequently substituted for it by Poets, who think that they are conferring honour upon themselves and their art, in proportion as they separate themselves from the sympathies of men, and indulge in arbitrary and capricious habits of expression, in order to furnish food for fickle tastes, and fickle appetites, of their own creation[1].

I cannot, however, be insensible to the present outcry against the triviality and meanness, both of thought and language, which some of my contemporaries have occasionally introduced into their metrical compositions; and I acknowledge that this defect, where it exists, is more dishonourable to the Writer's own character than false refinement or arbitrary innovation, though I should contend at the same time, that it is far less pernicious in the sum of its consequences. From such verses the Poems in these volumes will be found distinguished at least by one mark of difference, that each of them has a worthy *purpose*. Not that I always began to write with a distinct purpose formally conceived; but habits of meditation have, I trust, so prompted and regulated my feelings, that my descriptions of such objects as strongly excite

[1] It is worth while here to observe, that the affecting parts of Chaucer are almost always expressed in language pure and universally intelligible even to this day.

those feelings, will be found to carry along with them a *purpose*. If this opinion be erroneous, I can have little right to the name of a Poet. For all good poetry is the spontaneous overflow of powerful feelings: and though this be true, Poems to which any value can be attached were never produced on any variety of subjects but by a man who, being possessed of more than usual organic sensibility, had also thought long and deeply. For our continued influxes of feeling are modified and directed by our thoughts, which are indeed the representatives of all our past feelings; and, as by contemplating the relation of these general representatives to each other, we discover what is really important to men, so, by the repetition and continuance of this act, our feelings will be connected with important subjects, till at length, if we be originally possessed of much sensibility, such habits of mind will be produced, that, by obeying blindly and mechanically the impulses of those habits, we shall describe objects, and utter sentiments, of such a nature, and in such connection with each other, that the understanding of the Reader must necessarily be in some degree enlightened, and his affections strengthened and purified.

It has been said that each of these poems has a purpose. Another circumstance must be mentioned which distinguishes these Poems from the popular Poetry of the day; it is this, that the feeling therein developed gives importance to the action and situation, and not the action and situation to the feeling.

A sense of false modesty shall not prevent me from asserting, that the Reader's attention is pointed to this mark of distinction, far less for the sake of these particular Poems than from the general importance of the subject. The subject is indeed important! For the human mind is capable of being excited without the application of gross and violent stimulants; and he must have a very faint perception of its beauty and dignity who does not know this, and who does not further know, that one being is elevated above another, in proportion as he possesses this capability. It has therefore appeared to me, that to endeavour to produce or enlarge this capability is one of the best services in which, at any period, a Writer can be engaged; but this service, excellent at all times, is especially so at the present day. For a multitude of causes, unknown to former times, are now acting with a combined force to blunt the discriminating powers of the mind, and, unfitting it for all voluntary exertion, to reduce it to a state of almost savage torpor. The most effective of these causes are the great national events which are daily taking place, and the increasing accumulation of men in cities, where the uniformity of their occupations produces a craving for extraordinary incident, which the rapid communication of intelligence hourly gratifies. To this tendency of life and manners the literature and theatrical exhibitions of the country have conformed themselves. The invaluable works of our elder writers, I had almost said the works of Shakspeare and Milton, are driven into neglect by frantic novels, sickly and stupid German Tragedies, and deluges of idle and extravagant stories in verse.—When I think upon this degrading thirst after outrageous stimulation, I am almost ashamed to have spoken of the feeble endeavour made in these volumes to counteract it; and, reflecting upon the magnitude of the general evil, I should be oppressed with no dishonourable melancholy, had I not a deep impression of certain inherent and indestructible qualities of the human mind, and likewise of certain powers in the great and permanent objects that act upon it, which are equally inherent and indestructible; and were there not added to this impression a belief, that the time is approaching when the evil will be systematically opposed, by men of greater powers, and with far more distinguished success.

Having dwelt thus long on the subjects and aim of these Poems, I shall request the Reader's permission to apprise him of a few circumstances relating to their *style*, in order, among other reasons, that he may not censure me for not having performed what I never attempted. The Reader will find that personifications of abstract ideas rarely occur in these volumes; and are utterly rejected, as an ordinary device to elevate the style, and raise it above prose. My purpose was to imitate, and, as far as possible, to adopt the very language of men; and assuredly such personifications do not make any natural or regular part of that language. They are, indeed, a figure of speech occasionally prompted by passion, and I have made use of them as such; but have endeavoured utterly to reject them as a mechanical device of style, or as a family language which Writers in metre seem to lay claim to by prescription. I have wished to keep the Reader in the company of flesh and blood, persuaded that by so doing I shall interest him. Others who pursue a different track will interest him likewise; I do not interfere with their claim, but wish to prefer a claim of my own. There will also be found in these volumes little of what is usually called poetic diction; as much pains has been taken to avoid it as is ordinarily taken to produce it; this has been done for the reason already alleged, to bring my language near to the language of men; and further, because the pleasure which I have proposed to myself to impart, is of a kind very different from that which is supposed by many persons to be the proper object of poetry. Without being culpably particular, I do not know how to give my Reader a more exact notion of the style in which it was my wish and intention to write, than by informing him that I have at all times endeavoured to look steadily at my subject; consequently, there is I hope in these Poems little falsehood of description, and my ideas are expressed in language fitted to their respective importance. Something must have been gained by this practice, as it is friendly to one property of all good poetry, namely, good sense: but it has necessarily cut me off from a large portion of phrases and figures of speech which from father to son have long been regarded as the common inheritance of Poets. I have also thought it expedient to restrict myself still further, having abstained from the use of many expressions, in themselves proper and beautiful, but which have been foolishly repeated by bad Poets, till such feelings of disgust are connected with them as it is scarcely possible by any art of association to overpower.

If in a poem there should be found a series of lines, or even a single line, in which the language, though naturally arranged, and according to the strict laws of metre, does not differ from that of prose, there is a numerous class of critics, who, when they stumble upon these prosaisms, as they call them, imagine that they have made a notable discovery, and exult over the Poet as over a man ignorant of his own profession. Now these men would establish a canon of criticism which the Reader will conclude he must utterly reject, if he wishes to be pleased with these volumes. And it would be a most easy task to prove to him, that not only the language of a large portion of every good poem, even of the most elevated character, must necessarily, except with reference to the metre, in no respect differ from that of good prose, but likewise that some of the most interesting parts of the poems will be found to be strictly the language of prose when prose is well written. The truth of this assertion might be demonstrated by innumerable passages from almost all the poetical writings, even of Milton himself. To illustrate the subject in a general manner, I will here adduce a short composition of Gray, who was at the head of those who, by their reasonings, have attempted to widen the space of separation betwixt Prose and Metrical composition, and was more than any other man curiously elaborate in the structure of his own poetic diction.

In vain to me the smiling mornings shine,
And reddening Phoebus lifts his golden fire:
The birds in vain their amorous descant join,
Or cheerful fields resume their green attire.
These ears, alas! for other notes repine;
A different object do these eyes require;
My lonely anguish melts no heart but mine;
And in my breast the imperfect joys expire;
Yet morning smiles the busy race to cheer,
And new-born pleasure brings to happier men;
The fields to all their wonted tribute bear;
To warm their little loves the birds complain.
I fruitless mourn to him that cannot hear,
And weep the more because I weep in vain.

It will easily be perceived, that the only part of this Sonnet which is of any value is the lines printed in Italics; it is equally obvious, that, except in the rhyme, and in the use of the single word " fruitless " for fruitlessly, which is so far a defect, the language of these lines does in no respect differ from that of prose.

By the foregoing quotation it has been shown that the language of Prose may yet be well adapted to Poetry; and it was previously asserted, that a large portion of the language of every good poem can in no respect differ from that of good Prose. We will go further. It may be safely affirmed, that there neither is, nor can be, any *essential* difference between the language of prose and metrical composition. We are fond of tracing the resemblance between Poetry and Painting, and, accordingly, we call them Sisters: but where shall we find bonds of connection sufficiently strict to typify the affinity betwixt metrical and prose composition? They both speak by and to the same organs; the bodies in which both of them are clothed may be said to be of the same substance, their affections are kindred, and almost identical, not necessarily differing even in degree; Poetry[1] sheds no tears " such as Angels weep," but natural and human tears; she can boast of no celestial ichor that distinguishes her vital juices from those of prose; the same human blood circulates through the veins of them both.

If it be affirmed that rhyme and metrical arrangement of themselves constitute a distinction which overturns what has just been said on the strict affinity of metrical language with that of prose, and paves the way for other artificial distinctions which the mind voluntarily admits, I answer that the language of such Poetry as is here recommended is, as far as is possible, a selection of the language really spoken by men; that this selection, wherever it is made with true taste and feeling, will of itself form a distinction far greater than would at first be imagined, and will entirely separate the composition from the vulgarity and meanness of ordinary life; and, if metre be superadded thereto, I believe that a dissimilitude will be produced altogether sufficient for the gratification of a rational mind. What other distinction would we have? Whence is it to come? And where is it to exist? Not, surely, where the Poet speaks through the mouths of his characters: it

[1] I here use the word "Poetry" (though against my own judgment) as opposed to the word Prose, and synonymous with metrical composition. But much confusion has been introduced into criticism by this contradistinction of Poetry and Prose, instead of the more philosophical one of Poetry and Matter of Fact, or Science. The only strict antithesis to Prose is Metre; nor is this, in truth, a *strict* antithesis, because lines and passages of metre so naturally occur in writing prose, that it would be scarcely possible to avoid them, even were it desirable.

cannot be necessary here, either for elevation of style, or any of its supposed ornaments: for, if the Poet's subject be judiciously chosen, it will naturally, and upon fit occasion, lead him to passions the language of which, if selected truly and judiciously, must necessarily be dignified and variegated, and alive with metaphors and figures. I forbear to speak of an incongruity which would shock the intelligent Reader, should the Poet interweave any foreign splendour of his own with that which the passion naturally suggests: it is sufficient to say that such addition is unnecessary. And, surely, it is more probable that those passages, which with propriety abound with metaphors and figures, will have their due effect, if, upon other occasions where the passions are of a milder character, the style also be subdued and temperate.

But, as the pleasure which I hope to give by the Poems now presented to the Reader must depend entirely on just notions upon this subject, and, as it is in itself of high importance to our taste and moral feelings, I cannot content myself with these detached remarks. And if, in what I am about to say, it shall appear to some that my labour is unnecessary, and that I am like a man fighting a battle without enemies, such persons may be reminded, that, whatever be the language outwardly holden by men, a practical faith in the opinions which I am wishing to establish is almost unknown. If my conclusions are admitted, and carried as far as they must be carried if admitted at all, our judgments concerning the works of the greatest Poets both ancient and modern will be far different from what they are at present, both when we praise, and when we censure: and our moral feelings influencing and influenced by these judgments will, I believe, be corrected and purified.

Taking up the subject, then, upon general grounds, let me ask, what is meant by the word Poet? What is a Poet? To whom does he address himself? And what language is to be expected from him?—He is a man speaking to men: a man, it is true, endowed with more lively sensibility, more enthusiasm and tenderness, who has a greater knowledge of human nature, and a more comprehensive soul, than are supposed to be common among mankind; a man pleased with his own passions and volitions, and who rejoices more than other men in the spirit of life that is in him; delighting to contemplate similar volitions and passions as manifested in the goings-on of the Universe, and habitually impelled to create them where he does not find them. To these qualities he has added a disposition to be affected more than other men by absent things as if they were present; an ability of conjuring up in himself passions, which are indeed far from being the same as those produced by real events, yet (especially in those parts of the general sympathy which are pleasing and delightful) do more nearly resemble the passions produced by real events, than anything which, from the motions of their own minds merely, other men are accustomed to feel in themselves:—whence, and from practice, he has acquired a greater readiness and power in expressing what he thinks and feels, and especially those thoughts and feelings which, by his own choice, or from the structure of his own mind, arise in him without immediate external excitement.

But whatever portion of this faculty we may suppose even the greatest Poet to possess, there cannot be a doubt that the language which it will suggest to him, must often, in liveliness and truth fall short of that which is uttered by men in real life, under the actual pressure of those passions, certain shadows of which the Poet thus produces, or feels to be produced, in himself.

However exalted a notion we would wish to cherish of the character of a Poet, it is obvious, that while he describes and imitates passions, his employment is in some degree mechanical, compared with the freedom and power of real and substantial action and suffering. So that it will be the wish of the Poet to bring his feelings near to those of the persons whose feelings he describes, nay, for short spaces of time, perhaps, to let himself slip into an entire delusion, and even confound and identify his own feelings with theirs; modifying only the language which is thus suggested to him by a consideration that he describes for a particular purpose, that of giving pleasure. Here, then, he will apply the principle of selection which has been already insisted upon. He will depend upon this for removing what would otherwise be painful or disgusting in the passion; he will feel that there is no necessity to trick out or to elevate nature: and, the more industriously he applies this principle, the deeper will be his faith that no words, which *his* fancy or imagination can suggest, will be to be compared with those which are the emanations of reality and truth.

But it may be said by those who do not object to the general spirit of these remarks, that, as it is impossible for the Poet to produce upon all occasions language as exquisitely fitted for the passion as that which the real passion itself suggests, it is proper that he should consider himself as in the situation of a translator, who does not scruple to substitute excellencies of another kind for those which are unattainable by him; and endeavours occasionally to surpass his original, in order to make some amends for the general inferiority to which he feels that he must submit. But this would be to encourage idleness and unmanly despair. Further, it is the language of men who speak of what they do not understand; who talk of Poetry as of a matter of amusement and idle pleasure; who will converse with us as gravely about a *taste* for Poetry, as they express it, as if it were a thing as indifferent as a taste for rope-dancing, or Frontiniac or Sherry. Aristotle, I have been told, has said, that Poetry is the most philosophic of all writing: it is so: its object is truth, not individual and local, but general, and operative; not standing upon external testimony, but carried alive into the heart by passion; truth which is its own testimony, which gives competence and confidence to the tribunal to which it appeals, and receives them from the same tribunal. Poetry is the image of man and nature. The obstacles which stand in the way of the fidelity of the Biographer and Historian, and of their consequent utility, are incalculably greater than those which are to be encountered by the Poet who comprehends the dignity of his art. The Poet writes under one restriction only, namely, the necessity of giving immediate pleasure to a human Being possessed of that information which may be expected from him, not as a lawyer, a physician, a mariner, an astronomer, or a natural philosopher, but as a Man. Except this one restriction, there is no object standing between the Poet and the image of things; between this, and the Biographer and Historian, there are a thousand.

Nor let this necessity of producing immediate pleasure be considered as a degradation of the Poet's art. It is far otherwise. It is an acknowledgment of the beauty of the universe, an acknowledgment the more sincere, because not formal, but indirect; it is a task light and easy to him who looks at the world in the spirit of love: further, it is a homage paid to the native and naked dignity of man, to the grand elementary principle of pleasure, by which he knows, and feels, and lives, and moves. We have no sympathy but what is propagated by pleasure: I would not be misunderstood; but wherever we sympathise with pain, it will be found that the sympathy is produced and carried on by subtle combinations with pleasure. We have no knowledge, that is, no general principles drawn from the contemplation of particular facts, but what has been built up by pleasure, and exists in us by pleasure alone. The Man of science, the Chemist and Mathematician, whatever difficulties and disgusts they may have had to struggle with, know and feel this. However painful may be the objects with which the Anatomist's knowledge is connected, he feels that his knowledge is pleasure; and where he has no pleasure he has no knowledge. What then does the Poet? He considers man and the objects that surround him as acting and re-acting upon each other, so as to produce an infinite complexity of pain and pleasure; he considers man in his own nature and in his ordinary life as contemplating this with a certain quantity of immediate knowledge, with certain convictions, intuitions, and deductions, which from habit acquire the quality of intuitions; he considers him as looking upon this complex scene of ideas and sensations, and finding everywhere objects that immediately excite in him sympathies which, from the necessities of his nature, are accompanied by an over-balance of enjoyment.

To this knowledge which all men carry about with them, and to these sympathies in which, without any other discipline than that of our daily life, we are fitted to take delight, the Poet principally directs his attention. He considers man and nature as essentially adapted to each other, and the mind of man as naturally the mirror of the fairest and most interesting properties of nature. And thus the Poet, prompted by this feeling of pleasure, which accompanies him through the whole course of his studies, converses with general nature, with affections akin to those, which, through labour and length of time, the Man of science has raised up in himself, by conversing with those particular parts of nature which are the objects of his studies. The knowledge both of the Poet and the Man of science is pleasure; but the knowledge of the one cleaves to us as a necessary part of our existence, our natural and unalienable inheritance; the other is a personal and individual acquisition, slow to come to us, and by no habitual and direct sympathy connecting us with our fellow-beings. The Man of science seeks truth as a remote and unknown benefactor; he cherishes and loves it in his solitude: the Poet, singing a song in which all human beings join with him, rejoices in the presence of truth as our visible friend and hourly companion. Poetry is the breath and finer spirit of all knowledge; it is the impassioned expression which is in the countenance of all Science. Emphatically may it be said of the Poet, as Shakspeare hath said of man, "that he looks before and after." He is the rock of defence for human nature; an upholder and preserver, carrying everywhere with him relationship and love. In spite of difference of soil and climate, of language and manners, of laws and customs: in spite of things silently gone out of mind, and things violently destroyed; the Poet binds together by passion and knowledge the vast empire of human society, as it is spread over the whole earth, and over all time. The objects of the Poet's thoughts are everywhere; though the eyes and senses of man are, it is true, his favourite guides, yet he will follow wheresoever he can find an atmosphere of sensation in which to move his wings. Poetry is the first and last of all knowledge—it is as immortal as the heart of man. If the labours of Men of science should ever create any material revolution, direct or indirect, in our condition, and in the impressions which we habitually receive, the Poet will sleep then no more than at present; he will be ready to follow the steps of the Man of science, not only in those general indirect effects, but he will be at his side, carrying sensation into the midst of the objects of the science itself. The remotest discoveries of the Chemist, the Botanist, or Mineralogist, will be as proper objects of the Poet's art as any upon which it can be employed, if the time should ever come when these things shall be familiar to us, and the relations under which they are contemplated by the followers of these respective sciences shall be manifestly and palpably material to us as enjoying and suffering beings. If the time should ever come when what is now called science, thus familiarised to men, shall be ready to put on, as it were, a form of flesh and blood, the Poet will lend his divine spirit to aid the transfiguration, and will welcome the Being thus produced, as a dear and genuine inmate of the household of man.—It is not, then, to be supposed that any one, who holds that sublime notion of Poetry which I have attempted to convey, will break in upon the sanctity and truth of his pictures by transitory and accidental ornaments, and endeavour to excite admiration of himself by arts, the necessity of which must manifestly depend upon the assumed meanness of his subject.

What has been thus far said applies to Poetry in general; but especially to those parts of composition where the Poet speaks through the mouths of his characters; and upon this point it appears to authorise the conclusion that there are few persons of good sense, who would not allow that the dramatic parts of composition are defective, in proportion as they deviate from the real language of nature, and are coloured by a diction of the Poet's own, either peculiar to him as an individual Poet or belonging simply to Poets in general; to a body of men who, from the circumstance of their compositions being in metre, it is expected will employ a particular language.

It is not, then, in the dramatic parts of composition that we look for this distinction of language; but still it may be proper and necessary where the Poet speaks to us in his own person and character. To this I answer by referring the Reader to the description before given of a Poet. Among the qualities there enumerated as principally conducing to form a Poet, is implied nothing differing in kind from other men, but only in degree. The sum of what was said is, that the Poet is chiefly distinguished from other men by a greater promptness to think and feel without immediate external excitement, and a greater power in expressing such thoughts and feelings as are produced in him in that manner. But these passions and thoughts and feelings are the general passions and thoughts and feelings of men. And with what are they connected? Undoubtedly with our moral sentiments and animal sensations, and with the causes which excite these; with the operations of the elements, and the appearances of the visible universe; with storm and sunshine, with the revolutions of the seasons, with cold and heat, with loss of friends and kindred, with injuries and resentments, gratitude and hope, with fear and sorrow. These, and the like, are the sensations and objects which the Poet describes, as they are the sensations of other men, and the objects which interest them. The Poet thinks and feels in the spirit of human passions. How, then, can his language differ in any material degree from that of all other men who feel vividly and see clearly? It might be *proved* that it is impossible. But supposing that this were not the case, the Poet might then be allowed to use a peculiar language when expressing his feelings for his own gratification, or that of men like himself. But Poets do not write for Poets alone, but for men. Unless therefore we are advocates for that admiration which subsists upon ignorance, and that pleasure which arises from hearing what we do not understand, the Poet must descend from this supposed height; and, in order to excite rational sympathy, he must express himself as other men express themselves. To this it may be added, that while he is only selecting from the real language of men, or, which amounts to the same thing, composing accurately in the spirit of such selection, he is treading upon safe ground, and we know what we are to expect from him. Our feelings are the same with respect to metre; for, as it may be proper to remind the Reader, the distinction of metre is regular and uniform, and not, like that which is produced by what is usually called POETIC DICTION, arbitrary, and subject to infinite caprices upon which no calculation whatever can be made. In the one case, the Reader is utterly at the mercy of the Poet, respecting what imagery or diction he may choose to connect with the passion; whereas, in the other, the metre obeys certain laws, to which the Poet and Reader both willingly submit because they are certain, and because no interference is made by them with the passion, but such as the concurring testimony of ages has shown to heighten and improve the pleasure which co-exists with it.

It will now be proper to answer an obvious question, namely, Why, professing these opinions, have I written in verse? To this, in addition to such answer as is included in what has been already said, I reply, in the first place, Because, however I may have restricted myself, there is still left open to me what confessedly constitutes the most valuable object of all writing, whether in prose or verse; the great and universal passions of men, the most general and interesting of their occupations, and the entire world of nature before me—to supply endless combinations of forms and imagery. Now, supposing for a moment that whatever is interesting in these objects may be as vividly described in prose, why should I be condemned for attempting to superadd to such description the charm which, by the consent of all nations, is acknowledged to exist in metrical language? To this, by such as are yet unconvinced, it may be answered that a very small part of the pleasure given by Poetry depends upon the metre, and that it is injudicious to write in metre, unless it be accompanied with the other artificial distinctions of style with which metre is usually accompanied, and that, by such deviation, more will be lost from the shock which will thereby be given to the Reader's associations than will be counterbalanced by any pleasure which he can derive from the general power of numbers. In answer to those who still contend for the necessity of accompanying metre with certain appropriate colours of style in order to the accomplishment of its appropriate end, and who also, in my opinion, greatly underrate the power of metre in itself, it might, perhaps, as far as relates to these Volumes, have been almost sufficient to observe, that poems are extant, written upon more humble subjects, and in a still more naked and simple style, which have continued to give pleasure from generation to generation. Now, if nakedness and simplicity be a defect, the fact here mentioned affords a strong presumption that poems somewhat less naked and simple are capable of affording pleasure at the present day; and, what I wished *chiefly* to attempt, at present, was to justify myself for having written under the impression of this belief.

But various causes might be pointed out why, when the style is manly, and the subject of some importance, words metrically arranged will long continue to impart such a pleasure to mankind as he who proves the extent of that pleasure will be desirous to impart. The end of Poetry is to produce excitement in co-existence with an overbalance of pleasure; but, by the supposition, excitement is an unusual and irregular state of the mind; ideas and feelings do not, in that state, succeed each other in accustomed order. If the words, however, by which this excitement is produced be in themselves powerful, or the images and feelings have an undue proportion of pain connected with them, there is some danger that the excitement may be carried beyond its proper bounds. Now the co-presence of something regular, something to which the mind has been accustomed in various moods and in a less excited state, cannot but have great efficacy in tempering and restraining the passion by an intertexture of ordinary feeling, and of feeling not strictly and necessarily connected with the passion. This is unquestionably true; and hence, though the opinion will at first appear paradoxical, from the tendency of metre to divest language, in a certain degree, of its reality, and thus to throw a sort of half-consciousness of unsubstantial existence over the whole composition, there can be little doubt but that more pathetic situations and sentiments, that is, those which have a greater proportion of pain connected with them, may be endured in metrical composition, especially in rhyme, than in prose. The metre of the old ballads is very artless; yet they contain many passages which would illustrate this opinion; and, I hope, if the following Poems be attentively perused, similar instances will be found in them. This opinion may be further illustrated by appealing to the Reader's own experience of the reluctance with which he comes to the re-perusal of the distressful parts of "Clarissa Harlowe," or the "Gamester;" while Shakspeare's writings, in the most pathetic scenes, never act upon us, as pathetic, beyond the bounds of pleasure—an effect which, in a much greater degree than might at first be imagined, is to be ascribed to small, but continual and regular impulses of pleasurable surprise from the metrical arrangement.—On the other hand (what it must be allowed will much more frequently happen) if the Poet's words should be incommensurate with the passion, and inadequate to raise the Reader to a height of desirable excitement, then, (unless the Poet's choice of his metre has been grossly injudicious) in the feelings of pleasure which the Reader has been accustomed to connect with metre in general, and in the feeling, whether cheerful or melancholy, which he has been accustomed to connect with that particular movement of metre, there will be found something which will greatly contribute to impart passion to the words, and to effect the complex end which the Poet proposes to himself.

If I had undertaken a SYSTEMATIC defence of the theory here maintained, it would have been my duty to develope the various causes upon which the pleasure received from metrical language depends. Among the chief of these causes is to be reckoned a principle which must be well known to those who have made any of the Arts the object of accurate reflection; namely, the pleasure which the mind derives from the perception of similitude in dissimilitude. This principle is the great spring of the activity of our minds, and their chief feeder. From this principle the direction of the sexual appetite, and all the passions connected with it, take their origin: it is the life of our ordinary conversation; and upon the accuracy with which similitude in dissimilitude, and dissimilitude in similitude are perceived, depend our taste and our moral feelings. It would not be a useless employment to apply this principle to the consideration of metre, and to show that metre is hence enabled to afford much pleasure, and to point out in what manner that pleasure is produced. But my limits will not permit me to enter upon this subject, and I must content myself with a general summary.

I have said that poetry is the spontaneous overflow of powerful feelings: it takes its origin from emotion recollected in tranquillity: the emotion is contemplated till, by a species of reaction, the tranquillity gradually disappears, and an emotion, kindred to that which was before the subject of contemplation, is gradually produced, and does itself actually exist in the mind. In this mood successful composition generally begins, and in a mood similar to this it is carried on; but the emotion, of whatever kind, and in whatever degree, from various causes, is qualified by various pleasures, so that in describing any passions whatsoever, which are voluntarily described, the mind will, upon the whole, be in a state of enjoyment. If Nature be thus cautious to preserve in a state of enjoyment a being so employed, the Poet ought to profit by the lesson held forth to him, and ought especially to take care, that, whatever passions he communicates to his Reader, those passions, if his Reader's mind be sound and vigorous, should always be accompanied with an overbalance of pleasure. Now the music of harmonious metrical language, the sense of difficulty overcome, and the blind association of pleasure which has been previously received from works of rhyme or metre of the same or similar construction, an indistinct perception perpetually renewed of language closely resembling that of real life, and yet, in the circumstance of metre, differing from it so widely—all these imperceptibly make up a complex feeling of delight, which is of the most important use in tempering the painful feeling always found intermingled with powerful descriptions of the deeper passions. This effect is always produced in pathetic and impassioned poetry; while, in lighter compositions, the ease and gracefulness with which the Poet manages his numbers are themselves confessedly a principal source of the gratification of the Reader. All that it is *necessary* to say, however, upon this subject, may be effected by affirming, what few persons will deny, that, of two descriptions, either of passions, manners, or characters, each of them equally well executed, the one in prose and the other in verse, the verse will be read a hundred times where the prose is read once.

Having thus explained a few of my reasons for writing in verse, and why I have chosen subjects from common life, and endeavoured to bring my language near to the real language of men, if I have been too minute in pleading my own cause, I have at the same time been treating a subject of general interest; and for this reason a few words shall be added with reference solely to these particular poems, and to some defects which will probably be found in them. I am sensible that my associations must have sometimes been particular instead of general, and that, consequently, giving to things a false importance, I may have sometimes written upon unworthy subjects; but I am less apprehensive on this account, than that my language may frequently have suffered from those arbitrary connections of feelings and ideas with particular words and phrases, from which no man can altogether protect himself. Hence I have no doubt, that, in some instances, feelings, even of the ludicrous, may be given to my Readers by expressions which appeared to me tender and pathetic. Such faulty expressions, were I convinced they were faulty at present, and that they must necessarily continue to be so, I would willingly take all reasonable pains to correct. But it is dangerous to make these alterations on the simple authority of a few individuals, or even of certain classes of men; for where the understanding of an Author is not convinced, or his feelings altered, this cannot be done without great injury to himself: for his own feelings are his stay and support; and, if he set them aside in one instance, he may be induced to repeat this act till his mind shall lose all confidence in itself, and become utterly debilitated. To this it may be added, that the critic ought never to forget that he is himself exposed to the same errors as the Poet, and, perhaps, in a much greater degree: for there can be no presumption in saying of most readers, that it is not probable they will be so well acquainted with the various stages of meaning through which words have passed, or with the fickleness or stability of the relations of particular ideas to each other; and, above all, since they are so much less interested in the subject, they may decide lightly and carelessly.

Long as the Reader has been detained, I hope he will permit me to caution him against a mode of false criticism which has been applied to Poetry, in which the language closely resembles that of life and nature. Such verses have been triumphed over in parodies, of which Dr. Johnson's stanza is a fair specimen:—

I put my hat upon my head
And walked into the Strand,
And there I met another man
Whose hat was in his hand.

Immediately under these lines let us place one of the most justly-admired stanzas of the "Babes in the Wood."

These pretty Babes with hand in hand
Went wandering up and down;
But never more they saw the Man
Approaching from the Town.

In both these stanzas the words, and the order of the words, in no respect differ from the most unimpassioned conversation. There are words in both, for example, "the Strand," and "the Town," connected with none but the most familiar ideas; yet the one stanza we admit as admirable, and the other as a fair example of the superlatively contemptible. Whence arises this difference? Not from the metre, not from the language, not from the order of the words; but the *matter* expressed in Dr. Johnson's stanza is contemptible. The proper method of treating trivial and simple verses, to which Dr. Johnson's stanza would be a fair parallelism, is not to say, this is a bad kind of poetry, or, this is not poetry; but, this wants sense; it is neither interesting in itself, nor can *lead* to anything interesting; the images neither originate in that sane state of feeling which arises out of thought, nor can excite thought or feeling in the Reader. This is the only sensible manner of dealing with such verses. Why trouble yourself about the species till you have previously decided upon the genus? Why take pains to prove that an ape is not a Newton, when it is self-evident that he is not a man?

One request I must make of my reader, which is, that in judging these Poems he would decide by his own feelings genuinely, and not by reflection upon what will probably be the judgment of others. How common is it to hear a person say, I myself do not object to this style of composition, or this or that expression, but, to such and such classes of people it will appear mean or ludicrous! This mode of criticism, so destructive of all sound unadulterated judgment, is almost universal: let the Reader then abide, independently, by his own feelings, and, if he finds himself affected, let him not suffer such conjectures to interfere with his pleasure.

If an Author, by any single composition, has impressed us with respect for his talents, it is useful to consider this as affording a presumption, that on other occasions where we have been displeased, he, nevertheless, may not have written ill or absurdly; and further, to give him so much credit for this one composition as may induce us to review what has displeased us, with more care than we should otherwise have bestowed upon it. This is not only an act of justice, but, in our decisions upon poetry especially, may conduce, in a high degree, to the improvement of our own taste; for an *accurate* taste in poetry, and in all the other arts, as Sir Joshua Reynolds has observed, is an *acquired* talent, which can only be produced by thought and a long-continued intercourse with the best models of composition. This is mentioned, not with so ridiculous a purpose as to prevent the most inexperienced Reader from judging for himself, (I have already said that I wish him to judge for himself;) but merely to temper the rashness of decision, and to suggest, that, if Poetry be a subject on which much time has not been bestowed, the judgment may be erroneous; and that, in many cases, it necessarily will be so.

Nothing would, I know, have so effectually contributed to further the end which I have in view, as to have shown of what kind the pleasure is, and how that pleasure is produced, which is confessedly produced by metrical composition essentially different from that which I have here endeavoured to recommend: for the Reader will say that he has been pleased by such composition; and what more can be done for him? The power of any art is limited; and he will suspect, that, if it be proposed to furnish him with new friends, that can be only upon condition of his abandoning his old friends. Besides, as I have said, the Reader is himself conscious of the pleasure which he has received from such composition, composition to which he has peculiarly attached the endearing name of Poetry; and all men feel an habitual gratitude, and something of an honourable bigotry, for the objects which have long continued to please them: we not only wish to be pleased, but to be pleased in that particular way in which we have been accustomed to be pleased. There is in these feelings enough to resist a host of arguments; and I should be the less able to combat them successfully, as I am willing to allow, that, in order entirely to enjoy the Poetry which I am recommending, it would be necessary to give up much of what is ordinarily enjoyed. But, would my limits have permitted me to point out how this pleasure is produced, many obstacles might have been removed, and the Reader assisted in perceiving that the powers of language are not so limited as he may suppose; and that it is possible for poetry to give other enjoyments, of a purer, more lasting, and more exquisite nature. This part of the subject has not been altogether neglected, but it has not been so much my present aim to prove, that the interest excited by some other kinds of poetry is less vivid, and less worthy of the nobler powers of the mind, as to offer reasons for presuming, that if my purpose were fulfilled, a species of poetry would be produced, which is genuine poetry; in its nature well adapted to interest mankind permanently, and likewise important in the multiplicity and quality of its moral relations.

From what has been said, and from a perusal of the Poems, the Reader will be able clearly to perceive the object which I had in view: he will determine how far it has been attained; and, what is a much more important question, whether it be worth attaining: and upon the decision of these two questions will rest my claim to the approbation of the Public.

APPENDIX.

"By what is usually called Poetic Diction." [See p. 195.]

Perhaps, as I have no right to expect that attentive perusal, without which, confined, as I have been, to the narrow limits of a preface, my meaning cannot be thoroughly understood, I am anxious to give an exact notion of the sense in which the phrase poetic diction has been used; and for this purpose, a few words shall here be added, concerning the origin and characteristics of the phraseology, which I have condemned under that name.

The earliest poets of all nations generally wrote from passion excited by real events; they wrote naturally, and as men: feeling powerfully as they did, their language was daring, and figurative. In succeeding times Poets, and Men ambitious of the fame of Poets, perceiving the influence of such language, and desirous of producing the same effect without being animated by the same passion, set themselves to a mechanical adoption of these figures of speech, and made use of them, sometimes with propriety, but much more frequently applied them to feelings and thoughts with which they had no natural connection whatsoever. A language was thus insensibly produced, differing materially from the real language of men in *any situation*. The Reader or Hearer of this distorted language found himself in a perturbed and unusual state of mind: when affected by the genuine language of passion he had been in a perturbed and unusual state of mind also: in both cases he was willing that his common judgment and understanding should be laid asleep, and he had no instinctive and infallible perception of the true to make him reject the false; the one served as a passport for the other. The emotion was in both cases delightful, and no wonder if he confounded the one with the other, and believed them both to be produced by the same, or similar causes. Besides, the Poet spake to him in the character of a man to be looked up to, a man of genius and authority. Thus, and from a variety of other causes, this distorted language was received with admiration; and Poets, it is probable, who had before contented themselves for the most part with misapplying only expressions which at first had been dictated by real passion, carried the abuse still further, and introduced phrases composed apparently in the spirit of the original figurative language of passion, yet altogether of their own invention, and characterised by various degrees of wanton deviation from good sense and nature.

It is indeed true, that the language of the earliest Poets was felt to differ materially from ordinary language, because it was the language of extraordinary occasions; but it was really spoken by men, language which the Poet himself had uttered when he had been affected by the events which he described, or which he had heard uttered by those around him. To this language it is probable that metre of some sort or other was early superadded. This separated the genuine language of Poetry still further from common life, so that whoever read or heard the poems of these earliest Poets felt himself moved in a way in which he had not been accustomed to be moved in real life, and by causes manifestly different from those which acted upon him in real life. This was the great temptation to all the corruptions which have followed: under the protection of this feeling succeeding Poets constructed a phraseology which had one thing, it is true, in common with the genuine language of poetry, namely, that it was not heard in ordinary conversation; that it was unusual. But the first Poets, as I have said, spake a language which, though unusual, was still the language of men. This circumstance, however, was disregarded by their successors; they found that they could please by easier means: they became proud of modes of expression which they themselves had invented, and which were uttered only by themselves. In process of time metre became a symbol or promise of this unusual language, and whoever took upon him to write in metre, according as he possessed more or less of true poetic genius, introduced less or more of this adulterated phraseology into his compositions, and the true and the false were inseparably interwoven until, the taste of men becoming gradually perverted, this language was received as a natural language: and at length, by the influence of books upon men, did to a certain degree really become so. Abuses of this kind were imported from one nation to another, and with the progress of refinement this diction became daily more and more corrupt, thrusting out of sight the plain humanities of nature by a motley masquerade of tricks, quaintnesses, hieroglyphics, and enigmas.

It would not be uninteresting to point out the causes of the pleasure given by this extravagant and absurd diction. It depends upon a great variety of causes, but upon none, perhaps, more than its influence in impressing a notion of the peculiarity and exaltation of the Poet's character, and in flattering the Reader's self-love by bringing him nearer to a sympathy with that character; an effect which is accomplished by unsettling ordinary habits of thinking, and thus assisting the Reader to approach to that perturbed and dizzy state of mind in which if he does not find himself, he imagines that he is *balked* of a peculiar enjoyment which poetry can and ought to bestow.

The sonnet quoted from Gray, in the Preface, except the lines printed in Italics, consists of little else but this diction, though not of the worst kind; and indeed, if one may be permitted to say so, it is far too common in the best writers both ancient and modern. Perhaps in no way, by positive example, could more easily be given a notion of what I mean by the phrase *poetic diction* than by referring to a comparison between the metrical paraphrase which we have of passages in the Old and New Testament, and those passages as they exist in our common Translation. See Pope's "Messiah" throughout; Prior's "Did sweeter sounds adorn my flowing tongue," &c. &c. "Though I speak with the tongues of men and of angels," &c. &c. 1st Corinthians, chap. xiii. By way of immediate example take the following of Dr. Johnson:—

Turn on the prudent Ant thy heedless eyes,
Observe her labours, Sluggard, and be wise;
No stern command, no monitory voice,
Prescribes her duties, or directs her choice;
Yet, timely provident, she hastes away
To snatch the blessings of a plenteous day;
When fruitful Summer loads the teeming plain,
She crops the harvest, and she stores the grain.
How long shall sloth usurp thy useless hours,
Unnerve thy vigour, and enchain thy powers?
While artful shades thy downy couch enclose,
And soft solicitation courts repose,

Amidst the drowsy charms of dull delight,
Year chases year with unremitted flight,
Till Want now following, fraudulent and slow,
Shall spring to seize thee, like an ambush'd foe.

From this hubbub of words pass to the original. "Go to the Ant, thou Sluggard, consider her ways, and be wise: which having no guide, overseer, or ruler, provideth her meat in the summer, and gathereth her food in the harvest. How long wilt thou sleep, O Sluggard? when wilt thou arise out of thy sleep? Yet a little sleep, a little slumber, a little folding of the hands to sleep. So shall thy poverty come as one that travelleth, and thy want as an armed man." Proverbs, chap. vi.

One more quotation, and I have done. It is from Cowper's Verses supposed to be written by Alexander Selkirk:—

Religion! what treasure untold
Resides in that heavenly word!
More precious than silver and gold,
Or all that this earth can afford.
But the sound of the church-going bell
These valleys and rocks never heard,
Ne'er sighed at the sound of a knell,
Or smiled when a sabbath appeared.

Ye winds, that have made me your sport,
Convey to this desolate shore
Some cordial endearing report
Of a land I must visit no more.
My Friends, do they now and then send
A wish or a thought after me?
O tell me I yet have a friend,
Though a friend I am never to see.

This passage is quoted as an instance of three different styles of composition. The first four lines are poorly expressed; some Critics would call the language prosaic; the fact is, it would be bad prose, so bad, that it is scarcely worse in metre. The epithet "church-going" applied to a bell, and that by so chaste a writer as Cowper, is an instance of the strange abuses which Poets have introduced into their language, till they and their Readers take them as matters of course, if they do not single them out expressly as objects of admiration. The two lines "Ne'er sighed at the sound," &c., are, in my opinion, an instance of the language of passion wrested from its proper use, and, from the mere circumstance of the composition being in metre, applied upon an occasion that does not justify such violent expressions; and I should condemn the passage, though perhaps few Readers will agree with me, as vicious poetic diction. The last stanza is throughout admirably expressed: it would be equally good whether in prose or verse, except that the Reader has an exquisite pleasure in seeing such natural language so naturally connected with metre. The beauty of this stanza tempts me to conclude with a principle which ought never to be lost sight of, and which has been my chief guide in all I have said,—namely, that in works of *imagination and sentiment*, for of these only have I been treating, in proportion as ideas and ieelings are valuable, whether the composition be in prose or in verse, they require and exact one and the same language. Metre is but adventitious to composition, and the phraseology for which that passport is necessary, even where it may be graceful at all, will be little valued by the judicious.

APPENDIX III

WORDSWORTH'S PREFACE TO THE *POEMS* OF 1815

The powers requisite for the production of poetry are: first, those of Observation and Description,—*i.e.* the ability to observe with accuracy things as they are in themselves, and with fidelity to describe them, unmodified by any passion or feeling existing in the mind of the describer; whether the things depicted be actually present to the senses, or have a place only in the memory. This power, though indispensable to a Poet, is one which he employs only in submission to necessity, and never for a continuance of time: as its exercise supposes all the higher qualities of the mind to be passive, and in a state of subjection to external objects, much in the same way as a translator or engraver ought to be to his original. 2ndly, Sensibility,—which, the more exquisite it is, the wider will be the range of a poet's perceptions; and the more will he be incited to observe objects, both as they exist in themselves and as re-acted upon by his own mind. (The distinction between poetic and human sensibility has been marked in the character of the Poet delineated in the original preface.) 3rdly, Reflection,—which makes the Poet acquainted with the value of actions, images, thoughts, and feelings; and assists the sensibility in perceiving their connection with each other. 4thly, Imagination and Fancy,—to modify, to create, and to associate. 5thly, Invention,—by which characters are composed out of materials supplied by observation; whether of the Poet's own heart and mind, or of external life and nature; and such incidents and situations produced as are most impressive to the imagination, and most fitted to do justice to the characters, sentiments, and passions, which the Poet undertakes to illustrate. And, lastly, Judgment,—to decide how and where, and in what degree, each of these faculties ought to be exerted; so that the less shall not be sacrificed to the greater; nor the greater, slighting the less, arrogate, to its own injury, more than its due. By judgment, also, is determined what are the laws and appropriate graces of every species of composition[1].

[1] As sensibility to harmony of numbers, and the power of producing it, are invariably attendants upon the faculties above specified, nothing has been said upon those requisites.

The materials of Poetry, by these powers collected and produced, are cast, by means of various moulds, into divers forms. The moulds may be enumerated, and the forms specified, in the following order. 1st, The Narrative,—including the Epopœia, the Historic Poem, the Tale, the Romance, the Mock-heroic, and, if the spirit of Homer will tolerate such neighbourhood, that dear production of our days, the metrical Novel. Of this Class, the distinguishing mark is, that the Narrator, however liberally his speaking agents be introduced, is himself the source from which everything primarily flows. Epic Poets, in order that their mode of composition may accord with the elevation of their subject, represent themselves as *singing* from the inspiration of the Muse, "Arma virumque *cano;*" but this is a fiction, in modern times, of slight value: the "Iliad" or the "Paradise Lost" would gain little in our estimation by being chanted. The other poets who belong to this class are commonly content to *tell* their tale;—so that of the whole it may be affirmed that they neither require nor reject the accompaniment of music.

2ndly, The Dramatic,—consisting of Tragedy, Historic Drama, Comedy, and Masque, in which the Poet does not appear at all in his own person, and where the whole action is carried on by speech and dialogue of the agents; music being admitted only incidentally and rarely. The Opera may be placed here, inasmuch as it proceeds by dialogue; though depending, to the degree that it does, upon music, it has a strong claim to be ranked with the lyrical. The characteristic and impassioned Epistle, of which Ovid and Pope have given examples, considered as a species of monodrama, may, without impropriety, be placed in this class.

3rdly, The Lyrical,—containing the Hymn, the Ode, the Elegy, the Song, and the Ballad; in all which, for the production of their *full* effect, an accompaniment of music is indispensable.

4thly, The Idyllium,—descriptive chiefly either of the processes and appearances of external nature, as the "Seasons" of Thomson; or of characters, manners, and sentiments, as are Shenstone's "Schoolmistress," "The Cotter's Saturday Night" of Burns, "The Twa Dogs" of the same Author; or of these in conjunction with the appearances of Nature, as most of the pieces of Theocritus, the "Allegro" and "Penseroso" of Milton, Beattie's "Minstrel," Goldsmith's "Deserted Village." The Epitaph, the Inscription, the Sonnet, most of the epistles of poets writing in their own persons, and all loco-descriptive poetry, belong to this class.

5thly, Didactic,—the principal object of which is direct instruction; as the Poem of Lucretius, the "Georgics" of Virgil, "The Fleece" of Dyer, Mason's "English Garden," &c.

And, lastly, philosophical Satire, like that of Horace and Juvenal; personal and occasional Satire rarely comprehending sufficient of the general in the individual to be dignified with the name of poetry.

Out of the three last has been constructed a composite order, of which Young's "Night Thoughts," and Cowper's "Task," are excellent examples.

It is deducible from the above, that poems, apparently miscellaneous, may with propriety be arranged either with reference to the powers of mind *predominant* in the production of them; or to the mould in which they are cast; or, lastly, to the subjects to which they relate. From each of these considerations, the following Poems have been divided into classes; which, that the work may more obviously correspond with the course of human life, and for the sake of exhibiting in it the three requisites of a legitimate whole, a beginning, a middle and an end, have been also arranged, as far as it was possible, according to an order of time, commencing with Childhood, and terminating with Old Age, Death, and Immortality. My guiding wish was, that the small pieces of which these volumes consist, thus discriminated, might be regarded under a two-fold view; as composing an entire work within themselves, and as adjuncts to the philosophical Poem, "The Recluse." This arrangement has long presented itself habitually to my own mind. Nevertheless, I should have preferred to scatter the contents of these volumes at random, if I had been persuaded that, by the plan adopted, anything material would be taken from the natural effect of the pieces, individually, on the mind of the unreflecting Reader. I trust there is a sufficient variety in each class to prevent this; while, for him who reads with reflection, the arrangement will serve as a commentary unostentatiously directing his attention to my purposes, both particular and general But, as I wish to guard against the possibility of misleading by this classification, it is proper first to remind the Reader, that certain poems are placed according to the powers of mind, in the Author's conception, predominant in the production of them; *predominant*, which implies the exertion of other faculties in less degree. Where there is more imagination than fancy in a poem, it is placed under the head of imagination, and *vice versâ*. Both the above classes might without impropriety have been enlarged from that consisting of "Poems founded on the Affections;" as might this latter from those, and from the class "proceeding from Sentiment and Reflection." The most striking characteristics of each piece, mutual illustration, variety, and proportion, have governed me throughout.

None of the other Classes, except those of Fancy and Imagination, require any particular notice. But a remark of general application may be made. All Poets, except the dramatic, have been in the practice of feigning that their works were composed to the music of the harp or lyre: with what degree of affectation this has been done in modern times, I leave to the judicious to determine. For my own part, I have not been disposed to violate probability so far, or to make such a large demand upon the Reader's charity. Some of these pieces are essentially lyrical; and, therefore, cannot have their due force without a supposed musical accompaniment; but, in much the greatest part, as a substitute for the classic lyre or romantic harp, I require nothing more than an animated or impassioned recitation, adapted to the subject. Poems, however humble in their kind, if they be good in that kind, cannot read themselves; the law of long syllable and short must not be so inflexible,—the letter of metre must not be so impassive to the spirit of versification,—as to deprive the Reader of all voluntary power to modulate, in subordination to the sense, the music of the poem;—in the same manner as his mind is left at liberty, and even summoned, to act upon its thoughts and images. But, though the accompaniment of a musical instrument be frequently dispensed with, the true Poet does not therefore abandon his privilege distinct from that of the mere Proseman;

> He murmurs near the running brooks
> A music sweeter than their own.

Let us come now to the consideration of the words Fancy and Imagination, as employed in the classification of the following Poems. "A man," says an intelligent author, "has imagination in proportion as he can distinctly copy in idea the impressions of sense: it is the faculty which *images* within the mind the phenomena of sensation. A man has fancy in proportion as he can call up, connect, or associate, at pleasure, those internal images (φαντάζειν is to cause to appear) so as to complete ideal representations of absent objects. Imagination is the power of depicting, and fancy of evoking and combining. The imagination is formed by patient observation; the fancy by a voluntary activity in shifting the scenery of the mind. The more accurate the imagination, the more safely may a painter, or a poet, undertake a delineation, or a description, without the presence of the objects to be characterised. The more versatile the fancy, the more original and striking will be the decorations produced."—*British Synonyms discriminated, by W. Taylor.*

Is not this as if a man should undertake to supply an account of a building, and be so intent upon what he had discovered of the foundation, as to conclude his task without once looking up at the superstructure? Here, as in other instances throughout the volume, the judicious Author's mind is enthralled by Etymology; he takes up the original word as his guide and escort, and too often does not perceive how soon he becomes its prisoner, without liberty to tread in any path but that to which it confines him. It is not easy to find out how imagination, thus explained, differs from distinct remembrance of images; or fancy from quick and vivid recollection of them: each is nothing more than a mode of memory. If the two words bear the above meaning, and no other, what term is left to designate that faculty of which the Poet is "all compact;" he whose eye glances from earth to heaven, whose spiritual attributes body forth what his pen is prompt in turning to shape; or what is left to characterise Fancy, as insinuating herself into the heart of objects with creative activity?—Imagination, in the sense of the word as giving title to a class of the following Poems, has no reference to images that are merely a faithful copy, existing in the mind, of absent external objects; but is a word of higher import, denoting operations of the mind upon those objects, and processes of creation or of composition, governed by certain fixed laws. I proceed to illustrate my meaning by instances. A parrot *hangs* from the wires of his cage by his beak or by his claws; or a monkey from the bough of a tree by his paws or his tail. Each creature does so literally and actually. In the first Eclogue of Virgil, the shepherd, thinking of the time when he is to take leave of his farm, thus addresses his goats:—

> Non ego vos posthac viridi projectus in antro
> Dumosa *pendere* procul de rupe videbo.
>
> ———half way down
> *Hangs* one who gathers samphire,

is the well-known expression of Shakspeare, delineating an ordinary image upon the cliffs of Dover. In these two instances is a slight exertion of the faculty which I denominate imagination, in the use of one word: neither the goats nor the samphire-gatherer do literally hang, as does the parrot or the monkey; but, presenting to the senses something of such an appearance, the mind in its activity, for its own gratification, contemplates them as hanging.

> As when far off at sea a fleet descried
> *Hangs* in the clouds, by equinoctial winds
> Close sailing from Bengala, or the isles
> Of Ternate or Tidore, whence merchants bring
> Their spicy drugs; they on the trading flood
> Through the wide Ethiopian to the Cape
> Ply, stemming nightly toward the Pole: so seemed
> Far off the flying Fiend.

Here is the full strength of the imagination involved in the word *hangs*, and exerted upon the whole image: First, the fleet, an aggregate of many ships, is represented as one mighty person, whose track, we know and feel, is upon the waters; but, taking advantage of its appearance to the senses, the Poet dares to represent it as *hanging in the clouds*, both for the gratification of the mind in contemplating the image itself, and in reference to the motion and appearance of the sublime objects to which it is compared.

From impressions of sight we will pass to those of sound; which, as they must necessarily be of a less definite character, shall be selected from these volumes:

> Over his own sweet voice the Stock-dove *broods;*

of the same bird,

> His voice was *buried* among trees,
> Yet to be come at by the breeze;

> O, Cuckoo! shall I call thee *Bird*,
> Or but a wandering *Voice?*

The stock-dove is said to *coo*, a sound well imitating the note of the bird; but, by the intervention of the metaphor *broods*, the affections are called in by the imagination to assist in marking the manner in which the bird reiterates and prolongs her soft note, as if herself delighting to listen to it, and participating of a still and quiet satisfaction, like that which may be supposed inseparable from the continuous process of incubation. "His voice was buried among trees," a metaphor expressing the love of *seclusion* by which this Bird is marked; and characterising its note as not partaking of the shrill and the piercing, and therefore more easily deadened by the intervening shade; yet a note so peculiar and withal so pleasing, that the breeze, gifted with that love of the sound which the Poet feels, penetrates the shades in which it is entombed, and conveys it to the ear of the listener.

> Shall I call thee Bird,
> Or but a wandering Voice?

This concise interrogation characterises the seeming ubiquity of the voice of the cuckoo, and dispossesses the creature almost of a corporeal existence; the Imagination being tempted to this exertion of her power by a consciousness in the memory that the cuckoo is almost perpetually heard throughout the season of spring, but seldom becomes an object of sight.

Thus far of images independent of each other, and immediately endowed by the mind with properties that do not inhere in them, upon an incitement from properties and qualities the existence of which is inherent and obvious. These processes of imagination are carried on either by conferring additional properties upon an object, or abstracting from it some of those which it actually possesses, and thus enabling it to re-act upon the mind which hath performed the process, like a new existence.

I pass from the Imagination acting upon an individual image to a consideration of the same faculty employed upon images in a conjunction by which they modify each other. The Reader has already had a fine instance before him in the passage quoted from Virgil, where the apparently perilous situation of the goat, hanging upon the shaggy precipice, is contrasted with that of the shepherd contemplating it from the seclusion of the cavern in which he lies stretched at ease and in security. Take these images separately, and how unaffecting the picture compared with that produced by their being thus connected with, and opposed to, each other!

As a huge stone is sometimes seen to lie
Couched on the bald top of an eminence,
Wonder to all who do the same espy
By what means it could thither come, and whence,
So that it seems a thing endued with sense,
Like a sea-beast crawled forth, which on a shelf
Of rock or sand reposeth, there to sun himself.

Such seemed this Man; not all alive or dead
Nor all asleep, in his extreme old age.

* * * * *

Motionless as a cloud the old Man stood,
That heareth not the loud winds when they call,
And moveth altogether if it move at all.

In these images, the conferring, the abstracting, and the modifying powers of the Imagination, immediately and mediately acting, are all brought into conjunction. The stone is endowed with something of the power of life to approximate it to the sea-beast; and the sea-beast stripped of some of its vital qualities to assimilate it to the stone; which intermediate image is thus treated for the purpose of bringing the original image, that of the stone, to a nearer resemblance to the figure and condition of the aged Man; who is divested of so much of the indications of life and motion as to bring him to the point where the two objects unite and coalesce in just comparison. After what has been said, the image of the cloud need not be commented upon.

Thus far of an endowing or modifying power: but the Imagination also shapes and *creates;* and how? By innumerable processes; and in none does it more delight than in that of consolidating numbers into unity, and dissolving and separating unity into number,—alternations proceeding from, and governed by, a sublime consciousness of the soul in her own mighty and almost divine powers. Recur to the passage already cited from Milton. When the compact Fleet, as one Person, has been introduced "sailing from Bengala," "They," *i.e.* the "merchants," representing the fleet resolved into a multitude of ships, "ply" their voyage towards the extremities of the earth: "So," (referring to the word "As" in the commencement) "seemed the flying Fiend;" the image of his Person acting to recombine the multitude of ships into one body,—the point from which the comparison set out. "So seemed," and to whom seemed? To the heavenly Muse who dictates the poem, to the eye of the Poet's mind, and to that of the Reader, present at one moment in the wide Ethiopian, and the next in the solitudes, then first broken in upon, of the infernal regions!

Modo me Thebis, modo ponit Athenis.

Hear again this mighty Poet,—speaking of the Messiah going forth to expel from heaven the rebellious angels,

Attended by ten thousand thousand Saints
He onward came: far off his coming shone,—

the retinue of Saints, and the Person of the Messiah himself, lost almost and merged in the splendour of that indefinite abstraction "His coming!"

As I do not mean here to treat this subject further than to throw some light upon the present Volumes, and especially upon one division of them, I shall spare myself and the Reader the trouble of considering the Imagination as it deals with thoughts and sentiments, as it regulates the composition of characters, and determines the course of actions: I will not consider it (more than I have already done by implication) as that power which, in the language of one of my most esteemed Friends, "draws all things to one; which makes things animate or inanimate, beings with their attributes, subjects with their accessories, take one colour and serve to one effect[1]." The grand store-houses of enthusiastic and meditative Imagination, of poetical, as contra-distinguished from human and dramatic Imagination, are the prophetic and lyrical parts of the Holy Scriptures, and the works of Milton; to which I cannot forbear to add those of Spenser. I select these writers in preference to those of ancient Greece and Rome, because the anthropomorphitism of the Pagan religion subjected the minds of the greatest poets in those countries too much to the bondage of definite form; from which the Hebrews were preserved by their abhorrence of idolatry. This abhorrence was almost as strong in our great epic Poet, both from circumstances of his life, and from the constitution of his mind. However imbued the surface might be with classical literature, he was a Hebrew in soul; and all things tended in him towards the sublime.

[1] Charles Lamb upon the genius of Hogarth.

Spenser, of a gentler nature, maintained his freedom by aid of his allegorical spirit, at one time inciting him to create persons out of abstractions; and, at another, by a superior effort of genius, to give the universality and permanence of abstractions to his human beings, by means of attributes and emblems that belong to the highest moral truths and the purest sensations,—of which his character of Una is a glorious example. Of the human and dramatic Imagination the works of Shakespeare are an inexhaustible source.

> I tax not you, ye Elements, with unkindness,
> I never gave you kingdoms, call'd you Daughters!

And if, bearing in mind the many Poets distinguished by this prime quality, whose names I omit to mention; yet justified by recollection of the insults which the ignorant, the incapable, and the presumptuous, have heaped upon these and my other writings, I may be permitted to anticipate the judgment of posterity upon myself, I shall declare (censurable, I grant, if the notoriety of the fact above stated does not justify me) that I have given in these unfavourable times, evidence of exertions of this faculty upon its worthiest objects, the external universe, the moral and religious sentiments of Man, his natural affections, and his acquired passions; which have the same ennobling tendency as the productions of men, in this kind, worthy to be holden in undying remembrance.

To the mode in which Fancy has already been characterised as the power of evoking and combining, or, as my friend Mr. Coleridge has styled it, "the aggregative and associative power," my objection is only that the definition is too general. To aggregate and to associate, to evoke and to combine, belong as well to the Imagination as to the Fancy; but either the materials evoked and combined are different; or they are brought together under a different law, and for a different purpose. Fancy does not require that the materials which she makes use of should be susceptible of change in their constitution, from her touch; and, where they admit of modification, it is enough for her purpose if it be slight, limited, and evanescent. Directly the reverse of these, are the desires and demands of the Imagination. She recoils from everything but the plastic, the pliant, and the indefinite. She leaves it to Fancy to describe Queen Mab as coming,

> In shape no bigger than an agate-stone
> On the fore-finger of an alderman.

Having to speak of stature, she does not tell you that her gigantic Angel was as tall as Pompey's Pillar; much less that he was twelve cubits, or twelve hundred cubits high; or that his dimensions equalled those of Teneriffe or Atlas;—because these, and if they were a million times as high it would be the same, are bounded: The expression is, "His stature reached the sky!" the illimitable firmament!—When the Imagination frames a comparison, if it does not strike on the first presentation, a sense of the truth of the likeness, from the moment that it is perceived, grows—and continues to grow—upon the mind; the resemblance depending less upon outline of form and feature, than upon expression and effect; less upon casual and outstanding, than upon inherent and internal, properties: moreover, the images invariably modify each other.—The law under which the processes of Fancy are carried on is as capricious as the accidents of things, and the effects are surprising, playful, ludicrous, amusing, tender, or pathetic, as the objects happen to be appositely produced or fortunately combined. Fancy depends upon the rapidity and profusion with which she scatters her thoughts and images; trusting that their number, and the felicity with which they are linked together, will make amends for the want of individual value: or she prides herself upon the curious subtilty and the successful elaboration with which she can detect their lurking affinities. If she can win you over to her purpose, and impart to you her feelings, she cares not how unstable or transitory may be her influence, knowing that it will not be out of her power to resume it upon an apt occasion. But the Imagination is conscious of an indestructible dominion;—the Soul may fall away from it, not being able to sustain its grandeur; but, if once felt and acknowledged, by no act of any other faculty of the mind can it be relaxed, impaired, or diminished.—Fancy is given to quicken and to beguile the temporal part of our nature, Imagination to incite and to support the eternal.—Yet is it not the less true that Fancy, as she is an active, is also, under her own laws and in her own spirit, a creative faculty. In what manner Fancy ambitiously aims at a rivalship with Imagination, and Imagination stoops to work with the materials of Fancy, might be illustrated from the compositions of all eloquent writers, whether in prose or verse; and chiefly from those of our own Country. Scarcely a page of the impassioned parts of Bishop Taylor's Works can be opened that shall not afford examples.—Referring the Reader to those inestimable volumes, I will content myself with placing a conceit (ascribed to Lord Chesterfield) in contrast with a passage from the "Paradise Lost":—

> The dews of the evening most carefully shun,
> They are the tears of the sky for the loss of the sun.

After the transgression of Adam, Milton, with other appearances of sympathising Nature, thus marks the immediate consequence,

> Sky lowered, and, muttering thunder, some sad drops
> Wept at completion of the mortal sin.

The associating link is the same in each instance: Dew and rain, not distinguishable from the liquid substance of tears, are employed as indications of sorrow. A flash of surprise is the effect in the former case; a flash of surprise, and nothing more; for the nature of things does not sustain the combination. In the latter, the effects from the act, of which there is this immediate consequence and visible sign, are so momentous, that the mind acknowledges the justice and reasonableness of the sympathy in nature so manifested; and the sky weeps drops of water as if with human eyes, as " Earth had before trembled from her entrails, and Nature given a second groan."

Finally, I will refer to Cotton's " Ode upon Winter," an admirable composition, though stained with some peculiarities of the age in which he lived, for a general illustration of the characteristics of Fancy. The middle part of this ode contains a most lively description of the entrance of Winter, with his retinue, as "A palsied king," and yet a military monarch,—advancing for conquest with his army; the several bodies of which, and their arms and equipments, are described with a rapidity of detail, and a profusion of *fanciful* comparisons, which indicate on the part of the poet extreme activity of intellect, and a correspondent hurry of delightful feeling. Winter retires from the foe into his fortress, where

> ——a magazine
> Of sovereign juice is cellared in;
> Liquor that will the siege maintain
> Should Phœbus ne'er return again.

Though myself a water-drinker, I cannot resist the pleasure of transcribing what follows, as an instance still more happy of Fancy employed in the treatment of feeling than, in its preceding passages, the Poem supplies of her management of forms.

> 'Tis that, that gives the poet rage,
> And thaws the gelid blood of age;
> Matures the young, restores the old,
> And makes the fainting coward bold.
>
> It lays the careful head to rest,
> Calms palpitations in the breast,
> Renders our lives' misfortune sweet;
>
> * * * *
>
> Then let the chill Sirocco blow,
> And gird us round with hills of snow,
> Or else go whistle to the shore,
> And make the hollow mountains roar,

Whilst we together jovial sit
Careless, and crowned with mirth and wit,
Where, though bleak winds confine us home
Our fancies round the world shall roam.

We'll think of all the Friends we know,
And drink to all worth drinking to;
When having drunk all thine and mine,
We rather shall want healths than wine.

But where Friends fail us, we'll supply
Our friendships with our charity;
Men that remote in sorrows live,
Shall by our lusty brimmers thrive.

We'll drink the wanting into wealth,
And those that languish into health,
The afflicted into joy; th' opprest
Into security and rest.

The worthy in disgrace shall find
Favour return again more kind,
And in restraint who stifled lie,
Shall taste the air of liberty.

The brave shall triumph in success,
The lover shall have mistresses,
Poor unregarded Virtue, praise,
And the neglected Poet, bays.

Thus shall our healths do others good,
Whilst we ourselves do all we would;
For, freed from envy and from care,
What would we be but what we are?

When I sate down to write this Preface, it was my intention to have made it more comprehensive; but, thinking that I ought rather to apologise for detaining the reader so long, I will here conclude.

ESSAY, SUPPLEMENTARY TO PREFACE [1815]

With the young of both sexes, Poetry is, like love, a passion; but, for much the greater part of those who have been proud of its power over their minds, a necessity soon arises of breaking the pleasing bondage; or it relaxes of itself;—the thoughts being occupied in domestic cares, or the time engrossed by business. Poetry then becomes only an occasional recreation; while to those whose existence passes away in a course of fashionable pleasure, it is a species of luxurious amusement.

In middle and declining age, a scattered number of serious persons resort to poetry, as to religion, for a protection against the pressure of trivial employments, and as a consolation for the afflictions of life. And, lastly, there are many, who, having been enamoured of this art in their youth, have found leisure, after youth was spent, to cultivate general literature; in which poetry has continued to be comprehended *as a study*.

Into the above classes the Readers of poetry may be divided; Critics abound in them all; but from the last only can opinions be collected of absolute value, and worthy to be depended upon, as prophetic of the destiny of a new work. The young, who in nothing can escape delusion, are especially subject to it in their intercourse with Poetry. The cause, not so obvious as the fact is unquestionable, is the same as that from which erroneous judgments in this art, in the minds of men of all ages, chiefly proceed; but upon Youth it operates with peculiar force. The appropriate business of poetry, (which, nevertheless, if genuine, is as permanent as pure science,) her appropriate employment, her privilege and her *duty*, is to treat of things not as they *are*, but as they *appear;* not as they exist in themselves, but as they *seem* to exist to the *senses*, and to the *passions*. What a world of delusion does this acknowledged obligation prepare for the inexperienced! what temptations to go astray are here held forth for them whose thoughts have been little disciplined by the understanding, and whose feelings revolt from the sway of reason!—When a juvenile Reader is in the height of his rapture with some vicious passage, should experience throw in doubts, or common-sense suggest suspicions, a lurking consciousness that the realities of the Muse are but shows, and that her liveliest excitements are raised by transient shocks of conflicting feeling and successive assemblages of contradictory thoughts—is ever at hand to justify extravagance, and to sanction absurdity. But, it may be asked, as these illusions are unavoidable, and, no doubt, eminently useful to the mind as a process, what good can be gained by making observations, the tendency of which is to diminish the confidence of youth in its feelings, and thus to abridge its innocent and even profitable pleasures? The reproach implied in the question could not be warded off, if Youth were incapable of being delighted with what is truly excellent; or, if these errors always terminated of themselves in due season. But, with the majority, though their force be abated, they continue through life. Moreover, the fire of youth is too vivacious an element to be extinguished or damped by a philosophical remark; and, while there is no danger that what has been said will be injurious or painful to the ardent and the confident, it may prove beneficial to those who, being enthusiastic, are, at the same time, modest and ingenuous. The intimation may unite with their own misgivings to regulate their sensibility, and to bring in, sooner than it would otherwise have arrived, a more discreet and sound judgment.

If it should excite wonder that men of ability, in later life, whose understandings have been rendered acute by practice in affairs, should be so easily and so far imposed upon when they happen to take up a new work in verse, this appears to be the cause;—that, having discontinued their attention to poetry, whatever progress may have been made in other departments of knowledge, they have not, as to this art, advanced in true discernment beyond the age of youth. If, then, a new poem fall in their way, whose attractions are of that kind which would have enraptured them during the heat of youth, the judgment not being improved to a degree that they shall be disgusted, they are dazzled; and prize and cherish the faults for having had power to make the present time vanish before them, and to throw the mind back, as by enchantment, into the happiest season of life. As they read, powers seem to be revived, passions are regenerated, and pleasures restored. The Book was probably taken up after an escape from the burden of business, and with a wish to forget the world, and all its vexations and anxieties. Having obtained this wish, and so much more, it is natural that they should make report as they have felt.

If Men of mature age, through want of practice, be thus easily beguiled into admiration of absurdities, extravagances, and misplaced ornaments, thinking it proper that their understandings should enjoy a holiday, while they are unbending their minds with verse, it may be expected that such Readers will resemble their former selves also in strength of prejudice, and an inaptitude to be moved by the unostentatious beauties of a pure style. In the higher poetry, an enlightened Critic chiefly looks for a reflection of the wisdom of the heart and the grandeur of the imagination. Wherever these appear, simplicity accompanies them; Magnificence herself when legitimate, depending upon a simplicity of her own, to regulate her ornaments. But it is a well-known property of human nature, that our estimates are ever governed by comparisons, of which we are conscious with various degrees of distinctness. Is it not, then, inevitable (confining these observations to the effects of style merely) that an eye, accustomed to the glaring hues of diction by which such Readers are caught and excited, will for the most part be rather repelled than attracted by an original Work, the colouring of which is disposed according to a pure and refined scheme of harmony? It is in the fine arts as in the affairs of life, no man can *serve* (*i.e.* obey with zeal and fidelity) two Masters.

As Poetry is most just to its own divine origin when it administers the comforts and breathes the spirit of religion, they who have learned to perceive this truth, and who betake themselves to reading verse for sacred purposes, must be preserved from numerous illusions to which the two Classes of Readers, whom we have been considering, are liable. But, as the mind grows serious from the weight of life, the range of its passions is contracted accordingly; and its sympathies become so exclusive, that many species of high excellence wholly escape, or but languidly excite, its notice. Besides, men who read from religious or moral inclinations, even when the subject is of that kind which they approve, are beset with misconceptions and mistakes peculiar to themselves. Attaching so much importance to the truths which interest them, they are prone to overrate the Authors by whom those truths are expressed and enforced. They come prepared to impart so much passion to the Poet's language, that they remain unconscious how little, in fact, they receive from it. And, on the other hand, religious faith is to him who holds it so momentous a thing, and error appears to be attended with such tremendous consequences, that, if opinions touching upon religion occur which the Reader condemns, he not only cannot sympathise with them, however animated the expression, but there is, for the most part, an end put to all satisfaction and enjoyment. Love, if it before existed, is converted into dislike; and the heart of the Reader is set against the Author and his book.—To these excesses, they, who from their professions ought to be the most guarded against them, are perhaps the most liable; I mean those sects whose religion, being from the calculating understanding, is cold and formal. For when Christianity, the religion of humility, is founded upon the proudest faculty of our nature, what can be expected but contradictions? Accordingly, believers of this cast are at one time contemptuous; at another, being troubled, as they are and must be, with inward misgivings, they are jealous and suspicious;—and at all seasons, they are under temptation to supply by the heat with which they defend their tenets, the animation which is wanting to the constitution of the religion itself.

Faith was given to man that his affections, detached from the treasures of time, might be inclined to settle upon those of eternity;—the elevation of his nature, which this habit produces on earth, being to him a presumptive evidence of a future state of existence; and giving him a title to partake of its holiness. The religious man values what he sees chiefly as an "imperfect shadowing forth" of what he is incapable of seeing. The concerns of religion refer to indefinite objects, and are too weighty for the mind to support them without relieving itself by resting a great part of the burthen upon words and symbols. The commerce between Man and his Maker cannot be carried on but by a process where much is represented in little, and the Infinite Being accommodates himself to a finite capacity. In all this may be perceived the affinity between religion and poetry; between religion—making up the deficiencies of reason by faith; and poetry—passionate for the instruction of reason; between religion—whose element is infinitude, and whose ultimate trust is the supreme of things, submitting herself to circumscription, and reconciled to substitutions; and poetry—ethereal and transcendent, yet incapable to sustain her existence without sensuous incarnation. In this community of nature may be perceived also the lurking incitements of kindred error;—so that we shall find that no poetry has been more subject to distortion, than that species, the argument and scope of which is religious; and no lovers of the art have gone farther astray than the pious and the devout.

Whither then shall we turn for that union of qualifications which must necessarily exist before the decisions of a critic can be of absolute value? For a mind at once poetical and philosophical; for a critic whose affections are as free and kindly as the spirit of society, and whose understanding is severe as that of dispassionate government? Where are we to look for that initiatory composure of mind which no selfishness can disturb? For a natural sensibility that has been tutored into correctness without losing anything of its quickness; and for active faculties, capable of answering the demands which an Author of original imagination shall make upon them, associated with a judgment that cannot be duped into admiration by aught that is unworthy of it?—among those and those only, who, never having suffered their youthful love of poetry to remit much of its force, have applied to the consideration of the laws of this art the best power of their understandings. At the same time it must be observed—that, as this Class comprehends the only judgments which are trust-worthy, so does it include the most erroneous and perverse. For to be mistaught is worse than to be untaught; and no perverseness equals that which is supported by system, no errors are so difficult to root out as those which the understanding has pledged its credit to uphold. In this Class are contained censors, who, if they be pleased with what is good, are pleased with it only by imperfect glimpses, and upon false principles; who, should they generalise rightly, to a certain point, are sure to suffer for it in the end; who, if they stumble upon a sound rule, are fettered by misapplying it, or by straining it too far; being incapable of perceiving when it ought to yield to one of higher order. In it are found critics too petulant to be passive to a genuine poet, and too feeble to grapple with him; men, who take upon them to report of the course which *he* holds whom they are utterly unable to accompany,—confounded if he turn quick upon the wing, dismayed if he soar steadily "into the region;"—men of palsied imaginations and indurated hearts; in whose minds all healthy action is languid, who therefore feed as the many direct them, or, with the many, are greedy after vicious provocatives;—judges, whose censure is auspicious, and whose praise ominous! In this class meet together the two extremes of best and worst.

The observations presented in the foregoing series are of too ungracious a nature to have been made without reluctance; and, were it only on this account, I would invite the reader to try them by the test of comprehensive experience. If the number of judges who can be confidently relied upon be in reality so small, it ought to follow that partial notice only, or neglect, perhaps long continued, or attention wholly inadequate to their merits—must have been the fate of most works in the higher departments of poetry; and that, on the other hand, numerous productions have blazed into popularity, and have passed away, leaving scarcely a trace behind them: it will be further found, that when Authors shall have at length raised themselves into general admiration and maintained their ground, errors and prejudices have prevailed concerning their genius and their works, which the few who are conscious of those errors and prejudices would deplore; if they were not recompensed by perceiving that there are select Spirits for whom it is ordained that their fame shall be in the world an existence like that of Virtue, which owes its being to the struggles it makes, and its vigour to the enemies whom it provokes;—a vivacious quality, ever doomed to meet with opposition, and still triumphing over it; and, from the nature of its dominion, incapable of being brought to the sad conclusion of Alexander when he wept that there were no more worlds for him to conquer.

Let us take a hasty retrospect of the poetical literature of this Country for the greater part of the last two centuries, and see if the facts support these inferences.

Who is there that now reads the " Creation " of Dubartas? Yet all Europe once resounded with his praise; he was caressed by kings; and, when his Poem was translated into our language, the "Faery Queen" faded before it. The name of Spenser, whose genius is of a higher order than even that of Ariosto, is at this day scarcely known beyond the limits of the British Isles. And if the value of his works is to be estimated from the attention now paid to them by his countrymen, compared with that which they bestow on those of some other writers, it must be pronounced small indeed.

> The laurel, meed of mighty conquerors
> And poets *sage*—

are his own words; but his wisdom has, in this particular, been his worst enemy: while its opposite, whether in the shape of folly or madness, has been *their* best friend. But he was a great power, and bears a high name: the laurel has been awarded to him.

A dramatic Author, if he write for the stage, must adapt himself to the taste of the audience, or they will not endure him; accordingly the mighty genius of Shakspeare was listened to. The people were delighted: but I am not sufficiently versed in stage antiquities to determine whether they did not flock as eagerly to the representation of many pieces of contemporary Authors, wholly undeserving to appear upon the same boards. Had there been a formal contest for superiority among dramatic writers, that Shakspeare, like his predecessors Sophocles and Euripides, would have often been subject to the mortification of seeing the prize adjudged to sorry competitors, becomes too probable, when we reflect that the admirers of Settle and Shadwell were, in a later age, as numerous, and reckoned as respectable in point of talent, as those of Dryden. At all events, that Shakspeare stooped to accommodate himself to the People, is sufficiently apparent; and one of the most striking proofs of his almost omnipotent genius, is, that he could turn to such glorious purpose those materials which the prepossessions of the age compelled him to make use of. Yet even this marvellous skill appears not to have been enough to prevent his rivals from having some advantage over him in public estimation; else how can we account for passages and scenes that exist in his works, unless upon a supposition that some of the grossest of them, a fact which in my own mind I have no doubt of, were foisted in by the Players, for the gratification of the many?

But that his Works, whatever might be their reception upon the stage, made but little impression upon the ruling Intellects of the time, may be inferred from the fact that Lord Bacon, in his multifarious writings, nowhere either quotes or alludes to him[1]. His dramatic excellence enabled him to resume possession of the stage after the Restoration; but Dryden tells us that in his time two of the plays of Beaumont and Fletcher were acted for one of Shakspeare's. And so faint and limited was the perception of the poetic beauties of his dramas in the time of Pope, that, in his Edition of the Plays, with a view of rendering to the general reader a necessary service, he printed between inverted commas those passages which he thought most worthy of notice.

At this day, the French Critics have abated nothing of their aversion

[1] The learned Hakewill (a third edition of whose book bears date 1635), writing to refute the error "touching Nature's perpetual and universal decay," cites triumphantly the names of Ariosto, Tasso, Bartas, and Spenser, as instances that poetic genius had not degenerated; but he makes no mention of Shakspeare.

to this darling of our Nation: "the English, with their bouffon de Shakspeare," is as familiar an expression among them as in the time of Voltaire. Baron Grimm is the only French writer who seems to have perceived his infinite superiority to the first names of the French Theatre; an advantage which the Parisian Critic owed to his German blood and German education. The most enlightened Italians, though well acquainted with our language, are wholly incompetent to measure the proportions of Shakspeare. The Germans only, of foreign nations, are approaching towards a knowledge and feeling of what he is. In some respects they have acquired a superiority over the fellow-countrymen of the Poet: for among us it is a current, I might say, an established opinion, that Shakspeare is justly praised when he is pronounced to be "a wild irregular genius, in whom great faults are compensated by great beauties." How long may it be before this misconception passes away, and it becomes universally acknowledged that the judgment of Shakspeare in the selection of his materials, and in the manner in which he has made them, heterogeneous as they often are, constitute a unity of their own, and contribute all to one great end, is not less admirable than his imagination, his invention, and his intuitive knowledge of human nature?

There is extant a small Volume of miscellaneous poems, in which Shakspeare expresses his own feelings in his own person. It is not difficult to conceive that the Editor, George Steevens, should have been insensible to the beauties of one portion of that Volume, the Sonnets; though in no part of the writings of this Poet is found, in an equal compass, a greater number of exquisite feelings felicitously expressed. But, from regard to the Critic's own credit, he would not have ventured to talk of an[1] act of parliament not being strong enough to compel the perusal of those little pieces, if he had not known that the people of England were ignorant of the treasures contained in them: and if he had not, moreover, shared the too common propensity of human nature to exult over a supposed fall into the mire of a genius whom he had been compelled to regard with admiration, as an inmate of the celestial regions—"there sitting where he durst not soar."

Nine years before the death of Shakspeare, Milton was born; and early in life he published several small poems, which, though on their first appearance they were praised by a few of the judicious, were afterwards neglected to that degree, that Pope in his youth could

[1] This flippant insensibility was publicly reprehended by Mr. Coleridge in a course of Lectures upon Poetry given by him at the Royal Institution. For the various merits of thought and language in Shakspeare's Sonnets, see Numbers, 27, 29, 30, 32, 33, 54, 64, 66, 68, 73, 76, 86, 91, 92, 93, 97, 98, 105, 107, 108, 109, 111, 113, 114, 116, 117, 129, and many others.

borrow from them without risk of its being known. Whether these poems are at this day justly appreciated, I will not undertake to decide: nor would it imply a severe reflection upon the mass of readers to suppose the contrary; seeing that a man of the acknowledged genius of Voss, the German poet, could suffer their spirit to evaporate; and could change their character, as is done in the translation made by him of the most popular of those pieces. At all events, it is certain that these Poems of Milton are now much read, and loudly praised; yet were they little heard of till more than 150 years after their publication; and of the Sonnets, Dr. Johnson, as appears from Boswell's Life of him, was in the habit of thinking and speaking as contemptuously as Steevens wrote upon those of Shakspeare.

About the time when the Pindaric odes of Cowley and his imitators, and the productions of that class of curious thinkers whom Dr. Johnson has strangely styled metaphysical Poets, were beginning to lose something of that extravagant admiration which they had excited, the "Paradise Lost" made its appearance. "Fit audience find though few," was the petition addressed by the Poet to his inspiring Muse. I have said elsewhere that he gained more than he asked; this I believe to be true; but Dr. Johnson has fallen into a gross mistake when he attempts to prove, by the sale of the work, that Milton's Countrymen were "*just* to it" upon its first appearance. Thirteen hundred Copies were sold in two years; an uncommon example, he asserts, of the prevalence of genius in opposition to so much recent enmity as Milton's public conduct had excited. But, be it remembered that, if Milton's political and religious opinions, and the manner in which he announced them, had raised him many enemies, they had procured him numerous friends; who, as all personal danger was passed away at the time of publication, would be eager to procure the master-work of a man whom they revered, and whom they would be proud of praising. Take, from the number of purchasers, persons of this class, and also those who wished to possess the Poem as a religious work, and but few I fear would be left who sought for it on account of its poetical merits. The demand did not immediately increase; "for," says Dr. Johnson, "many more readers" (he means persons in the habit of reading poetry) "than were supplied at first the Nation did not afford." How careless must a writer be who can make this assertion in the face of so many existing title-pages to belie it! Turning to my own shelves, I find the folio of Cowley, seventh edition, 1681. A book near it is Flatman's Poems, fourth edition, 1686; Waller, fifth edition, same date. The Poems of Norris of Bemerton not long after went, I believe, through nine editions. What further demand there might be for these works I do not know; but I well remember, that, twenty-five years ago, the booksellers' stalls in London swarmed with the folios of Cowley. This is not mentioned in disparagement of that able writer and amiable man; but merely to show—that, if Milton's work were not more read, it was not because readers did not exist at the time. The early editions of the "Paradise Lost" were printed in a shape which allowed them to be sold at a low price, yet only three thousand copies of the Work were sold in eleven years; and the Nation, says Dr. Johnson, had been satisfied from 1623 to 1664, that is, forty-one years, with only two editions of the Works of Shakspeare; which probably did not together make one thousand Copies; facts adduced by the critic to prove the "paucity of Readers."—There were readers in multitudes; but their money went for other purposes, as their admiration was fixed elsewhere. We are authorised, then, to affirm, that the reception of the "Paradise Lost," and the slow progress of its fame, are proofs as striking as can be desired that the positions which I am attempting to establish are not erroneous[1].—How amusing to shape to one's self such a critique as a Wit of Charles's days, or a Lord of the Miscellanies or trading Journalist of King William's time, would have brought forth, if he had set his faculties industriously to work upon this Poem, everywhere impregnated with *original* excellence.

So strange indeed are the obliquities of admiration, that they whose opinions are much influenced by authority will often be tempted to think that there are no fixed principles[2] in human nature for this art to rest upon. I have been honoured by being permitted to peruse in MS. a tract composed between the period of the Revolution and the close of that century. It is the Work of an English Peer of high accomplishments, its object to form the character and direct the studies of his son. Perhaps nowhere does a more beautiful treatise of the kind exist. The good sense and wisdom of the thoughts, the delicacy of the feelings, and the charm of the style, are, throughout, equally conspicuous. Yet the Author, selecting among the Poets of his own country those whom he deems most worthy of his son's perusal, particularises only Lord Rochester, Sir John Denham, and Cowley. Writing about the same time, Shaftesbury, an author at present unjustly depreciated, describes the English Muses as only yet lisping in their cradles.

The arts by which Pope, soon afterwards, contrived to procure to

[1] Hughes is express upon this subject: in his dedication of Spenser's Works to Lord Somers, he writes thus. "It was your Lordship's encouraging a beautiful edition of 'Paradise Lost' that first brought that incomparable Poem to be generally known and esteemed."

[2] This opinion seems actually to have been entertained by Adam Smith, the worst critic, David Hume not excepted, that Scotland, a soil to which this sort of weed seems natural, has produced.

himself a more general and a higher reputation than perhaps any English Poet ever attained during his life-time, are known to the judicious. And as well known is it to them that, the undue exertion of those arts is the cause why Pope has for some time held a rank in literature, to which, if he had not been seduced by an over-love of immediate popularity, and had confided more in his native genius, he never could have descended. He bewitched the nation by his melody, and dazzled it by his polished style, and was himself blinded by his own success. Having wandered from humanity in his Eclogues with boyish inexperience, the praise, which these compositions obtained, tempted him into a belief that Nature was not to be trusted, at least in pastoral Poetry. To prove this by example, he put his friend Gay upon writing those Eclogues which their author intended to be burlesque. The instigator of the work, and his admirers, could perceive in them nothing but what was ridiculous. Nevertheless, though these Poems contain some detestable passages, the effect, as Dr. Johnson well observes, "of reality and truth became conspicuous even when the intention was to show them grovelling and degraded." The Pastorals, ludicrous to such as prided themselves upon their refinement, in spite of those disgusting passages, "became popular, and were read with delight, as just representations of rural manners and occupations."

Something less than sixty years after the publication of the "Paradise Lost" appeared Thomson's "Winter;" which was speedily followed by his other Seasons. It is a work of inspiration; much of it is written from himself, and nobly from himself. How was it received? "It was no sooner read," says one of his contemporary biographers, "than universally admired: those only excepted who had not been used to feel, or to look for anything in poetry, beyond a *point* of satirical or epigrammatic wit, a smart *antithesis* richly trimmed with rhyme, or the softness of an *elegiac* complaint. To such his manly classical spirit could not readily commend itself; till, after a more attentive perusal, they had got the better of their prejudices, and either acquired or affected a truer taste. A few others stood aloof, merely because they had long before fixed the articles of their poetical creed, and resigned themselves to an absolute despair of ever seeing anything new and original. These were somewhat mortified to find their notions disturbed by the appearance of a poet, who seemed to owe nothing but to nature and his own genius. But, in a short time, the applause became unanimous; every one wondering how so many pictures, and pictures so familiar, should have moved them but faintly to what they felt in his descriptions. His digressions too, the overflowings of a tender benevolent heart, charmed the reader no less; leaving him in doubt, whether he should more admire the Poet or love the Man."

This case appears to bear strongly against us:—but we must distinguish between wonder and legitimate admiration. The subject of the work is the changes produced in the appearances of nature by the revolution of the year: and, by undertaking to write in verse, Thomson pledged himself to treat his subject as became a Poet. Now, it is remarkable that, excepting the nocturnal Reverie of Lady Winchilsea, and a passage or two in the "Windsor Forest" of Pope, the poetry of the period intervening between the publication of the "Paradise Lost" and the "Seasons" does not contain a single new image of external nature; and scarcely presents a familiar one from which it can be inferred that the eye of the Poet had been steadily fixed upon his object, much less that his feelings had urged him to work upon it in the spirit of genuine imagination. To what a low state knowledge of the most obvious and important phenomena had sunk, is evident from the style in which Dryden has executed a description of Night in one of his Tragedies, and Pope his translation of the celebrated moonlight scene in the "Iliad." A blind man, in the habit of attending accurately to descriptions casually dropped from the lips of those around him, might easily depict these appearances with more truth. Dryden's lines are vague, bombastic, and senseless[1]; those of Pope, though he had Homer to guide him, are throughout false and contradictory. The verses of Dryden, once highly celebrated, are forgotten; those of Pope still retain their hold upon public estimation,—nay, there is not a passage of descriptive poetry, which at this day finds so many and such ardent admirers. Strange to think of an enthusiast, as may have been the case with thousands, reciting those verses under the cope of a moonlight sky, without having his raptures in the least disturbed by a suspicion of their absurdity!—If these two distinguished writers could habitually think that the visible universe was of so little consequence to a poet, that it was scarcely necessary for him to cast his eyes upon it, we may be assured that those passages of the elder poets which faithfully and poetically describe the phenomena of nature, were not at that time holden in much estimation, and that there was little accurate attention paid to those appearances.

Wonder is the natural product of Ignorance; and as the soil was *in*

1 CORTES *alone in a night-gown.*

All things are hush'd as Nature's self lay dead;
The mountains seem to nod their drowsy head.
The little Birds in dreams their songs repeat,
And sleeping Flowers beneath the Night-dew sweat:
Even Lust and Envy sleep; yet Love denies
Rest to my soul, and slumber to my eyes."

DRYDEN'S *Indian Emperor.*

such good condition at the time of the publication of the "Seasons," the crop was doubtless abundant. Neither individuals nor nations become corrupt all at once, nor are they enlightened in a moment. Thomson was an inspired poet, but he could not work miracles; in cases where the art of seeing had in some degree been learned, the teacher would further the proficiency of his pupils, but he could do little *more;* though so far does vanity assist men in acts of self-deception, that many would often fancy they recognized a likeness when they knew nothing of the original. Having shown that much of what his biographer deemed genuine admiration must in fact have been blind wonderment —how is the rest to be accounted for?—Thomson was fortunate in the very title of his poem, which seemed to bring it home to the prepared sympathies of every one: in the next place, notwithstanding his high powers, he writes a vicious style; and his false ornaments are exactly of that kind which would be most likely to strike the undiscerning. He likewise abounds with sentimental common-places, that, from the manner in which they were brought forward, bore an imposing air of novelty. In any well-used copy of the "Seasons" the book generally opens of itself with the rhapsody on love, or with one of the stories (perhaps "Damon and Musidora"); these also are prominent in our collections of Extracts, and are the parts of his Work which, after all, were probably most efficient in first recommending the author to general notice. Pope, repaying praises which he had received, and wishing to extol him to the highest, only styles him "an elegant and philosophical Poet;" nor are we able to collect any unquestionable proofs that the true characteristics of Thomson's genius as an imaginative poet[1] were perceived, till the elder Warton, almost forty years after the publication of the "Seasons," pointed them out by a note in his Essay on the "Life and Writings of Pope." In the "Castle of Indolence" (of which Gray speaks so coldly) these characteristics were almost as conspicuously displayed, and in verse more harmonious, and diction more pure. Yet that fine poem was neglected on its appearance, and is at this day the delight only of a few!

When Thomson died, Collins breathed forth his regrets in an Elegiac Poem, in which he pronounces a poetical curse upon *him* who should regard with insensibility the place where the Poet's remains were deposited. The Poems of the mourner himself have now passed through innumerable editions, and are universally known; but if, when Collins

[1] Since these observations upon Thomson were written, I have perused the second edition of his "Seasons," and find that even *that* does not contain the most striking passages which Warton points out for admiration; these, with other improvements, throughout the whole work, must have been added at a later period.

died, the same kind of imprecation had been pronounced by a surviving admirer, small is the number whom it would not have comprehended. The notice which his poems attained during his lifetime was so small, and of course the sale so insignificant, that not long before his death he deemed it right to repay to the bookseller the sum which he had advanced for them, and threw the edition into the fire.

Next in importance to the "Seasons" of Thomson, though at considerable distance from that work in order of time, come the "Reliques of Ancient English Poetry;" collected, new-modelled, and in many instances (if such a contradiction in terms may be used) composed by the Editor, Dr. Percy. This work did not steal silently into the world, as is evident from the number of legendary tales, that appeared not long after its publication; and had been modelled, as the authors persuaded themselves, after the old Ballad. The Compilation was however ill suited to the then existing taste of city society; and Dr. Johnson, 'mid the little senate to which he gave laws, was not sparing in his exertions to make it an object of contempt. The critic triumphed, the legendary imitators were deservedly disregarded, and, as undeservedly, their ill-imitated models sank, in this country, into temporary neglect; while Bürger, and other able writers of Germany, were translating or imitating these Reliques, and composing, with the aid of inspiration thence derived, poems which are the delight of the German nation. Dr. Percy was so abashed by the ridicule flung upon his labours from the ignorance and insensibility of the persons with whom he lived, that, though while he was writing under a mask he had not wanted resolution to follow his genius into the regions of true simplicity and genuine pathos (as is evinced by the exquisite ballad of "Sir Cauline" and by many other pieces), yet when he appeared in his own person and character as a poetical writer, he adopted, as in the tale of the "Hermit of Warkworth," a diction scarcely in any one of its features distinguishable from the vague, the glossy, and unfeeling language of his day. I mention this remarkable fact[1] with regret, esteeming the genius of Dr. Percy in this kind of writing superior to that of any other man by whom in modern times it has been cultivated. That even Bürger (to whom Klopstock gave, in my hearing, a commendation which he denied

[1] Shenstone, in his "Schoolmistress," gives a still more remarkable instance of this timidity. On its first appearance, (see D'Israeli's 2nd Series of the "Curiosities of Literature") the Poem was accompanied with an absurd prose commentary, showing, as indeed some incongruous expressions in the text imply, that the whole was intended for burlesque. In subsequent editions, the commentary was dropped, and the People have since continued to read in seriousness, doing for the Author what he had not courage openly to venture upon for himself.

to Goethe and Schiller, pronouncing him to be a genuine poet, and one of the few among the Germans whose works would last) had not the fine sensibility of Percy, might be shown from many passages, in which he has deserted his original only to go astray. For example,

Now daye was gone, and night was come,
And all were fast asleepe,
All save the Lady Emeline,
Who sate in her bowre to weepe:

And soone she heard her true Love's voice
Low whispering at the walle,
Awake, awake, my dear Ladye,
'Tis I thy true-love call.

Which is thus tricked out and dilated:

Als nun die Nacht Gebirg' und Thal
Vermummt in Rabenschatten,
Und Hochburgs Lampen überall
Schon ausgeflimmert hatten,
Und alles tief entschlafen war;
Doch nur das Fräulein immerdar,
Voll Fieberangst, noch wachte,
Und seinen Ritter dachte:
Da horch! Ein süsser Liebeston
Kam leis' empor geflogen.
"Ho, Trudchen, ho! Da bin ich schon!
Frisch auf! Dich angezogen!"

But from humble ballads we must ascend to heroics.

All hail, Macpherson! hail to thee, Sire of Ossian! The Phantom was begotten by the snug embrace of an impudent Highlander upon a cloud of tradition—it travelled southward, where it was greeted with acclamation, and the thin Consistence took its course through Europe, upon the breath of popular applause. The Editor of the "Reliques" had indirectly preferred a claim to the praise of invention, by not concealing that his supplementary labours were considerable! how selfish his conduct, contrasted with that of the disinterested Gael, who, like Lear, gives his kingdom away, and is content to become a pensioner upon his own issue for a beggarly pittance!—Open this far-famed Book!—I have done so at random, and the beginning of the "Epic Poem Temora," in eight Books, presents itself. "The blue waves of Ullin roll in light. The green hills are covered with day. Trees shake their dusky heads in the breeze. Grey torrents pour their noisy streams. Two green hills with aged oaks surround a narrow plain. The blue course of a stream is there. On its banks stood Cairbar of Atha. His spear supports the king; the red eyes of his fear are sad. Cormac rises on his soul with all his ghastly wounds." Precious memorandums from the pocket-book of the blind Ossian!

If it be unbecoming, as I acknowledge that for the most part it is, to speak disrespectfully of Works that have enjoyed for a length of time a widely-spread reputation, without at the same time producing irrefragable proofs of their unworthiness, let me be forgiven upon this occasion.—Having had the good fortune to be born and reared in a mountainous country, from my very childhood I have felt the falsehood that pervades the volumes imposed upon the world under the name of Ossian. From what I saw with my own eyes, I knew that the imagery was spurious. In nature everything is distinct, yet nothing defined into absolute independent singleness. In Macpherson's work, it is exactly the reverse; everything (that is not stolen) is in this manner defined, insulated, dislocated, deadened,—yet nothing distinct. It will always be so when words are substituted for things. To say that the characters never could exist, that the manners are impossible, and that a dream has more substance than the whole state of society, as there depicted, is doing nothing more than pronouncing a censure which Macpherson defied; when, with the steeps of Morven before his eyes, he could talk so familiarly of his Car-borne heroes;—of Morven, which, if one may judge from its appearance at the distance of a few miles, contains scarcely an acre of ground sufficiently accommodating for a sledge to be trailed along its surface.—Mr. Malcolm Laing has ably shown that the diction of this pretended translation is a motley assemblage from all quarters; but he is so fond of making out parallel passages as to call poor Macpherson to account for his "*ands*" and his "*buts!*" and he has weakened his argument by conducting it as if he thought that every striking resemblance was a *conscious* plagiarism. It is enough that the coincidences are too remarkable for its being probable or possible that they could arise in different minds without communication between them. Now as the Translators of the Bible, and Shakspeare, Milton, and Pope, could not be indebted to Macpherson, it follows that he must have owed his fine feathers to them; unless we are prepared gravely to assert, with Madame de Staël, that many of the characteristic beauties of our most celebrated English Poets are derived from the ancient Fingallian; in which case the modern translator would have been but giving back to Ossian his own.—It is consistent that Lucien Buonaparte, who could censure Milton for having surrounded Satan in the infernal regions with courtly and regal splendour, should pronounce the modern Ossian to be the glory of Scotland;—a country that has produced a Dunbar, a Buchanan, a Thomson, and a Burns! These opinions are of ill omen for the Epic ambition of him who has given them to the world.

Yet, much as those pretended treasures of antiquity have been admired, they have been wholly uninfluential upon the literature of the Country. No succeeding writer appears to have caught from them a ray of inspiration; no author, in the least distinguished, has ventured formally to imitate them—except the boy, Chatterton, on their first appearance. He had perceived, from the successful trials which he himself had made in literary forgery, how few critics were able to distinguish between a real ancient medal and a counterfeit of modern manufacture; and he set himself to the work of filling a magazine with *Saxon Poems*,—counterparts of those of Ossian, as like his as one of his misty stars is to another. This incapability to amalgamate with the literature of the Island, is, in my estimation, a decisive proof that the book is essentially unnatural; nor should I require any other to demonstrate it to be a forgery, audacious as worthless.—Contrast, in this respect, the effect of Macpherson's publication with the "Reliques" of Percy, so unassuming, so modest in their pretensions!—I have already stated how much Germany is indebted to this latter work; and for our own country, its poetry has been absolutely redeemed by it. I do not think that there is an able writer in verse of the present day who would not be proud to acknowledge his obligations to the "Reliques;" I know that it is so with my friends; and, for myself, I am happy in this occasion to make a public avowal of my own.

Dr. Johnson, more fortunate in his contempt of the labours of Macpherson than those of his modest friend, was solicited not long after to furnish Prefaces biographical and critical for the works of some of the most eminent English Poets. The booksellers took upon themselves to make the collection; they referred probably to the most popular miscellanies, and, unquestionably, to their books of accounts; and decided upon the claim of authors to be admitted into a body of the most eminent, from the familiarity of their names with the readers of that day, and by the profits, which, from the sale of his works, each had brought and was bringing to the Trade. The Editor was allowed a limited exercise of discretion, and the Authors whom he recommended are scarcely to be mentioned without a smile. We open the volume of Prefatory Lives, and to our astonishment the *first* name we find is that of Cowley!—What is become of the morning-star of English Poetry? Where is the bright Elizabethan constellation? Or, if names be more acceptable than images, where is the ever-to-be-honoured Chaucer? where is Spenser? where Sidney? and, lastly, where he, whose rights as a poet, contra-distinguished from those which he is universally allowed to possess as a dramatist, we have vindicated,—where Shakspeare?—These, and a multitude of others not unworthy to be placed near them, their contemporaries and successors, we have *not*. But in their stead, we have (could better be expected when precedence was to be settled by an abstract of reputation at any given period made, as in this case before us?) Roscommon, and Stepney, and Phillips, and Walsh, and Smith, and Duke, and King, and Spratt—Halifax, Granville, Sheffield, Congreve, Broome, and other reputed Magnates—metrical writers utterly worthless and useless, except for occasions like the present, when their productions are referred to as evidence what a small quantity of brain is necessary to procure a considerable stock of admiration, provided the aspirant will accommodate himself to the likings and fashions of his day.

As I do not mean to bring down this retrospect to our own times, it may with propriety be closed at the era of this distinguished event. From the literature of other ages and countries, proofs equally cogent might have been adduced, that the opinions announced in the former part of this Essay are founded upon truth. It was not an agreeable office, nor a prudent undertaking, to declare them; but their importance seemed to render it a duty. It may still be asked, where lies the particular relation of what has been said to these Volumes?—The question will be easily answered by the discerning Reader who is old enough to remember the taste that prevailed when some of these poems were first published, seventeen years ago; who has also observed to what degree the poetry of this Island has since that period been coloured by them; and who is further aware of the unremitting hostility with which, upon some principle or other, they have each and all been opposed. A sketch of my own notion of the constitution of Fame has been given; and, as far as concerns myself, I have cause to be satisfied. The love, the admiration, the indifference, the slight, the aversion, and even the contempt, with which these Poems have been received, knowing, as I do, the source within my own mind, from which they have proceeded, and the labour and pains, which, when labour and pains appeared needful, have been bestowed upon them, must all, if I think consistently, be received as pledges and tokens, bearing the same general impression, though widely different in value;—they are all proofs that for the present time I have not laboured in vain; and afford assurances, more or less authentic, that the products of my industry will endure.

If there be one conclusion more forcibly pressed upon us than another by the review which has been given of the fortunes and fate of poetical Works, it is this,—that every author, as far as he is great and at the same time *original*, has had the task of *creating* the taste by which he is to be enjoyed: so has it been, so will it continue to be. This remark was long since made to me by the philosophical Friend for the separation of whose poems from my own I have previously expressed my regret. The predecessors of an original Genius of a high order will have smoothed the way for all that he has in common with them;—and much he will have in common; but, for what is peculiarly his own, he will be called upon to clear and often to shape his own road:—he will be in the condition of Hannibal among the Alps.

And where lies the real difficulty of creating that taste by which a truly original poet is to be relished? Is it in breaking the bonds of custom, in overcoming the prejudices of false refinement, and displacing the aversions of inexperience? Or, if he labour for an object which here and elsewhere I have proposed to myself, does it consist in divesting the reader of the pride that induces him to dwell upon those points wherein men differ from each other, to the exclusion of those in which all men are alike, or the same; and in making him ashamed of the vanity that renders him insensible of the appropriate excellence which civil arrangements, less unjust than might appear, and Nature illimitable in her bounty, have conferred on men who may stand below him in the scale of society? Finally, does it lie in establishing that dominion over the spirits of readers by which they are to be humbled and humanised, in order that they may be purified and exalted?

If these ends are to be attained by the mere communication of *knowledge*, it does *not* lie here.—Taste, I would remind the reader, like Imagination, is a word which has been forced to extend its services far beyond the point to which philosophy would have confined them. It is a metaphor, taken from a *passive* sense of the human body, and transferred to things which are in their essence *not* passive,—to intellectual *acts* and *operations*. The word, Imagination, has been overstrained, from impulses honourable to mankind, to meet the demands of the faculty which is perhaps the noblest of our nature. In the instance of Taste, the process has been reversed; and from the prevalence of dispositions at once injurious and discreditable, being no other than that selfishness which is the child of apathy,—which, as Nations decline in productive and creative power, makes them value themselves upon a presumed refinement of judging. Poverty of language is the primary cause of the use which we make of the word, Imagination; but the word, Taste, has been stretched to the sense which it bears in modern Europe by habits of self-conceit, inducing that inversion in the order of things whereby a passive faculty is made paramount among the faculties conversant with the fine arts. Proportion and congruity, the requisite knowledge being supposed, are subjects upon which taste may be trusted; it is competent to this office;—for in its intercourse with these the mind is *passive*, and is affected painfully or pleasurably as by an instinct. But the profound and the exquisite in feeling, the lofty and universal in thought and imagination; or, in ordinary language, the pathetic and the sublime;—are neither of them, accurately speaking, objects of a faculty which could ever without a sinking in the spirit of Nations have been designated by the metaphor—*Taste*. And why? Because without the exertion of a co-operating *power* in the mind of the Reader, there can be no adequate sympathy with either of these emotions: without this auxiliary impulse, elevated or profound passion cannot exist.

Passion, it must be observed, is dervied from a word which signifies *suffering;* but the connection which suffering has with effort, with exertion, and *action*, is immediate and inseparable. How strikingly is this property of human nature exhibited by the fact, that, in popular language, to be in a passion, is to be angry!—But,

> Anger in hasty *words* or *blows*
> Itself discharges on its foes.

To be moved, then, by a passion, is to be excited, often to external, and always to internal, effort; whether for the continuance and strengthening of the passion, or for its suppression, accordingly as the course which it takes may be painful or pleasurable. If the latter, the soul must contribute to its support, or it never becomes vivid,—and soon languishes, and dies. And this brings us to the point. If every great poet with whose writings men are familiar, in the highest exercise of his genius, before he can be thoroughly enjoyed, has to call forth and to communicate *power*, this service, in a still greater degree falls upon an original writer, at his first appearance in the world.—Of genius the only proof is, the act of doing well what is worthy to be done, and what was never done before: Of genius, in the fine arts, the only infallible sign is the widening the sphere of human sensibility, for the delight, honour, and benefit of human nature. Genius is the introduction of a new element into the intellectual universe: or, if that be not allowed, it is the application of powers to objects on which they had not before been exercised, or the employment of them in such a manner as to produce effects hitherto unknown. What is all this but an advance, or a conquest, made by the soul of the poet? Is it to be supposed that the reader can make progress of this kind, like an Indian prince or general—stretched on his palanquin, and borne by his slaves? No; he is invigorated and inspirited by his leader, in order that he may exert himself; for he cannot proceed in quiescence, he cannot be carried like a dead weight. Therefore to create taste is to call forth and bestow power, of which knowledge is the effect; and *there* lies the true difficulty.

As the pathetic participates of an *animal* sensation, it might seem—that, if the springs of this emotion were genuine, all men, possessed of competent knowledge of the facts and circumstances, would be instantaneously affected. And, doubtless, in the works of every true poet will be found passages of that species of excellence, which is proved by effects immediate and universal. But there are emotions of the pathetic that are simple and direct, and others—that are complex and revolutionary; some—to which the heart yields with gentleness; others —against which it struggles with pride; these varieties are infinite as the combinations of circumstance and the constitutions of character. Remember, also, that the medium through which, in poetry, the heart is to be affected, is language; a thing subject to endless fluctuations and arbitrary associations. The genius of the poet melts these down for his purpose; but they retain their shape and quality to him who is not capable of exerting, within his own mind, a corresponding energy. There is also a meditative, as well as a human, pathos; an enthusiastic, as well as an ordinary, sorrow; a sadness that has its seat in the depths of reason, to which the mind cannot sink gently of itself—but to which it must descend by treading the steps of thought. And for the sublime,— if we consider what are the cares that occupy the passing day, and how remote is the practice and the course of life from the sources of sublimity, in the soul of Man, can it be wondered that there is little existing preparation for a poet charged with a new mission to extend its kingdom, and to augment and spread its enjoyments?

Away, then, with the senseless iteration of the word, *popular*, applied to new works in poetry, as if there were no test of excellence in this first of the fine arts but that all men should run after its productions, as if urged by an appetite, or constrained by a spell!—The qualities of writing best fitted for eager reception are either such as startle the world into attention by their audacity and extravagance; or they are chiefly of a superficial kind, lying upon the surfaces of manners; or arising out of a selection and arrangement of incidents, by which the mind is kept upon the stretch of curiosity, and the fancy amused without the trouble of thought. But in everything which is to send the soul into herself, to be admonished of her weakness, or to be made conscious of her power;—wherever life and nature are described as operated upon by the creative or abstracting virtue of the imagination; wherever the instinctive wisdom of antiquity and her heroic passions uniting, in the heart of the poet, with the meditative wisdom of later ages, have produced that accord of sublimated humanity, which is at once a history of the remote past and a prophetic enunciation of the remotest future, *there*, the poet must reconcile himself for a season to few and scattered hearers.—Grand thoughts (and Shakspeare must often have sighed over this truth), as they are most naturally and most fitly conceived in solitude, so can they not be brought forth in the midst of plaudits, without some violation of their sanctity. Go to a silent exhibition of the productions of the sister Art, and be convinced that the qualities which dazzle at first sight, and kindle the admiration of the multitude, are essentially different from those by which permanent influence is secured. Let us not shrink from following up these principles as far as they will carry us, and conclude with observing—that there never has been a period, and perhaps never will be, in which vicious poetry, of some kind or other, has not excited more zealous admiration, and been far more generally read, than good; but this advantage attends the good, that the *individual*, as well as the species, survives from age to age; whereas, of the depraved, though the species be immortal, the individual quickly *perishes;* the object of present admiration vanishes, being supplanted by some other as easily produced; which, though no better, brings with it at least the irritation of novelty,—with adaptation, more or less skilful, to the changing humours of the majority of those who are most at leisure to regard poetical works when they first solicit their attention.

Is it the result of the whole, that, in the opinion of the Writer, the judgment of the People is not to be respected? The thought is most injurious; and, could the charge be brought against him, he would repel it with indignation. The People have already been justified, and their eulogium pronounced by implication, when it was said, above—that, of *good* poetry, the *individual*, as well as the species, *survives*. And how does it survive but through the People? What preserves it but their intellect and their wisdom?

> —Past and future, are the wings
> On whose support, harmoniously conjoined,
> Moves the great Spirit of human knowledge—
>
> *MS.*

The voice that issues from this Spirit, is that Vox Populi which the Deity inspires. Foolish must he be who can mistake for this a local acclamation, or a transitory outcry—transitory though it be for years, local though from a Nation. Still more lamentable is his error who can believe that there is anything of divine infallibility in the clamour of that small though loud portion of the community, ever governed by factitious influence, which, under the name of the Public, passes itself, upon the unthinking, for the People. Towards the Public, the Writer hopes that he feels as much deference as it is entitled to: but to the People, philosophically characterised, and to the embodied spirit of their knowledge, as far as it exists and moves, at the present, faithfully supported by its two wings, the past and the future, his devout respect, his reverence, is due. He offers it willingly and readily; and, this done, takes leave of his Readers, by assuring them—that, if he were not persuaded that the contents of these Volumes, and the Work to which they are subsidiary, evince something of the "Vision and the Faculty divine;" and that, both in words and things, they will operate in their degree, to extend the domain of sensibility for the delight, the honour, and the benefit of human nature, notwithstanding the many happy hours which he has employed in their composition, and the manifold comforts and enjoyments they have procured to him, he would not, if a wish could do it, save them from immediate destruction;—from becoming at this moment, to the world, as a thing that had never been.

NOTE ON THE WORDSWORTH ESSAYS

It has been thought desirable to give these Prefaces and Essays in the text of the Poet's last revision; but some important changes from the 1815 version ought to be recorded, as in one place Coleridge refers to and quotes from a passage not to be found in the current text. Mere changes in the form of expression—e.g. the general substitution of impersonal for personal statements—have been disregarded. The Preface and Appendix to *Lyrical Ballads* were reprinted in the 1815 volumes unaltered from the version of 1802 and 1805.

p. 185, l. 3: "Low and rustic life" instead of "Humble, etc."

p. 186, l. 16: "the understanding of the being to whom we address ourselves, if he be in a healthful state of association, must necessarily be in some degree enlightened, and his affections ameliorated."

p. 186. The paragraph beginning "It has been said" has been much reduced from a longer section which reads thus:

I have said that each of these poems has a purpose. I have also informed my Reader what this purpose will be found principally to be: namely to illustrate the manner in which our feelings and ideas are associated in a state of excitement. But, speaking in language somewhat more appropriate, it is to follow the fluxes and refluxes of the mind when agitated by the great and simple affections of our nature. This object I have endeavoured in these short essays to attain by various means; by tracing the maternal passion through many of its more subtile windings, as in the poems of the Idiot Boy and the Mad Mother; by accompanying the last struggles of a human being, at the approach of death, cleaving in solitude to life and society, as in the Poem of the Forsaken Indian; by showing, as in the Stanzas entitled We are Seven, the perplexity and obscurity which in childhood attend our notion of death, or rather our utter inability to admit that notion; or by displaying the strength of fraternal, or to speak more philosophically, of moral attachment when early associated with the great and beautiful objects of nature, as in The Brothers; or, as in the Incident of Simon Lee, by placing my Reader in the way of receiving from ordinary moral sensations another and more salutary impression than we are accustomed to receive from them. It has also been part of my general purpose to attempt to sketch characters under the influence of less impassioned feelings, as in the Two April Mornings, The Fountain, The Old Man Travelling, The Two Thieves, &c. characters of which the elements are simple, belonging rather to nature than to manners, such as exist now, and will probably always exist, and which from their constitution may be distinctly and profitably contemplated. I will not abuse the indulgence of my Reader by dwelling longer upon this subject; but it is proper that I should mention one other circumstance which distinguishes these poems from the popular Poetry of the day; it is this, that the feeling therein developed gives importance to the action and situation, and not the action and situation to the feeling. My meaning will be rendered perfectly intelligible by referring my Reader to the Poems entitled POOR SUSAN and the CHILDLESS FATHER, particularly to the last Stanza of the latter Poem.

p. 191, l. 15: "his situation is altogether slavish and mechanical," instead of "his employment, etc."

p. 192, l. 4: "strength and divinity" instead of "competence and confidence."

p. 198, l. 21. Here follows this paragraph, afterwards omitted:

We see that Pope, by the power of verse alone, has contrived to render the plainest common sense interesting, and even frequently to invest it with the appearance of passion. In consequence of these convictions I related in metre the Tale of GOODY BLAKE and HARRY GILL, which is one of the rudest of this collection. I wished to draw attention to the truth, that the power of the human imagination is sufficient to produce such changes even in our physical nature as might almost appear miraculous. The truth is an important one; the fact (for it is a *fact*) is a valuable illustration of it: and I have the satisfaction of knowing that it has been communicated to many hundreds of people who would never have heard of it, had it not been narrated as a Ballad, and in a more impressive metre than is usual in Ballads.

p. 198, l. 30: before "I may have, etc.," read "sometimes from diseased impulses."

p. 202, l. 10: "The agitation and confusion of mind were, etc." instead of "The emotion was, etc."

p. 205, l. 2. The Appendix thus concludes:

The beauty of this stanza tempts me here to add a sentiment which ought to be the pervading spirit of a system, detached parts of which have been imperfectly explained in the Preface,—namely that in proportion as ideas and feelings are valuable whether the composition be in prose or in verse, they require and exact one and the same language.

p. 206. The Preface begins with two paragraphs about the placing of the prose matter. They have now no interest or importance. The note at the foot of p. 206 does not appear in 1815.

p. 208, l. 40. Here follows this paragraph, afterwards omitted:

It may be proper in this place to state, that the Extracts in the 2nd Class entitled "Juvenile Pieces," are in many places altered from the printed copy, chiefly by omission and compression. The slight alterations of another kind were for the most part made not long after the publication of the Poems from which the Extracts are taken. These Extracts seem to have a title to be placed here, as they were the productions of youth, and represent implicitly some of the features of a youthful mind, at a time when images of nature supplied to it the place of thought, sentiment, and almost of action; or, as it will be found expressed, of a state of mind when

> the sounding cataract
> Haunted me like a passion : the tall rock,
> The mountain, and the deep and gloomy wood,
> Their colours and their forms were then to me
> An appetite, a feeling and a love,
> That had no need of a remoter charm,
> By thought supplied, or any interest
> Unborrowed from the eye—

I will own that I was much at a loss what to select of these descriptions; and perhaps it would have been better either to have reprinted the whole, or suppressed what I have given.

The "Extracts" referred to are those from *An Evening Walk* and *Descriptive Sketches*, for a note on which see under p. 45, l. 22.

p. 211, l. 6. This paragraph, in 1815, reads thus: "From images of sight we will pass to those of sound:"

p. 214, l. 22. Here follows this paragraph, afterwards omitted:

I dismiss this subject with observing—that, in the series of Poems placed under the head of Imagination, I have begun with one of the earliest processes of Nature in the development of this faculty. Guided by one of my own primary consciousnesses, I have represented a commutation and transfer of internal feelings, co-operating with external accidents to plant, for immortality, images of sound and sight, in the celestial soil of the Imagination. The Boy, there introduced, is listening, with something of a feverish and restless anxiety, for the recurrence of the riotous sounds which he had previously excited; and, at the moment when the intenseness of his mind is beginning to remit, he is surprised into a perception of the solemn and tranquillizing images which the Poem describes.—The Poems next in succession exhibit the faculty exerting itself upon various objects of the external universe; then follow others, where it is employed upon feelings, characters, and actions; and the Class is concluded with imaginative pictures of moral, political, and religious sentiments.

The reference in the beginning of this paragraph is to the piece "There was a Boy."

p. 216, l. 10. Here follows this paragraph, afterwards omitted:

Awe-stricken as I am by contemplating the operations of the mind of this truly divine Poet, I scarcely dare venture to add that, "An address to an Infant," which the Reader will find under the Class of Fancy in the present Volumes, exhibits something of this communion and interchange of instruments and functions between the two powers; and is, accordingly, placed last in the class, as a preparation for that of Imagination which follows.

p. 217. After the poem comes a paragraph, of which the important part is this:

It remains that I should express my regret at the necessity of separating my compositions from some beautiful Poems of Mr. Coleridge, with which they have been long associated in publication. The feelings. with which that joint publication was made, have been gratified; its end is answered, and the time is come when considerations of general propriety dictate the separation....

p. 217. In 1815 the Essay begins thus:

By this time, I trust that the judicious Reader, who has now first become acquainted with these poems, is persuaded that a very senseless outcry has been raised against them and their Author.—Casually, and very rarely only, do I see any periodical publication, except a daily newspaper; but I am not wholly unacquainted with the spirit in which my most active and persevering Adversaries have maintained their hostility; nor with the impudent falsehoods and base artifices to which they have had recourse. These, as implying a consciousness on their parts that attacks honestly and fairly conducted would be unavailing, could not but have been regarded by me with triumph; had they been accompanied with such display of talents and information as might give weight to the opinions of the Writers, whether favourable or unfavourable. But the ignorance of those who have chosen to stand forth as my enemies, as far as I am acquainted with their enmity, has unfortunately been still more gross than their disingenuousness, and their incompetence more flagrant than their malice. The effect in the eyes of the discerning is indeed ludicrous: yet, contemptible as such men are, in return for the forced compliment paid me by their long-continued notice (which, as I have appeared so rarely before the public, no one can say has been solicited) I entreat them to spare themselves. The lash, which they are aiming at my productions, does, in fact, only fall on phantoms of their own brain; which, I grant, I am innocently instrumental in raising.—By what fatality the orb of my genius (for genius none of them seem to deny me) acts upon these men like the moon upon a certain description of patients, it would be irksome to inquire; nor would it consist with the respect which I owe myself to take further notice of opponents whom I internally despise.

Other alterations in the Essay are not important.

G. S.

APPENDIX IV

LIST OF WORKS

I. Coleridge's Works, 1794—1817

It will be a convenience to have a list of Coleridge's principal activities up to the publication of *Biographia Literaria*.

(1) 1794. Act I of *The Fall of Robespierre*. By S. T. Coleridge, of Jesus College, Cambridge. Acts II and III were by Southey.

(2) 1794–5. Verses contributed to *The Morning Chronicle*, including the *Address to a Young Jackass* and the *Sonnets on Eminent Characters*. One poem, *To Fortune*, really appeared in 1793 (Nov. 7) and is therefore S. T. C.'s first printed work.

(3) 1795. *A Moral and Political Lecture delivered at Bristol*. By S. T. Coleridge, of Jesus College, Cambridge. Afterwards reprinted as the first of two *Conciones ad Populum* (1795).

(4) 1795. *Conciones ad Populum, Or addresses to the People*. By S. T. Coleridge. Contains 3 and another pamphlet *On the present war*.

(5) 1795. *The Plot Discovered: or An Address to the People against Ministerial Treason*. By S. T. Coleridge.

(6) 1795. *An Answer to 'A Letter to Edward Long Fox, M.D.'* A short anonymous prose pamphlet.

(7) 1796. *The Watchman*. Published by the Author, S. T. Coleridge. A periodical essay, ten numbers issued, March 1 to May 13.

(8) 1796. *Poems on Various Subjects*. By S. T. Coleridge, late of Jesus College, Cambridge. Contains the *Monody on Chatterton*, *Religious Musings* and various sonnets, here called "Effusions"—a few by Lamb.

(9) 1796. A sheet of selected sonnets. For an account of this see note to p. 7, l. 21.

(10) 1796. *Ode on the Departing Year*. By S. T. Coleridge.

(11) 1797. *Poems*. By S. T. Coleridge. Second Edition. Containing the better part of 8 with contributions from Charles Lamb and Charles Lloyd.

(12) 1798. *Fears in Solitude...To which are added France, an Ode, and Frost at Midnight*. By S. T. Coleridge.

(13) 1798. *Lyrical Ballads*. Anonymous. Coleridge's contributions were *The Ancient Mariner*, *The Foster-Mother's Tale* (a passage from the tragedy *Osorio* afterwards recast as *Remorse*), *The Nightingale* (replacing *Lewti*, at first included, and actually printed, but withdrawn before publication), *The Dungeon* (also from *Osorio*).

(14) 1797–1802. Contributions to *The Morning Post*—many verses and political articles, the latter reprinted by his daughter in *Essays on his Own Times* (1850).

(15) 1800. Contributions to Southey's *Annual Anthology* (*Lewti*, *The Mad Ox*, *This Lime-tree bower*, *Fire, Famine and Slaughter* and others).

(16) 1800. *Lyrical Ballads.* 2nd edition. This was to have contained *Christabel*; but the only new Coleridge contribution is *Love*—i.e., "All thoughts, all passions, all delights."

(17) 1800. *The Piccolomini* or the first part of *Wallenstein*, A Drama in Five Acts. Translated from the German of Frederick Schiller. By S. T. Coleridge.

(18) 1800. *The Death of Wallenstein.* A Tragedy in Five Acts. Translated from the German of Frederick Schiller. By S. T. Coleridge.

(19) 1803. *Poems.* By S. T. Coleridge. Third Edition, a reprint, with changes, of 8 and 11.

(20) 1806, etc. Contributions to *The Courier.* Various Verses.

(21) 1808. Lectures at the Royal Institution. No report exists.

(22) 1809–10. *The Friend: A Literary, Moral and Political Weekly Paper, Excluding Personal and Party Politics, and the Events of the Day.* Conducted by S. T. Coleridge, of Grasmere, Westmoreland. Twenty-eight parts issued, the first June 1, 1809, the last March 15, 1810. It will be seen that "weekly" has to be generously interpreted.

(23) 1809–10. Letters to *The Courier*, "On the Spaniards," reprinted in *Essays on his Own Times.*

(24) 1811. Contributions to *The Courier.* A long series of articles. Reprinted in *Essays on his Own Times* (1850).

(25) 1811–12. Lectures on Shakespeare, Milton, etc. at Crane Court and the Surrey Institution; modern reprint in Bohn (*Lectures and Notes on Shakespeare*, etc.).

(26) 1812. Contributions to Southey's *Omniana, or Horae Otiosiores.* Modern reprint in Bohn (*Table Talk and Omniana*).

(27) 1813. *Remorse; a Tragedy.* In five Acts. By S. T. Coleridge. First written as *Osorio.* Successfully produced at Drury Lane, Jan. 1813, and ran twenty nights.

(28) 1813–14. Lectures on Shakespeare and Milton at Bristol. Brief reports exist, reprinted in *Lectures* (Bohn).

(29) 1814. *Essays on the Fine Arts*, contributed to *Felix Farley's Bristol Journal.* Reprinted by Cottle in his *Early Recollections*; modern reprint, *Miscellanies* (Bohn).

(30) 1814. Contributions to *The Courier*—six *Letters to Judge Fletcher concerning his Charge to the Grand Jury of the County of Wexford*, reprinted in *Essays on his Own Times.*

(31) 1816. *Christabel, Kubla Khan, The Pains of Sleep.* By S. T. Coleridge, Esq.

(32) 1816. *The Statesman's Manual, or The Bible the Best Guide to Political Skill and Foresight: A Lay Sermon, addressed to the Higher Classes of Society.* By S. T. Coleridge, Esq.

(33) 1817. *A Lay Sermon, addressed to the Higher and Middle Classes, on the existing Distresses and Discontents.* By S. T. Coleridge, Esq. (32 and 33 reprinted in *Biographia Literaria and Lay Sermons*, Bohn).

(34) 1817. *Biographia Literaria: or Biographical Sketches of my Literary Life and Opinions.* By S. T. Coleridge, Esq.

(35) 1817. *Sibylline Leaves: A Collection of Poems.* By S. T. Coleridge, Esq. This reprints the principal poems already published together with pieces hitherto unpublished.

In 1847 appeared an elaborate new edition of *Biographia Literaria*, with some alterations apparently authorised, under the joint editorship of Coleridge's nephew, Henry Nelson Coleridge, and his wife, Sara, the poet's daughter. This contains a mass of very useful annotations together with a long biographical appendix (of great value in its day), and an even longer introduction dealing with Coleridge's alleged plagiarisms and his theological teaching. The present edition follows (in the main) the text of 1847 and occasional references are given to the notes, especially those dealing with Coleridge's more obscure quotations. The somewhat defensive account of Coleridge issuing from two editors closely connected with him by family ties and community of interests will always have value; but for modern students there is more profit in the masterly Life of Coleridge by J. Dykes Campbell prefixed to the *Poetical Works* (Macmillan) and published separately in volume form, especially when supplemented by the *Letters of Samuel Taylor Coleridge* in two volumes, edited by his grandson, Ernest Hartley Coleridge. A complete collection of the known letters has still to be made.

No new edition of *Biographia Literaria* (other than bare reprints of the text) appeared till 1907, when it was edited by Mr J. Shawcross (Oxford University Press, 2 vols.) with a valuable introduction and notes embodying a special study of Coleridge's theory of the imagination and his obligations to German writers. It is the standard edition, a necessary part of the English scholar's library.

II. Wordsworth's Works, 1793—1815

The following list gives the works of Wordsworth up to the date of *Biographia*.

(1) [1793] *A Letter to the Bishop of Landaff on the Extraordinary Avowal of his Political Principles contained in the Appendix to his Late Sermon. By a Republican.* A prose pamphlet. It was never published by Wordsworth and did not appear in print till 1876 when it was included in Grosart's edition of the prose works, under the title *Apology for the French Revolution.*

(2) 1793. *An Evening Walk. An Epistle in Verse. Addressed to a Young Lady, from the Lakes of the North of England.* By W. Wordsworth, B.A., of St John's, Cambridge.

(3) 1793. *Descriptive Sketches. In Verse. Taken during a Pedestrian Tour in the Italian, Grison, Swiss and Savoyard Alps.* By W. Wordsworth, B.A., of St John's, Cambridge.

(4) 1798. *Lyrical Ballads, with a few other Poems.* The volume was published anonymously, and no indication of joint authorship was given.

(5) 1800. *Lyrical Ballads, with other Poems.* In Two Volumes. By W. Wordsworth. Second Edition. All the new matter (except Coleridge's *Love*)

is Wordsworth's. The edition is important as containing the first form of Wordsworth's famous Preface enunciating his view of poetry. There are also some variations of text.

(6) 1802. *Lyrical Ballads, with Pastoral and Other Poems.* In two volumes. By W. Wordsworth. Third Edition. There are further changes in text; the Preface is greatly expanded, and there is a new Appendix, on "what is usually called Poetic Diction."

(7) 1805. *Lyrical Ballads, with Pastoral and other Poems.* In two volumes. By W. Wordsworth. Fourth Edition. Textual changes.

(8) 1807. *Poems, in Two Volumes.* By William Wordsworth, Author of the Lyrical Ballads. This contains entirely new matter, including such important things as the *Immortality* ode and a number of the best sonnets. There is a very useful modern facsimile reprint, edited by Thomas Hutchinson, whose notes are of great interest.

(9) 1809. *Concerning the Relations of Great Britain, Spain and Portugal, to Each Other, and to the Common Enemy, at this Crisis; and specifically as affected by the Convention of Cintra.* By William Wordsworth. A valuable prose pamphlet, usually referred to briefly as "The Convention of Cintra."

(10) 1814. *The Excursion, being a Portion of the Recluse, a Poem.* By William Wordsworth. Contains also Wordsworth's prose *Essay on Epitaphs.*

(11) 1815. *Poems by William Wordsworth; Including Lyrical Ballads, and the Miscellaneous Pieces of the Author. With Additional Poems, a New Preface, and a Supplementary Essay. In Two Volumes.* This very important edition reprints (with textual changes) the *Lyrical Ballads* and the *Poems* of 1807 together with much new matter arranged in the now familiar Wordsworthian categories, Poems referring to the Period of Childhood, Juvenile Pieces, Poems founded on the Affections, Poems of the Fancy, Poems of the Imagination, Poems Proceeding from Sentiment and Reflection, Miscellaneous Sonnets, Sonnets dedicated to Liberty, Poems on the Naming of Places, Inscriptions, Poems referring to the Period of Old Age, Epitaphs and Elegiac Poems, Ode. There is a new Preface and Supplementary Essay, in Vol. I, the Preface and Appendix to *Lyrical Ballads* being reprinted at the end of Vol. II. It is to these two volumes that Coleridge frequently refers in *Biographia.*

(12) *The White Doe of Rylstone; or the Fate of the Nortons.* A Poem. By William Wordsworth. Also contains *The Force of Prayer; or the Founding of Bolton Priory.*

G. S.

APPENDIX V

STAGES IN THE GROWTH OF *BIOGRAPHIA LITERARIA*

The following facts may be a useful supplement to the passages of the Introduction that deal with the origin and development of *Biographia Literaria*. In September 1814, Coleridge, broken in health by his laudanum habit, wrote from Ashley, near Bath, to Daniel Stuart, editor of *The Courier*, a very interesting letter describing the regimen by which he was attempting to conquer his fatal weakness. He was then nearly forty-two and had another twenty years of life before him:

...And now, having for the very first time in my whole life opened out my whole feelings and thoughts concerning my past fates and fortunes, I will draw anew on your patience, by a detail of my present operations. My medical friend is so well satisfied of my convalescence, and that nothing now remains, but to superinduce *positive* health on a system from which disease and its *removable* causes have been driven out, that he has not merely consented to, but advised my leaving Bristol, for some rural retirement. I could indeed pursue nothing uninterruptedly in that city. Accordingly, I am now joint tenant with Mr Morgan, of a sweet little cottage, at Ashley, half a mile from Box, on the Bath road. I breakfast every morning before nine; work till one, and walk or read till three. Thence, till tea-time, chat or read some lounge-book, or correct what I have written. From six to eight work again; from eight till bed-time, play whist, or the little mock billiard called bagatelle, and then sup and go to bed. My morning hours, as the longest and most important division, I keep sacred to my most important Work, which is printing at Bristol; two of my friends having taken upon themselves the risk. It is so long since I have conversed with you, that I cannot say, whether the subject will, or will not be interesting to you. The title is "Christianity, the one true Philosophy; or, Five Treatises on the Logos, or Communicative Intelligence, natural, human, and divine." To which is prefixed a prefatory Essay, on the laws and limits of toleration and liberality, illustrated by fragments of AUTO-biography. The *first* Treatise—Logos Propaideuticos, or the Science of systematic thinking in ordinary life. The *second*—Logos Architectonicus, or an attempt to apply the constructive, or Mathematical process to Metaphysics and Natural Theology. The *third*—Ὁ Λόγος ὁ θεάνθρωπος (the divine logos incarnate)—a full commentary on the Gospel of St John, in development of St Paul's doctrine of preaching Christ alone, and Him crucified. The *fourth*—on Spinoza and Spinozism, with a life of B. Spinoza. This entitled Logos Agonistes. The *fifth* and last, Logos Alogos (i.e., Logos Illogicus), or on modern Unitarianism, its causes and effects. The whole will be comprised in two portly octavos, and the second treatise will be the only one which will, and from the nature of the subject must, be unintelligible to the great majority even of well-educated readers. The purpose of the whole is a philosophical defence of the Articles of the Church, as far as they respect doctrine, as points of faith. If originality be any merit, this work will have that, at all events, from the first page to the last.

This, of course, is nothing but one of those elaborate efflorescences of self-deception in which Coleridge's life is unhappily fertile. How long he followed his methodical course of philosophy tempered with billiards we cannot say; but by March 1815 he is at Calne writing an agonised appeal to Cottle—for what purpose Cottle at least had no doubt.

CALNE, *March* 7, 1815.

DEAR COTTLE,

You will wish to know something of myself. In health, I am not worse than when at Bristol I was best; yet fluctuating, yet unhappy! in circumstances "poor indeed!" I have collected my scattered, and my manuscript poems, sufficient to make one volume. Enough I have to make another. But till the latter is finished, I cannot without great loss of character, publish the former on account of the arrangement, besides the necessity of correction. For instance, I earnestly wish to begin the volumes, with what has never been seen by any, however few, such as a series of Odes on the different sentences of the Lord's Prayer, and more than all this, to finish my greater work on "Christianity, considered as Philosophy, and as the only Philosophy." All the materials I have in no small part, reduced to form, and written, but, oh me! what can I do, when I am so poor, that in having to turn off every week, from these to some mean subject for the newspapers, I distress myself, and at last neglect the greater wholly, to do little of the less. If it were in your power to receive my manuscripts, (for instance what I have ready for the press of my poems) and by setting me forward with *thirty* or *forty* pounds, taking care that what I send, and would make over to you, would more than secure you from loss, I am sure you would do it. And I would die (after my recent experience of the cruel and insolent spirit of calumny,) rather than subject myself, as a slave, to a club of subscribers to my poverty.

If I were to say I am easy in my conscience, I should add to its pains by a lie; but this I can truly say, that my embarrassments have not been occasioned by the bad parts, or selfish indulgences of my nature. I am at present five and twenty pounds in arrears, my expenses being at £2. 10*s*. per week. You will say I ought to live for less, and doubtless I might, if I were to alienate myself from all social affections, and from all conversation with persons of the same education. Those who severely blame me, never ask, whether at any time in my life, I had for myself and my family's wants, £50 beforehand.

Heaven knows of the £300 received, through you, what went to myself. No! bowed down under manifold infirmities, I yet dare appeal to God for the truth of what I say; I have remained poor by always having been poor, and incapable of pursuing any one great work, for want of a competence beforehand.

S. T. COLERIDGE.

"This (says Cottle) was precisely the termination I was prepared to expect. I had never before, through my whole life refused Mr C. an application for money; yet I now hesitated: assured that the sum required, was not meant for the discharge of board, (for which he paid nothing) but for the purchase of opium, the expense of which, for years, had amounted nearly to the two pounds ten shillings per week. Under this conviction, and after a painful conflict, I sent Mr C. on the next day, a friendly letter, declining his request in the kindest manner I could, but enclosing a five pound note. It happened that my letter to Mr Coleridge passed on the road, another letter from him to myself, far more harrowing than the first. This was the *last* letter I ever received from Mr C."

No mention is made, it will be seen, of any progress with the "Auto-biographical fragments" which were to preface the great Treatise; but something was being done, for at the end of July 1815 Coleridge writes thus to Dr Brabant of Devizes:

Saturday, 29 *July*, 1815.

My dear Sir,—The necessity of extending what I first intended as a preface to an Autobiographia Literaria, or Sketches of my literary life and opinions, as far as poetry and poetical criticism are concerned, has confined me to my study from eleven to four and from six till ten, since I last left you. I have just finished it, having only the correction of the MS. to go through. I have given a full account (*raisonné*) of the controversy concerning Wordsworth's Poems and Theory, in which my name has been so constantly included. I have no doubt that Wordsworth will be displeased, but I have done my duty to myself and to the public, in, as I believe, completely subverting the theory and in proving that the poet himself has never acted on it except in particular stanzas, which are the blots of his composition. One long passage, a disquisition on the powers of Association, with the history of the opinions on this subject, from Aristotle to Hartley, and on the generic difference between the faculties of Fancy and Imagination, I did not indeed altogether insert, but I certainly extended and elaborated with a view to *your* perusal, as laying the foundation stones of the Constructive or Dynamic Philosophy in opposition to the merely Mechanic.

It is clear that by the summer of 1815 Coleridge was attempting to produce, not, indeed, those visionary volumes "of not less than six hundred pages each," but two volumes of more manageable scope and dimensions. The great Treatise, the elaborately promised Philosophy of All Philosophies, remained a delusion, almost a delirium, to the end of his life, though he constantly professed his ability to produce and complete it at any moment. Some matter, presumably intended for this Treatise, still exists; but Mr Ernest Hartley Coleridge, who reports upon it, is careful not to exaggerate its value. By October 1815, the two actual, as distinguished from the imagined, volumes had begun to take shape, Volume 1 a literary autobiography [*Biographia Literaria*],

Volume II a collection of his scattered poems [*Sibylline Leaves*]. Thus he writes to Daniel Stuart under the date named:

I have sent to the Printer at Bristol (Mr Gutch an old schoolfellow) two volumes, the first, Biographical Sketches of my literary life and opinions (with the principles on which they are grounded and the arguments by which they were deduced) in politics, religion, philosophy and *poetry*—the latter in the hope of settling the controversy on the nature of *poetic* diction. I fear that my reasonings may not please Wordsworth; but I am convinced that the detection of the faults in his poetry is indispensable, to a rational appreciation of his merits. The second volume entitled Sibylline Leaves, contains all the Poems I think worthy of publication (exclusive of those in my "Poems" published in 1794), about one third or little more from MSS., and all corrected and finished to the best of my power. For the last four months, I have never worked less than six hours every day—namely, from ten to four; and more I cannot do, if I am to have any time for reading and reflection, which I do not include in the six hours.

I am now at work on a Tragedy and a dramatic entertainment one half of my time; and the other half, I give to the Work on which I would wish to ground my reputation with posterity, if I should have any—a Work, for which I have been collecting the materials for the last fifteen years almost incessantly. Its Title will be Logosophia, or on the Logos, human and divine, in six Treatises. The *first*, a philosophic compendium of the history of philosophy, from Pythagoras to the present day, with miscellaneous investigations on Toleration and the obstacles to just reasoning. (No such work exists, at least, in our language; for Brucker is a wilderness, in six huge Quartos, and he was no philosopher, and Enfield's Abridgement is below criticism.) The *second*, the science of connected [*reasoning*] (with the history of Logic from Aristotle to Condillac) free from [illegible] pedantry, and applied to the purposes of real life—the Bar, the Pulpit, the Senate, and rational conversation. The *third*, the science of premises, or, transcendental philosophy, i.e., the examination of the premises which, in ordinary and practical reasoning, are taken for granted. (As the whole proceeds on actual constructions in the mind, I might call it Intellectual Geometry.) The *fourth*, a detailed commentary on the Gospel of St John, to which the former is introductory—the object of both to prove, that Christianity is true philosophy, and of course, that all true philosophy is Christianity. The *fifth*, on the Mystics and Pantheists, with the lives of Giordano Bruno, Jacob Behmen, George Fox, and Benedict Spinoza; with an analysis of their systems, etc. The *sixth*, on the causes and consequences of Unitarianism. It will comprise two large octavo volumes, six hundred pages each. God knows, whether I shall meet with patronage, to enable me to publish it. I am most willing to work hard, and wish for nothing more, than merely to be enabled to work. But what can I do, if I am to starve while I am working! And I declare to God! I see little other prospect. Would to God, I had been bred a shoemaker! If twenty or thirty of those, who think well of my powers, would agree to receive my manuscripts, such as they themselves should approve, and to allow me on the receipt such a sum, as would simply enable me to live (the money always posterior to the MSS. received), I might be useful; otherwise I must sink,.......

Let us consider what had happened, first, to deflect Coleridge's mind from the cherished Treatise towards a pair of less ambitious volumes, and next to give one of those volumes, the *Biographia*, its peculiar character—for, as every one must have noted, there is very little autobiography in it. It begins, as an autobiography should, with Coleridge himself; but, after uttering a protest against Reviewers, it digresses into barren regions of Germanised philosophy, and ends by being all about Wordsworth. In a footnote to his invaluable memoir, Dykes Campbell says, " In the unprinted correspondence of this period I see indications which lead me to believe that the only prose contemplated at first was to take the form of a preface to the poems; and that this preface grew into a literary autobiography." How does it come about that the "fragments of AUTO-biography" referred to in September 1814, have to be " extended " in July 1815, and have developed, by October 1815, into an autobiography which proves to be mainly about somebody else? The explanation is quite simple, and can be stated in the form of three facts: (1) the publication of *The Excursion* in July 1814; (2) the appearance of Jeffrey's attack upon that poem in *The Edinburgh Review*, Nov. 1814; (3) the publication of Wordsworth's collected *Poems* in March 1815, with all its attendant essays. As the Introduction points out, the primal origin of *Biographia* has to be sought in the first acquaintance of our two poets twenty years before. The immediate origin must be sought in the *Poems* of 1815—or rather, in the attached essays. Wordsworth and Coleridge represented to the public a community of method, style and purpose, and were thought of together as inevitably (and unwarrantably) as were Rossetti and Burne-Jones at the other end of the century. Wordsworth himself believed in that community much more than Coleridge; and the famous Preface of 1800 represents not merely what Wordsworth thought about poetry, but what Wordsworth thought that Coleridge thought about poetry. That Coleridge always had his doubts may be seen from the letters of 1802 quoted in the note to p. 54, l. 29; but he had divined the essential greatness of Wordsworth as clearly as he had detected his essential weakness; and in the poet of *Tintern Abbey* and the *Intimations* he hailed the first great contemplative poet of modern life, one who would outsing Lucretius and give the world what even yet it does not possess, a great philosophical poem. It is part of Coleridge's greatness as a critic that he recognised not merely what quality of poet Wordsworth was, but what quantity of poet Wordsworth was. He believed, and he never wavered in his belief, that in Wordsworth there had arisen the greatest personality in poetry since Milton; and from him he confidently expected a constructive achievement in verse worthy to stand beside *Paradise Lost*. *The Prelude*, first known to Coleridge completely at the beginning of 1807, had raised his hopes to the highest. If this was merely the preparatory exercise, what might not be expected from the finished work! And then, seven years later, came *The Excursion*....

Coleridge's disappointment was deep indeed. Instead of the great philosophical poem, co-extensive with human thought and as noble as its theme, he found a series of melancholy anecdotes in a country churchyard narrated with all the protracted elaboration of the obvious that is one of Wordsworth's greatest weaknesses. He allowed his disappointment to leak out, first in a letter to Lady Beaumont, and next in a letter to Wordsworth himself, in which, with courageous and friendly frankness, he expressed his dissent as freely as his admiration. Thus he writes to Lady Beaumont:

April 3, 1815.

...Of *The Excursion*, excluding the tale of the ruined cottage, which I have ever thought the finest poem in our language, comparing it with any of the same or similar *length*, I can truly say that one half the number of its beauties would make all the beauties of all his contemporary poets collectively mount to the balance:—but yet—the fault may be in my own mind—I do not think, I did not feel, it equal to the work on the growth of his own spirit [i.e. *The Prelude*]. As proofs meet me in every part of *The Excursion* that the poet's genius has not flagged, I have sometimes fancied that, having by the conjoint operation of his own experiences, feelings, and reason, *himself* convinced *himself* of truths, which the generality of persons have either taken for granted from their infancy, or, at least, adopted in early life, he has attached all their own depth and weight to doctrines and words, which come almost as truisms or commonplaces to others. From this state of mind, in which I was comparing Wordsworth with himself, I was roused by the infamous "Edinburgh" review of the poem. If ever guilt lay on a writer's head, and if malignity, slander, hypocrisy, and self-contradictory baseness can constitute guilt, I dare openly, and openly (please God!) I will, impeach the writer of that article of it. These are awful times—a dream of dreams! To be a prophet is and ever has been, an unthankful office.

It is evident that some rumour of Coleridge's dissatisfaction reached Wordsworth and that Wordsworth was disposed to ask about it—even though, in a letter to a correspondent unknown, he expressed his doubts whether Coleridge had read three pages of the poem. This is Coleridge's reply; it is the best, the bravest, the most manly of his letters:

CALNE, *May* 30, 1815.

My Honoured Friend,—On my return from Devizes, whither I had gone to procure some vaccine matter (the small-pox having appeared in Calne, and Mrs Morgan's sister believing herself never to have had it), I found your letter: and I will answer it immediately, though to answer it as I could wish to do would require more recollection and arrangement of thought than is always to be commanded on the instant. But I dare not trust my own habit of procrastination, and, do what I would, it would be impossible in a single letter to give more than *general* convictions. But, even after a tenth or twentieth letter, I should still be disquieted as knowing how poor a substitute must letters be for a *vivâ voce* examination of a work with its author, line by line. It is most uncomfortable from many, many causes, to express anything but sympathy, and congratulation to an absent friend, to whom for the more substantial third of a life we have been habituated to look up: especially where a love, though increased by many and different influences, yet begun and throve and knit its joints in the perception of his superiority. It is not in *written words*, but by the hundred modifications that looks make and tone, and denial of the *full* sense of the very words used, that one can reconcile the struggle between sincerity and diffidence, between the persuasion that I am in the right, and that as deep though not so vivid conviction, that it may be the positiveness of ignorance rather than the certainty of insight. Then come the human frailties, the dread of giving pain, or exciting suspicions of alteration and dyspathy, in short, the almost inevitable insincerities between imperfect beings, however sincerely attached to each other. It is hard (and I am Protestant enough to doubt whether *it is* right) to confess the whole truth (even *of* one's self, human nature scarce endures it, even *to* one's self) but to me it is still harder to do this of and to a revered friend....

I feared that had I been silent concerning "the Excursion," Lady Beaumont would have drawn some strange inference; and yet I had scarcely sent off the letter before I repented that I had not run that risk rather than have approach to dispraise communicated to you by a third person. But what did my criticism amount to, reduced to its full and naked sense? This, that *comparatively* with the *former* poem, "The Excursion," as far as it was new to me, had disappointed my expectations; that the excellencies were so many and of so high a class that it was impossible to attribute the inferiority, if any such really existed, to any flagging of the writer's own genius—and that I conjectured that it might have been occasioned by the influence of self-established convictions having given to certain thoughts and expressions a depth and force which they had not for readers in general. In order, therefore, to explain the *disappointment*, I must recall to your mind what my *expectations* were: and, as these again were founded on the supposition that (in whatever order it might be published) the poem on the growth of your own mind was as the ground plot and the roots, out of which "The Recluse" was to have sprung up as the tree, as far as [there was] the same sap in both I expected them, doubtless, to have formed one complete whole; but in matter, form, and product to be different, each not only a distinct but a different work. In the first I had found "themes by thee first sung aright,"

> Of smiles spontaneous and mysterious fears
> (The first-born they of reason and twin-birth)
> Of tides obedient to external force,
> And currents self-determined, as might seem,
> Or by some central breath; of moments awful,
> Now in thy inner life, and now abroad,
> When power stream'd from thee, and thy soul received
> The light reflected as a light bestowed;

Of fancies fair, and milder hours of youth,
Hyblæan murmurs of poetic thought
Industrious in its joy, in vales and glens
Native or outland, lakes and famous hills!
Or on the lonely highroad, when the stars
Were rising; or by secret mountain streams,
The guides and the companions of thy way;
Of more than *fancy*—of the *social sense*
Distending wide, and man beloved as man,
Where France in all her towns lay vibrating,
Ev'n as a bark becalm'd beneath the burst
Of Heaven's immediate thunder, when no cloud
Is visible, or shadow on the main!
For Thou wert there, thy own brows garlanded,
Amid the tremor of a realm aglow,
Amid a mighty nation jubilant,
When from the general heart of human kind
Hope sprang forth, like a full-born Deity!
Of that dear Hope afflicted, and amaz'd,
So homeward summon'd! thenceforth calm and sure
From the dread watch-tower of man's absolute self,
With light unwaning on her eyes, to look
Far on! herself a glory to behold,
The Angel of the vision! Then (last strain)
Of duty, chosen laws controlling choice,
Action and Joy! *An Orphic song indeed,*
A song divine of high and passionate truths,
To their own music chaunted!

Indeed, through the whole of that Poem, *με Αὔρα τις εἰσέπνευσε μουσικωτάτη*. This I considered as "The Excursion"; and the second, as "The Recluse," I had (from what I had at different times gathered from your conversation on the Place [Grasmere]) anticipated as commencing with you set down and settled in an abiding home, and that with the description of that home you were to begin a *philosophical poem*, the *result* and fruits of a spirit so framed and so disciplined as had been told in the former.

Whatever in Lucretius is poetry is not philosophical, whatever is philosophical is not poetry; and in the very pride of confident hope I looked forward to "The Recluse" as the *first* and *only* true philosophical poem in existence. Of course, I expected the colours, music, imaginative life, and passion of *poetry*; but the matter and arrangement of *philosophy*; not doubting from the advantages of the subject that the totality of a system was not only capable of being harmonised with, but even calculated to aid, the unity (beginning, middle, and end) of a poem. Thus, whatever the length of the work might be, still it was a *determinate* length; of the subjects announced, each would have its own appointed place, and excluding repetitions, each would relieve and rise in interest above the other. I supposed you first to have meditated the faculties of man in the abstract, in their correspondence with his sphere of action, and, first in the feeling, touch, and taste, then in the eye, and last in the ear,—to have laid a solid and immovable foundation for the edifice by removing the sandy sophisms of Locke, and the mechanic dogmatists, and demonstrating that the senses were living growths and developments of the mind and spirit, in a much juster as well as higher sense, than the mind can be said to be formed by the senses. Next, I understood that you would take the human race in the concrete, have exploded the absurd notion of Pope's "Essay on Man," Darwin, and all the countless believers even (strange to say) among Christians of man's having progressed from an ourang-outang state—so contrary to all history, to all religion, nay, to all possibility—to have affirmed a Fall in some sense, as a fact, the possibility of which cannot be understood from the nature of the will, but the reality of which is attested by experience and conscience. Fallen men contemplated in the different ages of the world, and in the different states—savage, barbarous, civilised, the lonely cot, or borderer's wigwam, the village, the manufacturing town, seaport, city, universities, and, not disguising the sore evils under which the whole creation groans, to point out, however, a manifest scheme of redemption, of reconciliation from this enmity with Nature—what are the obstacles, the *Antichrist* that must be and already is—and to conclude by a grand didactic swell on the necessary identity of a true philosophy with true religion, agreeing in the results and differing only as the analytic and synthetic process, as discursive from intuitive, the former chiefly useful as perfecting the latter; in short, the necessity of a general revolution in the modes of developing and disciplining the human mind by the substitution of life and intelligence (considered in its different powers from the plant up to that state in which the difference of degree becomes a new kind (man self-consciousness), but yet not by essential opposition) for the philosophy of mechanism, which, in everything that is most worthy of the human intellect, strikes *Death*, and cheats itself by mistaking clear images for distinct conceptions, and which idly demands conceptions where intuitions alone are possible or adequate to the majesty of the Truth. In short, facts elevated into theory—theory into laws—and laws into living and intelligent powers—true idealism necessarily perfecting itself in realism, and realism refining itself into idealism.

Such or something like this was the plan I had supposed that you were engaged on. Your own words will therefore explain my feelings, viz., that your object "was not to convey recondite, or refined truths, but to place commonplace truths in an interesting point of view." Now this I suppose to have been in your two volumes of poems, as far as was desirable or possible, without an insight into the whole truth. How can common truths be made permanently interesting but by being *bottomed* on our common nature? It is only by the profoundest insight into numbers and quantity that a sublimity and even religious wonder become attached to the simplest operations of arithmetic, the most evident properties of the circle or triangle. I have only to finish a preface, which I shall have done in two, or, at farthest, three days; and I will then, dismissing all comparison either with the poem on the growth of your own support, or with the imagined plan of "The Recluse," state fairly my main objections to "The Excursion" as it is. But it would have been alike unjust both to you and to myself, if I had led you to suppose that any disappointment I may have felt arose wholly or chiefly from the passages I do not like, or from the poem considered irrelatively....

God bless you! I am, and never have been other than your most affectionate

S. T. Coleridge.

In fact, Coleridge was saying of *The Excursion* what Jeffrey had said just before and what many readers have said since, "This will never do." Certainly *The Excursion* does not contain the worst of Wordsworth; but just as certainly it does not contain his best. The charge laid by Matthew Arnold against Shelley, viz. the want of a sound subject-matter, might have been laid with greater cogency against *The Excursion*. It is in nine books and nine thousand lines, and it seems to be just one unhappy story told over and over again. It has its fine and noble passages; but they are not strong enough or numerous enough to carry off the effect of its relentless garrulity and its almost unvaried lugubriousness. We come to it, as Coleridge did, prepared by *The Prelude* and the fine passage of *The Recluse* quoted in the preface, to find an utterance,

> Of Truth, of Grandeur, Beauty, Love, and Hope,
> And melancholy Fear subdued by Faith;
> Of blessed consolations in distress;
> Of moral strength, and intellectual Power;
> Of joy in widest commonalty spread;

and we find instead three elderly persons and one who was never young sitting in a churchyard and "thinking of the old 'uns" at immoderate length. The poet of *The Thorn*, who is also the prose defender of *The Thorn* as a piece of systematic garrulity, is too obviously discernible in *The Excursion*. The usual defence is that *The Excursion* is only part of a great projected poem and that we should not judge it till we know the whole. The obvious answer is that *The Excursion* is all there is of it to know, and that it is always unsafe to judge a poem by the parts that were never written. I hope, too, it is not unkind to point out that Wordsworth's philosophical poem like Coleridge's philosophical treatise was never finished.

The letter to Lady Beaumont clearly indicates the double purpose at work in Coleridge's mind. It was one thing to say that *The Excursion* was beneath Wordsworth, and quite another to say that *The Excursion* was beneath contempt. Disappointed as he was by *The Excursion*, Coleridge was stung into active indignation by the ribald obtuseness of Jeffrey.

Si natura negat, facit indignatio versus; and out of a mingled desire to disentangle the best of Wordsworth from the worst and to defend him as a purely inspired poet of lofty aims against the coarse malice of reviewers, Coleridge shook off his apathy and began to develop his first autobiographical sketch into a reasoned and self-sacrificing exposition of a great poet's genius. Hence the too frequent appearance of the now negligible Jeffrey in allusions or lengthy notes which the editors of 1847 wisely mitigated or omitted as they could. When, very shortly after, came Wordsworth's own two volumes of 1815 with the *Lyrical Ballads* essays retained in full and buttressed by two new pieces of massy prose criticism that showed, nevertheless, distinct signs of a faulty foundation, Coleridge felt that he must speak out clearly on the whole subject. Observe that sentence in the letter to Dr Brabant, " The necessity of extending what I first intended as a preface to an Autobiographia Literaria." Observe, too, that we hear nothing of Coleridge's intention to issue a work in two volumes, the first in prose and the second in verse, until after the appearance of Wordsworth's two volumes. We may assume that the one suggested the other. In fact, the volumes of 1815 with their essays new and old had taken Coleridge back again to the great days of 1797 and re-opened the glorious controversy about the nature and language of poetry. There was, as Coleridge had always known, something wrong with a theory that offered equal justification for *Andrew Jones* and *Lucy Gray*, and something wrong with a poet who was conscious of no difference between them. Wordsworth had to be defended against himself as well as against Jeffrey. In the "fragments of Auto-biography" Coleridge saw a chance of making his own position clear; and thus it comes about that the book which begins with Coleridge ends with Wordsworth. The *Biographia* grew out of the necessities of the moment, and we must be grateful to those necessities; for without them it would probably never have grown at all. Chapters I to III are mainly autobiographical, and represent, no doubt, the "fragments of AUTO-biography" first mentioned to Stuart in the letter of September 1814, before *The Excursion* and its reviewer had given a specific direction and purpose to the writer's desultory prose. It may be mentioned that a long footnote to Chapter III (omitted by the 1847 editors) in which precise charges of malice are brought against Jeffrey, makes no allusion whatever to his review of *The Excursion*. Up to that point Coleridge seems more concerned to defend Southey than to defend Wordsworth, who is, in fact, very little mentioned. With Chapter IV, however, Wordsworth definitely appears. The first part of the chapter deals entirely with *Lyrical Ballads* and its Preface; but later there are allusions to the volumes of 1815, which had just been published. Then the fatal words " fancy " and " imagination " are mentioned and away goes our Logosophist in hot pursuit through Hartley and Hobbes and Spinoza and Des Cartes and Schelling and Kant, for nine long chapters, " and finds no end, in wandering mazes lost." Becoming at last aware that if he did not soon pull up he would actually achieve those " two volumes of not less than six hundred pages each" instead of writing a defence of Wordsworth, he sought for some quick way of getting back to his subject, and found it by writing a letter to himself advising himself to stop, printed the letter at the end of Chapter XIII, and returned abruptly to Wordsworth in Chapter XIV almost where he had left him in Chapter V. But from this point the allusions to *The Excursion* and *Poems* of 1815 become more detailed and exact, actual pages being cited in the text. All thoughts of autobiography are abandoned, and the book really ends with Wordsworth, though, for reasons to be given presently, it was continued for another hundred and sixty pages.

So far we have dealt with the composition of the book—its sudden development, under the stimulus of *The Excursion*, *The Edinburgh Review* and the *Poems* of 1815, from a desultory and prefatory autobiographical fragment into a critical examination and defence of Wordsworth's poetical achievement. The printing and publication form a separate chapter of its history—a chapter of accidents. First we have Coleridge announcing in July 1816, with characteristic optimism, that it was printed:

8 *July*, 1816.

...From several causes my literary reputation has been lately on the increase and as two dramatic pieces of mine will be brought out at Drury Lane at or before Christmas, and as the *poems* of my maturer years, and my *literary life*, (which *are* printed and have passed the revision of the first Critics of this country, and of those who exert most influence in the higher circles from their rank, and on the Public by their connection with the most important of our works of periodical criticism) will appear at the same time, I have every reason to hope that the disposition to enquire after my works will become still more extended....

As a matter of fact Coleridge was at this time supplying copy so copiously that the limits of a single volume were exceeded and the *Biographia* had to overflow into a second volume of its own; and so the original scheme of a work in two volumes, one of prose and one of verse, broke down. Before the end of 1816 troubles had arisen with the printers at Bristol, and after some delay and much irritation the work was transferred for completion to Messrs Gale and Fenner in London, for whom Coleridge had written the *Lay Sermon*. The second volume of *Biographia* had then reached p. 128, i.e. Chapter XXI. To make this volume uniform in size with the first Coleridge had to provide another 160 pages of matter. As usual he began to think of something else:

...I often converse better than I can compose; and hence too, it is, that a collection of my letters written before my mind was so much oppressed would, in the opinion of all who have ever seen any number of them, be thrice the value of my set publications. Take as a specimen—'s Letters, which never received a single correction, or that letter addressed to myself as from a friend, at the close of the first volume of the Literary Life, which was written without taking my pen off the paper except to dip it in the inkstand.

However, he writes thus to Rest Fenner, the publisher, in Sept. 1816,

22 *Sept.* 1816.

...The scheme of my labours is this;—having despatched the Lay Sermon addressed to the Labouring Classes, and, if I do not succeed, to give it up, and, at all events, to commence the next week with the matter which I have been forced by the blunder and false assurance of the printer to add to the "Literary Life," in order to render the volumes of something like the same size. I not only shall not, but I cannot think of or do anything till the three volumes complete are in Mr Gale's House....

The additional matter was thus provided: another critical chapter on Wordsworth was written (Ch. XXII), and then (the original impulse having died away) recourse was had to old material—the three *Satyrane's Letters* from *The Friend*, and the lengthy criticism in *The Courier* of Maturin's utterly unimportant tragedy *Bertram*. This was rounded off with a diffuse and speculative chapter, slightly personal but mainly theological, and in that unhappy fashion the volume was padded out to the requisite size. Even as late as March 1817 we find Coleridge exclaiming with irritation at receiving a sheet of *Zapolya* instead of *Biographia*. But all things come to an end, even the delays of printers; and *Biographia Literaria* actually emerged into published existence in the summer of 1817, followed soon afterwards by *Sibylline Leaves*, dissociated from it and issued as a separate publication.

G. S.

NOTES

CHAPTER I

p. 1, l. 21. **true nature of poetic diction.** The stages of this "long continued controversy" are (1) *Lyrical Ballads* (1798), written, according to the preliminary *Advertisement*, "as experiments...to ascertain how far the language of conversation in the middle and lower classes of society is adapted to the purposes of poetic pleasure"; (2) *Lyrical Ballads*, 2 vols. (1800), in which the *Advertisement* of (1) becomes a lengthy *Preface* denying to poetry a conventional diction of its own and assigning as its proper vocabulary "a selection of the real language of men in a state of vivid sensation"; (3) *Lyrical Ballads* (1802), in which the *Preface* of (2) is enlarged, and defended by an *Appendix on what is usually called Poetic Diction*; (4) Wordsworth's *Poems*, 2 vols. (1815) with a new *Preface*, and (5) The *Essay supplementary to the Preface*, also contained in Vol. 1 of the *Poems* of 1815.

p. 1, l. 26. **a small volume.** No. 8 in the list of works.

p. 2, footnote. **The authority of Milton.** Double epithets, like everything else in poetry, must be justified solely by success, not by age, precedent or authority. In the year of *Biographia* was published the first volume of a poet remarkable for his coinage of double epithets; but the "rapier-pointed epigram," the "sky-searching lark" and the "deep-brow'd Homer" of Keats's earliest poems are certainly not less happy than the "heart high-sorrowful," the "droop-headed flowers" or the "azure-lidded sleep" of his latest.

p. 2, footnote. **Ut tanquam scopulum, etc.** From the *Noctes Atticae* of Aulus Gellius (2nd century A.D.), Bk. 1, Chap. 10. The passage reads: "Vive ergo moribus praeteritis; loquere verbis praesentibus; atque id, quod a C. Caesare, excellentis ingenii ac prudentiae viro, in primo *De Analogia* libro, scriptum est, habe semper in memoria atque in pectore, ut tanquam scopulum, sic fugias inauditum atque insolens verbum." It may be rendered thus: "Order your life according to the manners of older times, but speak in the language of the present; and keep always in mind and soul what Caesar—a man of extraordinary genius and sagacity—has written in the first book of his *Analogy*: Like a dangerous rock shun the new and unusual word." Caesar's treatise *De Analogia* has not come down to us.

p. 2, l. 19. **pruned the double epithets.** The passage in the text was used almost word for word twenty years earlier in the preface to the second edition of the *Poems* (1797), and repeated later; but a comparison of the three editions (8, 11, 19 in List of Works) shows that the alleged rigour of the pruning was one of Coleridge's fancies. Some rather egregious examples in 8 disappear from 11 and 19, among them, "tyrant-murdered multitudes," "wildly-bowered sequestered walk" and "nature's bosom-startling call"; "rapture-trembling Seraphim" appears in 8 and 11, but is expunged from 19; but after all revisions the pages of the early poems abound in double epithets. Here are some that appear throughout: "toy-bewitched," "moon-glittering bulk," "lone-glittering," "king-polluted," "sloth-jaundiced." "Sorrow-shrivelled captive" see-saws in various editions between the Chatterton *Monody* and *The Man of Ross*, and is finally retained in the latter.

p. 3, l. 2. **date of the present work.** 1815 when it was being written, and so anterior to 31, 32 and 33 in the List of Works.

p. 3, l. 3. **with my name.** But his name had appeared in Nos. 12, 17, 18, 19, 22 and 27 of the List.

p. 3, l. 5. **the three or four poems.** His contributions to *Lyrical Ballads*. See List of Works, Nos. 13 and 16.

p. 3, footnote. **See the criticisms.** The criticisms of *Lyrical Ballads* to which Coleridge refers, that in *The Critical Review*, Oct., 1798, and that in *The Monthly Review*, May, 1799, were on the whole remarkably friendly in general tone. *The Ancient Mariner* was a stumbling-block to both reviewers. This is what the *Monthly* critic says of the Coleridge pieces:

"The author's first piece, the *Rime of the ancyent marinere*, in imitation of the *style* as well as of the spirit of the elder poets, is the strangest story of a cock and a bull that we ever saw on paper: yet, though it seems a rhapsody of unintelligible wildness and incoherence, (of which we do not perceive the drift, unless the joke lies in depriving the wedding guest of his share of the feast,) there are in it poetical touches of an exquisite kind.

"*The Dramatic Fragment* [i.e. *The Foster-Mother's Tale*], if it intends anything, seems meant to throw disgrace on the savage liberty preached by some modern *philosophes*....*The Nightingale* sings a strain of true and beautiful poetry;—Miltonic, yet original; reflective, and interesting in an uncommon degree."

And he concludes his survey of the volume by saying: "So much genius and originality are discovered in this publication, that we wish to see another from the same hand, written on more elevated subjects and in a more cheerful disposition."

The *Critical* author (of whom we shall speak further below) must be quoted upon Wordsworth as well as Coleridge:

"In a very different style of poetry, is the Rime of the Ancyent Marinere; a ballad (says the advertisement) 'professedly written in imitation of the *style*, as well as of the spirit of the elder poets.' We are tolerably conversant with the early English poets; and can discover no resemblance whatever, except in antiquated spelling and a few obsolete words. This piece appears to us perfectly original in style as well as in story. Many of the stanzas are laboriously beautiful; but in connection they are absurd or unintelligible. Our readers may exercise their ingenuity in attempting to unriddle what follows:

'The roaring wind! it roar'd far off,
It did not come anear;
But with its sound it shook the sails
That were so thin and sere.

The upper air bursts into life,
And a hundred fire-flags sheen
To and fro they are hurried about;
And to and fro, and in and out
The stars dance on between.

The coming wind doth roar more loud;
The sails do sigh, like sedge:
The rain pours down from one black cloud,
And the moon is at its edge.

Hark! hark! the thick black cloud is cleft,
And the moon is at its side:
Like waters shot from some high crag,
The lightning falls with never a jag
A river steep and wide.

The strong wind reach'd the ship: it roar'd
And dropp'd down, like a stone!
Beneath the lightning and the moon
The dead men gave a groan.'

We do not sufficiently understand the story to analyse it. It is a Dutch attempt at German sublimity. Genius has here been employed in producing a poem of little merit.

With pleasure we turn to the serious pieces, the better part of the volume. The Foster-Mother's Tale is in the best style of dramatic narrative. The Dungeon, and the Lines upon the Yew-tree Seat, are beautiful:...Admirable as this poem [The Female Vagrant] is, the author seems to discover still superior powers in the Lines written near Tintern Abbey. On reading this production, it is impossible not to lament that he should ever have condescended to write such pieces as the Last of the Flock, the Convict, and most of the ballads. In the whole range of English poetry, we scarcely recollect any thing superior to a part of the following passage [ll. 66–112]:

...And so I dare to hope...
All my moral being...

The 'experiment,' we think, has failed, not because the language of conversation is little adapted to 'the purposes of poetic pleasure,' but because it has been tried upon uninteresting subjects. Yet every piece discovers genius; and, ill as the author has frequently employed his talents, they certainly rank him with the best of living poets."

Really, considering that the anonymous little volume of *Lyrical Ballads* was issued as the uncompromising manifesto of a poetic revolution, we cannot feel that these notices lacked sympathy or understanding. Now the *Critical* reviewer, who was so severe on *The Ancient Mariner*, was Robert Southey, with whom Coleridge had been intimately associated. Southey, thinking that he was referred to in the "Nehemiah Higginbottom" sonnets (see pp. 14–15 of the present volume) no doubt wrote his attack on *The Ancient Mariner* as a counterblast to what he thought was an attack on himself, and was so pleased with his "German sublimity" phrase that he repeated it in a letter to William Taylor of Norwich (Sept. 1798). The whole incident is not very creditable to Southey, and should not be forgotten when we consider Coleridge's generous praise of his fellow-poet in *Biographia Literaria*. Lamb, who had been temporarily infected by Southey with unfriendliness to Coleridge, nevertheless protested strongly against the attack on *The Ancient Mariner*: "If you wrote that review in 'Crit. Rev.,' I am sorry you are so sparing of praise to the 'Ancient Marinere';—so far from calling it, as you do, with some wit, but more severity, 'A Dutch Attempt, etc.,' I call it a right English attempt, and a successful one, to dethrone German simplicity. You have selected a passage fertile in unmeaning miracles, but have passed by fifty passages as miraculous as the miracles they celebrate. I have never so deeply felt the pathetic as in that part,

> A spring of love gush'd from my heart,
> And I bless'd them unaware—

It stung me into high pleasure through sufferings. Lloyd does not like it; his head is too metaphysical, and your taste too correct; at least I must allege something against you both, to excuse my own dotage—

> So lonely 'twas, that God himself
> Scarce seemèd there to be! etc., etc.

But you allow some elaborate beauties—you should have extracted 'em. 'The Ancient Marinere' plays more tricks with the mind than that last poem [i.e. *Tintern Abbey*] which is yet one of the finest written."

To complete the comedy of errors we may add that very soon Wordsworth was among those who published condemnations of *The Ancient Mariner*; for to the next edition (1800) of *Lyrical Ballads* he added a most egregious note finding many fanciful faults with the poem. Once more Lamb, who seems to have been the only man with spirit fine enough to appreciate this wonderful piece, spoke up in a letter of defence, which drew from Wordsworth a reply of solemn rebuke and advice. But the note was omitted in the next edition. See *Lyrical Ballads* (ed. Sampson), pp. 178–180, and Lamb's Letters, to Wordsworth (Jan. 30, 1801) and to Manning (Feb. 15, 1801). Coleridge took it all without complaint or protest. Among his faults a want of magnanimity had no place.

p. 3, l. 28. **a very severe master.** The Rev. James Boyer, or Bowyer (b. 1736), was educated at Christ's Hospital and Balliol. He resigned his Mastership in 1799. The classic account of Boyer is to be found in Lamb's essay *Christ's Hospital Five and Thirty Years Ago*, to which the reader should need no more than a bare reference. De Quincey, by the way, ridicules the assertion of Coleridge that Boyer was a sound teacher, and dismisses him scornfully as a bloody-minded pedant, constitutionally incapable of fine discrimination. It was Coleridge's habit, he pointed out, to imagine that the geese of his youth were swans. But, after all, Coleridge knew Boyer, De Quincey didn't.

p. 3, l. 31. **Virgil.** Coleridge retained this preference, if we may judge from *Table-Talk*, in which he exclaims, "If you take from Virgil his diction and metre, what do you leave him?"

p. 3, l. 34. **silver and brazen ages.** Roman literature is commonly divided into these periods: I. The Bronze Age (240–80 B.C.), the age of primitive or tentative literature, that includes the dramatists Naevius, Ennius, Pacuvius, Accius, Plautus and Terence. Naevius and Ennius were also epic poets, the latter the founder (in a sense) of Latin poetry II. The Golden Age, from Cicero to Augustus (80 B.C.–14 A.D.), the classic period in which flourished the best-known Roman writers, Cicero, Caesar, Livy, Lucretius, Virgil, Horace, Catullus, Propertius, Tibullus and Ovid. III. The Silver Age, from Tiberius to Trajan (14–117 A.D.), in which the outstanding figures are Silius Italicus, Statius, Persius, Juvenal, Martial, Petronius, Tacitus, Quintilian and the two Plinies. IV. The Age of Decadence, from 117 onwards, that includes such writers as Claudian, Suetonius, and Apuleius. Coleridge excludes from the great age, not only Terence (2nd century B.C.) but also Lucretius and Catullus (ob. circ. 55 B.C.), and limits the golden age to the actual Augustan period, in which Virgil and Horace are the most brilliant figures. Coleridge, with his philosophical interests, would as naturally prefer Lucretius to Virgil as a serious English reader would prefer (say) Wordsworth to Tennyson. The comparison must not be pressed too far.

p. 4, l. 11. **Didymus.** An Alexandrian Greek (63 B.C.–10 A.D.) who lived and worked in Rome. He was a critic, grammarian and lexicographer of monumental industry.

p. 4, l. 14. **our own English compositions.** It is interesting to note that, at the end of the eighteenth century, close attention was given, at a famous classical school, to the art of writing English.

p. 4, l. 25. **the manchineel.** A West Indian tree with a poisonous milky sap and an acrid fruit resembling an apple. It was supposed to be so poisonous that people died from merely sleeping in its shade. By 1797 Coleridge had evidently forgotten the ban on the Manchineel, for in his lines *To the Revd. George Coleridge* this passage occurs:

> But, like a tree with leaves of feeble stem,
> If the clouds lasted, and a sudden breeze
> Ruffled the boughs, they on my head at once
> Dropped the collected shower; and some most false,
> False and fair foliag'd as the Manchineel,
> Have tempted me to slumber in their shade
> E'en 'mid the storm; then breathing subtlest damps,
> Mix'd their own venom with the rain from Heaven,
> That I woke poison'd!

p. 4, l. 27. **Alexander and Clytus.** Clitus, a Macedonian, one of Alexander's friends and generals, had saved the monarch's life in an unequal combat during the great battle of the Granicus (B.C. 334). A few years later, at a banquet where the bluff soldier was vigorously and perhaps rather stupidly outspoken, and all parties rather drunk, an altercation arose, which presently developed into a furious quarrel, at the climax of which Alexander snatched a spear from a soldier and ran it through the body of his friend and saviour. Suddenly sobered, he saw what he had done, and in the anguish of remorse was hardly restrained from killing himself. See Plutarch's Life of Alexander for a vivid account of the incident.

p. 5, l. 1. **index expurgatorius.** The "index expurgatorius" is the list of books permitted by the Roman Church to be read after the omission of passages dangerous to faith or morals. It might be urged against Coleridge that the stock-phrases of law and legislation have at least the sanction of age or tradition; but there is nothing whatever to be said in favour of the forms and expressions inflicted upon the English language by some journalists and most officials.

p. 5, l. 38. **Ne falleretur, etc.** No source has been found for this passage, and H. N. Coleridge, in the edition of 1847, assigns it to Coleridge himself, adding that *incalescentia* is a good word not countenanced by any classic writer of Rome. Mr Shawcross concurs, and records his suspicion of *genuina* as a substantive—which it does not seem to be in this passage. But surely it is hard to believe that, at this moment, and with no visible provocation, Coleridge decided to write in Latin instead of English. Very likely he found the passage, or something like it, in a post-classical source not yet traced. It may be rendered thus: "In order that it might not be deluded by sonorous periods and flowing rhythm, elaborate ornaments and flowers of rhetoric, but might penetrate beneath the surface of the language and examine the nature and depth of the foundation and the supports of the superstructure, and discover whether the figures of speech were mere enamel meant only for ornament, or the native colour and genuine warmth of blood flowing from the very heart of the subject matter."

p. 6, l. 15. **Mr Bowles's sonnets.** There is nothing unusual in the disproportionate influence exercised by a trivial book or utterance upon a youthful and ardent mind. It is the quality of the mind that matters, not the quality of the influence. The Reverend William Lisle Bowles (1762–1850), Prebendary of Salisbury and Rector of Bremhill, owes his immortality, not to his verses, but to the mere chance that a great combustible mind took fire from the feeble sparks of poetry he struck out. The ignition might easily have come from any other man or book. Bowles's *Fourteen Sonnets written chiefly on Picturesque Spots during a Journey* (1789) was reprinted with additions in 1789, 1794, 1796, 1800 and 1802; an indication that the gently sentimental utterances of this sequestered parson were pleasing to many ears tired of the brilliant rhymes flashed out by polished wits. Bowles kindled the ardour of still another poet, but not in the same way; for certain strictures on Pope contained in his edition of that writer in 1806 brought down upon him the fiery wrath of Byron, the conflagration being fierce and protracted. The reader may like to see a characteristic specimen of Bowles. The sonnet given below is plainly one of the admired ones as Coleridge modelled his own *Sonnet to the Otter* upon it.

Sonnet VII

To the River Itchin, near Winton.

Itchin, when I behold thy banks again,
  Thy crumbling margin, and thy silver breast,
  On which the self-same tints still seem to rest,
Why feels my heart the shiv'ring sense of pain?
Is it—that many a summer's day has past
  Since, in life's morn, I carol'd on thy side?
  Is it—that oft, since then, my heart has sigh'd,
As Youth, and Hope's delusive gleams, flew fast?
  Is it—that those, who circled on thy shore,
  Companions of my youth, now meet no more?

Whate'er the cause, upon thy banks I bend
  Sorrowing, yet feel such solace at my heart,
As at the meeting of some long-lost friend,
  From whom in happier hours, we wept to part.

p. 6, l. 18. **modes of teaching.** This passage may usefully remind the reader that disputes between the advocates of "humanistic" and of "useful" studies are not a new thing vainly invented at recent educational conferences or in recent newspaper discussions. The modern attack upon "bookish" education may be dated from Rousseau's *Emile* published in 1762. In France, as someone has wittily remarked, Rousseau's doctrines produced a Revolution; in England they produced *Sandford and Merton*. That classic of "practical" education by Thomas Day (1748–89) appeared in three volumes between 1783 and 1789 and had considerable influence upon theories of teaching. Day had proposed marriage to each of two sisters, neither of whom would have him, but each of whom in turn was married to **Richard Lovell Edgeworth** (1744–1817), Day's close friend and fellow-student, a highly interesting person of an ingenious and mechanical turn of mind. In collaboration with his famous daughter Maria (author of *Castle Rackrent*, *The Absentee* and *Ormond*) he wrote in 1798 a book called *Practical Education* and in 1809 another called *Professional Education*. In both these works he attacks University education, mainly on three grounds, first the excessive amount of time spent on Latin and Greek to the neglect of the mother tongue, secondly the inclusion of Latin versification in the curriculum, and thirdly the exclusion from the curriculum of all forms of art and craft work. Edgeworth was in fact a twentieth century educationist writing a hundred years too soon. It is almost certainly Edgeworth whom Coleridge had in mind when he wrote this passage. But Edgeworth was not the only man attacking the Universities at this time. Two essays by Sydney Smith in *The Edinburgh Review* (1809–1810) take just the same lines as Edgeworth's books. For Coleridge's views on Bell and Lancaster and on "improving" books as a substitute for fairy tales see subsequent notes.

p. 6, l. 22. **in whose halls.** From Wordsworth's sonnet beginning,

It is not to be thought of that the Flood
Of British freedom.

p. 6, l. 37. **neque enim debet., etc.** "For the fact that a writer is living should not hinder the success of his works. Can it be just that the honour and influence of a writer who is among us shall wane as though we had had too much of him, whereas, had he flourished among men of a bygone age, we should search not only for his books, but also for portraits of him? But it is perverse and pernicious to refuse to admire a man who is worthy of the highest esteem, simply because we are able to see him and meet him, and to give him not merely our praise but our affection too."

p. 7, l. 10. **a Grecian.** The name given to boys in the highest form at Christ's Hospital. See Lamb's *Recollections of Christ's Hospital*.

p. 7, l. 11. **Dr Middleton.** Thomas Fanshawe Middleton (1769–1822) became first Bishop of Calcutta in 1814. He was supposed to have died on the voyage—hence the elegiac tone of the following quotation.

p. 7, l. 13. **qui laudibus.** From Petrarch's Latin Epistles, Bk. I, Ep. I. Francesco Petrarca (1304–1374) the great Italian poet and scholar is renowned first of all for songs and sonnets in Italian enshrining his romantic passion for Laura de Sade, and next for an ardent zeal in the cause of classical study, reflected in his own numerous Latin compositions. The passage may be rendered thus: "Who was wont to honour with generous praise my talents and my writings and thus to spur my ambition. Not everything is buried in the earth; love never dies; grief never dies; to behold the faces of those we loved is a boon denied; but it is still ours to weep and remember."

p. 7, l. 21. **enthusiastically delighted.** So reverential was the youthful Coleridge that, in his 1796 volume, he would not use the word "sonnet," but bestowed upon his (and Lamb's) compositions the hapless title "Effusions." Thus he writes: "Of the following Poems a considerable number are styled *Effusions* in defiance of Churchill's line:

Effusion on Effusion *pour* away.

I could recollect no title more descriptive of the manner and matter of the Poems—I might indeed have called the majority of them Sonnets—but they do not possess that *oneness* of thought which I deem indispensable in a Sonnet—and (not a very honorable motive perhaps) I was fearful that the title *Sonnet* might have reminded my reader of the Poems of the Revd. W. L. Bowles—a comparison with whom would have sunk me below that mediocrity, on the surface of which I am at present enabled to float." Lamb protested energetically against "Effusions" in a letter (Dec. 2, 1796) when the Second Edition was under consideration: "What you do retain tho', call sonnets for God's sake, and not effusions—spite of your ingenious anticipation of ridicule in your Preface." Accordingly, the "effusions" retained in the new edition were called "sonnets." The sonnet-form, which Wordsworth was to use so wonderfully some ten years later, attracted Coleridge in his early days of poetry. One striking proof of this remains. In 1796 Coleridge sent to Thelwall "a sheet of Sonnets collected by me for the use of a few friends who payd the printing. There you will see my opinion of Sonnets" (Letter to Thelwall, Dec. 17, 1796). Only one copy of this pamphlet is known to exist—the very one referred to—for it is bound up with Coleridge's own copy of Bowles's *Sonnets and Other Poems* (1796) presented to Mrs Thelwall by S. T. C. and inscribed to her in his own hand on the fly-leaf. He says: "Dear Mrs Thelwall, I entreat your acceptance of this volume, which has given me more pleasure, and done my heart more good, than all the other books I ever read, excepting my Bible...." The precious volume is in the Dyce Collection at South Kensington Museum. The pamphlet is a small octavo sheet of sixteen pages, the first two occupied by an introduction and the remainder by twenty-eight sonnets, two on a page. The introduction begins with the statement, "I have selected the following SONNETS from various Authors for the purpose of binding them up with the Sonnets of the Rev. W. L. Bowles." The essay, which has no great critical value, was used by Coleridge as a preface to the group of sonnets in his *Poems* of 1797. The twenty-eight selected examples are thus distributed: Coleridge, Southey, Lamb, Lloyd, 4 each, Bowles 3, Charlotte Smith 2, Bamfield, Thomas Warton, Henry Brooke, W. Sotheby, Thomas Russel, Thomas Dermody, Anna Seward, 1 each.

The reader interested in Coleridge's youthful preferences will find a complete list on p. 1141 of E. Hartley Coleridge's edition of the Poetical Works. It is scarcely necessary to add that Coleridge soon learned to look with less admiring eyes upon the Bowles and the Charlotte Smith school of composition.

p. 7, l. 29. **the three or four following publications.** The successive editions of the sonnets with additional numbers.

p. 7, l. 40. **At a very premature age.** Lamb's loving and exquisite invocation remains the classic picture of Coleridge in his boyhood: "Come back into memory, like as thou wert in the dayspring of thy fancies, with hope like a fiery column before thee—the dark pillar not yet turned—Samuel Taylor Coleridge—Logician, Metaphysician, Bard! —How have I seen the casual passer through the Cloisters stand still, intranced with admiration (while he weighed the disproportion between the *speech* and the *garb* of the young Mirandola), to hear thee unfold, in thy deep and sweet intonations, the mysteries of Iamblichus, or Plotinus (for even in those years thou waxedst not pale at such philosophic draughts), or reciting Homer in his Greek, or Pindar—while the walls of the old Grey Friars re-echoed to the accents of the *inspired charity-boy!*"

p. 8, l. 5. **two or three compositions.** Coleridge's *juvenilia* will be found in the Dykes Campbell or E. H. Coleridge editions of the poems. One of them, *Dura Navis* (written in his fifteenth year), begins thus:

> To tempt the dangerous deep, too venturous youth,
> Why does thy breast with fondest wishes glow?
> No tender parent there thy cares shall sooth,
> No much lov'd Friend shall share thy every woe.

To this poem Coleridge appended in after years a note that may be worth quoting: "I well remember old Jemmy Bowyer, the plagose Orbilius of Christ's Hospital, but an admirable educer no less than Educator of the Intellect, bade me leave out as many epithets as would turn the whole into eight-syllable lines, and then ask myself if the exercise would not be greatly improved. How often have I thought of the proposal since then, and how many thousand bloated and puffing lines have I read, that, by this process, would have tripped over the tongue excellently. Likewise I remember that he told me on the same occasion—'Coleridge! the connections of a Declamation are not the transitions of Poetry—bad, however, as they are, they are better than "Apostrophes" and "O thou's," for at the worst they are something like common sense. The others are the grimaces of Lunacy.'"

p. 8, l. 15. **Of providence, etc.** Milton, *Paradise Lost*, Bk. II, ll. 559–561.

p. 8, l. 22. **an amiable family.** Coleridge had befriended a younger boy named Evans, whose widowed mother and her three daughters, resident in London, repaid him with the affectionate attentions so dear to a friendless lad far removed from home. This, according to Coleridge, began in 1788, when he was sixteen. With the eldest daughter, Mary, he fell in love, after the usual manner of "the growing boy," and, what is less usual, remained in love even through the distractions of Cambridge. In 1794 he declared his passion in writing; but Mary replied with a kind and firm letter that ended his hopes for ever. The story is quite a serious chapter in Coleridge's life, and is best studied in his letters.

p. 8, l. 33. **a long and blessed interval.** The interval that includes such landmarks as (1) his meetings with Lamb (1795) and their *symposia* of egg-hot and tobacco in "the little smoky room at The Salutation and the Cat where we have sat together through the winter nights, beguiling the cares of life with Poesy"; (2) the interest and excitement of preparing for Cottle the Bristol publisher his first volume of poems; (3) his meeting with Wordsworth (1795 or 1796), their long talks, and the resulting *Lyrical Ballads* (1798). The magical, radiant Coleridge of this period, dear to all young lovers of poetry, and dear to the unhappy poet himself as he saw the image mistily "in the dark backward and abysm of time," is imperishably preserved for us in Hazlitt's essay *My First Acquaintance with Poets.*

p. 9, l. 2. **Lewesdon Hill.** This poem, by William Crowe (1745–1829), an odd and attractive character, was published in 1788. The spot described is in the west of Dorsetshire. As the poem is not generally known, a quotation will be useful:

> How changed is thy appearance, beauteous hill!
> Thou hast put off thy wintry garb, brown heath
> And russet fern, thy seemly-colour'd cloak
> To bide the hoary frosts and dripping rains
> Of chill December, and art gaily robed
> In livery of the spring: upon thy brow
> A cap of flowery hawthorn, and thy neck
> Mantled with new-sprung furze and spangles thick
> Of golden bloom: nor lack thee tufted woods
> Adown thy sides: Tall oaks of lusty green,
> The darker fir, light ash, and the nesh tops
> Of the young hazel join, to form thy skirts
> In many a wavy fold of verdant wreath.
> So gorgeously hath Nature drest thee up
> Against the birth of May; and vested so,
> Thou dost appear more gracefully array'd
> Than Fashion's worshippers; whose gaudy shews,
> Fantastical as are a sick man's dreams,
> From vanity to costly vanity
> Change oftener than the moon. Thy comely dress,
> From sad to gay returning with the year,
> Shall grace thee still till Nature's self shall change.

p. 9, l. 6. **the writings of Pope.** The dates of the poems referred to are, *Essay on Man,* 1733–4, *Rape of the Lock,* 1714, *Iliad,* 1715–20.

p. 9, l. 23. **a sorites.** A sorites in logic is a "heap" or series of syllogisms linked together in such a way that the predicate of each proposition forms the subject of the next, the conclusion being formed by a return to the first proposition. The usual example of the common or Aristotelian form is this: Caius is a man—All men are finite beings—All finite beings are sentient—All sentient beings seek happiness—Therefore Caius seeks happiness.

p. 9, l. 29. **Darwin's Botanic Garden.** The difference between the Wordsworthian and the Darwinian view of poetry is so important as to necessitate a somewhat extended note. Erasmus Darwin (1731–1802), grandfather of the great Charles, was himself a distinguished physician and biologist with views that, to an acute modern critic of evolutionary theory, approach nearer to essential truth than the conclusions of *The Origin of Species* (see Samuel Butler's *Evolution Old and New*). To the general reader, however, Erasmus Darwin is best known, at least by name, as author of *The Botanic Garden*, an elaborate exposition of the Linnean system written in the fanciful manner of Pope's *Rape of the Lock*. The second part of the poem, called *The Loves of the Plants*, in four cantos with elaborate explanatory notes putting scientifically the facts that were put fancifully in the text, was the first to be published (1789); the first part, *The Economy of Vegetation*, also in four cantos with elaborate notes, appeared in 1792. Horace Walpole writing in May of that year says:

"Dr Darwin has appeared, superior in some respects to the former part. The *Triumph of Flora* beginning at the fifty-ninth line, is most beautifully and enchantingly imagined: and the twelve verses that by miracle describe and comprehend the creation of the universe out of chaos, are in my opinion the most sublime passage in any author, or in any of the few languages with which I am acquainted." And he goes on to praise "the imagination, harmony, and expression of the versification" of "this glorious work." Here are the twelve lines that Walpole found sublime:

> "LET THERE BE LIGHT!" proclaim'd the ALMIGHTY LORD,
> Astonish'd Chaos heard the potent word;
> Through all his realms the kindling Ether runs,
> And the mass starts into a million suns;
> Earths round each sun with quick explosions burst,
> And second planets issue from the first;
> Bend, as they journey with projectile force,
> In bright ellipses their reluctant course;
> Orbs wheel in orbs, round centres centres roll,
> And form, self-balanced, one revolving Whole.
> —Onward they move amid their bright abode,
> Space without bound, THE BOSOM OF THEIR GOD!"

Here are a few specimens of what may be called the general texture of the work:

> Hence ductile CLAYS in wide expansion spread,
> Soft as the Cygnet's down, their snow-white bed;
> With yielding flakes successive forms reveal,
> And change obedient to the whirling wheel.
> First CHINA's sons, with early art elate,
> Form'd the gay tea-pot, and the pictured plate;
> Saw with illumin'd brow and dazzled eyes
> In the red stove vitrescent colours rise;
> Speck'd her tall beakers with enamel'd stars,
> Her monster-josses, and gigantic jars;
> Smear'd her huge dragons with metallic hues,
> With golden purples and cobaltic blues;

Bade on wide hills her porcelain castles glare,
And glazed Pagodas tremble in the air.

* * * * * *

Gnomes! as you now dissect with hammers fine
The granite-rock, the nodul'd flint calcine;
Grind with strong arm, the circling chertz betwixt,
Your pure Ka-o-lins and Pe-tun-tses mixt;
O'er each red saggar's burning cave preside
The keen-eyed Fire-Nymphs blazing by your side;
And pleased on WEDGEWOOD ray your partial smile,
A new Etruria decks Britannia's isle.—
Charm'd by your touch, the flint liquescent pours,
Through finer sieves, and falls in whiter showers;
Charm'd by your touch, the kneaded clay refines,
The biscuit hardens, the enamel shines;
Each nicer mould a softer feature drinks,
The bold Cameo speaks, the soft Intaglio thinks.
(*Economy of Vegetation*, Canto II.)

SYLPHS! YOU, retiring to sequester'd bowers,
Where oft your PRIESTLEY woos your airy powers,
On noiseless step or quivering pinion glide,
As sits the Sage with Science by his side;
To his charm'd eye in gay undress appear,
Or pour your secrets on his raptured ear.
How nitrous Gas from iron ingots driven
Drinks with red lips the purest breath of heaven;
How, while Conferva from its tender hair
Gives in bright bubbles empyrean air,
The crystal floods phlogistic ores calcine,
And the pure ETHER marries with the MINE.
(*Economy of Vegetation*, Canto IV.)

When o'er the cultured lawns and dreary wastes
Retiring Autumn flings her howling blasts,
Bends in tumultuous waves the struggling woods,
And showers their leafy honours on the floods,
In withering heaps collects the flowery spoil,
And each chill insect sinks beneath the soil;
Quick flies fair TULIPA the loud alarms,
And folds her infant closer in her arms;
In some lone cave, secure pavilion, lies,
And waits the courtship of serener skies.—
So, six cold moons, the Dormouse charm'd to rest,
Indulgent Sleep! beneath thy eider breast,
In fields of Fancy climbs the kernel'd groves,
Or shares the golden harvest with his loves.—
Then bright from earth amid the troubled sky
Ascends fair COLCHICA with radiant eye,
Warms the cold bosom of the hoary year,
And lights with Beauty's blaze the dusky sphere.
Three blushing Maids the intrepid Nymph attend,
And *six* gay Youths, enamour'd train! defend.

So shines with silver guards the Georgian star,
And drives on Night's blue arch his glittering car;
Hangs o'er the billowy clouds his lucid form,
Wades through the mist, and dances in the storm.
(*Loves of the Plants*, Canto I.)

The lengthy and interesting notes are not necessary to our present purpose and are therefore omitted. As Coleridge remarks on p. 12 it is necessary for the reader to be "acquainted with the general style of composition that was at that time deemed poetry in order to understand and account for the effect produced" on him by Bowles. Darwin's *Botanic Garden* thus deserves notice at length because it is an epitome (if anything so diffuse can be called an epitome) of all that Wordsworth and Coleridge revolted from themselves, and turned the taste of England from for ever. The artistic creed embodied in Darwin is this, that the expression of fact in unusual language, with the addition of rhyme and metre, constitutes Poetry. That is, if you call a spade a spade you are talking prose; if you call it an agricultural implement you are getting towards poetry; and if you address it as,

Metallic Blade, wedded to ligneous Rod,
Wherewith the rustic Swain upturns the Sod,

you have attained poetry. The absurdity of this view is delightfully, but perhaps not quite intentionally, exposed in Canning's parody called *The Loves of the Triangles*, which appeared in *The Anti-Jacobin* for April 16, April 23 and May 7, 1798. Thus, Euclid's compact and perspicuous prose tells us, "The angles at the base of an isosceles triangle are equal to one another; and if the equal sides are produced, the angles at the other side of the base are equal." Versified in Darwinian fashion by the parodist this appears as follows:

'Twas thine alone, O Youth of Giant Frame,
ISOSCELES! that rebel heart to tame!
In vain coy MATHESIS thy presence flies:
Still turn her fond hallucinating eyes;
Thrills with *Galvanic* fire each tortuous nerve,
Throb her blue veins, and dies her cold reserve.
Yet strives the Fair, till in the Giant's breast
She sees the mutual passion flame confess'd:
Where'er he moves, she sees his tall limbs trace
Internal Angles equal at the Base;
Again she doubts him: but *produced at will*,
She sees *th'external Angles equal still*.

The Darwinian prose notes and comments (which are part of the fun) are omitted. The whole parody is so much like the original that it may almost be said to fail as a caricature. The reader who turns from *The Botanic Garden* (1789–92) to the *Tintern Abbey* lines (1798) can feel the essential difference between the false and the true in poetry and measure the magnitude of what may be called the Wordsworthian revolution.

p. 9, l. 36. **a contribution.** This cannot now be traced.

p. 10, l. 1. **preference of Collins's odes.** The superiority of Collins to Gray was a prime article of faith in the Wordsworth-Coleridge circle—and elsewhere. The reader who turns to Ward's *English Poets*,

Vol. III, will find, in successive contributions, the superiority of Collins urged by Swinburne and the superiority of Gray by Matthew Arnold.

p. 10, l. 14. **Youth at the prow.** It may be pointed out, on the other hand, that the "concretion" or personification in this familiar line does not depend upon majuscules, but is secured by the imaging of one figure "on the prow" and the other "at the helm." Abstractions do not steer even poetical ships.

p. 11, l. 2. **his Gradus.** Coleridge here adds this note: "In the *Nutricia* of Politian there occurs this line:

Pura coloratos interstrepit unda lapillos.

Casting my eye on a University prize-poem, I met this line:

Lactea purpureos interstrepit unda lapillos.

Now look out in the Gradus for *Purus*, and you find as the first synonym *lacteus*; for *coloratus*, and the first synonym is *purpureus*. I mention this by way of elucidating one of the most ordinary processes in the *ferrumination* of these centos." Angelo Ambrogini (1454–1494) (called Poliziano or Politianus from Montepulciano, his birthplace) was a Renaissance scholar and poet who may be read about at length in J. A. Symonds's *Renaissance in Italy*.

p. 11, l. 31. **that to which we return.** Upon this principle the *Elegy* of Gray is triumphantly vindicated.

p. 12, l. 1. **French tragedies.** No importance need be attached to Coleridge's view of French tragedy, of which he knew very little. The present statement, for instance, is ridiculous.

p. 12, l. 24. **The reader must, etc.** See note above on *The Botanic Garden*. Bowles's *Monody at Matlock* appeared in 1791, the *Vision of Hope*, 1796. The latter piece Coleridge admired with a difference even in the year of its publication, for thus he writes to Thelwall: "Bowles (the bard of my idolatry) has written a poem lately without plan or meaning, though the component parts are divine."

p. 12, l. 28. **it is peculiar, etc.** This is a necessary consequence of Coleridge's principle, enun ciatedby Wordsworth in the Preface of 1815, "that every author, as far as he is great and at the same time *original*, has had the task of *creating* the taste by which he is to be enjoyed."

p. 12, l. 30. **The poems of West.** There are two eighteenth century poets of this name. Richard West (1716–1742) wrote, during his brief life, an *Imitation of Tibullus* and an *Ode to May*. His untimely death drew from Gray, his intimate friend, the sonnet ruthlessly criticised in Wordsworth's Preface to *Lyrical Ballads*. But no doubt Coleridge was referring to Gilbert West (1703–1756) who translated the Odes of Pindar with an interesting preface, as well as Apollonius and Lucian, and wrote *On the Abuse of Travelling* and *Education* (both in imitation of Spenser) and a hopeless poetic drama (full of odes) entitled *The Institution of the Order of the Garter*.

p. 12, l. 32. **the best of Warton's.** Thomas Warton (1728–1790), an Oxford scholar, Professor of Poetry, Professor of Ancient History, and Poet Laureate, is remembered chiefly as the author of a *History of English Poetry* in four volumes (1774–81) that did much to assist the reaction of taste from eighteenth century elegance back to the writers of an older and less artificial period. He was, as well, a diligently imitative versifier, choosing Milton's minor poems as the models for his best work.

p. 12, l. 35. **Percy's collection.** Thomas Percy (1729–1811), Bishop of Dromore, a busy man of letters with interests ranging from the theatre to theology (taking Icelandic poetry on the way) is most famous for his *Reliques of English Poetry* (3 vols. 1765), in which he included poems from an old MS. volume (since reprinted in full), poems from other MS. collections, poems from old broadsides, Scottish ballads, and songs from the Elizabethan and later miscellanies. There were also some later, even contemporary poems. Of the 180 poems in the *Reliques* 45 were from the first-named source, the MS. volume, which "I rescued (says Percy) from destruction, and begged at the hands of my worthy friend Humphrey Pitt, Esq.... I saw it lying dirty on the floor under a Bureau in ye Parlour: being used by the maids to light the fire." The volume dates from about the middle of the seventeenth century. Percy's versions were a little sophisticated, but his volumes did incalculable service to poetry in freshening the drawing-room atmosphere with breezes from the ancient hills. Percy was a herald of the Romantic Revolt. Wordsworth and Scott both professed their admiration for the *Reliques*—the latter's account of his first acquaintance with Percy being a classic page of the autobiographical fragment that opens Lockhart's *Life*.

p. 13, footnote. **Cowper's Task, etc.** William Cowper (1731–1800) published *The Task* in 1785. James Thomson (1700–1748) published *The Seasons* in sections, *Winter* 1726, *Summer* 1727, *Spring* 1728, the whole being completed in 1730. The reference to blank verse indicates that Coleridge was thinking of *The Seasons* and not of *The Castle of Indolence* (1746), which is written in the Spenserian stanza. The "many years after" Bowles to which Coleridge postpones his knowledge of Cowper must be liberally interpreted. It is probable that he knew the works of Cowper earlier and the works of Bowles later than he believed in 1815. He was well acquainted with Cowper in 1796, as a reference to Lamb's letters of that year will show. His cherished phrase "the divine chit-chat of Cowper" occurs in his correspondence of 1796.

p. 13, l. 11. **the Destiny of Nations.** The poem so called (it is a collection of fragments) is in the main composed of Coleridge's contributions to Bk. II of Southey's *Joan of Arc* (1796). Coleridge intended to expand or complete this under the title *The Progress of Liberty or Vision of the Maid of Orleans* for his volume of 1797. Some additions were made, but Lamb dealt with them frankly, not to say fiercely, in a letter to Coleridge of Feb. 5, 1795. The lines were therefore left out and were not republished till 1817 when they appeared in *Sibylline Leaves*.

p. 13, l. 12. **Remorse.** See Nos. 13 and 27 of the list of works. The original *Osorio* will be found in Dykes Campbell's and E. H. Coleridge's editions of the Poetical Works.

p. 13, l. 19. **a copy of verses.** The *Address to a Young Jackass and its Tethered Mother*, first published in the *Morning Chronicle*, Dec. 30, 1794, and included in the volume of 1796. But it should be **noted that the words (from Horace, *Satires*, I, iv) "sermoni propiora,"** i.e. "nearer to prose" or "in a conversational style" were not used of this poem at all and did not appear in the volume of 1796. They were used in 1797 as a motto to a very different piece, *Reflections on Leaving a Place of Retirement*. In Coleridge's poems the motto appears as "sermoni propriora,"—hence Lamb's famous version "properer for a sermon." The same form appears in the 1817 edition of *Biog. Lit.* Perhaps it was an intentional variation of the word.

p. 13, l. 27. **three sonnets.** Cottle quotes a letter (1797) referring to these sonnets: "I sent to the *Monthly Magazine* [Nov. 1797] three mock Sonnets in ridicule of my own Poems, and Charles Lloyd's, and Charles Lamb's etc., etc., exposing that affectation of unaffectedness, of jumping and misplaced accent, in commonplace epithets, flat lines forced into poetry by italics (signifying how well and mouthishly the author would read them), puny pathos, etc., etc. The instances were all taken from myself and Lloyd and Lamb." In the magazine they are headed "SONNETS, attempted in the manner of 'CONTEMPORARY WRITERS.'" Sonnet II is headed "To Simplicity," Sonnet III "On a ruined House in a Romantic Country." But Coleridge sophisticated the first sonnet when he reprinted it in the *Biog. Lit.* of 1817. The version in *The Monthly Magazine* contains six examples of words in capitals and italics; the version in *Biographia Literaria* contains twenty-three! The editors of 1847 ignored all the typographical oddities, and, as the whole matter is quite unimportant, there is little to be gained by disturbing their reading. Perhaps, however, we might record that in the first version l. 4 of Sonnet I begins "Eve darkens," and that l. 8 of Sonnet II reads "Grow cool and *miff*, O! I am *very* sad." Coleridge had evidently forgotten all about "Nehemiah Higginbottom" when he found it necessary to denounce burlesques and imitations in the severe note on p 44 and the passage on p. 126.

p. 13, l. 31. **licentious.** Not, of course, in its modern restricted meaning.

p. 15, footnote. **severe epigram.** Coleridge is here quite at fault. The epigram was published in the *Morning Post*, Jan. 24, 1800, with this heading: "To Mr Pye, on his *Carmen Seculare* (a title which has by various persons who have heard it, been thus translated, 'A Poem *an age long*')." There is some point in saying of a *Carmen Saeculare* that it "must eternal be"; none in saying it of *The Ancient Mariner*.

CHAPTER II

p. 16, l. 7. **genus irritabile vatum.** Horace, *Epistles*, II, ii, l. 102, "the touchy race of poets."

p. 16, l. 28. **There's no philosopher.** From Coleridge's poem, *Recantation, illustrated in the Story of the Mad Ox.*

p. 17, l. 16. **commanding Genius.** Coleridge's distinction between "absolute" and "commanding" genius is not very happily expressed by those words. But his meaning is clear. An "absolute" genius (e.g. Shakespeare or Beethoven) acts in a world of his own creation; a "commanding" genius (e.g. Napoleon) acts in the external world of fact, and his power may be constructive or destructive.

p. 17, l. 28. **Palmyra.** The famous city in Western Asia where the great queen Zenobia reigned and the great critic Longinus taught. The most generally accessible account of Palmyra is contained in Chapter XI of Gibbon's *Decline and Fall*. An elaborate volume on the ruins of Palmyra by Wood and Dawkin had been published in 1753 and may have suggested the allusion to Coleridge.

p. 18, l. 15. **grew immortal.** From Pope's *Satires and Epistles of Horace Imitated*, Bk. II, Ep. I, *To Augustus*, ll. 69–72:

> Shakespear (whom you and ev'ry Play-house bill
> Style the divine, the matchless, what you will)
> For gain, not glory, wing'd his roving flight,
> And grew Immortal in his own despite.

p. 18, l. 16. **one whom he had celebrated.** No convincing identification has ever been made of the persons addressed or referred to in the *Sonnets*.

p. 18, footnote. **the essentials of the Greek stage.** As a Greek play was acted without any break or pause, there could obviously be no change of scene or time. Thus, the action of a Greek play had to be such as could take place in one spot (unity of place) and in one day (unity of time), not as in *Cymbeline* where the scene of action changes from Britain to Rome and back again, or as in *A Winter's Tale* where the time of action is spread over seventeen years. Out of the Greek unities of place and time naturally sprang a third, unity of action; for a story so limited in space and time could have no embroideries or digressions such as the grave-diggers' scene in *Hamlet* or the tavern scenes in *King Henry IV*. Aristotle's view of this unity can be gathered from his doctrine that a play "should be an imitation of an action that is one and entire, the parts of it being so connected, that if any one of them be either transposed or taken away, the whole will be destroyed or changed; for whatever may be either retained or omitted, without making any sensible difference, is not properly a part." The French seventeenth-century tragic writers, who followed the model of the Greeks very closely, adhered to the Greek unities, even though the French plays had normally five acts instead of the continuous action of their models—compare, for instance, the *Phèdre* of Racine with the *Hippolytus* of Euripides. The French writers insisted further that in a play there should be unity of kind, that is, a tragic play must not contain anything comic, nor a comic play anything tragic—nothing like (for instance) the Fool in *King Lear* or the church scene in *Much Ado about Nothing*. French misapprehension and depreciation of Shakespeare can therefore be understood; and it was the French dramatists (rather than the Greek) who influenced English eighteenth-century criticism in favour of "the unities." Coleridge seems to suggest that it was his own criticism that first defended Shakespeare from condemnation for his disregard of these unities. Such a claim will not bear examination. (For Coleridge's public pronouncements on this matter see his *Lectures*, Bohn ed., pp. 51–54, 121–124.) Pope's Preface (which should be read by every student) is a tribute of praise paid to the embodiment of Originality by the embodiment of Correctness. Pope tries very hard to make the best of both Shakespeare and the Unities; but he nowhere suggests that Shakespeare failed for not following them, and he says expressly that "to judge of Shakespeare by Aristotle's rules, is like trying a man by the laws of one country, who acted under those of another." Dr Johnson, whose Preface is a landmark of literary criticism, has something to say in dispraise of Shakespeare, but, in all essentials, his essay is a magnificent defence of the Shakespearean or "mingled" drama against the critics who demanded unity of kind and action: "Shakespeare's plays are not in the rigorous and critical sense either tragedies or comedies, but compositions of a distinct kind; exhibiting the real state of sublunary nature, which partakes of good and evil, joy and sorrow, mingled with endless variety of proportion and innumerable modes of combination; and expressing the course of the world, in which the loss of one is the gain of another; in whioh, at the same time, the reveller is hasting to his wine, and the mourner burying his friend; in which the malignity of one is sometimes defeated by the frolick of another; and many mischiefs and many benefits are done and hindered without design.

"Out of this chaos of mingled purposes and casualties, the ancient poets, according to the laws which custom had prescribed, selected some the crimes of men, and some their absurdities; some the momentous vicissitudes of life, and some the lighter occurrences; some the terrors of distress, and some the gayeties of prosperity. Thus rose the two modes of imitation, known by the names of *tragedy* and *comedy*, compositions intended to promote different ends by contrary means, and considered as so little allied, that I do not recollect among the Greeks or Romans a single writer who attempted both.

"Shakespeare has united the powers of exciting laughter and sorrow not only in one mind, but in one composition. Almost all his plays are divided between serious and ludicrous characters, and, in the successive evolutions of the design, sometimes produce seriousness and sorrow, and sometimes levity and laughter.

"That this is a practice contrary to the rules of criticism will be readily allowed; but there is always an appeal open from criticism to nature...."

Coleridge himself could hardly have put the case for Shakespeare more convincingly. It may be added that Horace Walpole, the embodiment of eighteenth century elegance, defended Shakespeare vigorously against the strictures of Voltaire, and scattered among his letters many passages of just and appreciative criticism.

p. 18, footnote. **Mr. Schlegel.** August Wilhelm von Schlegel (1767–1845), the famous German critic, was a great admirer of Shakespeare, whose works he translated (1798–1810). In 1808 he gave at Vienna a series of lectures on dramatic art and literature (English translation in Bohn's Library) which greatly influenced the course of criticism. Coleridge was also lecturing in 1808, but unfortunately nothing is extant to show how far he was independent of Schlegel, whose work he undoubtedly used in his later lectures. But the general course of Coleridge's own letters and reported conversation of this period, apart from his subsequent work, clearly proves his essential originality in creative criticism. He was a much more highly endowed critic than Schlegel and had the inestimable advantage of being Shakespeare's countryman and fellow poet, and not merely his German translator. However, Coleridge's mind was often at its best under the impulses derived from other (and sometimes greatly inferior) persons, and so there is no need to minimise what he owed to Schlegel—or Bowles.

p. 19, l. 33. **persecution of Burleigh.** There are several traditional stories indicating a certain obtuseness of the great Lord Burghley to the merits of Spenser; but there is no evidence of specific persecution. The poems of Spenser were all written before the calamities that overwhelmed him, so the "melancholy grace" of his compositions can hardly be attributed to that cause. The terrible events that drove him from Ireland barely alive happened in October, 1598, and he died in January, 1599. None of his known works was written in that short interval.

p. 20, l. 3. **Darkness before.** From Wordsworth's tribute to Milton, *Prelude*, Bk. III, l. 285.

p. 20, l. 10. **argue not.** Milton, Sonnet XVII, *To Cyriack Skinner, upon his Blindness.*

p. 21, l. 32. **stereotype pieces.** Coleridge suggests, by this printing-house simile, that sententious passages and stock descriptions in the epigrammatic manner of Pope can be strung together mechanically and convey the impression of success. This is not true of Pope himself as Coleridge acknowledges in the subsequent note. The imitators of Pope who may have written in that manner have not survived; and, in any case, faults in the imitators of a certain style do not necessarily imply defects in the style itself.

p. 22, footnote. **one of my Lectures.** No such lecture survives.

p. 22, footnote. **Sir Joshua Reynolds.** The sentiment here attributed to Reynolds is not discoverable in the *Discourses.*

p. 22, footnote. **As when the moon.** The reader will find translations of this famous passage by Chapman, Pope and Tennyson in *Cambridge Readings in Literature*, Bk. IV. A comparison is instructive.

p. 22, footnote. **article on Chalmers's British Poets.** H. N. Coleridge (edition of 1847) writes: "The article to which the Author refers was written by Mr Southey, and may be found in Vol. XI of *The Quarterly Review*, p. 480. But it contains nothing corresponding to Mr Coleridge's remark, whose reference is evidently mistaken."

p. 23, footnote. **Fletcher's lines.** Coleridge is referring to the edition of Beaumont and Fletcher by Theobald, Seward and Simpson (1750). The lines are from Act I, Sc. ii, l. 133. The Spenser reference is to *Julye*, 21–24.

p. 23, l. 3. **lowest mechanic crafts.** It is difficult to avoid seeing here a reference to William Gifford (1756–1826) the shoemaker's apprentice who became editor of *The Anti-Jacobin* and *The Quarterly Review*. His implacable opposition to all writers of supposed "liberal" tendencies gained him in life certain sinecures and in death a tomb in the Abbey.

p. 24, l. 12. **anonymous critics.** *The Edinburgh Review, The Quarterly Review* and *Blackwood's Magazine* at this time exercised considerable influence on the public mind by their coarse and violent attacks—usually inflamed by political rancour—upon distinguished writers of the day. Wordsworth, Coleridge, Hazlitt, Keats, Shelley, Lamb, Leigh Hunt and others suffered disgraceful treatment at the hands of these anonymous reviewers. Jeffrey, Gifford, Lockhart and "Christopher North" were among the chief offenders, and must bear editorial responsibility for the articles written by others.

p. 24, l. 13. **synodical individuals.** This phrase has not been found in Marvell. Coleridge's magniloquent language refers to the traditional editorial plural still to be found in the leading articles of our periodicals.

p. 24, l. 15. **Paras.** Pariahs, members of the lowest caste.

p. 26, footnote. **Dryden's famous line.** *Absalom and Achitophel,* I, 163:

> Great Wits are sure to Madness near alli'd,
> And thin Partitions do their Bounds divide.

p. 26, l. 21. **constitutional indolence.** Coleridge was not unconscious of his fatal defects.

p. 27, l. 32. **Sic vos, etc.**. "Thus you, but not for yourselves, produce honey, O Bees!" Tradition says that a poetaster Bathyllus having claimed for himself the honour of producing certain adulatory verses to Augustus, really written by Virgil, the indignant poet wrote "Sic vos, non vobis" four times as the beginning of four lines, and challenged his rival to complete them. As Bathyllus could not, Virgil wrote thus:

> Hos ego versiculos feci: tulit alter honores.
> Sic vos, non vobis, nidificatis aves,
> Sic vos, non vobis, vellera fertis oves,
> Sic vos, non vobis, mellificatis apes,
> Sic vos, non vobis, fertis aratra boves.

CHAPTER III

p. 28, l. 4. **I owe full two-thirds.** The principal periodicals from 1798–1815, furnish no evidence of special and wide-spread animosity. The most implacable of Coleridge's critics was his former adorer Hazlitt, whose main charge against Coleridge was apostasy from the cause of revolution. But Hazlitt's principal attacks are later than *Biographia.*

p. 28, l. 8. **Beauties, etc.** "Beauties" of authors, (e.g. Dodd's *Beauties of Shakespeare*) and "E egant Extracts" of verse and prose were familiar volumes at the end of the eighteenth century and may now be easily acquired from the cheaper boxes of the second-hand booksellers. "Anas" are collections of anecdotes, etc., the word "ana" being the termination of such words as *Ménagiana* (a famous French collection) *Shakespeariana,* etc.

p. 29, l. 2. **Averroes.** Averroes (1126–1196) a famous Moorish philosopher born at Cordova.

p. 29, l. 28. **no unfriendly disposition.** In the edition of 1817 Coleridge here had a long footnote containing specific charges of malice against Jeffrey. There is little to gain by quoting it here in full. The reader will find it in most reprints of *Biographia.* Jeffrey defended himself in the *Edinburgh* notice of *Biographia,* and the editors of 1847 omitted the note, retaining however the latter part of it, which was transferred to p. 24, where it is now the footnote beginning "If it were worth while, etc."

p. 30, l. 20. **constitute my whole publicity.** But see List of Works.

p. 30, l. 29. **I changed my plan.** Too much importance need not be attached to this explanation. Coleridge sometimes changed his plan by defect rather than by design. Many of his lectures were given extempore, and wandered so far from the supposed subject that the ground originally planned could not be covered. See the Bohn ed. of the *Lectures*, introductory pages.

p. 30, l. 36. **Bacon, Harrington, etc.** Bacon (1561–1626) the greatest of English philosophers; James Harrington (1611–1677), author of *The Commonwealth of Oceana*, a political Utopia written (after the execution of Charles I) to suggest a form of government for "Oceana," i.e. England; Machiavelli (1469–1527), the Florentine statesman, author of *The Prince*; and Spinoza (1632–1677) author of *Tractatus Politicus*, a discussion of certain dangers in monarchical and aristocratical government, are grouped by Coleridge as serious political philosophers in contrast to Hume (1711–1776), philosopher and historian, author of *Political Discourses*; Condillac (1715–1780) a distinguished French philosopher, and Voltaire (1694–1778) one of the greatest of French writers and political critics, who are evidently to be considered among "the unworthy." Such a view of the last three, and especially of Condillac and Voltaire, seems now absurd; but, in 1815, the French philosophers of the eighteenth century being, if not the fathers, then at least the forefathers, of the Revolution, were all suspected and traduced by the orthodox. Hume's close association with the French writers naturally brought him under condemnation.

p. 31, l. 5. **not in irrecoverable conversation.** Coleridge did not maintain this reticence. His recorded Table-talk deals freely with contemporaries.

p. 31, l. 12. **Sint unicuique, etc.** Apparently a rendering of 1 Cor. iii. 8: " and every man shall receive his own reward "; but it is not the Vulgate version.

p. 31, l. 23. **his earlier publications.** Southey's first works are, (1) *The Fall of Robespierre* (1794), act 1 being by Coleridge; (2) Poems by R. Lovell and R. Southey (1795); *Joan of Arc* (1796); *Minor Poems*, 2 vols. (1797–1799).

p. 31, l. 40. **Strada's Prolusions.** Famiano Strada (1572–1649), the Jesuit historian, author of *De Bello Belgico*, wrote also *Prolusiones et Paradeigmata Eloquentiae*, literary commentaries on the classics of ancient literature.

p. 32, l. 5. **agreed far more, etc.** That is, he took Warton's (the romantic) view of poetry rather than Johnson's (the formal or classical). See note to p. 12, l. 32 for a reference to Warton.

p. 32, l. 8. **Sir Philip Sidney.** Sidney's *Apologie for Poetrie*, written in 1581, was first published in 1594, eight years after its author's death. The edition of 1594 was registered as *The Defence of Poesie*; that of a few months later (1595) was registered as *An Apologie for Poetrie*, under which title it is commonly known. No such statement as that made by Coleridge is to be found in it, though probably Sidney would not have disowned the sentiment; for, in its insistence upon the virtue of sincerity and the viciousness of artificial diction, *The Apologie* may be taken as a commentary on his own famous line, "Fool! said my Muse, look in thy heart and write." The only direct reference in the essay to an old ballad is, in fact, rather contradictory of Coleridge's statement: "I never heard the old song of *Percy* and *Douglas*, that I found not my heart moved more than with a Trumpet; and yet is it sung but by some blind Crowder, with no rougher voice than rude style; which being so evil apparelled in the dust and cobwebs of that uncivil age, what would it work, trimmed in the gorgeous eloquence of *Pindar*?" Probably Coleridge remembered the first part of this passage and associated it with another, much later in the essay, in which Sidney denounces the false diction of some versifiers: "Now for the outside of it [i.e. lyric poetry], which is words, or (as I may term it) Diction, it is even well worse; so is that honey-flowing Matron Eloquence apparelled, or rather disguised, in a Courtesan-like painted affectation. One time with so far-fetched words, that many seem Monsters, but must seem strangers to any poor Englishman. Another time with coursing of a Letter, as if they were bound to follow the method of a Dictionary: another time with figures and flowers, extremely winter-starved." There is another passage of Sidney so appropriate to the general argument as to deserve quotation, though it refers to prose oratory: "I have found in divers small learned Courtiers a more sound style than in some professors of learning; of which I can guess no other cause but that the Courtier following that which by practice he findeth fittest to nature, therein (though he know it not) doth according to art, though not by art; where the other, using art to show art and not hide art (as in these cases he should do) flieth from nature, and indeed abuseth art."

p. 32, l. 15. **when all his works shall be collected.** The collected edition of Southey is in ten volumes (1837–38). It is one of the ironies of literary history that Southey is remembered now as a poet only by a few of the despised minor poems, later generations of readers having agreed to ignore the epics upon which he (and Coleridge) based his hopes of immortality.

p. 32, l. 33. **of him that reads, etc.** The passage cannot be found in Jeremy Taylor, to whom Coleridge attributed it in 1817.

p. 32, l 36. **lofty address of Bacon.** At the beginning of *Novum Organum*.

p. 32, l. 40. **from Pindar's.** The quotation is from Pindar's First Olympic Ode. It is thus translated by the Gilbert West referred to in an earlier note:

Fate hath in various stations rank'd mankind:
  In royal power the long gradations end.
By that horizon prudently confin'd,
  Let not thy hopes to farther views extend.
Long mayst thou wear the regal crown!
  And may the Bard his wish receive,
  With thee, and such as thee to live,
Around his native Greece for wisdom known.

p. 33, l. 25. **St. Nepomuc.** John Nepomucky—(c pronounced like ts)—(1300–1383) was drowned in the Moldau by order of the Emperor Wenceslaus. He became the patron saint of Bohemia. Cecilia, a martyr of the second century, is the traditional patron of music. Her association with the art appears to have arisen from a misunderstanding of a sentence in the old legend, "*cantantibus organis* illa in corde sua soli domino decantabat"—i.e. she sang in her heart to God alone, while *others* were making music; but the words were applied to Cecilia herself.

p. 33, l. 33. **the Thalaba, etc.** *Thalaba the Destroyer* (1801), *Madoc* (1805), *Chronicle of the Cid* (1808), *The Curse of Kehama* (1810), *Roderick* (1814).

p. 34, l. 1. **se cogitare, etc.** Adapted from Pliny's *Letters*, Bk. VII, Ep. 17. It may be rendered thus: "...that he reflects on the importance of publishing any of his compositions: and cannot bring himself to believe that any work which he wishes to please all men for all time does not deserve to be frequently revised."

p. 34, l. 10. **periturae parcere chartae.** From Juvenal, *Sat.* I, 18

stulta est clementia, cum tot ubique
Vatibus occurras, periturae parcere chartae.

"It is a foolish mercy, when everywhere you encounter so many alleged poets, to spare the paper which is sure to be spoilt by someone else."

p. 34, l. 34. **Raphael's figures.** Raphael's pictures, especially those painted under the influence of Perugino, contain several examples of trees like "knitting needles and broom-twigs." See, for instance, the familiar portrait of Maddalena Doni (Pitti Palace, Florence) and the Madonna del Cardellino (Uffizi, Florence). The "gallipots" are not obvious in any.

p. 35, l. 11. **fixed canons of criticism.** "Fixed canons of criticism" are a delusion. There are no such things, though each generation believes that it possesses them. Criticism can merely say what has been; it cannot say finally what may be. **It is an art, not an exact science.** General principles may be drawn from the nature of the various arts and the practice of the various artists, and they may be discussed in essays of permanent value—the *Laocoon* of Lessing, for example; but critical art, like creative art, cannot become "fixed"; if it does, it perishes. Criticism is attendant upon creation, and must advance with it. All advance in music, for instance, has had to be won against the "fixed canons" of academic criticism. It was not the absence of "fixed canons" that made critics of Coleridge's time condemn the poetry of Wordsworth; it was the belief that they possessed such canons and that, judged by them, Wordsworth's poetry would "never do." Wordsworth himself says: "For to be mistaught is worse than to be untaught; and no perverseness equals that which is supported by system, no errors are so difficult to root out as those which the understanding has pledged its credit to uphold." (Essay Supplementary to Preface, p. 221 of the present volume.) The search for an infallible "absolute" in criticism, in science, in philosophy, and in religion, is like the search for an elixir of life, fascinating but hopeless, an end towards which man may travel hopefully, but at which he must never expect to arrive.

p. 35, l. 22. **Haec ipsi, etc.** The deprecatory motto adopted by Southey for his *Minor Poems* (1815) . It is adapted from Martial, XIII, 2, 8: Nos haec novimus esse nihil. "That these things nothing are, full well we know," is Cotton's rendering.

p. 35, l. 25. **the prudery of Spratt.** The life of Cowley was written by his fellow poet Bishop Thomas Sprat in a spirit of stately eulogy that could admit nothing so easy and familiar as the unpremeditated style of letters. As almost the only works of Cowley still read are his prose

Essays (with verses attached) it is possible that the suppressed letters may have had more interest for modern readers than the once famous "Pindariques."

p. 35, l. 29. **Swift and his correspondents.** The rhyming epistles that passed between the Dean and his friends, especially Dr Sheridan, will be found, with "the riddles, conundrums, etc.," in Swift's collected poems. His adventures in "tri-syllable rhymes" carry him as far as

> But, jest apart, restore, you capon ye,
> My twelve thirteens and sixpence-ha'penny.

and, in quadrisyllables as far as,

> For this I will not dine with Agmondisham,
> And for his victuals, let a ragman dish 'em.

Coleridge's comparison of Southey with Swift is not very happy. Swift is best forgotten in his trifles; Southey best remembered in his.

p. 37, l. 26. **Milton.** Coleridge is probably referring to a passage in *The Second Defence of the People of England*, originally written in Latin. The usual English rendering reads thus: "And with respect to myself, though I have accurately examined my conduct, and scrutinized my soul, I call thee, O God, the searcher of hearts, to witness, that I am not conscious, either in the more early or in the later periods of my life, of having committed any enormity, which might deservedly have marked me out as a fit object for such a calamitous visitation [i.e. his blindness]. But since my enemies boast that this affliction is only a retribution for the transgressions of my pen, I again invoke the Almighty to witness, that I never, at any time, wrote anything which I did not think agreeable to truth, to justice, and to piety. This was my persuasion then, and I feel the same persuasion now. Nor was I ever prompted to such exertions by the influence of ambition, by the lust of lucre or of praise; it was only by the conviction of duty and the feeling of patriotism, a disinterested passion for the extension of civil and religious liberty." See also the deeply interesting autobiographical passages elsewhere in the *Defensio Secunda*.

CHAPTER IV

p. 40, l. 10. **the two volumes.** See list of W. W.'s works, nos. 4 to 7.

p. 42, footnote. **a bull.** Coleridge attempted several times to give a philosophical explanation of bulls; but he can scarcely be said, either here or elsewhere, to have made the matter any clearer. We still know what a bull is, in spite of his explanation.

p. 43, l. 23. **I admitted.** So did Wordsworth himself to some extent. *The Convict* with its strong revolutionary and humanitarian sentiments expressed in the gay anapaestic measure of Tom Moore was omitted from all editions after 1798. *A Character in the Antithetical Manner*, first published in 1800, disappears from subsequent editions, one cannot say why, as it is quite inoffensive. The very feeblest of the poems, *Andrew Jones*, first published in 1800, was obstinately retained in all subsequent editions of *Lyrical Ballads* and included in the collected volumes of 1815. Wordsworth wrote in 1800 a lengthy note in defence of *The Thorn*, the best parts of which need none; but *Goody Blake and Harry Gill* was neither dropped nor defended, and Simon Lee's ankles have continued to swell in all editions of Wordsworth.

p. 43, l. 26. **Alice Fell.** First published in the *Poems* of 1807.

p. 43, l. 30. **two subsequent volumes.** *Poems* (1807).

p. 43, l. 39. **Marini.** Giambattista Marini or Marino (1569–1629) a Neapolitan poet, friend of Tasso. His poems were remarkable for an affectation of manner that, in his followers, became grotesque.

p. 44, footnote. **preface to the recent collection.** The *Preface* to the edition of 1815. Possibly such a passage as the following was in Coleridge's mind: "And if, bearing in mind the many Poets distinguished by this prime quality, whose names I omit to mention; yet justified by recollection of the insults which the ignorant, the incapable, and the presumptuous, have heaped upon these and my other writings, I may be permitted to anticipate the judgment of posterity upon myself, I shall declare (censurable, I grant, if the notoriety of the fact above stated does not justify me) that I have given in these unfavourable times, evidence of the exertions of this faculty upon its worthiest objects, the external universe, the moral and religious sentiments of Man, his natural affections, and his acquired passions; which have the same ennobling tendency as the productions of men, in this kind, worthy to be holden in undying remembrance." See p. 214 of the present volume.

p. 44, footnote. **Xanthias.** The slave of the god Dionysos in *The Frogs* of Aristophanes. The lines are thus rendered by Prof. Gilbert Murray:

D. And weren't *you* frighten'd at his awful threats
And language?
X. I? I never cared a rap.

p. 44, l. 15. **Bacchus and the frogs.** Gilbert Murray thus renders the passage which Coleridge quotes:

FROGS. Brekekekex co-ax!
DIONYSOS. A plague on all of your swarming packs.
There's nothing in you except co-ax!

* * * *

I don't care how you scold.
FR. Then all day long
We will croak you a song
As loud as our throats can hold.
Brekekekex co-ax, co-ax!!
D. Brekekekex co-ax, co-ax!!
I'll see you don't outdo me in that.
FR. Well, you shall never beat *us,—that's flat!*
D. I'll make you cease your song
If I shout for it all day long;
My lungs I'll tax
With co-ax, co-ax
—I assure you they're thoroughly strong—
Until your efforts at last relax:
Brekekekex co-ax, co-ax!!

p. 45, l. 12. **Descriptive Sketches.** Not the first publication, but the second. See list of Wordsworth's works, 2 and 3. The student who desires to follow the course of Wordsworth's developing poetic faculty, and especially to discern the effect of Coleridge's influence upon him, should be careful to read these early poems in the original, unrevised editions of 1793. Both forms are fully printed in the Oxford Wordsworth. The reader who turns to *Descriptive Sketches* from Darwin's *Botanic Garden,* completed the year before, will be able to appreciate Coleridge's point about "the emergence of an original poetic genius."

p. 45, l. 29. **the Storm.** *Descriptive Sketches* 332–347 (1793), 270–284 (last version). Coleridge is quoting from the text used in the extracts given in the *Poems* of 1815. In the original version the passage begins thus:

Tis storm; and hid in mist from hour to hour
All day the floods a deeper murmur pour,
And mournful sounds, as of a Spirit lost,
Pipe wild along the hollow-blustering coast,
Till the Sun walking on his western field
Shakes from behind the clouds his flashing shield.
Triumphant, etc.

p. 46, l. 2. **the butterfly.** In the edition of 1817 this footnote appears: "The fact, that in Greek Psyche is the common name for the soul, and the butterfly, is thus alluded to in the following stanzas from an unpublished poem of the author":—the quotation then follows.

p. 46, l. 11. **my twenty-fourth year.** The date of the first meeting of Wordsworth and Coleridge has never been precisely settled. It was probably near the end of 1795. But this is not important. The much more important meeting is the second, towards the end of 1796, for the regular intercourse of the young poets (Coleridge aged 24, Wordsworth 26) began from this time, Wordsworth moving from Racedown to Alfoxden in 1797 in order to be near Coleridge at Nether Stowey.

p. 46, l. 14. **a manuscript poem.** *Guilt and Sorrow: or Incidents upon Salisbury Plain,* written with alterations and enlargements between 1791 and 1794, but not published fully till 1842. The woman's narrative in it (somewhat less than half the original poem) was published separately in *Lyrical Ballads* (1798) under the title *The Female Vagrant.* Continual alterations in the text indicate Wordsworth's dissatisfaction with the form and the matter of this excessively gloomy poem. As a product of his Godwinian or Revolutionary period, it would naturally displease the Wordsworth of later days.

p. 46, l. 20. **Lines on revisiting the Wye.** The *Tintern Abbey* lines. See especially ll. 58–102.

p. 47, footnote. **'Mid stormy vapours.** Lines 317–324 (1793). Coleridge is quoting from the extract contained in the *Poems* of 1815. The text in this passage is the same as in the original edition. A comparison with the text as finally altered in 1845 is instructive:

And what if ospreys, cormorants, herons cry,
Amid tempestuous vapours driving by,
Or hovering over wastes too bleak to rear
That common growth of earth, the foodful ear;
Where the green apple shrivels on the spray,
And pines the unripened pear in summer's kindliest ray;
Contentment shares the desolate domain
With Independence, child of high Disdain.

p. 47, l. 16. **for the common view.** The rediscovery of the thrill in common things, the attaching of "thoughts that do often lie too deep for tears" even to "the meanest flower that blows" is rightly indicated as Wordsworth's greatest contribution to human life.

p. 47, l. 17. **the dew drops.** Here follows, in the edition of 1817, a long quotation from *The Friend*, p. 76, No. 5:

"To find no contradiction in the union of old and new; to contemplate the ANCIENT of days and all his works with feelings as fresh, as if all had then sprang forth at the first creative fiat; characterizes the mind that feels the riddle of the world, and may help to unravel it. To carry on the feelings of childhood into the powers of manhood; to combine the child's sense of wonder and novelty with the appearances, which every day for perhaps forty years had rendered familiar:

> With sun and moon and stars throughout the year,
> And man and woman;

this is the character and privilege of genius, and one of the marks which distinguish genius from talents. And therefore is it the prime merit of genius and its most unequivocal mode of manifestation, so to represent familiar objects as to awaken in the minds of others a kindred feeling concerning them and that freshness of sensation which is the constant accompaniment of mental, no less than of bodily, convalescence. Who has not a thousand times seen snow fall on water? Who has not watched it with a new feeling, from the time that he has read Burns' comparison of sensual pleasure:

> To snow that falls upon a river,
> A moment white—then gone for ever!

"In poems, equally as in philosophic disquisitions, genius produces the strongest impressions of novelty, while it rescues the most admitted truths from the impotence caused by the very circumstance of their universal admission. Truths of all others the most awful and mysterious yet being at the same time of universal interest, are too often considered as *so* true, that they lose all the life and efficiency of truth, and lie bed-ridden in the dormitory of the soul, side by side with the most despised and exploded errors." Coleridge apologizes for the long quotation on the ground that *The Friend* had so few readers that it was as unknown as a volume in manuscript. What Coleridge rightly calls a *rifaciment* rather than a new edition of *The Friend* was published a year after *Biographia*. The Burns quotation often cited by Coleridge is from *Tam o' Shanter*:

> But pleasures are like poppies spread:
> You seize the flow'r, its bloom is shed;
> Or like the snow falls in the river,
> A moment white—then melts for ever.

p. 47, l. 28. **apposite.** Printed "opposite" in 1817, 1847 and in most subsequent editions; but it is obviously wrong.

p. 48, footnote. **to indorse.** Milton uses the general, unrestricted sense in

> elephants indorst with towers of archers. (*P.R.* III, 329.)

p. 48, footnote. **senses of both.** In 1817 this sentence followed: "Thus too 'mister' and 'master,' both hasty mispronunciations of the same word 'magister,' 'mistress,' and 'miss,' 'if' and 'give,' etc. etc There is a sort, etc."

p. 49, l. 1. **delirium from mania**. The editors of 1847 here add a quotation from *Table-Talk* as a footnote: "You may conceive the difference in kind between the Fancy and the Imagination in this way; that if the check of the senses and the reason were withdrawn, the first would become delirium and the last mania. The fancy brings together images which have no connection natural or moral, but are yoked together by the poet by means of some accidental coincidence; as in the well-known passage in *Hudibras*;

> The Sun had long since in the lap
> Of Thetis taken out his nap,
> And like a lobster boil'd, the morn
> From black to red began to turn.

The Imagination modifies images, and gives unity to variety: it sees all things in one, *il più nell' uno*. There is the epic imagination, the perfection of which is in Milton; and the dramatic, of which Shakespeare is the absolute master. The first gives unity by throwing back into the distance; as after the magnificent approach of the Messiah to battle; the poet, by one touch from himself,—

> Far off their coming shone—

makes the whole one image. And so at the conclusion of the description of the entranced Angels, in which every sort of image from all the regions of earth and air is introduced to diversify and illustrate, the reader is brought back to the simple image by—

> He called so loud, that all the hollow deep
> Of Hell resounded.

The dramatic imagination does not throw back but brings close; it stamps all nature with one, and that its own, meaning, as in Lear throughout."

Coleridge several times attempted to differentiate Imagination and Fancy.

p. 49, l. 3. **Lutes, laurels, etc.** Otway, *Venice Preserved*, Act v, Sc. ii:

> Murmuring streams, soft shades, and springing flowers!
> Lutes, Laurels, seas of milk, and ships of amber!

p. 49, l. 5. **What! have his daughters, etc.** *King Lear*, Act III, Sc. iv.

p. 49, l. 6. **the preceding apostrophe**. Act. III, Sc. ii.

p. 49, l. 28. **Mr. W. Taylor's recent volume.** Wordsworth's reference to this volume in his Preface to the *Poems* of 1815 should be considered carefully. See p. 209, the passage beginning "Let us come now."

p. 50, footnote. **the moral sophisms of Hobbes.** This is not the place for any discussion of a mere *obiter dictum* occurring in a footnote; but the matter cannot be left without some reference. Thomas Hobbes (1588–1679), the rationalist philosopher of Malmesbury, incurred much opposition from the orthodox on account of his ethical and political doctrines. His works are not easily accessible, the only one at all well known to general readers being *Leviathan* (1651—Camb. Univ. Press, 1904). Coleridge disliked him, and, indeed, underrated him; but he is not so easily confuted as Coleridge thought. Hobbes nowhere bases any doctrine upon a supposed synonymity of "obligation" and "compulsion." Those who wish to pursue the matter further may be referred to the treatise *Of Liberty and Necessity* (1654) which Coleridge seems to have had in mind.

p. 50, l. 16. **My friend has drawn, etc.** In the Preface to *Poems* (1815). See p. 206 of this volume.

p. 51, l. 1. **Hooker's.** Richard Hooker (1554?–1600), one of the first of great English prose writers, was an Exeter man, educated there and at Corpus Christi College, Oxford. He attained no high preferment, and died Rector of Bishopsbourne, Canterbury. His greatest work is called *Of the Lawes of Ecclesiastical Politie*. Everyone should read, or have read, his Life by Izaak Walton. Coleridge's quotations, substantially but not verbally correct, are taken from the opening paragraphs of *Ecclesiastical Polity*.

CHAPTER XIV

This begins the most important part of *Biographia Literaria*.

p. 52, l. 1. **the first year.** See note to p. 46, l. 11.

p. 52, l. 23. **the plan of the Lyrical Ballads.** Wordsworth's account dictated many years later to Miss Fenwick is somewhat different and probably more accurate:

"I will here mention one of the most remarkable facts in my own poetic history, and that of Mr Coleridge. In the spring of the year 1798, he, my sister, and myself, started from Alfoxden pretty late in the afternoon, with a view to visit Lynton and the Valley of Stones near it; and as our united funds were very small, we agreed to defray the expense of the tour by writing a poem, to be sent to the *New Monthly Magazine*, set up by Phillips, the bookseller, and edited by Dr Aikin. Accordingly we set off, and proceeded along the Quantock Hills, towards Watchet; and in the course of this walk was planned the poem of *The Ancient Mariner*, founded on a dream, as Mr Coleridge said, of his friend Mr Cruikshank. Much the greatest part of the story was Mr Coleridge's invention; but certain parts I myself suggested: for example, some crime was to be committed which should bring upon the Old Navigator, as Coleridge afterwards delighted to call him, the spectral persecution, as a consequence of that crime, and his own wanderings. I had been reading in Shelvocke's *Voyages*, a day or two before, that, while doubling Cape Horn, they frequently saw albatrosses in that latitude, the largest sort of sea-fowl, some extending their wings twelve or thirteen feet. 'Suppose,' said I, 'you represent him as having killed one of these birds on entering the South Sea, and that the tutelary spirits of these regions take upon them to avenge the crime.' The incident was thought fit for the purpose, and adopted accordingly. I also suggested the navigation of the ship by the dead men, but do not recollect that I had anything more to do with the scheme of the poem. The gloss with which it was subsequently accompanied was not thought of by either of us at the time; at least not a hint of it was given to me, and I have no doubt it was a gratuitous after-thought. We began the composition together, on that to me memorable evening: I furnished two or three lines at the beginning of the poem, in particular—

> And listen'd like a three year's child;
> The Mariner had his will.

These trifling contributions, all but one (which Mr C. has with unnecessary scrupulosity recorded), slipt out of his mind, as well they might. As we endeavoured to proceed conjointly (I speak of the same evening), our respective manners proved so widely different, that it would have been quite presumptuous in me to do anything but separate from an undertaking upon which I could only have been a clog. We returned after a few days from a delightful tour, of which I have many pleasant, and some of them droll enough, recollections. We returned by Dulverton to Alfoxden. *The Ancient Mariner* grew and grew till it became too important for our first object, which was limited to our expectation of five pounds; and we began to talk of a volume which was to consist, as Mr Coleridge has told the world, of Poems chiefly on natural subjects taken from common life, but looked at, as much as might be, through an imaginative medium."

p. 53, l. 10. **The Dark Ladie and the Christabel.** Neither poem was ever published in *Lyrical Ballads*, or, indeed, ever finished. *The Dark Ladie* appeared in 1834, *Christabel* in 1816. The poem *Love* (Vol. II of *Lyrical Ballads*, 1800) was intended as an Introduction to *The Dark Ladie*; but only a few stanzas of the main poem were written. To the end of his life, Coleridge, with characteristic self-deception, protested his ability to complete *Christabel* at any moment. It remains, however, as it was left in 1800.

p. 53, l. 22. **the language of ordinary life.** These words are not actually used. It may be useful to collect the principal attempts of Wordsworth to explain what he meant:

1798, the language of conversation in the middle and lower classes of life.

1800, a selection of the real language of men in a state of vivid sensation.

ib. I propose to my self to imitate, and, as far as possible, to adopt the very language of men (so in 1802 and 1805).

ib. to bring my language near to the language of men (so in 1802 and 1805).

1802, a language [i.e. the "mechanical poetic diction"] differing materially from the real language of men *in any situation*.

1805, a selection of language really used by men.

ib. a selection of the language really spoken by men.

ib. the real language of nature.

ib. selecting from the real language of men.

p. 54, l. 23. **in his recent collection.** The *Poems* of 1815, in which the *Lyrical Ballads* preface is transferred to the end, its place being taken by a new Preface. See Appendix II and III to the present volume.

p. 54, l. 29. **to declare once for all, etc.** The reader should notice Coleridge's statements made in 1802—the Preface having first appeared in 1800:

(1) From a letter to W. Sotheby, 13 July 1802.

"I was much pleased with your description of Wordsworth's character as it appeared to you. It is in a few words, in half a dozen strokes, like one of Mortimer's figures, a fine portrait. The word 'homogeneous' gave me great pleasure, as most accurately and happily expressing him. I must set you right with regard to my perfect coincidence with his poetic creed. It is most certain that the heads of our mutual conversations, etc., and the passages, were indeed partly taken from note of mine; for it was at first intended that the preface should be written by me. And it is likewise true that I warmly accord with Wordsworth in his abhorrence of these poetic licenses, as they are called, which are indeed mere tricks of convenience and laziness. *Ex. gr.* Drayton has these lines:

> Ouse having Ouleney past, as she were waxed mad
> From her first stayder course immediately doth gad,
> And in meandered gyres doth whirl herself about,
> *That, this* way, here and there, backward in and out.
> And like a wanton girl oft doubling in her gait
> In labyrinthian turns and twinings intricate, etc.

The first poets, observing such a stream as this, would say with truth and beauty, 'it *strays*'; and now every stream shall *stray*, wherever it prattles on its *pebbled way*, instead of its bed or channel. And I have taken the instance from a poet from whom as few instances of this vile, commonplace, trashy style could be taken as from any writer [namely], from Bowles' execrable translation of that lovely poem of Dean Ogle's (vol. II, p. 27). I am confident that Bowles good-naturedly translated it in a hurry, merely to give him an excuse for printing the admirable original. In my opinion, every phrase, every metaphor, every personification, should have its justifying clause in some *passion*, either of the poet's mind or of the characters described by the poet. But metre itself implies a passion, that is, a state of excitement both in the poet's mind, and is expected, in part, of the reader; and, though I stated this to Wordsworth, and he has in some sort stated it in his preface, yet he has not done justice to it, nor has he, in my opinion, sufficiently answered it. In my opinion, poetry justifies as poetry, independent of any other passion, some new combinations of language and *commands* the omission of many others allowable in other compositions. Now Wordsworth, *me saltem judice*, has in his system not sufficiently admitted the former, and in his practice has too frequently sinned against the latter. Indeed, we have had lately some little controversy on the subject, and we begin to suspect that there is somewhere or other a radical difference in our opinions. *Dulce est inter amicos rarissimâ dissensione condere plurimas consentiones*, saith St Augustine, who said more good things than any saint or sinner that I ever read in Latin."

(2) From a letter to Southey, 29 July 1802.

"Of course Darwin and Wordsworth having given each a defence of their mode of poetry, and a disquisition on the nature and essence of poetry in general, I shall necessarily be led rather deeper, and these I shall treat of either first or last. But I will apprise you of one thing, that although Wordsworth's preface is half a child of my own brain, and arose out of conversations so frequent that, with few exceptions, we could scarcely either of us, perhaps, positively say which first started any particular thought (I am speaking of the Preface as it stood in the second volume), yet I am far from going all lengths with Wordsworth. He has written lately a number of Poems (thirty-two in all), some of them of considerable length (the longest one hundred and sixty lines), the greater number of these, to my feelings, very excellent compositions, but here and there a daring humbleness of language and versification, and a strict adherence to matter of fact, even to prolixity, that startled me. His alterations, likewise, in 'Ruth' perplexed me, and I have thought and thought again, and have not had my doubts solved by Wordsworth. On the contrary, I rather suspect that somewhere or other there is a radical difference in our theoretical opinions respecting poetry; this I shall endeavour to go to the bottom of, and, acting the arbitrator between the old school and the new school, hope to lay down some plain and perspicuous, though not superficial canons of criticism respecting poetry. What an admirable definition Milton gives, quite in an 'obiter' way, when he says of poetry, that it is 'simple, sensuous, passionate!' It truly comprises the whole that can be said on the subject. In the new edition of the L. Ballads there is a valuable appendix, which I am sure you must like, and in the Preface itself considerable additions; one on the dignity and nature of the office and character of a Poet, that is very grand, and of a sort of Verulamian power and majesty, but it is, in parts (and this is the fault, *me judice*, of all the latter half of that Preface), obscure beyond any necessity, and the extreme elaboration and almost constrainedness of the diction contrasted (to my feelings) somewhat harshly with the general style of the Poems, to which the Preface is an introduction. Sara (why, dear Southey! will you write it always Sarah? *Sara*, methinks, is associated with times that you and I cannot and do not wish ever to forget), Sara said, with some acuteness, that she wished all that part of the Preface to have been in blank verse, and *vice versâ*, etc. However, I need not say, that any diversity of opinion on the subject between you and myself, or Wordsworth and myself, can only be small, taken in a *practical* point of view."

p. 55, l. 32. **Bathyllus.** The twenty-ninth ode of Anacreon. The *Alexis* of Virgil is the second Eclogue.

p. 56, l. 5. **The final definition.** This should be compared with the detailed discussion and defence of an almost identical definition in *Lectures*, Bohn ed. pp. 47–49.

p. 56, l. 28. **a series of striking lines or distiches.** Coleridge was thinking particularly of Pope's couplets.

p. 57, l. 2. **Praecipitandus, etc.** From chapter CXVIII of the *Satyricon* of Petronius, perhaps, but not certainly, the Petronius who was the arbiter of taste and fashion in the Rome of Nero. The whole passage deserves to be cited: "There is that grand subject, our Civil Wars; whoever attempts it, unless he be fully accomplished in literature, will sink under the task. For the thing to be done is not to comprise a series of facts in verse; an historian can much better execute such a narrative; but *the free spirit must be hurried along* through mazy involutions, divine interventions, marvellous machinery and elaborate conceptions; so that we may recognise rather the inspired frenzy of the poet, than the scrupulous veracity of the narrator of attested facts." The passage is meant as a criticism of Lucan's historical poem the *Pharsalia*.

p. 57, l. 8. **Jeremy Taylor.** Taylor's elaborate similes will be familiar, in quotation, to most readers. The comparison of a man's life to the rising and setting of the sun (*Holy Dying*) and the comparison of a good man's prayer to the soaring of a lark (Sermon, *The Return of Prayers*) are two of the best known. (For the former, see note to p. 126, l. 21.) A passage from his funeral sermon on the Countess of Carbery may be quoted as an immediate illustration: "There is no age of man but it hath proper to itself some posterns and outlets for death, besides those infinite and open ports out of which myriads of men and women every day pass into the dark and the land of forgetfulness. Infancy hath life but *in effigie*, or like a spark dwelling in a pile of wood; the candle is so newly lighted, that every little shaking of the taper, and every ruder breath of air puts it out, and it dies. Childhood is so tender, and yet so unwary; so soft to all the impressions of chance, and yet so forward to run into them, that God knew there could be no security without the care and vigilance of an angel-keeper: and the eyes of parents and the arms of nurses, the provisions of art and all the effects of human love and providence are not sufficient to keep one child from horrid mischiefs, from strange and early calamities and deaths, unless a messenger be sent from heaven to stand sentinel...."

p. 57, l. 8. **Burnet's Theory of the Earth.** Thomas Burnet (1635–1715) must not be confused with William III's bishop and historian Gilbert Burnet. Thomas was a Cambridge scholar who became Master of the Charterhouse. His *Archaeologia Philosophica* gave offence by its treatment of the early stories of the Old Testament as allegories. His *Telluris Theoria Sacra*, written first in Latin and afterwards rendered into English—recomposed rather than merely rendered—is one of the curiosities of literature. It is in four books of several chapters each. Book I deals with the Deluge and Dissolution of the Earth; Book II with the primeval Earth and Paradise; Book III with the Conflagration; Book IV with the new Heavens and new Earth and the Consummation of all things. Coleridge is referring to the chapters in Book III describing the destruction of the world by fire and the second coming of Christ. Here is a typical passage:

"Earthquakes and subterraneous eruptions will tear the body and bowels of the earth; and thunders and convulsive motions of the air rend the skies. The waters of the sea will boil and struggle with streams of sulphur that run into them; which will make them fume, and smoke, and roar, beyond all storms and tempests; and these noises of the sea will be answered again from the land, by falling rocks and mountains. This is a small part of the disorders of that day.

"But it is not possible, from any station, to have a full prospect of this last scene of the earth; for it is a mixture of fire and darkness. This new temple is filled with smoke, while it is consecrating, and none can enter into it. But I am apt to think, if we could look down upon this burning world from above the clouds, and have a full view of it, in all its parts, we should think it a lively representation of hell itself. For fire and darkness are the two chief things by which that state, or that place, uses to be described; and they are both here mingled together, with all other ingredients that make that tophet that is prepared of old (Isa. xxx.). Here are lakes of fire and brimstone; rivers of melted glowing matter; ten thousand volcanoes vomiting flames all at once; thick darkness, and pillars of smoke twisted about with wreaths of flame, like fiery snakes; mountains of earth thrown up into the air, and the heavens dropping down in lumps of fire. These things will all be literally true, concerning that day, and that state of the earth. And if we suppose Beelzebub, and his apostate crew, in the midst of this fiery furnace (and I know not where they can be else), it will be hard to find any part of the universe, or any state of things, that answers to so many of the properties and characters of hell as this which is now before us.

"But if we suppose the storm over, and that the fire hath got an entire victory over all other bodies, and subdued every thing to itself, the conflagration will end in a deluge of fire, or in a sea of fire, covering the whole globe of the earth: for, when the exterior region of the earth is melted into a fluor, like molten glass, or running metal, it will, according to the nature of other fluids, fill all vacuities and depressions, and fall into a regular surface, at an equal distance everywhere, from its centre. This sea of fire, like the first abyss, will cover the face of the whole earth, make a kind of second chaos, and leave a capacity for another world to rise from it. But that is not our present business. Let us only, if you please to take leave of this subject, reflect, upon this occasion, on the vanity and transient glory of all this habitable world; how, by the force of one element breaking loose upon the rest, all the varieties of nature, all the works of art, all the labours of men, are reduced to nothing; all that we admired and adored before as great and magnificent, is obliterated, or vanished; and another form and face of things, plain, simple, and everywhere the same, overspreads the whole earth. Where are now the great empires of the world, and their great imperial cities? Their pillars, trophies, and monuments of glory? Shew me where they stood, read the inscription, tell me the victor's name. What remains, what impressions, what difference or distinction do you see in this mass of fire? Rome itself, eternal Rome, the great city, the empress of the world, whose domination and superstition, ancient and modern, make a great part of the history of this earth; what is become of her now? She laid her foundations deep, and her palaces were strong and sumptuous: she glorified herself, and lived deliciously; and said in her heart, I sit a queen, and shall see no sorrow. But her hour is come, she is wiped away from the face of the earth, and buried in perpetual oblivion. But it is not cities only, and works of men's hands, but the everlasting hills, the mountains and rocks of the earth, are melted as wax before the sun; and their place is nowhere found. Here stood the Alps, a prodigious range of stone, the load of the earth, that covered many countries, and reached their arms from the ocean to the Black sea; this huge mass of stone is softened and dissolved, as a tender cloud into rain. Here stood the African mountains, and Atlas with his top above the clouds. There was frozen Caucasus, and Taurus, and Imaus, and the mountains of Asia. And yonder, towards the north, stood the Riphæan hills, clothed in ice and snow. All these are vanished, dropt away as the snow upon their heads, and swallowed up in a red sea of fire (Rev. xv. 3.). 'Great and marvellous are thy works, Lord God almighty; just and true are thy ways, thou King of saints. Hallelujah.'"

The reader can now decide how far he agrees with Coleridge that such passages are "poetry of the highest order...without metre." Coleridge did not cite the magnificent prose of Milton, possibly because he did not wish to call a poet to bear witness for the poetry of prose.

p. 58, l. 2. **laxis effertur habenis.** "is borne onwards with loose reins"—possibly a reminiscence of "laxis...immissus habenis," (Virg. *Georg.* II, 364).

p. 58, l. 12. **Sir John Davies.** Sir John Davies (1570–1626) wrote, with smaller things, two lengthy poems, *Nosce Teipsum* (its subject the

"Soul of Man and the Immortality thereof") and *Orchestra, or a Poeme of Dauncing*. Coleridge quotes from Section IV of the first. The original verses run thus:

Doubtless, this could not be, but that she turns
Bodies to Spirits, by sublimation strange;
As fire converts to fire the things it burns;
As we our meats into our nature change.

From their gross matter she abstracts the forms,
And draws a kind of quintessence from things;
Which to her proper nature she transforms,
To bear them light on her celestial wings.

This doth she, when from things particular,
She doth abstract the universal kinds,
Which bodyless and immaterial are,
And can be only lodg'd within our minds.

CHAPTER XV

This chapter is based upon the fourth lecture of the course on Shakespeare and Milton given by Coleridge in 1811–12. See also the Lectures of 1818 (Bohn, pp. 218–223).

p. 59, footnote. **a Greek monk.** According to *Anima Poetae* the Greek monk is Naucratius and the panegyrized patriarch Theodorus Chersites.

p. 59, l. 25. **The man that hath not music.** The line should end "in himself," not "in his soul." *M. of V.* v. i.

p. 60, l. 14. **poeta nascitur.** This proverb cannot be traced to any particular author. The curious reader will find many references to similar phrases in Walsh's *Handy-Book of Literary Curiosities*.

p. 61, l. 40. **Which shoots.** A line slightly altered from Coleridge's *France: an Ode*.

p. 62, l. 4. **Behold yon row.** These lines and those following were composed by Coleridge as an illustration of this passage.

p. 62, l. 16. **Shakespeare.** The quotations are taken from sonnets 33 and 107.

p. 63, l. 1. **Inopem, etc.** Ovid. *Met.* III, 466. "Plenty has made me poor."

p. 63, l. 20. **Γονίμου μέν κ.τ.λ.** Aristophanes, *Frogs*, 96–97.

Search as you will, you'll find no poet now
With grit in him to wake a word of power.

p. 63. l. 36. **poetry is the blossom, etc.** Compare the famous passage in Wordsworth's *Preface* to *Lyrical Ballads*: "Poetry is the breath and finer spirit of all knowledge; it is the impassioned expression which is in the countenance of all Science.

p. 64, l. 18. **no automaton of genius.** In *Lectures*, pp. 223–230 will be found a more extended statement of this view—the section entitled "Shakespeare's Judgment equal to his Genius." *The Spectator*, No 160, fairly represents the "elegant" view of Shakespeare as an untutored genius, spoken through, rather than speaking: "Among great geniuses those few draw the admiration of all the world upon them, and stand up as the prodigies of mankind, who, by the mere strength of natural parts, and without any assistance of art or learning, have produced works that were the delight of their own times and the wonder of posterity. There appears something nobly wild and extravagant in these great natural geniuses that is infinitely more beautiful than all turn and polishing of what the French call a *bel esprit*, by which they would express a genius refined by conversation, reflection, and the reading of the most polite authors.... Many of these great natural geniuses that were never disciplined and broken by rules of art, are to be found among the ancients....Our countryman Shakespeare was a remarkable instance of this first kind of great geniuses." This paper is always attributed to Addison.

p. 64, l. 34. **We must be free.** From Wordsworth's sonnet "It is not to be thought of, etc."

CHAPTER XVI

p. 66, l. 20. **Dante in his tract, etc.** Dante's treatise *De Vulgari Eloquentia*, written in Latin about 1305–9, is a fragment containing less than half the matter proposed. An Italian translation (used by Coleridge) was published in 1529. In this tract, Dante reviews the many dialects current in Italy to discover one worthy vernacular, and decides that they are all faulty and that the noble mother tongue of Italy must be the one that is the basis of them all, or to which they all tend to approximate—"we declare the illustrious, cardinal, courtly and curial vernacular language in Italy to be that which belongs to all the towns in Italy but does not appear to belong to any one of them, and by which all the municipal dialects of the Italians are measured, weighed and compared." This illustrious vernacular he declares specially suited to poetry. The statement attributed to Dante by Coleridge does not appear in the treatise. The nearest approach to it is found in Book II, ch. i: "We declare in the first place that the illustrious Italian vernacular is equally fit for use in prose and in verse. But because prose writers rather get this language from poets, and because poetry seems to remain a pattern to prose writers, and not the converse, which things appear to confer a certain supremacy on verse, let us first disentangle this language as to its use in metre....Let us then first inquire whether all those who write verse in the vernacular should use this illustrious language; and as far as a superficial consideration of the matter goes, it would seem that they should, because every one who writes verse ought to adorn his verse as far as he is able. Wherefore, since nothing affords so great an adornment as the illustrious vernacular does, it would seem that every writer of verse ought to employ it....This illustrious language, then, just like our behaviour in other matters and our dress, demands men of like quality to its own; for munificence demands men of great resources, and the purple, men of noble character, and in the same way this illustrious language seeks for men who excel in genius and knowledge, and despises others....And since language is as necessary an instrument of our thought as a horse is of a knight, and since the best horses are suited to the best knights, as has been said, the best language will be suited to the best thoughts. But the best thoughts cannot exist except where knowledge and genius are found; therefore the best language is only suitable in those in whom knowledge and genius are found." And his conclusion, therefore, is that this illustrious vernacular should be used only by the true poets, and not by every scribbler of indifferent verse. So, by inversion we may attribute to Dante the sentiment that the true poets are in a special sense the custodians of the noble mother tongue.

It is pertinent to the general subject of *Biographia* to note what Dante means by the "adornment" of verse:

"As to the statement that every one ought to adorn his verse as far as he can, we declare that it is true; but we should not describe an ox with trappings or a swine with a belt as adorned, nay rather we laugh at them as disfigured; for adornment is the addition of some suitable thing." The case could not be put more clearly. A reference to the quotations from Darwin will indicate that putting girdles on swine was the approved poetic device of the time.

The quotations above are all taken from the translation of *De Vulgari Eloquentia* by Mr A. G. Ferrers Howell in the Temple Classics.

p. 66, l. 24. **Animadverte, etc.** The edition of 1817 gives a reference to Hobbes's *Examinatio et Emendatio Mathematicae hodiernae*, [Dial. II, Vol. IV, p. 83 of Molesworth's edition of the Latin Works]. The whole passage of quotations may be rendered thus: "Observe how prone men are to fall from the wrong use of words into wrong notions about things!" [Hobbes.]

"Indeed, there are plenty of things in a life so short and a world so obscure as ours, to the study of which time may be devoted, so that there is no need to spend time in finding a meaning for confused discussions, capable of many interpretations. Alas! what disasters have been caused by cloudy words which, whilst they say so much, convey no meaning;—call them rather clouds, from which burst hurricanes and thunderstorms both in church and state! And that was just as true in our opinion which Plato says in the Gorgias: 'Anyone who knows terms will know things also'; and that which Epictetus said: 'the study of terms is the beginning of instruction'; and this is a wise saying in the writings of Galenus, 'Confusion in the use of terms begets confusion in the knowledge of things.' A fine saying indeed is that of J. C. Scaliger in Book I *Concerning Plants*: 'The first duty (says he) of the wise man is to think well in order that he may live for himself: the next is to speak well in order that he may live for his country.'" [Sennertus.]

The Sennertus referred to is Daniel Sennert (1572–1637), a German physician and professor, for whom see Bayle's Dictionary. The edition of 1847 gives a reference to "p. 193, *De nominibus novis Paracelsicis* in his folio works, Leyden, 1676. The words in brackets are not in the original, and there are several omissions. The sentence cited as from the Gorgias is not contained, I believe, in that dialogue." It may be added that *ut nihil dicunt* should probably be *ut nihil dicant*.

p. 67, l. 14. **beauty and harmony of the colours.** These lines might have been written to describe the peculiar beauty of Turner, who, three years younger than Coleridge, had by the date of *Biographia* produced the best of his early pictures, including "A Frosty Morning" and "Crossing the Brook" (to which the words of Coleridge seem specially to apply) and was on the eve of the visit to Italy that inspired his most glorious visions. But there is no evidence that Coleridge knew anything of Turner —there is certainly no reference to him in any published Coleridgiana; and it must be added that the most Turneresque of poets is one to whom Coleridge was distinctly tepid—Shelley.

p. 67, l. 16. **novelty of subject...avoided.** Coleridge might have named a French artist Chardin (1699–1779), who, living in the most brilliant and artificial period of French history, and contemporary, almost, with Watteau, Boucher, Greuze and Fragonard, is famous for the beauty and sincerity that mark his representations of the most homely scenes and objects.

p. 67, l. 20. **especially those of Italy.** The greatest of this period were Boiardo (1430–1494), Ariosto (1474–1533) and Tasso (1544–1595).

p. 67, l. 33. **in the art.** The distinction is still more apparent in music. In the works of the older masters, Bach, Handel, Haydn and Mozart, we have the perfection of "pattern" music, i.e., music following prescribed forms and deriving its beauty from the expression attained in and by those forms. Thus, some of the instrumental fugues and fugal choruses of Bach are among the greatest of compositions, and are as well the most elaborately and intricately formal. In Beethoven, the expressiveness, or dramatic power, tends to overflow, almost to shatter, the traditional forms; and in the modern school we have dramatic force, expressiveness or pictorialism, secured without any of the formal "patterning" of the old masters. The sounds have become symbols to be interpreted by the hearer. It would be difficult to find music more unlike in form and in purpose than the piano preludes of Bach and the piano preludes of Debussy. In all forms of art the danger lies in extremes. The purely formal musician is arid and unprofitable; the formless impressionist is "full of sound and fury signifying nothing."

p. 68, l. 6. **Alonzo and Imogen.** A poem by Matthew Gregory Lewis (1775–1818) who was educated at Westminster and Oxford and employed in the diplomatic service, but owes his fame (such as it is), as well as his nickname "Monk," to his melodramatic romance *Ambrosio, or the Monk*. His *Castle Spectre* and *Bravo of Venice* were famous on the stage of their day. To *Tales of Wonder* edited by himself and containing thirty-two poems by himself, Scott, and others, he contributed *Alonzo the Brave and Fair Imogene* from his famous romance. The "measure" can be taken from the following quotation. Imogene is unfaithful to the absent Alonzo, and at her marriage (to another) a mysterious being appears:

His visor was closed, and gigantic his height;
  His armour was sable to view:
All pleasure and laughter were hushed at his sight;
The dogs, as they eyed him, drew back in affright;
  The lights in the chamber burnt blue!

All present then uttered a terrified shout;
  All turned with disgust from the scene.
The worms they crept in, and the worms they crept out,
And sported his eyes and his temples about,
  While the spectre addressed Imogene.

p. 68, l. 18. **that man of genius**. Sara Coleridge (1847) suggests that her father's requirements are fulfilled in the person of Mr H. Taylor—i.e., Sir Henry Taylor, author of interesting memoirs and of the drama *Philip van Artevelde* with its one memorable line "The world knows nothing of its greatest men." The modern reader (who certainly knows nothing of Sir Henry Taylor) will be more inclined to adduce two poets from "the groves of Isis and Cam," Matthew Arnold and Alfred Tennyson.

p. 69, footnote. **An artist**. Sir Joshua Reynolds, in the second of his *Discourses*. The following passages may be quoted: "To a young man just arrived in Italy, many of the present painters of that country are ready enough to obtrude their precepts, and to offer their own performances as examples of that perfection which they affect to recommend. The Modern, however, who recommends himself as a standard, may justly be suspected as ignorant of the true end, and unacquainted with the proper object, of the art which he professes. To follow such a guide will not only retard the student, but mislead him.

"On whom then can he rely, or who shall show him the path that leads to excellence? The answer is obvious: those great masters who have travelled the same road with success are the most likely to conduct others. The works of those who have stood the test of ages have a claim to that respect and veneration to which no modern can pretend. The duration and stability of their fame is sufficient to evince that it has not been suspended upon the slender thread of fashion and caprice, but bound to the human heart by every tie of sympathetic approbation....

"An eye critically nice can only be formed by observing well-coloured pictures with attention; and by close inspection and minute examination, you will discover, at last, the manner of handling, the artifices of contrast, glazing, and other expedients by which good colourists have raised the value of their tints, and by which nature has been so happily imitated....

"With respect to the pictures that you are to choose for your models, I could wish that you would take the world's opinion rather than your own. In other words, I would have you choose those of established reputation rather than follow your own fancy. If you should not admire them at first, you will, by endeavouring to imitate them, find that the world has not been mistaken."

p. 69, footnote. **Harris of Salisbury**. James Harris (1709–1780), was born at Salisbury and educated at Oxford. He offers an interesting combination of scholar, gentleman, philosopher and man of affairs, His *Art and Happiness* (1744) and *Hermes* (1751) stirred up considerable attention, traces of which can be found in the allusions of Coleridge and Hazlitt. Harris, who was himself a member of Parliament and lord of the Admiralty, is also remembered as the father of the first Earl of Malmesbury, a distinguished ambassador, who edited his father's works in two massive quartos, 1801. Probably Coleridge was referring to the passage concluding *Philological Inquiries*, pt II, chap. xii:

"'Tis not however improbable that some intrepid spirit may demand again, *What avail these subtleties?—Without so much trouble, I can be full enough pleased.*—I KNOW WHAT I LIKE.—We answer, *And so does the Carrion-crow, that feeds upon a carcase.* The difficulty lies not in knowing WHAT *we like*; but in knowing HOW *to like*, and WHAT IS WORTH LIKING. Till these Ends are obtained, we may admire *Dursey* before *Milton*; a smoaking Boor of *Hemskirk*, before an APOSTLE of *Raphael*.

"Now as to the knowing, HOW TO LIKE, and then WHAT IS WORTH LIKING; the first of these, being the OBJECT of *Critical* DISQUISITION, has been attempted to be shewn thro' the course of *these Inquiries*.

"As to the second, WHAT IS WORTH OUR LIKING, this is best known by studying *the best* AUTHORS, beginning from the GREEKS; then passing to the LATINS; nor on any account excluding those, who have excelled among the MODERNS.

"And here, if, while we peruse some Author of high rank, we perceive we don't instantly relish him, let us not be disheartened—let us even FEIGN a *Relish*, till we find a *Relish* come. A *morsel* perhaps pleases us—Let us cherish it—*Another Morsel* strikes us—let us cherish this also—Let us thus proceed, and steadily persevere, till we find we can relish, *not Morsels*, but *Wholes*; and feel that, what began in FICTION, terminates in REALITY. The Film being in this manner removed, we shall discover *Beauties*, which we never imagined; and contemn for *Puerilities*, what we once *foolishly* admired.

"One thing however in this process is indispensibly required: we are *on no account* to expect that FINE THINGS SHOULD DESCEND TO US; our taste, if possible, MUST BE MADE TO ASCEND TO THEM.

"This is the Labour, this the Work; there is *Pleasure* in the Success, and *Praise* even in the Attempt.

"This Speculation applies not to Literature only: it applies to Music, to *Painting*, and, as they are all *congenial*, to all the *liberal* Arts. We should in each of them endeavour to investigate WHAT IS BEST, and there (if I may so express myself) *there* to fix our abode.

"By only seeking and perusing what is *truly* excellent, and by contemplating always *this* and *this alone*, the Mind insensibly becomes *accustomed* to it, and finds that *in this alone* it can acquiesce with content. It happens indeed *here*, as in a subject far more important, I mean in a *moral* and a *virtuous* CONDUCT. IF WE CHUSE THE BEST LIFE, USE WILL MAKE IT PLEASANT."

CHAPTER XVII

p. 72, l. 5. **converted into mere artifices**. See the Preface (*L.B.*) and Appendix on Poetic Diction, generally.

p. 72, l. 19. **within the last ten or twelve years.** To this period belong, for instance, the poems of Scott, a fair amount of Byron and the early poems of Shelley.

p. 73, l. 37. **low and rustic life.** It may be interesting to note that Irish writers like J. M. Synge and Lady Gregory have sought to create a modern Irish vernacular literature from the language of the peasants. Thus writes Synge in the preface to *The Playboy of the Western World*: "In writing...I have used one or two words only that I have not heard among the country people of Ireland or spoken in my own nursery before I could read the newspapers. A certain number of the phrases I employ I have heard also from herds and fishermen along the coast from Kerry to Mayo, or from beggar-women and ballad-singers nearer Dublin....When I was writing *The Shadow of the Glen* some years ago, I got more aid than any learning could have given me from a chink in the floor of the old Wicklow house where I was staying, that let me hear what was being said by the servant girls in the kitchen." And this, in practice, is how it turns out: "Let you wait, to hear me talking, till we're astray in Erris, when Good Friday's by, drinking a sup from a well, and making mighty kisses with our wetted mouths, or gaming in a gap of sunshine, with yourself stretched back unto your necklace, in the flowers of the earth....If the mitred bishops seen you that time, they'd be the like of the holy prophets, I'm thinking, do be straining the bars of Paradise to lay eyes on the Lady Helen of Troy, and she abroad, pacing back and forward, with a nosegay in her golden shawl." Wordsworth might have agreed with Synge's theory, but would he have recognised the result as the language of "low and rustic life"?

p. 74, l. 6. **an imitation as distinguished, etc.** Coleridge made several attempts to state in set terms the difference between an imitation and a likeness. See, for instance, *Lectures*, p. 122, *Miscellanies*, pp. 45, 46, *Table Talk*, p. 239. The distinction, stated crudely, comes to this: if you make an impression on wax with an engraved seal, the impression is a copy or "likeness," the engraving on the seal being an "imitation."

p. 74, l. 27. **The Mad Mother.** So called in *L.B.* The title was dropped later. It is the poem beginning "Her eyes are wild."

p. 75, l. 10. **Dr. Henry More.** Henry More (1614–1687), the Cambridge Platonist," was educated at Eton and Christ's College. The edition of 1817 gives a reference to *Enthusiasmus Triumphatus*: "For a man illiterate, as he was, [i.e., a certain 'enthusiast,' David George], but of good parts, by constant reading of the Bible will naturally contract a more winning and commanding Rhetorick than those that are learned, the intermixture of tongues and of artificial phrases deforming their style and making it sound more after the manner of men, though ordinarily there may be more of God in it than in that of the enthusiast."

p. 76, l. 9. **the principle of Aristotle.** "It is not the poet's province to relate such things as have actually happened, but such as might have happened, such as are possible, according either to probable or necessary consequence....Poetry is chiefly conversant about general truth, History about particular." (*Poetics*, Pt. II, Sect. vi.)

p. 78, l. 1. **acknowledges in a note.** This note first appeared in *L.B.* of 1800. It is important enough to be quoted:

"Note to *The Thorn.*—This Poem ought to have been preceded by an introductory Poem, which I have been prevented from writing by never having felt myself in a mood when it was probable that I should write it well.—The character which I have here introduced speaking is sufficiently common. The Reader will perhaps have a general notion of it, if he has ever known a man, a Captain of a small trading vessel, for example, who, being past the middle age of life, had retired upon an annuity or small independent income to some village or country town of which he was not a native, or in which he had not been accustomed to live. Such men, having little to do, become credulous and talkative from indolence; and from the same cause, and other pre-disposing causes by which it is probable that such men may have been affected, they are prone to superstition. On which account it appeared to me proper to select a character like this to exhibit some of the general laws by which superstition acts upon the mind. Superstitious men are almost always men of slow faculties and deep feelings: their minds are not loose but adhesive; they have a reasonable share of imagination, by which word I mean the faculty which produces impressive effects out of simple elements; but they are utterly destitute of fancy, the power by which pleasure and surprise are excited by sudden varieties of situation and an accumulated imagery.

"It was my wish in this poem to show the manner in which such men cleave to the same ideas; and to follow the turns of passions, always different, yet not palpably different, by which their conversation is swayed. I had two objects to attain; first, to represent a picture which should not be unimpressive, yet consistent with the character that should describe it; secondly, while I adhered to the style in which such persons describe, to take care that words, which in their minds are impregnated with passion, should likewise convey passion to Readers who are not accustomed to sympathize with men feeling in that manner or using such language. It seemed to me that this might be done by calling in the assistance of Lyrical and rapid Metre. It was necessary that the Poem, to be natural, should in reality move slowly; yet I hoped, that, by the aid of the metre, to those who should at all enter into the spirit of the Poem, it would appear to move quickly. The Reader will have the kindness to excuse this note, as I am sensible that an introductory Poem is necessary to give this Poem its full effect.

"Upon this occasion I will request permission to add a few words closely connected with the Thorn and many other Poems in these Volumes. There is a numerous class of readers who imagine that the same words cannot be repeated without tautology: this is a great error; virtual tautology is much oftener produced by using different words when the meaning is exactly the same. Words, a Poet's words more particularly, ought to be weighed in the balance of feeling, and not measured by the space which they occupy upon paper. For the Reader cannot be too often reminded that Poetry is passion: it is the history or science of feelings: now every man must know that an attempt is rarely made to communicate impassioned feelings without something of an accompanying consciousness of the inadequateness of our powers, or the deficiencies of language. During such efforts there will be a craving in the mind, and as long as it is unsatisfied the Speaker will cling to the same words, or words of the same character. There are also various other reasons why repetition and apparent tautology are frequently beauties of the highest kind. Among the chief of these reasons is the interest which the mind attaches to words, not only as symbols of the passion, but as *things*, active and efficient, which are of themselves part of the passion. And further, from a spirit of fondness, exultation, and gratitude, the mind luxuriates in the repetition of words which appear successfully to communicate its feelings. The truth of these remarks might be shown by innumerable passages from the Bible, and from the impassioned Poetry of every nation.

'Awake, awake, Deborah: awake, awake, utter a song:
Arise, Barak, and lead thy captivity captive, thou son of Abinoam.'
'At her feet he bowed, he fell, he lay down: at her feet he bowed, he fell; where he bowed there he fell down dead.'
'Why is his Chariot so long in coming? Why tarry the Wheels of his Chariot?'

Judges, chap. 5th, verses 12, 27 and part of 28. See also the whole of that tumultuous and wonderful Poem."

p. 78, l. 11. **the Nurse in Romeo and Juliet.** The point is dealt with in the *Lectures*, p. 86—part of the course delivered 1811–12.

p. 78, l. 22. **the last couplet of the third stanza.** The version given by Coleridge is that of *Lyrical Ballads* and *Poems* (1815). The reader will find it a useful exercise in criticism to compare Wordsworth's first and last thoughts on this point.

p. 79, l. 1. **four admirable lines.** That is, the passage beginning "As now to any eye." It is a little difficult to follow Coleridge's emphatic exception of this passage.

p. 82, l. 5. **Tom Brown.** Tom Brown (1663–1704) "of facetious memory," a voluminous author of satires, poems and pamphlets, is now quite forgotten, and not even recognised in his one contribution to current quotation "I do not like thee Dr Fell." **Sir Roger L'Estrange** (1616–1704) was an indefatigable translator and Royalist pamphleteer, remarkable for his vigour and coarseness. His papers *The Public Intelligencer* and *The Observator* entitle him to mention in the history of journalism. The difference intimated by Coleridge between these two writers and such writers as Hooker and Bacon is the difference between popular journalism and the "grand manner."

p. 82, l. 23. **use of the word "real."** Coleridge's disquisition is very interesting; but after all no precise definition of "real" is necessary: "we know what it is, and there's an end on't." Perhaps we know better what it is *not*; to call the moon "refulgent lamp of night" is to use language that is not "real" in any sense. Such language belongs to the world of sham and insincerity.

p. 82, l. 31. **Algernon Sidney.** Algernon Sidney (1622–1683), noblest victim of the persecution of free thought under Charles II, was arrested on a false charge of treason, sentenced to death by Judge Jeffreys, and beheaded. His *Discourses on Government* were published in 1698, after his death.

p. 83, l. 15. **as Dante, etc.** See quotation given in an earlier note.

p. 83, l. 18. **in a state of excitement.** These words are not used by Wordsworth. What he wrote was "the real language of men in a state of vivid sensation."

p. 84, l. 6. **by Mr. Wordsworth himself.** In a note to *The Thorn*, See note to p. 78, l. 1.

CHAPTER XVIII

p. 85, l. 23. **In distant countries.** *The Last of the Flock. L.B.* 1798.

p. 86, l. 30. **the sublime prayer.** There is nowhere in Milton any "prayer and hymn of praise" presented "as a fair specimen of common extemporary devotion." Perhaps Coleridge was thinking of the lines in *Paradise Lost* describing the unmeditated orisons of our first parents:

> Lowly they bow'd adoring, and began
> Their orisons, each morning duly paid
> In various style, for neither various style
> Nor holy rapture wanted they to praise
> Their Maker, in fit strains pronounc't or sung
> Unmeditated, such prompt eloquence
> Flow'd from their lips, in prose or numerous verse,
> More tuneable than needed lute or harp
> To add more sweetness.
>
> (v. 144–152.)

Their elaborate hymn of praise beginning "These are thy glorious works, Parent of good," extends from l. 153 to l. 208. Possibly, with this, Coleridge had in mind such a passage as Chapter XVI of *Eikonoklastes*, which attacks liturgical forms and defends extemporary devotions. See Vol. I, p. 431, etc. (Bohn). A much less worthy utterance on this subject is to be found in Section II of *Animadversions upon the Remonstrant's Defence concerning Smectymnuus*, Vol. III, p. 52, etc. (Bohn).

p. 86, l. 38. **The Vision, etc.** *Excursion*, I, 79. The passage is more fully discussed below.

p. 87, footnote. **Dr. Bell's invaluable system.** Andrew Bell (1753–1832), a St Andrews man, became superintendent of a large orphanage in Madras, where, owing to difficulties in obtaining teachers, he instituted a monitorial system, under which the elder pupils both taught and were taught. He published an account of his system in *An Experiment in Education* (1797). The system was taken up by Joseph Lancaster (1778–1838) with some modifications, and the two educationists became the leaders of rival parties. The Lancaster schools were undenominational and were attended largely by nonconformists; the Bell schools were Church of England. From Lancaster's efforts sprang the British and Foreign School Society, to which the disciples of Bell replied by founding the National Society for the Education of the Poor in the Principles of the Church of England. De Quincey makes elaborate fun of Coleridge's (and Southey's) advocacy of Bell and detestation of Lancaster. To such a pitch (he tells us) was the partizanship carried that people were heard asking each other, "Have you heard Coleridge lecture on *Bel and the Dragon*?" (De Quincey, *Works*, Vol. v, p. 196.)

p. 89, l. 40. **denied or doubted.** But evidently it was denied and doubted, otherwise Wordsworth would not have written such a passage as that in his Preface beginning "If in a poem there should be found, etc." See p. 188 of this volume.

p. 89, l. 41. **modes of expression, etc.** Coleridge extends Wordsworth's claim here. Wordsworth nowhere contends that poetry and prose must be identical in style, differing only in the circumstance of metre. What he says expressly is "*the language* of a large portion of every good poem...will be found to be strictly the language of prose, when prose is well written." The insistence on "language" must be noted. Wordsworth is denying that poetry has a special conventional *vocabulary* of its own. Examine, for instance, such lines as Addison's:

> Soon as soft vernal breezes warm the sky,
> Britannia's colours in the zephyrs fly.

Their sole claim to be poetry is that they call the winds "vernal breezes" and "zephyrs"—a matter of vocabulary. Addison's public devoutly believed that when you called the winds "soft vernal breezes," Italy "Ausonia's shores," the French "haughty Gauls" and the British forces "Britannia's graceful sons" you were writing poetry, just as the old style sporting journalist called the rain "Jupiter Pluvius" in the conviction that the heights of Parnassus were thus attained. It is this claim of an unnatural inflated vocabulary to be poetry, merely because it is unnatural and inflated, that Wordsworth patiently and exhaustively denies. The most richly-languaged of all our poets can thrill us to the heart with lines that in *language* are plain prose:

> We are such stuff
> As dreams are made on, and our little life
> Is rounded with a sleep.

p. 91, l. 41. **a lower species of wit.** Nevertheless, one of the tenderest poems in our language is an elaborate exercise in double and triple rhymes—Hood's *Bridge of Sighs*.

p. 92, l. 2. **poor Smart's distich.** Christopher Smart (1722–1771), a poet whose life was continuously unfortunate, partly through ill-luck and partly through his own improvidence and dissipation, is now remembered almost solely for the best parts of his *Song to David*. Coleridge's quotation comes from the lines *To the Rev. Mr Powell, on the Non-Performance of a Promise he made the Author of a Hare*:

> Thou valiant son of great Cadwallader,
> Hast thou a hare, or hast thou swallow'd her?

p. 92, l. 10. **The Children in the Wood.** See Preface (p. 199 of this volume).

p. 92, l. 26. **Tom Hickathrift, etc.** Lamb, Coleridge and Wordsworth were all admirers of the old wonder stories for children, and declared enemies of all juvenile compilations with an "improving" tendency. The stories mentioned were famous in their day, and two, at least, remain popular in this. *Goody Two Shoes* is alleged to have been written for Newbery, the bookseller of St Paul's Churchyard, by Oliver Goldsmith. *Little Red Riding Hood* was introduced from the French of Perrault (1628–1703), whose *Histoires ou Contes du Temps Passé* contains also such imperishable stories as *Bluebeard, Cinderella, Puss in Boots, Tom Thumb* and *The Sleeping Beauty*. Tom or Jack Hickathrift was a carter who killed a great giant with a cart-wheel as shield and axletree as weapon.

p. 92, l. 33. **Θαύματα θαυμαστότατα.** Marvels most marvellous.

p. 93, l. 1. **of Sterne.** *The Monk* is the title of three chapters in the early part of *A Sentimental Journey*, *The Dead Ass* of one in the middle, and *Maria* of three near the end—all told with the delicate and humorous pathos of which Sterne was a master. It will be obvious that these stories told in verse might be very good, but that, so told, they would be too unlike Sterne for any useful comparison to be made.

p. 93, l. 6. **Anecdote for Fathers, etc.** The first two poems appeared in *L.B.*, the last three in *Poems* (1807). Such poems would be "more delightful in prose" only if the prose were of a higher order than the verse. The question is not one of kind but of degree. The least happy parts of the specified poems are unsatisfactory, not because that kind of poem is bad, but because they are bad of their kind. The difference between,

> Her eyes are wild, her head is bare,
> The sun has burnt her coal black hair;

and,

> For still the more he works, the more
> His poor old ancles swell;

or between,

> And she is known to every star
> And every wind that blows;

and,

> I've measured it from side to side;
> 'Tis three feet long and two feet wide;

is simply that one succeeds in being good of its kind and the other doesn't. In all the examples the words are as simple as can be; but these simple words in one instance express what is essentially poetic, and in the other what is essentially prosaic. Prose is none the less prose for being in metre.

p. 93, l. 20. **a language different from that of prose.** This is very questionable. See the examples in the preceding note, and most of the *Tintern Abbey* lines and *Immortality* ode. Many supremely lovely poems and passages of Wordsworth are written in a language that is not different from prose. The metre, or better, the rhythm, of poetry is a quality in itself, and does not involve an obligation to use, or to refrain from using, any particular kind of language. Of course, the rhythm and the language must not be at variance. Thus, it might be observed that *Poor Susan* is partly unsuccessful, not because its language is different from that of prose, or like it; but because a pathetic little incident is told in a lively, lilting measure, suited to,

> I sprang to the saddle, and Joris, and he,
> I galloped, Dirck galloped, we galloped all three;

but not suited to,

> The streams will not flow and the hills will not rise,
> And the colours have all passed away from her eyes.

p. 94, l. 9. **sense of oddity and strangeness.** It is not the nature of the subject, or metrical form, or both together, that produces "a sense of oddity and strangeness," but a lack of style, or a lack of success, due partly to a somewhat inappropriate metre, and partly to the garrulity or want of conciseness that is a characteristic defect of Wordsworth. Compare, as an example of the last point,

> As it might be, perhaps, from bodings of his mind;

with the line as altered later:

> From bodings, as might be, that hung upon his mind.

The second, though not a very good line, is better than the first, because it avoids the slackness of "As it might be, perhaps." Wordsworth sometimes fails, not because his language is the language of prose, but because it is the language of bad prose.

p. 94, footnote. **the description of Night-Mair.**

> O sleep of horrors! Now run down and stared at
> By forms so hideous that they mock remembrance—

etc. as in quotation (Act IV, Sc. i). The last syllable of "nightmare" has nothing to do with horses. It means, as Coleridge suggests, a crushing terror.

p. 94, l. 19. **the preceding stanza.** Another stanza (as will be obvious) comes between.

p. 95, l. 6. **mordaunt.** A mordant is a substance used to prepare textile fabrics for receiving colours that would not "take" otherwise. Fabrics are usually treated with the mordant before the colour is applied.

p. 95, l. 24. **an after remark.** See later, p. 101.

p. 95, l. 30. **all the parts.** That is to say, a poem (like a person) must be true to itself if it is to be really likeable or successful.

p. 96, l. 21. **prove the point.** There are some sentences equally suited to prose and verse—this is evident to everybody. Further (Coleridge maintains) there are some sentences *not* equally suited to both. Wordsworth denies, or appears to deny, this, and Coleridge demands that he should make his denial good—that is, Wordsworth's denial of the second proposition is the point to be proved.

p. 97, l. 29. **Will Mr. Wordsworth say.** Wordsworth would probably have replied that these stanzas did not fall under his condemnation, because the language was natural to the poem, that is, it did not take the form of substituting artificial and inflated expressions for natural and simple ones. There is a world of difference between,

> He started up, and did himself prepayre
> In sun-bright arms and battailous array;
> For with that pagan proud he combat will that day;

and,

> Soon as soft vernal breezes warm the sky,
> Britannia's colours in the zephyrs fly.

p. 97, l. 32. **The Faery Queen.** The quotations are Bk. I, Can. 2, St. I, and Bk. I, Can. 5, St. 2.

p. 98, l. 18. **the style of prose.** No; but because it is the style of *bad* prose. Wordsworth's principle is as old (for instance) as Erasmus, who in a letter to Andreas Ammonius written from Cambridge, 21 Dec. 1513, says: Sunt qui poema non putent, nisi deos omneis e coelo mari terraque subinde advoces; nisi sexcentas infulcias fabulas. *Mihi semper placuit carmen quod a prosa, sed optima, non longe recederat.* (Ed. P. S. Allen, Vol. I, p. 545.) Mr Nichols renders it thus: There are some who do not count it poetry, unless you are constantly calling the gods out of Heaven to appear at sea or on land, and stuff your verse with hundreds of fables. For my part, I have always liked the poem which does not depart far from the best prose. (*Epistles of Erasmus*, Vol. II, 107.) Wordsworth's least happy moments are undeniably *prosa*, but are far indeed from being *prosa optima!*

p. 99, l. 21. **Will it be contended.** The reply might well be that the stanzas fail, not because they are prosaic, but because they are prosy. They are too dull to bother about; but their dulness has nothing to do with the form of language used.

p. 99, l. 24. **Daniel.** Samuel Daniel (1562–1619) survives for most readers in such a sonnet as "Care-charmer Sleep" rather than in his long poems. William Browne, in his *Britannia's Pastorals* (Bk II, The Second Song), taking a conspicuously friendly view of contemporary poets, calls Daniel "well-languaged" and thus briefly dismisses him. An epithet is scanty evidence one way or another. Drayton, upon whom Browne lavishes several ecstatic lines, calling him "Our second Ovid" and "All-loved Draiton," wrote more distinctly and frigidly of Daniel in his Elegy *To my dearly loved Friend Henry Reynolds, Esq.; of Poets and Poesy*:

> Amongst these Samuel Daniel, whom if I
> May speak of, but to censure do deny
> Only have heard some wise men him rehearse,
> To be too much historian in verse;
> His rhymes were smooth, his meters well did close,
> But yet his manner better fitted prose.

Drayton and Daniel were rivals, however; so perhaps his evidence must be taken with a difference. Coleridge's quotation is from Bk. I of *The History of the Civil Wars*, St. 7–9.

p. 99, l. 35. **Lamb's Dramatic Specimens.** Lamb's *Specimens of English Dramatic Poets who lived about the Time of Shakespeare* was published in 1808. The notes, as Coleridge indicates, are gems of criticism. This is the passage to which Coleridge refers:

> Ah, I remember well (and how can I
> But evermore remember well) when first
> Our flame began, when scarce we knew what was
> The flame we felt: when as we sat and sigh'd
> And look'd upon each other, and conceiv'd
> Not what we ail'd, yet something we did ail;
> And yet were well, and yet we were not well,
> And what was our disease we could not tell.
> Then would we kiss, then sigh, then look; and thus
> In that first garden of our simpleness
> We spent our childhood: but when years began
> To reap the fruit of knowledge: ah, how then
> Would she with graver looks, with sweet stern brow,
> Check my presumption and my forwardness;
> Yet still would give me flowers, still would me show,
> What she would have me, yet not have me know.

Lamb gives two other passages from *Hymen's Triumph* but adds no comment on the poet.

p. 100, footnote. **The Brothers.** *Lyrical Ballads* (1800). Coleridge quotes from the *text* of this edition; but a second *errata* list in that edition and the text of all subsequent editions give different readings at certain points. The reader should have the actual text of 1800, as Coleridge made more changes than he professed to make. This is how the lines run:

> James, pointing to its summit, over which
> They all had purposed to return together,
> Inform'd them that he there would wait for them:
> They parted, and his Comrades passed that way
> Some two hours after, but they did not find him
> At the appointed place, a circumstance
> Of which they took no heed: but one of them,
> Going by chance, at night, into the house
> Which at that time was James's home, there learned
> That nobody had seen him all that day:

The second *errata* list gives these variations:

> James pointed...
> And told them...
> ......but they did not find him
> Upon the Pillar—at the appointed place.
> Of this they took no heed: etc.

With a few trifling alterations this text stood till 1827, when the whole of the quoted passage disappeared, its place being taken by these lines:

> Upon its aery summit crowned with heath,
> The loiterer, not unnoticed by his comrades,
> Lay stretched at ease; but passing by the place
> On their return, they found that he was gone.
> No ill was feared; till one of them by chance
> Entering, when evening was far spent, the house
> Which at that time was James's home, there learned
> That nobody had seen him all that day.

A comparison of the versions will afford the reader a pleasing exercise in criticism.

p. 101, l. 3. **in the following words.** See the Preface, p. 195 of this volume; or rather, see the whole of the section pp. 189–195, beginning 'If it be affirmed, etc."

p. 101, l. 10. **a fool or madman.** But there is something in Wordsworth's contention. In the main, rhyme and metre are "controls" which the poet is obliged to observe, though now and then we find a poet like Swinburne who is carried away by his metrical exuberance. When he writes, for instance,

> Shrill shrieks in our faces the blind bland air that was mute as a maiden,

he is obviously writing for the rhythm's sake—it is metre, not meaning, that matters. But extravagances in imagery and diction are even less subject to restraint. Consider the following lines from the celebrated Doctor Watts's "Elegiac Thought on Miss Susan Warner who died of the Small-Pox, December 18, 1707 at One of the Clock in the Morning":

> Awake, my muse, range the wide world of souls,
> And seek Vernera fled: With upward aim
> Direct thy wing; for she was born from heaven,
> Fulfill'd her visit, and returned on high.
> The midnight watch of angels, that patrole
> The British sky, have noticed her ascent
> Near the meridian star; pursue the track
> To the bright confines of immortal day
> And paradise her home. Say, my Urania,
> (For nothing scapes thy search, nor canst thou miss
> So fair a spirit)....

And so forth. Surely it is obvious that the pious poet has been admirably controlled by his metre (such as it is), but has been wildly uncontrolled in his diction. See, too, the passages from Darwin quoted in note to p. 9, l. 29.

p. 101, l. 29. **the name of Taste.** This does not carry us very far. Wordsworth might well have replied that the orgy of exaggerated diction culminating in the excesses of Darwin originated in Taste—of the wrong sort. In every form of art the devotees of false decoration will claim for their preferences the sanction of Taste, and will denounce the admirers of a simpler style as barbarians without Taste. Thus, it was the cultivated Taste of France, embodied in Voltaire, that rejected Shakespeare as an uncouth barbarian.

p. 102, l. 18. **μόρφωσις, not ποίησις.** "Fashioning" not "creation"—the distinction that was in Whistler's mind when he described the usual sort of Academy picture as not "art" but "produce."

p. 102, l. 24. **and children only.** Better, "and only children put it to their mouths," his point being that children alone are deceived by a counterfeit.

p. 103, l. 9. **Dodsley's collection.** Robert Dodsley (1703–1764) was a weaver's apprentice, but ran away and became a footman. His bookish instincts led him to set up as a publisher, in which capacity he acted for Johnson, Pope, Goldsmith, Horace Walpole, and Lord Chesterfield. He founded *The Annual Register* and employed Burke as its editor. His *Select Collection of Old Plays* (1744) contributed to the later revival of interest in the Elizabethan and Jacobean dramatists. *A Collection of Poems by Various Hands* appeared in six volumes between 1748 and 1758. It contained contributions from the distinguished poets of the day as well as from the mere versifiers.

p. 103, l. 11. **the two Suttons.** " It was Daniel and Robert Sutton, the sons of a surgeon at Debenham, Suffolk, who during the years preceding 1765 so improved the practice of inoculation as to render it acceptable and popular. The operation was by this time overlaid with many accessories, preparatory and consequent—purges, emetics, bleedings, blisters and anodynes—so that the process had become a very serious and costly one. Daniel Sutton had the sagacity to select those remedies and means which were really helpful; and he set up as an empirical inoculator holding an infallible secret. People came to him in crowds, and his success was great. He published in his old age an account of his system: the chief points comprised the use of one puncture only, of spare diet, refrigerant drinks, and cool air. Daniel Sutton styled himself in 1769, ' Professor of Inoculation in the kingdom of Great Britain, and in all the dominions of his Britannic Majesty.' (*Dr John Fothergill and his Friends*; by R. Hingston Fox, M.D.)

CHAPTER XIX

p. 106, footnote. **the celebrated Mendelssohn.** Moses Mendelssohn (1729–1786) a Jewish philosopher, grandfather of the (now) still more "celebrated Mendelssohn," who was a boy of six when Coleridge was writing *Biographia*. The intervening Abraham used to complain good-humouredly that at first he was known as his father's son, and in later years as his son's father.

p. 107, l. 9. **Garve.** Christian Garve (1742–1798)—name pronounced in two syllables—a German moralist and critic, translator of Burke *On the Sublime and Beautiful*, succeeded the poet Gellert (1715–1769) as professor of philosophy at Leipsic. The edition of 1847 gives a reference to *Sammlung einiger Abhandlungen von Christian Garve*, Leipsic, 1779, pp. 233–4 "with slight alterations."

p. 107, l. 37. **Cotton.** Charles Cotton (1630–1687) is immortal as the "hearty, cheerful Mr Cotton" of Lamb's essay *New Year's Eve* (in which one of his poems is quoted in full) and as the continuator of Walton's *Compleat Angler*. His *Scarronides or Virgil Travestie* appeared first in 1664. Cotton was a sedulous translator, his best known work in this line being a version of Montaigne (1685). See Wordsworth's extended reference and quotation on pp. 216–217 of the present volume.

p. 108, l. 13. **The final e.** Coleridge's view of Chaucerian pronunciation must be received with caution. The final *e* is certainly not "sounded or dropt indifferently." The quotation that follows is taken from Bk. v of *Troilus and Criseyde*, l. 603, etc. The first line should read:

And after this he to the yatès wente.

Line 4 of the second stanza should read,

For sorwe of which myn hertë wol to-cleve!

"Malencolye" in the third stanza must be accented on the second syllable. Certain lines in the last stanza are better read thus:

> This song whan he thus songen haddė, sone
> * * * * * *
> He stood the brightė monė to biholde,
> And all his sorwe he to the monė tolde.

The quotation is left as Coleridge gave it, with the division into stanzas ignored.

p. 109, l. 37. **a former page.** p. 12.

p. 110, l. 2. **Drayton's Ideas.** A series of sixty-three sonnets in the Shakespearean form, including the magnificent "Since there's no help, come, let us kiss and part."

p. 110, l. 8. **The Synagogue.** Written by Christopher Harvie, and printed with *The Temple* in 1640. *The Temple* itself was first published in 1633, shortly after the death of its saintly author, whose Life, by Izaak Walton, should be a part of every Englishman's reading. Coleridge omits the characteristic last stanza of *Vertue*:

> Onely a sweet and vertuous soul,
> Like season'd timber, never gives;
> But though the whole world turn to coal,
> Then chiefly lives.

CHAPTER XX

p. 113, l. 9. **Lord Byron.** By the date at which Coleridge was writing, Byron had published Cantos 1 and 2 of *Childe Harold*, *The Giaour*, *The Bride of Abydos* and *The Corsair*.

p. 113, l. 14. **our illustrious Laureate.** Southey.

p. 114, l. 2. **The Recluse.** This was a long philosophical poem in three divisions, intended by Wordsworth to be his *magnum opus*, embodying his mature views of Man, Nature and Society. The existing nine books of *The Excursion* are a part of what was to have been the second division of *The Recluse*. Of the first division only a portion was written. The fragment was first published in 1889; but a long quotation had already appeared in the Preface to *The Excursion*. Of the third division nothing appears to exist.

p. 114, l. 7. **It seems, etc.** Adapted from *The Pet Lamb* (*L.B.* 1800). The references to the subsequent quotations are as follows: "The Child is father of the Man," from "My heart leaps up" (*Poems*, 1807); *Lucy Gray*, *Ruth* and *The Idle Shepherd-Boys* from *L.B.* 1800; *The Blind Highland Boy* from *Poems* (1807); the *Boy of Winander-Mere* (not so called by Wordsworth) is the passage beginning "There was a boy," part of *The Prelude* (Bk. v), but first published in *L.B.* 1800. After the third line of the quotation should come a line,

> Responsive to his call, with quivering peals,

To Joanna, the second of the *Poems on the Naming of Places* (*L.B.* 1800); *Song at the Feast of Brougham Castle* (*Poems*, 1807); the penultimate quoted stanza reads thus in the latest version:

Alas! the impassioned minstrel did not know
How, by Heaven's grace, this Clifford's heart was framed:
How he, long forced in humble walks to go,
Was softened into feeling, soothed, and tamed.

CHAPTER XXI

p. 120, l. 26. **the Edinburgh Review.** First number, Oct. 1802; *The Quarterly Review*, first number Feb. 1809; *Blackwood's Edinburgh Magazine*, first number, April 1817.

p. 121, l. 20. **No private grudge.** Lines written, apparently, for the present occasion.

p. 122, l. 8. **the illustrious Lessing.** Gotthold Ephraim Lessing (1729–1781), the great German dramatist and critic was, in a sense, the founder of modern criticism. His *Laocoon* (1766), in which he lays down the limits of various forms of art, is one of the books that every student of literature must know. Macaulay said that a reading of it formed an epoch in his mental history, and that he learned more from it than he had ever learned elsewhere. Another aesthetic treatise of the same sort is *How the Ancients Represented Death* (1769). It is the Preface to this work that Coleridge has chiefly in mind. See the Bohn volume containing this, *Laocoon* and other critical works. A book on Lessing is one of the many projected and desirable books that Coleridge did not write.

p. 124, l. 27. **O then, etc.** *Excursion*, I, 198, etc. Coleridge quotes from the first edition (1814). The latest version differs in details which the reader should consider. Jeffrey's review of *The Excursion* appeared in the *Edinburgh* for Nov. 1814. Coleridge is quite wrong in the particular accusation he makes against Jeffrey at this point. The actual quotation in the review begins at line 203 and ends at 218, and is preceded by the comment: "The young pedlar's sensations at sunrise are thus naturally recorded." No doubt the critic meant his "naturally" to be sarcastic, as his reference to the preceding quotation is described as "the beginning of the raving fit" and as "a good example of the forced and affected ecstasies in which this author abounds"; and a further quotation is introduced with the remark: "What follows about nature, triangles, stars, and the laws of light, is still more incomprehensible." But it is wrong to say that the lines quoted in the text are adduced "as a proof and example of an author's tendency to downright ravings, etc."

p. 125, l. 25. **in animam, etc.** From the apocryphal Wisdom of Solomon i, 4: "For into a malicious soul wisdom shall not enter." The Vulgate version is "in malevolam animam non introibit sapientia."

p. 125, l. 33. **This won't do.** Jeffrey's review of *The Excursion* begins thus: "This will never do! It bears no doubt the stamp of the author's heart and fancy: but unfortunately not half so visibly as that of his peculiar system. His former poems were intended to recommend that system, and to bespeak favour for it by their individual merit;—but this, we suspect, must be recommended by the system—and can only expect to succeed where it has been previously established. It is longer, weaker, and tamer, than any of Mr Wordsworth's other productions; with less boldness of originality, and less even of that extreme simplicity and lowliness of tone which wavered so prettily, in the *Lyrical Ballads*, between silliness and pathos. We have imitations of Cowper, and even of Milton here; engrafted on the natural drawl of the Lakers—and all diluted into harmony by that profuse and irrepressible wordiness which deluges all the blank verse of this school of poetry, and lubricates and weakens the whole structure of their style....The case of Mr Wordsworth, we perceive, is now manifestly hopeless; and we give him up as altogether incurable, and beyond the power of criticism. We cannot, indeed, altogether omit taking precautions now and then against the spreading of the malady; but for himself, though we shall watch the progress of his symptoms as a matter of professional curiosity and instruction, we really think it right not to harass him any longer with nauseous remedies."

And thereupon the critic-physician proceeds "to harass him" for the space of thirty pages. The review ends thus:

"Why should Mr Wordsworth have made his hero a superannuated Pedlar? What but the most wretched affectation or provoking perversity of taste, could induce any one to place his chosen advocate of wisdom and virtue in so absurd and fantastic a condition? Did Mr Wordsworth really imagine that his favourite doctrines were likely to gain anything in point of effect or authority, by being put into the mouth of a person accustomed to higgle about tape, or brass sleeve-buttons? Or is it not plain, that, independent of the ridicule and disgust which such a personification must excite in many of his readers, its adoption exposes his work throughout to the charge of revolting incongruity, and utter disregard of probability or nature? For, after he has thus wilfully debased his moral teacher by a low occupation, is there one word that he puts into his mouth, or one sentiment of which he makes him the organ, that has the most remote reference to that occupation? Is there anything in his learned, abstract, and logical harangues, that savours of the calling that is ascribed to him? Are any of their materials such as a pedlar could possibly have dealt in? Are the manners, the diction, the sentiments, in any the very smallest degree, accommodated to a person in that condition? or are they not eminently and conspicuously such as could not by possibility belong to it? A man who went about selling flannel and pocket-handkerchiefs in this lofty diction, would soon frighten away all his customers; and would infallibly pass either for a madman, or for some learned and affected gentleman, who, in a frolic, had taken up a character which he was peculiarly ill-qualified for supporting.

"The absurdity in this case is palpable and glaring: but it is exactly of the same nature with that which infects the whole substance of the work—a puerile ambition of singularity engrafted on an unlucky predilection for truisms; and an affected passion for simplicity and humble life, most awkwardly combined with a taste for mystical refinements, and all the gorgeousness of obscure phraseology. His taste for simplicity is evinced by sprinkling up and down his interminable declamations a few descriptions of baby-houses, and of old hats with wet brims; and his amiable partiality for humble life, by assuring us that a wordy rhetorician, who talks about Thebes, and allegorizes all the heathen mythology, was once a pedlar—and making him break in upon his magnificent orations with two or three awkward notices of something that he had seen when selling winter raiment about the country—or of the changes in the state of society, which had almost annihilated his former calling."

These quotations will enable the reader to understand Coleridge's present and subsequent allusions. There is no need for any discussion here of Jeffrey or *The Excursion*; but it may be pointed out that the critic's many interrogations can be answered, at least in part, from the poem itself.

p. 126, l. 7. **The gayest, etc.** Akenside, *Pleasures of the Imagination*, I, 20.

p. 126, l. 21. **Taylor's Holy Dying.** Chap I, sec. iii, " But as when the sun approaches towards the gates of the morning he first opens a little eye of heaven, and sends away the spirits of darkness, and gives light to a cock, and calls up the lark to matins, and by-and-by gilds the fringes of a cloud, and peeps over the eastern hills, thrusting out his golden horns, like those which decked the brows of Moses, when he was forced to wear a veil because himself had seen the face of God; and still, while a man tells the story, the sun gets up higher, till he shows a fair face and a full light, and then he shines one whole day, under a cloud often, and sometimes weeping great and little showers, and sets quickly: so is a man's reason and his life."

p. 126, l. 22. **emblem of power.** The representation of Moses with horns derives its authority from the Vulgate version of Exodus xxxiv, 29: Quod *cornuta* esset facies sua, ex consortio sermonis Domini." Those curious on the subject should consult *Horns of Honour* by F. T. Elworthy.

CHAPTER XXII

p. 128, l. 28. **Fidelity.** *Poems* (1807). The preceding stanza is:

It was a Cove, a huge Recess,
That keeps till June December's snow;
A lofty Precipice in front,
A silent Tarn below!
Far in the bosom of Helvellyn,
Remote from public Road or Dwelling,
Pathway, or cultivated land;
From trace of human foot or hand.

p. 130, . 13. **Cowley's Essay on Cromwell.** Abraham Cowley (1618–1667), born in London and educated at Westminster and Cambridge, is now little read as a poet; but his short prose essays with appended verses can still be enjoyed. A longer prose work is the one referred to by Coleridge: *A Vision, Concerning his late Pretended Highnesse Cromwell, the Wicked; Containing a Discourse in Vindication of him by a pretended Angel, and the Confutation thereof by the Author.* It contains three lengthy passages of verse.

p. 130, l. 14. **the Consolation of Boetius.** Boëthius (480?–524), statesman and philosopher, was a Roman senator in the days of Theodoric the Goth. He was cruelly put to death upon a false charge of treason. During his imprisonment he composed his *Consolation of Philosophy*, in alternate paragraphs of prose and verse. The treatise was favourite moral reading for many centuries in many lands, and numbers among its translators King Alfred and Chaucer. The best available account of Boëthius is in Chapter XXXIX of Gibbon.

p. 130, l. 14. **Argenis.** John Barclay (1582–1621), born in France of Scottish parentage, was notable for his attacks on the Jesuits. His *Argenis*, a sort of political romance or allegory, has been several times translated into English from its original Latin.

p. 130, l. 25. **Metastasio.** Pietro Bonaventura Trapessi (1698–1782) was called Metastasio ("changing" or "transformation") after his adoption by the famous jurist Gravina. His works are mainly dramas composed for musical setting. Thus, *Didone Abandonnata* has been set by at least thirty different composers, including Scarlatti, Porpora, Piccini, Paisiello, Paer and Mercadante. His *Semiramide* was set by Gluck, and was the first work in which that great musician essayed the style that he brought to perfection in his later classical operas. One of Metastasio's dramas *La Clemenza di Tito* was set (after much alteration) by Mozart. The awkwardness alluded to by Coleridge—i.e., the abrupt change of artistic plane from speech to song in the older forms of opera, has always been felt as a defect; but much had already been done in the way of improvement by the date of *Biographia*. Gluck (1714–1787) was the first musician to transform opera from a medley of dialogue and song into homogeneous music-drama. A little later, Mozart (1756–1791) showed in the elaborate concerted numbers of his greater operas how music purely and exquisitely formal could be charged with deep dramatic significance. The complete expansion of opera into music drama is best exemplified in Wagner's *Tristan und Isolde*, which is a continuous composition, with no separate numbers, and only three full closes, one at the end of each act.

p. 131, l. 12. **the exquisite stanzas.** See ante, p. 114. The quoted poem is one that underwent some remarkable transformations which the reader should notice. The piece first appeared in the *Poems* of 1807, where it gives the title to a long section of Vol. II, "The Blind Highland Boy; with Other Poems." In that edition the stanzas describing the blind boy's boating adventure appear thus:

In such a vessel ne'er before
Did human Creature leave the shore:
If this or that way he should stir
Woe to the poor blind Mariner!
    For death will be his doom.

Strong is the current; but be mild,
Ye waves and spare the helpless Child!
If ye in anger fret or chafe,
A Bee-hive would be ship as safe
    As that in which he sails.

But say, what was it? Thought of fear!
Well may ye tremble when ye hear!
—A Household Tub, like one of those
Which women use to wash their clothes,
    This carried the blind Boy.

Close to the water he had found
This Vessel, push'd it from dry ground
Went into it; and, without dread,
Following the fancies in his head,
    He paddled up and down.

A while he stood upon his feet;
He felt the motion—took his seat;
And dallied thus, till from the shore
The tide retreating more and more
    Had suck'd, and suck'd him in.

The unholy glee with which hostile critics fell upon the Household Tub can be imagined. In 1815 Wordsworth made a drastic change, to which he drew attention in an appended note: "It is recorded in Dampier's Voyages that a Boy, the Son of a Captain of a Man of War, seated himself in a Turtle-shell and floated in it from the shore to his Father's Ship, which lay at anchor at the distance of half-a-mile. Upon the suggestion of a Friend [Coleridge], I have substituted such a Shell for that less elegant vessel in which my blind voyager did actually intrust himself to the dangerous current of Loch Levin, as was related to me by an Eye-witness." See *Anima Poetae*, p. 207. In place of the quoted stanzas these appear:

In such a vessel never more
May human Creature leave the shore:
If this or that way he should stir,
Woe to the poor blind Mariner!
    For death will be his doom.

But say what bears him?—Ye have seen
The Indian's Bow, his arrows keen,
Rare beasts, and birds with plumage bright;
Gifts which, for wonder or delight,
    Are brought in ships from far.

Such gifts had those sea-faring men
Spread round that Haven in the glen;
Each hut, perchance, might have its own,
And to the Boy they all were known,
    He knew and prized them all.

And one, the rarest, was a Shell
Which he, poor Child, had studied well;
The Shell of a green Turtle, thin
And hollow;—you might sit therein,
    It was so wide and deep.

'Twas even the largest of its kind,
Large, thin, and light as birch-tree rind;
So light a Shell that it would swim,
And gaily lift its fearless brim
    Above the tossing waves.

And this the little blind Boy knew:
And he a story strange, yet true,
Had heard, how in a Shell like this
An English Boy, O thought of bliss!
    Had stoutly launched from shore;

Launched from the margin of a bay
Among the Indian Isles, where lay
His Father's ship, and had sailed far,
To join that gallant Ship of war,
    In his delightful Shell.

Our Highland Boy oft visited
The house which held this prize; and, led
By choice or chance, did thither come
One day when no one was at home,
    And found the door unbarred.

While there he sate, alone and blind,
That Story flashed upon his mind;—
A bold thought rouzed him, and he took
The Shell from out its secret nook,
    And bore it in his arms.

And with the happy burthen hied,
And pushed it from Loch Levin's side,—
Stepped into it; and, without dread,
Following the fancies in his head,
    He paddled up and down.

A while he stood upon his feet, etc.

There were further changes, and the reader should compare the final version (see Oxford Wordsworth, p. 296) with the quoted stanzas. One friendly critic of exquisite taste, preferred the Tub. Writing to acknowledge Wordsworth's gift of the 1815 volumes, Charles Lamb says: "I am afraid lest that substitution of a shell (a flat falsification of the history) for the household implement as it stood at first, was a kind of tub thrown out to the beast, or rather thrown out for him. The tub was a good honest tub in its place, and nothing could be fairly said against it. You say you made the alteration for the 'friendly reader,' but the malicious will take it to himself. Damn 'em; if you give 'em an inch, etc." (April 7, 1815.) Sara Coleridge, too, in editing her father's *Biographia* in 1847, adds a note regretting the substitution. But the Shell remains unto this day.

p. 131, l. 26. **'Tis gone—forgotten.** From the poem beginning "Once in a lonely Hamlet I sojourn'd" first published in 1807. The piece, however, was always known as *The Emigrant Mother*, though not printed with that title till 1820, when the text, too, underwent some modification. The first two lines were changed to:

'Tis gone—like dreams that we forget;
There was a smile or two—yet—yet
I can remember them, etc.

The last lines were still later altered to:

For they confound me; where—where is
That last, that sweetest smile of his?

p. 131, l. 37. **Thou hast a nest.** From the poem called *To a Sky-Lark*, first published in 1807. Wordsworth made several changes. Some of the lines were entirely omitted in 1827 and restored in 1832, and in place of the last four quoted lines, these were substituted in 1820:

What though my course be rugged and uneven,
To prickly moors and dusty ways confined,
Yet, hearing thee, or others of thy kind,
As full of gladness and as free of heaven,
I on the earth will go plodding on,
By myself, cheerfully, till the day is done.

The final version should also be observed.

p. 132, l. 9. **Close by a Pond.** From *Resolution and Independence*—usually referred to in the Wordsworth household as *The Leech-Gatherer*. It was first published in 1807. The whole stanza from which the present lines are quoted was omitted in 1820.

p. 132, l. 16. **And, still, etc.** Altered in 1820 to:

And, still as I drew near with gentle pace,
Upon the margin of that moorish flood, etc.

p. 132, l. 27. **But now, perplex'd.** In 1807 this had been,

And now, not knowing what the Old Man had said.

In 1820 it became:

—Perplexed, and longing to be comforted.

p. 132, l. 42. **especially characteristic of the author.** Wordsworth discusses some lines of it at length in the 1815 Preface. See p. 212 of the present volume.

p. 133, l. 21. **Aristotle pronounces.** Adapted from the passage in the *Poetics* where Aristotle says, "Poetry is a more philosophical and a more excellent thing than History: for Poetry is chiefly conversant about general truth, History about particular. In what manner, for example, any person of a certain character would speak or act, probably or necessarily—this is general; and this is the object of Poetry, even while it makes use of particular names. But what Alcibiades did, or what happened to him—this is particular truth." Sidney's elaboration of this passage in his *Apologie* is worth attention—history, he says, "being captive to the truth of a foolish world," is clearly inferior to poetry which "cometh unto you with a tale which holdeth children from play, and old men from the chimney-corner." The distinction has been made familiar in Matthew Arnold's paraphrase: "The superiority of poetry over history consists in its possessing a higher truth and a higher seriousness."

p. 133, l. 25. **Davenant's prefatory letter.** *The Authour's Preface to his much honour'd Friend Mr. Hobs*, introducing his poem *Gondibert*.

p. 134, l. 4. **the lines in The Excursion.** The referencc is to Bk. III, ll. 50–73, beginning,

Upon a semicirque of turf-clad ground.

What Coleridge says about the failure of elaborate description is admirably sound; but it should be pointed out that the rather minute description contained in the passage referred to is there, not for any merely picturesque purpose, but for its bearing on what follows. "The description [in Coleridge's words] is here necessary to the intelligibility of the tale."

p. 134, l. 24. **The fig-tree.** *P.L.* IX, 1101.

p. 135, l. 1. **head of Memnon.** One of two statues on the Nile said to utter sounds when struck by the first beams of the rising sun. It is not known certainly how the sounds could be produced by the mere action of light. Cambyses is alleged to have cleft the statue from head to waist in a vain attempt to discover the secret. Readers will recall the terrible vocal statues in Butler's *Erewhon*; but here the vocal agency was the wind, the hollow statues being, in effect, organ pipes. The fable, in

Coleridge's phrase, "is reversed," because the sound of Milton's line calls up the vision, whereas in the statue it was the light that awakened the sound.

p. 135, l. 15. **mean or ludicrous associations.** See the quotation from *The Edinburgh Review* in a preceding note.

p. 136, l. 12. **hysteron-proteron.** Literally "the latter former"—a figure of speech in which for emphasis the natural order of words is inverted. In general, it signifies a topsy-turvy method of expression—putting the cart before the horse.

p. 136, l. 22. **Antonine...Epictetus.** Two of the greatest pagan moralists were the "halting slave" Epictetus (1st century, A.D.) and the emperor Marcus Aurelius Antoninus (2nd century, A.D.)—hence Coleridge's antithesis.

p. 136, l. 24. **and rejoice.** This and the next quotation are from *The Excursion*, Bk. I, l. 75, etc. After "accomplishment of verse" should come five others:

(Which, in the docile season of their youth,
It was denied them to acquire, through lack
Of culture and the inspiring aid of books,
Or haply by a temper too severe,
Or a nice backwardness afraid of shame)
Nor having, etc.

p. 137, l. 18. **I think of Chatterton, etc.** From *Resolution and Independence.*

p. 137, l. 36. **The precepts of Horace.** Coleridge is supported by much in the general spirit of *De Arte Poetica* but not by any particular precepts. Perhaps the passages beginning at l. 112 and l. 409 may be held to apply—we will paraphrase them into modern terms: "If the words are out of keeping with the speaker's rank, stalls and gallery alike will roar with laughter. It will make a great difference whether it is a low comedy character or the hero that speaks, an old man well stricken in years or a young man in the first flush of youth, a lady of breeding or a busybody of a nurse, a man out and about on business or a farmer who never looks beyond his fields, an Arab or a Parisian, a man brought up in Kerry or a man brought up in Kent."

"It has been much discussed whether the best poetry originates in nature or in art. For my own part, I cannot see how mere study without a rich natural strain, or untutored natural parts alone, can accomplish anything: so much do they need each other and join amicably in co-operation."

Perhaps, too, Coleridge had in mind the oft-quoted *Difficile est proprie communia dicere*, which, elaborately as it has been discussed, bears a sound surface meaning, namely, that the difficulty of poetry is to individualise what is general, to express the abstract in the concrete, "to give to airy nothing, a local habitation and a name." The readers who would like to hear the line discussed should refer to Boswell under date 1776, where they will find Mr Wilkes and Dr Johnson arguing it out together.

p. 138, l. 9. **The Messiah.** Friedrich Gottlieb Klopstock (1724–1803), the author of an epic called *The Messiah*, took himself and his mission as a sacred poet with ultra-Miltonic seriousness. His great work is now little read; but he is deservedly honoured as a pioneer of native German literature at a time when French alone was considered worthy of patronage by the petty princelings of central Europe. Most English readers, it is to be feared, remember Klopstock for the ludicrous invocation in Letter XI of *The Sorrows of Werter*, and for Coleridge's muttered comment on the pastor's description of Klopstock as the German Milton—"A very *German* Milton, indeed!" See the third of *Satyrane's Letters* for Coleridge's account of a visit to Klopstock.

p. 138, l. 10. **Cumberland's Calvary.** Richard Cumberland (1732–1811) was a Cambridge man who entered the public service, and, becoming Secretary to the Board of Trade, naturally took to literature. He wrote much for the stage, his most popular works being *The Brothers, The West Indian* and *The Choleric Man*. His *Calvary* (1792) is a blank verse epic utterly forgotten save for this allusion of Coleridge's. Sara Coleridge has a lengthy note on it in the edition of 1847 to which the curious may be referred.

p. 138, l. 11. **illusion, contradistinguished from delusion.** In illusion we consent for the moment to accept the false as true, well knowing it to be false; in delusion we really take the false as true. To use a simple illustration, educated persons may enjoy the illusion of seeing a conjuror comb white rabbits from an old gentleman's beard, but they are not deluded into thinking the rabbits habitually nested there. Without a willing consent to illusion we could not accept Puck or Ariel or Caliban; but we are not expected to cherish a delusion that such beings have actual existence. What Coleridge means is that any elaborate or circumstantial attempt to make illusions into delusions is not only resented by the mind as an imposition: it is actually destructive of any enjoyment derivable from the illusion.

p. 139, l. 3. **Among the hills of Athol, etc.** *Excursion*, Bk. I, l. 108, etc. But the passage was altered later by excision, the teacher-step-father being suppressed. For the present version see Oxford Wordsworth, p. 758. A comparison should be made.

p. 139, l. 26. **the dramatic form in certain poems.** This is ambiguous. Perhaps Coleridge means what Browning calls "Dramatic Lyrics," i.e., those in which the matter is an utterance of some supposed character, e.g., *The Last of the Flock* (speaker, a ruined shepherd), *The Female Vagrant* (speaker, the vagrant woman), *The Mad Mother* (speaker, the mother) and *The Complaint of a Forsaken Indian Woman* (speaker, the woman). Or perhaps he means the poems in which there is dialogue or exchange of conversation, e.g., *Expostulation and Reply*, *We are Seven*, *Anecdote for Fathers*, and *The Brothers*. But the objection would apply equally to both forms. All the examples named are taken from *Lyrical Ballads*. In the *Poems* of 1807 and the additions of 1815 these forms are very little used.

p. 139, l. 40. **As instances.** Unfortunately it is not clear what instances are meant. C. is plainly not referring to the *Poems* of 1807, for his words do not apply to the second Celandine poem (pp. 27, 28), and p. 62 contains only the last five lines of *The Seven Sisters*. In Vol. I of 1815, pp. 27, 28 contain part of the *Anecdote for Fathers*, which certainly doesn't hasten to its point. But p. 62 is blank! There are equally strong reasons for thinking that Vol. I is not a misprint for Vol. II—unless, as Sara Coleridge suggests, p. 62 of Vol. II is meant, a page containing part of the *Song at the Feast of Brougham Castle*. But it is difficult to understand why that page is specially selected for censure. The lines of the *Excursion* referred to are certainly not the most admirable in that poem.

p. 140, l. 7. **Hercules, etc.** Hercules having killed his friend Iphitus was punished by a sickness, from which, however, an oracle promised him recovery if he went into bondage for three years. He therefore became servant to Omphale, Queen of Lydia, and with her did the work of a female slave, including the spinning of wool.

p. 140, l. 15. **They flash.** From the poem commonly called *The Daffodils*, though it was never given any title by Wordsworth. Not everyone will agree with Coleridge's charge of anti-climax.

p. 140, l. 25. **The second instance.** The reference is to *Gipsies* (pp. 11–12). Coleridge quotes from the volume of 1815. The later version is somewhat different. See Oxford Wordsworth, p. 192.

p. 141, l. 22. **the Ode.** *Intimations of Immortality, etc.*

p. 142, l. 26. **Spinoza and Behmen.** Baruch or Benedict Spinoza (1632–1677), born at Amsterdam of Spanish or Portuguese Jewish parentage, gave up the study of Jewish theology and devoted himself to philosophy. He was one of the first exponents of "monism," that is, the oneness of everything expressed in an infinity of modes. The One is God. His teaching is thus pantheistic. See his works (translated by R. H. M. Elwes, 2 vols.) and the essays by Matthew Arnold (*Essays in Criticism*) and Froude (*Short Studies*, I). JAKOP BÖHME (1575–1624), the celebrated mystic, was born near Görlitz, and, after being a herd-boy, followed the trade of a shoemaker. His work *Aurora* contains much lofty, mystical speculation, the central idea of which is that God is the One and the All, the primal and comprehensive Unity. Böhme claimed to be divinely illuminated and to perceive mysteries hidden from others. His influence was very wide. Sir Isaac Newton and William Law were among his admirers, and he still attracts many readers and devotees.

p. 142, l. 28. **ΕΝ ΚΑΙ ΠΑΝ.** The One and the All.

p. 142, l. 34. **Jacobi.** Friedrich Heinrich Jacobi (1743–1819), a German critical philosopher, who, according to Sara Coleridge's note in 1847, "wrote upon Spinoza and against Mendelssohn, on Realism and Idealism, on the Undertaking of Criticism to convert Reason into the Understanding, and other works of metaphysical controversy. His complete works in 5 vols., Leipsic, 1812–22, include his celebrated philosophical romances." Of the latter (*Woldemar* and *Edward Allwill's Correspondence*) Mrs Austin, the translator of Ranke, speaks very highly.

p. 142, l. 35. **Gleim.** Johann Wilhelm Ludwig Gleim (1719–1803) is called by Coleridge the "Tyrtaeus and Anacreon" of German poetry on account of his *Songs of a Prussian Grenadier*, which are naturally Tyrtaean in their patriotic fervour and Anacreontic in their soldierly praise of wine. Gleim was very hospitable and conducted a passionate correspondence with many literary friends.

p. 143, l. 15. **To whom the grave, etc.** These four lines were afterwards omitted by Wordsworth in consequence of Coleridge's criticism, and were replaced by the single line,

In darkness lost,—the darkness of the grave.

The idea that shocked Coleridge so deeply had no terrors for either

William or Dorothy Wordsworth. In Dorothy's *Journals*, that delightful and indispensable companion to her brother's (and Coleridge's) best poems, this entry occurs under date Thursday 29th April, 1802: "We then went to John's Grove, sate awhile at first; afterwards William lay, and I lay, in the trench under the fence—he with his eyes shut, and listening to the waterfalls and the birds. There was no one waterfall above another—it was a sound of waters in the air—the voice of the air. William heard me breathing, and rustling now and then, but we both lay still, and unseen by one another. He thought that it would be so sweet thus to lie in the grave, to hear the peaceful sounds of the earth, and just to know that our dear friends were near."

p. 144, l. 26. **has been already stated.** See Chapter XVI.

p. 145, l. 4. **untranslatableness.** See Chapter I.

p. 145, l. 29. **Sidonius Apollinaris.** Sidonius (430–483), Bishop of Clermont, wrote Latin letters and poems, the latter described as specially turgid and bombastic. He must not be confused with three other persons named Apollinaris, one of whom opposed the Arian heresy so vigorously that he plunged into a heresy of his own.

p. 145, l. 34. **by actual...experience.** See Chapter I.

p. 147, l. 5. **Makes audible.** From Coleridge's *To a Gentleman; composed on the Night after his Recitation of a Poem on the Growth of an Individual Mind.* The gentleman was Wordsworth, the poem *The Prelude*, the date January, 1807.

p. 147, l. 10. **page 25, vol. ii.** The reference is to *Star Gazers*, stanzas 3–6, first published in *Poems* (1807). The quotations that follow are from *Simon Lee* (*L.B.* 1798), *The Fountain* (*L.B.* 1800), *The Small Celandine* (*Poems*, 1807). The "sonnet on Buonaparte" is that beginning "I grieved for Bonaparte."

p. 148, l. 9. **resembles Samuel Daniel.** See a previous note. That Wordsworth knew and admired Daniel is evident from Bk. IV of *The Excursion* in which lines 324–331 are a quotation from the elder poet, supported by a note containing a further quotation.

p. 148, l. 24. **A poem is not necessarily obscure.** Coleridge is here glancing at the preface to the second edition of his own poems (1797) in which he says: "An Author is obscure when his conceptions are dim and imperfect, and his language incorrect, or unappropriate, or involved. A poem that abounds in allusions, like *The Bard* of Gray, or one that impersonates high and abstract truths, like Collins's *Ode on the Poetical Character*, claims not to be popular, but should be acquitted of obscurity. The deficiency is in the *Reader*."

p. 148, l. 27. **Fit audience.** *P.L.* VII, 31.

p. 148, l. 31. **Canzone, etc.** *Il Convivio*, Book II, Chap. I, Canzone prima, 53–55. See Oxford Dante, p. 251. In that text the last line reads:

Tanto la parli faticosa e forte.

p. 148, l. 38. **the flux and reflux.** A reference to that part of the *L.B.* Preface in which it is stated that one of the purposes of the poems is "to follow the fluxes and refluxes of the mind when agitated by the great and simple affections of our nature." The passage was omitted in later versions of the Preface. See p. 240.

p. 149, l. 5. **to charge Mr. Wordsworth.** What Wordsworth himself said about the poem is as follows: "To the attentive and competent reader the whole sufficiently explains itself; but there may be no harm in adverting here to particular feelings or *experiences* of my own mind on which the structure of the poem partly rests. Nothing was more difficult for me in childhood than to admit the notion of death as a state applicable to my own being. I have said elsewhere:

> A simple child
> That lightly draws its breath,
> And feels its life in every limb,
> What should it know of death?

But it was not so much from feelings of animal vivacity that my difficulty came as from a sense of the indomitableness of the Spirit within me. I used to brood over the stories of Enoch and Elijah, and almost to persuade myself that, whatever might become of others, I should be translated, in something of the same way, to heaven. With a feeling congenial to this, I was often unable to think of external things as having external existence, and I communed with all that I saw as something not apart from, but inherent in, my own immaterial nature. Many times while going to school have I grasped at a wall or tree to recall myself from this abyss of idealism to the reality. At that time I was afraid of such processes. In later periods of life I have deplored, as we all have reason to do, a subjugation of an opposite character, and have rejoiced over the remembrances, as is expressed in the lines—

> Obstinate questionings
> Of sense and outward things,
> Fallings from us, vanishings, etc.

To that dream-like vividness and splendour which invest objects of sight in childhood, every one, I believe, if he would look back, could bear testimony, and I need not dwell upon it here; but having in the poem regarded it as presumptive evidence of a prior state of existence, I think it right to protest against a conclusion, which has given pain to some good and pious persons that I meant to inculcate such a belief. It is far too shadowy a notion to be recommended to faith, as more than an element in our instincts of immortality. But let us bear in mind that, though the idea is not advanced in revelation, there is nothing there to contradict it, and the fall of man presents an analogy in its favour. Accordingly, a pre-existent state has entered into the popular creeds of many nations; and, among all persons acquainted with classic literature, is known as an ingredient in Platonic philosophy. Archimedes said that he could move the world if he had a point whereon to rest his machine. Who has not felt the same aspirations as regards the world of his own mind? Having to wield some of its elements when I was impelled to write this poem on the "Immortality of the Soul," I took hold of the notion of pre-existence as having sufficient foundation in humanity for authorizing me to make for my purpose the best use of it I could as a poet."

The Platonic view of pre-existence is put forward in the most famous of the dialogues, the *Phaedo*. Wordsworth had not Greek enough to be widely read in Plato; but he would certainly have heard Coleridge talk about a doctrine so congenial, and could easily pursue it in a translation. Here is a passage: "What you now advance," says Cebes, interrupting Socrates, "is only a necessary consequence of another principle that I have often heard you lay down, viz., that all our acquired knowledge is only remembrance. For if that principle be true, we must necessarily have learnt at another time what we call to mind in this. Now that's impossible, unless our soul had a being before its being invested with this human form...."

"What we now advance of equality is equally applicable to goodness, justice, sanctity, and, in a word, to all other things that have a real existence. So that of necessity we must have known all these things before we came into this world....And being possessed of that knowledge, if we did not forget apace every day, we should not only be born with it, but retain it all our lifetime. For to know is only to preserve the knowledge we have received, and not to lose it. And to forget is to lose the knowledge we enjoy before....Now if, after having possessed that knowledge before we were born, and having lost it since, we come to retrieve it by the ministry of our senses which we call learning, shall we not justly entitle it Remembrance?"

p. 149, l. 9. **Πολλά κ.τ.λ.** From Pindar's second Olympic Ode, Strophe v. Sara Coleridge in the edition of 1847 quotes the version by Cary, the translator of Dante:

> Beneath mine elbow a full quiver lies
> Of fleetest arrows, sounding to the wise;
> But for the crowd, they need interpreters.
> All else, expert by rule
> Are none of hers;
> Mere tongues in vehement gabble idly heard,
> Clamouring, like daws, at Jove's celestial bird.

p. 149, l. 22. **curiosa felicitas.** "Carefully sought happiness of phrase"—the tribute of Petronius to Horace. (*Satyricon*, Chap. CXVIII.)

p. 149, l. 38. **description of skating.** From the lines now entitled, with true Wordsworthian lengthiness, *Influences of Natural Objects in Calling Forth and Strengthening the Imagination in Boyhood and Early Youth*. The passage was written in 1799, and first published in *The Friend* (Dec. 28, 1809). where it was called *Growth of Genius from the Influences of Natural Objects on the Imagination in Boyhood and Early Youth*. Slightly altered, it now forms part of *The Prelude*, Bk. I, 401–463.

p. 150, l. 8. **The Green Linnet.** From *Poems* (1807). The reader should compare the last quoted stanza with the altered version now current.

p. 150, l. 26. **the blue-cap.** In *The Kitten and the Falling Leaves* (*Poems*, 1807), the lines beginning,

> That way look, my Infant, lo!

The description of the blue-cap and the noon-tide silence begins at l. 63:

> Where is he that giddy Sprite.

The poem to the cuckoo is the familiar piece beginning "O blithe New-comer" (*Poems*, 1807). The next reference is to one of the "Lucy" poems, (*L.B.* 1800).

p. 150, l. 43. **See vol. i, etc.** The reference is to the lines beginning,

> 'Tis said that some have died for love.

L.B. 1800.)

p. 151, l. 1. **The Affliction of Margaret.** From *Poems*, 1807, the lines beginning:

Where art thou, my beloved Son.

p. 151, l. 5. **The Mad Mother.** From *L.B.* 1798. The title is now dropped. The two quoted stanzas are not consecutive.

p. 151, l. 41. **mere and unmodified fancy.** This is certainly true; and is one of several objections to Wordsworth's specific division of his work into "Poems of the Fancy" and "Poems of the Imagination."

p. 152, l. 4. **add the gleam.** From *Elegiac Stanzas suggested by a Picture of Peele Castle in a Storm.* (*Poems*, 1807.) Mr Shawcross has an interesting note on this passage (Vol. II, p. 293) regretting that Coleridge's quotation has given currency to a false view of Wordsworth's art and general purpose. The lines, he says, are those "in which Wordsworth wished to characterize the errors, or at least the limitations, of the imagination in youth....Wordsworth has been held, on the strength of this passage, to conceive of the charm of art as something adventitious, which the artist or poet puts into nature and does not find there." And he attaches importance to the fact that in 1827 Wordsworth altered the lines to,

add a gleam
Of lustre, never known to sea or land,
But borrowed from the youthful poet's dream.

Perhaps he does not attach enough importance to the fact that Wordsworth afterwards reverted to the original reading, and that "the fond delusion of my heart" of 1807 became "the fond illusion" in the next edition, and remained so. Mr Shawcross is quite right in insisting that the poet does not "add" what is not there: he discerns and reveals, in the spirit of Blake's pregnant utterance, "A fool sees not the same tree that a wise man sees." But he does "add" to *our* vision. It is a great function of art to make visible "the light of common day," disregarded simply because it is common. We are not justified in assuming from the mood of resolute realism in which Wordsworth's elegiac utterance concludes that the young poet's vision was false. It was different, that is all. The gloom of the bereaved man's vision would certainly have been false to youth; and if any importance is to be attached to the Immortality ode, "the light that never was on sea or land," streams from the clouds of glory which it is youth's privilege to retain and maturity's tragedy to have lost.

p. 152, l. 13. **Yew Trees.** The lines beginning,

There is a Yew-tree, pride of Lorton Vale.

(*Poems*, 1815.) In the tenth line of the quotation all editions of Wordsworth read "pining."

p. 152, l. 42. **Or the 8th, 9th, etc.** The sonnets referred to are those beginning:

8th. Where lies the Land to which yon Ship must go?
9th. Even as a dragon's eye that feels the stress.
19th. O mountain Stream! the Shepherd and his Cot.
26th. Earth has not anything to shew more fair.
31st. Methought I saw the footsteps of a throne.
33rd. It is a beauteous Evening, calm and free.

The next references are (1) to the sonnet beginning, "Two Voices are there"; and to the Ode, *Intimations of Immortality*. These poems were all published in the wonderful volumes of 1807, which contain some of Wordsworth's finest poetry.

p. 154, l. 22. **White Doe.** This was published as a separate volume in 1815, though written several years earlier. The quoted lines begin at Canto First, l. 31. The two beginning "And right across, etc." are now omitted.

p. 155, l. 28. **Bartram's Travels.** *Travels through North and South Carolina*, etc., 1792.

p. 156, l. 2. **too petulant.** See Essay Supplementary to the Preface, p. 221 of the present volume. In the *Biographia* of 1817, after this paragraph came another, omitted by the editors of 1847, referring to Jeffrey and *The Edinburgh Review*: "Let not Mr Wordsworth be charged with having expressed himself too indignantly, till the wantonness and the systematic and malignant perseverance of the aggressions have been taken into fair consideration. I myself heard the commander in chief of this unmanly warfare make a boast of his private admiration of Wordsworth's genius. I have heard him declare, that whoever came into his room would probably find the *Lyrical Ballads* lying open on his table, and that (speaking exclusively of those written by Mr Wordsworth himself), he could nearly repeat the whole of them by heart. *But* a Review, in order to be a saleable article, must be *personal*, *sharp* and *pointed*: and *since then*, the Poet has made himself, and with himself all who were, or were supposed to be, his friends and admirers, the object of the critic's revenge—how? by having spoken of a work so conducted in the terms which it deserved! I once heard a clergyman in boots and buckskin avow, that he would cheat his own father *in a horse*. A moral system of a similar nature seems to have been adopted by too many anonymous critics. As we used to say at school, in reviewing they *make* being rogues; and he, who complains, is to be laughed at for his ignorance of *the game*. With the pen out of their hand they are *honorable men*. They exert indeed power (which is to that of the injured party who should attempt to expose their glaring perversions and misstatements, as twenty to one) to write down, and (where the author's circumstances permit) to *impoverish* the man, whose learning and genius they themselves in private have repeatedly admitted. They knowingly strive to make it impossible for the man even to publish[1] any future work without exposing himself to all the wretchedness of debt and embarrassment. But this is all *in their vocation*: and, bating what they do in their *vocation*, 'who can say that black is the white of their eye?'"

p. 156, l. 17. **such a criticism.** Compare with this sentence the general drift of Matthew Arnold's Introduction to his selections from Wordsworth.

p. 156, l. 20. **accelerated nor retarded.** This is the natural termina-

[1] Not many months ago an eminent bookseller was asked what he thought of ——? The answer was: "I have heard his powers very highly spoken of by some of our first-rate men; but I would not have a work of his if anyone would give it me: for he is spoken but slightly of, or not at all, in the Quarterly Review: and the Edinburgh, you know, is decided to cut him up!"

tion of Coleridge's discussion of Wordsworth. The chapter ends, however, with a further passage, for which see p. 178 of this volume. Following the chapter comes other matter, for an account of which see pp. 179–182. The whole work thus concludes:

"This has been my Object, and this alone can be my Defence—and O! that with this my personal as well as my *Literary Life* might conclude! the unquenched desire I mean, not without the consciousness of having earnestly endeavoured to kindle young minds, and to guard them against the temptations of Scorners, by showing that the Scheme of Christianity, as taught in the Liturgy and Homilies of our Church, though not discoverable by human Reason, is yet in accordance with it; that link follows link by necessary consequence; that Religion passes out of the ken of Reason only where the eye of Reason has reached its own Horizon; and that faith is then but its continuation: even as the Day softens away into the sweet Twilight, and Twilight, hushed and breathless, steals into the Darkness. It is Night, sacred Night! the upraised Eye views only the starry Heaven which manifests itself alone; and the outward Beholding is fixed in the sparks twinkling in the aweful depth, though Suns of other Worlds, only to preserve the Soul steady and collected in its pure *Act* of inward adoration to the great I AM, and to the filial WORD that re-affirmeth it from Eternity to Eternity, whose choral Echo is the universe."

ΘΕΩι ΜΟΝΩι ΔΟΞΑ.

CPSIA information can be obtained
at www.ICGtesting.com
Printed in the USA
LVHW041153210620
658620LV00001B/32

9 781107 536821